Y0-BDR-772

Woodrow Wilson and Far Eastern Policy
1913-1921

Woodrow Wilson
and
Far Eastern Policy
1913-1921

by Roy Watson Curry

1968
OCTAGON BOOKS, INC.
New York

Reprinted 1968
by special arrangement with Twayne Publishers, Inc.

OCTAGON BOOKS, INC.
175 FIFTH AVENUE
NEW YORK, N. Y. 10010

LIBRARY OF CONGRESS CATALOG CARD NUMBER: 68-22300

Printed in U.S.A. by
NOBLE OFFSET PRINTERS, INC.
NEW YORK 3, N. Y.

FOR MY BELOVED FATHER
AND MOTHER

History is not a record of all the facts:
that were impossible. It is a record of some
of the facts, selected for their significance,
and set forth in such order and combination, with such a touch of realizing imagination, with such colour and life as shall
cause them, if possible, to make the same
impression on us as they must have made
on those who were actors in the midst of
them.

—Woodrow Wilson

Preface

During the eight years, 1913-1921, while Woodrow Wilson was President of the United States, the transpiration of events in the Far East was momentous. In a quieter day they would have monopolized the attention of the American people. In fact, Far Eastern affairs occupied considerable public attention until the fateful August of 1914 when all else became a sideshow to the fierce European contest of arms on the ancient battlefields of Flanders. The engagement of Russia and Britain against Germany created a weakness in the Far Eastern balance of power, leaving Japan dominant in Asia. The triangular pattern of powers which the United States had been wont to offset against one another to preserve her own interests in China thus disappeared. Wilson was confronted with the problem of Japan's opportune expansion in China at the expense of America's traditional policy of the open door and its corollary for preservation of Chinese territorial and political integrity. The Philippines stood hostage for admitted American weakness in the Orient. A policy of cooperation with the European powers was now complicated by their engagement in the war and by Japan's active participation with them as an ally.

The present study attempts to recount the events of these years in the light of new materials now opened to scholarship. The conclusion emerges that the American treatment of events took place within the framework of traditional policy and to the increased tempo of suspicion between Japan and the United States. In these events Woodrow Wilson was the central figure, for while he initiated little in the way of Far Eastern policy, it was his final decision which bore responsibility for American action there. In the face of events he was flexible as to methods

7

adopted within a framework of the fixed principles comprising traditional American policy. It was his purpose "to serve" Asia, and this purpose gradually became identified with preserving America's position in China.

I am deeply indebted to Professor Paul H. Clyde of Duke University for my original interest in this subject. His friendly counsel, criticism, and encouragement have made completion of the study possible. My initial interest in Woodrow Wilson, the man, was aroused by my paternal grandmother, the late Mrs. John M. Curry.

Pursuit of this study has been an adventure in human helpfulness. I take sincere pleasure in acknowledging my indebtedness to the members of the staffs of the Duke University Library, the University of North Carolina Library, the Library of Congress, and the National Archives. I wish to express my particular appreciation to Henry M. Fuller, the reference librarian at Yale University; to Alexander Clark, Curator of Manuscripts at Princeton University, and to Miss Katharine Brand, Curator of the Wilson Papers in the Library of Congress. My sincerest appreciation is due to Mrs. Woodrow Wilson for permission to use the papers of her late husband. I wish to acknowledge the permission granted by the Yale University Library and Mr. Charles Seymour to use material from the Edward M. House and the Frank L. Polk papers. I am indebted to Mr. Allen W. Dulles for the use of quotations from the Robert Lansing papers. The Honorable Jonathan Daniels kindly granted the use of the papers of his father, Josephus Daniels.

I am also indebted to the Honorable Breckenridge Long for his conversation concerning the persons and events of this narrative, to Miss Laura Shearer Turnbull for an enlightening conversation on the Wilson materials, and to many others of friendly scholarship and interests who made this task rich in its human relationships. I am indeed grateful to Mrs. Margaret Neff for her efficient technical aid.

R. W. C.

Pittsburgh, Pennsylvania
May 19, 1955

Acknowledgements

The author wishes to acknowledge his indebtedness to:

Appleton, Century, Crofts for permission to quote from *The Good Fight* by Manuel L. Quezon and *The Cornerstone of Philippine Independence* by Francis B. Harrison.

Bobbs-Merrill for permission to quote from the *War Memoirs of Robert Lansing*.

Doubleday-Page and Company for permission to quote from *Woodrow Wilson Life and Letters*, IV and VI by Ray S. Baker and *Eight Years with Wilson's Cabinet, 1913-1920*, I, by David F. Houston.

Harcourt, Brace and Company for permission to quote from *The Far Eastern Policy of the United States* by A. Whitney Griswold; *An American Diplomat in China* by Paul S. Reinsch; and *The Autobiography of Lincoln Steffens*.

Houghton-Mifflin for permission to quote from *The Intimate Papers of Colonel House* edited by Charles Seymour.

The Johns Hopkins Press for permission to quote from *Diplomatic Commentaries* by Viscount Kikujiro Ishii and *The Origins of the Foreign Policy of Woodrow Wilson* by Harley Notter.

Peter Smith for permission to quote from *America's Siberian Adventure, 1918-1920* by William S. Graves.

Scribners' Sons for permission to quote from *American Chronicle* by Ray S. Baker.

The University of North Carolina Press for permission to quote from *The Wilson Era, Years of Peace, 1910-1917* by Josephus Daniels.

And to Mrs. Woodrow Wilson for permission to quote from *The Public Papers of Woodrow Wilson*, I and VI, edited by Ray S. Baker and William E. Dodd.

Contents

CHAPTER ONE

Money, Recognition, and Representation in China

THE SMALL CANNOT OPPOSE THE GREAT, THE FEW CANNOT
OPPOSE THE MANY, THE WEAK CANNOT OPPOSE THE STRONG.
—Chinese Proverb

Each man called by the American people to the high dignity of office as President of the United States must, in his own way and time, learn to function in the executive position. His duties are multiple, his responsibilities wide, his powers vast and of uncertain definition. Yet, his training is always inadequate for the task. Inadequate even when they included such distinctions as those Woodrow Wilson bore when inaugurated twenty-eighth President of the United States on March 4, 1913.

Since 1910, the reform Governor of New Jersey, Wilson had been previously the President of Princeton University, professor of jurisprudence and politics, historian, and publicist. Now fifty-six years of age, born in Virginia and reared in Georgia and North Carolina with a deep affection for the post-bellum South, a moralist with a strong appreciation for the liberalism of the Manchester School, Wilson was considered by many as the Democratic standard-bearer for reform in the turbulent era of criticism and self-examination engendered by the Progressives and the stir of issues of the new century.

Wilson was a complicated man whose personality, motives and policies were to be explored and explained by many people. To some he was a cold, dogmatic, ambitious opportunist.[1] To

13

others he was a warm-hearted, sensitive, scholarly, well-meaning man of liberal tendencies who sought to harness the forces of his day to serve progress at home and abroad.[2] More lately, he has been pictured as a fundamentally conservative figure, who, caught in the tides of Progressivism, swam with the current to enact into law certain basic and often inadequate measures for the solution of our national ills.[3]

He was, of course, all these men at different times, but he was never consistently any one of them. Personally he had little respect for consistency as such.[4] He revered traditional American ideals and objectives, but he accepted the evolutionary view of society as a growing organism.[5] His firm belief in moral principle as a guide for action supplied an ever-present standard by which he could chart his course. Yet Wilson was ever expedient in the achievement of his objectives. At first there appears a conflict in principle and expediency as a basis for action, but he viewed, "Only that is expedient which is just, but this is only another way of saying that only that is expedient which tallies with prevalent standards of judgment as to conduct and responsibilities."[6] He was apt to be flexible on matters of method, but on general policy principles he was unmovable.[7]

His chief talent was a capacity for growth. This was abetted by a curious and incisive mind. He was quick to grasp the essential points of a problem and to arrive at a conclusion.[8] He explained his method as a functioning executive to the journalist Lincoln Steffens:

> "An executive is a man of action, an intellectual — such as you and I"; he smiled — "An intellectual is inexecutive. In an executive job we are dangerous, unless we are aware of our limitations and take measures to stop our everlasting disposition to think, to listen, to — not act. I made up my mind long ago, when I got my first executive job, to open my mind for a while, hear everybody who came to me with advice, information — what you will — then, some day, the day when my mind felt like deciding, to shut it up and act. My decision might be right; it might be wrong. No matter. I would take a chance and do — something."[9]

This disrespect for consistency yet respect for traditional ideals and policies expeditiously achieved within a framework of moral principle, coupled with his capacity for growth, reveal something of the complexity of the man. At the same time an appreciation of these personal qualities is absolutely essential to an understanding of his decisions in foreign and domestic affairs.

Throughout the campaign of 1912 there had been but incidental mention of foreign policy. The Democratic platform had been silent on the subject save for minor planks on the Philippines and approval of Congressional action concerning the Russian Treaty of 1832. The election had been based squarely on domestic issues, in which Wilson felt himself thoroughly competent. As to international matters, he confessed to a Princeton friend shortly before the inauguration, "It would be the irony of fate if my administration had to deal chiefly with foreign affairs."[10]

Unfortunately, the President had but a veneer of knowledge of the world outside the borders of the United States. He had been twice to Britain, had traveled quickly through France, and had touched briefly on Italian soil. Of the Orient he had no more than an intelligent man's acquired information. Of the oriental nations, he was especially interested in China.[11] As President of Princeton, he had taken the initiative in obtaining Chinese students under the Boxer indemnity funds. He had interested himself in the Princeton Work in Peking, through which the University supported Y.M.C.A. activities there. A number of oriental students had been present on the campus. A cousin by marriage, Samuel J. Woodbridge, edited a Presbyterian missionary weekly in Shanghai. Wilson had entertained and associated with men of the world and listened to them speak on the Far East. Like many of his peers, he looked upon China as the newly-awakened giant of the Orient. With her huge population and an undeveloped hinterland of resources, she offered unparalleled opportunities for the development of American trade.[12]

After the November polls, the President-elect with his wife and three daughters went to Bermuda for a rest. There, according to Harley Notter, Wilson studied oriental problems and arranged to meet David Starr Jordan of Stanford for a discussion of them. He wrote the editor of the *Oriental Review* expressing his hope for enduring friendship between the United States and Japan, informed John S. Thomson that he was studying the Chinese situation and that his interest in her welfare was deep and permanent.[13] To Sun Yat-sen, who had sent congratulations upon the outcome of the American elections, Wilson replied: "Permit me to say that I have watched with the keenest interest the recent course of events in China and have felt the strongest sympathy with every movement which looks toward giving the people of the great empire of China the liberty for which they have so long been yearning and preparing themselves."[14] The International Consortium Loan and recognition of the Republic were being discussed in the press at the time.

One of the President-elect's first acts upon his return from Bermuda was to ask William Jennings Bryan, the old war horse of the Democratic party, yet three years younger than Wilson, to join the cabinet as Secretary of State.[15] This appointment was to have widespread effect on the early Far Eastern policy of the administration. A combination of circumstances brought about the appointment of Bryan to the first post in the Cabinet. "The Great Commoner," as he was called in the press, had a numerous following among the Democrats throughout the country. His influence and political friendships would greatly aid in getting through the administration's legislative program, which Wilson had already clearly formulated in his own mind. Bryan's support of Wilson at Baltimore was regarded as being important in the nomination of the New Jersey Governor. The office of Secretary of State was Bryan's by his position in the party and by political obligation.[16]

Colonel Edward M. House, a native Texan of independent means and political tastes, who had come gradually into the picture as a Wilson adviser during the pre-convention campaign, also urged the Bryan appointment. The President-elect sent House to Florida, where Bryan was then building a new home, to sound out "The Commoner" on the Wilson program. House found Bryan "really a fine man, full of democratic simplicity, earnest, patriotic, and of a fervently religious nature." The

Colonel wrote Wilson, "He has accepted all your conclusions so cordially that it has been a pleasure to me to discuss matters with him."[17]

The Press viewed Bryan's personal naïveté and simplicity as dangerous characteristics in a Secretary of State. Wilson, however, had long since believed that the Secretary was of a subordinate position, that the actual conduct of the office lodged with the President.[18] Bryan seems to have had the same attitude and was quite content to act in a secondary role to Wilson. Indeed, it is evident that in their early administration relations, both men made a point of getting along with one another. As time progressed, the two found they were joined by a strong bond of mutual opinion.

Bryan, like Wilson, was an idealist seeking the reign of practical justice and peace. Both men were sincere Christians believing also in the efficacy of Christianity to develop the proper virtues making for respect of individual rights and liberties. They held in common a belief in the need of a wider area of democratic freedom and opportunity for the individual. Both men feared the corruption of American ideals by corporate wealth whether functioning on a national or international level. Justice, peace, Christianity, and democracy were the key ideals which they served. They never disappeared as ideals, but as time transpired they were increasingly compromised with the realities of the present.

Unlike Wilson, Bryan knew something of the Orient from personal experience. In 1905-1907 "The Commoner" with his family had made a world tour. The young Japanese, who had lived with the Bryans in Nebraska and had adopted the name Bryan Yamashita,[19] arranged a magnificent reception for the party in Japan. As an honored guest at a banquet feting Admiral Heihachiro Togo, hero of the Russo-Japanese War, Bryan, a severe abstainer from alchohol, toasted the Admiral in water, mischievously remarking that had the hero's victory been on champagne, he would have toasted him in that liquid. The American was received by the Emperor and made the customary bows to the throne. Bryan publicly spoke complimentary of the ruler granting his people a constitution and moving gradually into a representative system of government.[20]

The Bryans visited Korea as the country was on the eve of being taken over by the Japanese. In China, they found the Empire coming apart. There the Bryan party moved about less noticed and contrasted the squalor and disorder of the port cities with the efficiency and courtesy of their reception in Japan. They next visited the Philippines where they found the influence of American ideas spreading and met Emilio Aguinaldo, the lately pacified leader of the insurrection against American rule. Bryan was constrained in his speeches and thus disappointed the Filipinos who admired him as the spokesman of anti-imperialism in America.[21] The party proceeded by way of South East Asia through India, Russia, Europe to the United States.[22] It was against this background that the Secretary now viewed the affairs of the world.

Realizing his lack of experience in foreign affairs, Bryan persuaded Huntington Wilson, who was considered an authority on the Far East, to remain from the Taft administration as Counselor in the Department of State. Soon after the new administration was underway, Counselor Wilson was called to the White House to give his views on foreign affairs. He believed implicitly in the "dollar diplomacy" of the Taft administration, and that night he argued for recognition of Huerta in Mexico, continuation of government support of the bankers in the Six Power Consortium Loan, and the non-recognition of the Chinese Republic. He was received coldly and never again consulted. The Counselor remembered Bryan as being so busy with political appointments in those days that he had little time to study the problems of the Department. Later, he recalled seizing the Secretary "one night on a windy street corner to try to explain to him the intricacies of the China Consortium."[23]

There was much to explain about the Consortium loan. Wilson was well aware of the narrative for the negotiations had been much in the news. The loan negotiations and recognition of the so-called Republic of China were recognized as pending business for the new President.

The Taft administration, in implementing its policy of cooperation with the interested powers in Asia, had attempted to strengthen America's voice in the policies of the powers there. By pressuring American capital to invest in China, it hoped to create a means of fostering the open door, preserving the political and territorial integrity of China, and opening the opportunities for American business, especially in Manchuria. When a consortium of British, French, and German bankers secured the right to build the Hukuang railway through central and southern China, the State Department instigated the formation of an American group of bankers headed by J. P. Morgan and Company. By diplomatic means it accomplished the reluctant admission of the American group to the Consortium, in May, 1911. The outbreak of the revolution in China, however, prevented the beginning of railway construction for two years, but the Americans shared in the initial loans to the enterprise.[24]

Soon after admission to the Consortium, the American group was invited to underwrite a loan to provide funds for stabilizing Chinese and Manchurian finances. The Americans, with Chinese consent, proceeded to internationalize the loan by opening it to other members of the Consortium. Of the ten million pounds sought, four hundred thousand pounds were actually advanced.[25] This sum was later repaid under the Reorganization Loan of 1913, negotiation of which now became the primary interest of the powers.

The newly-established, so-called Republic, saddled with liabilities and in desperate straits for financial aid, turned to the Consortium bankers for funds. Between February 28 and March 9, 1912, some 3,100,000 taels were loaned by the group as emergency aid to the new government. In consideration for this assistance, Yuan Shih-k'ai, President of the Peking government, assured the Consortium, provided it offered equal terms with other bankers, "the firm option of undertaking the comprehensive loan for general reorganization purposes. . . ."[26] This offer was to haunt Yuan for the Powers used it as a bona fide agreement. Under its terms, they forced the hard-pressed Chinese to forego loans negotiated with independent Belgian and

English firms.[27] Peking could not afford to oppose the demands of the Consortium in these instances, because her need of funds was so desperate.

Meanwhile, in June, 1912, Japanese and Russian groups were admitted to the group of international bankers, thus forming the Six Power Consortium. Negotiations for the reorganization loan proceeded slowly through the remainder of 1912 and the winter of the new year. The bankers were concerned to see that the loan was adequately secured. Recognizing as they did the internal chaotic state of political and financial affairs, the irresponsibility of Chinese officials in seeking credits, certainly as a business venture the loan was essentially unattractive. On the surface, therefore, the stringent conditions under which they agreed to issue the loan were justified. The groups retained power to approve the purposes for which the loan was spent. China was required to create an audit system employing foreign advisers to supervise the expenditures for the purposes of reorganization. The salt taxes, pledged for repayment of the loan, were also to be administered under a foreign director. The first series of 60,000,000 pounds was to be taken at a fixed price by the Consortium, which was thereafter assured an option on the subsequent series at market price. Agents from the consortium "should be" appointed for a five year term to assist in the administration of the reorganization for which the loan was being made.[28]

It is difficult, of course, to say to what extent the conditions of the loan represented merely bankers' caution. They served so admirably to provide opportunities for the advancement of foreign control over the financial and indirectly the political life of the Chinese people. Great Britain, France, and Germany had constantly used their financial and economic advantages as a means of coercing China for their own purposes. Russia looked upon its loans as a means of enhancing control over Manchuria and Mongolia, while Japan had but awakened to the possibilities of erecting an Asiatic empire through financial domination.[29] American self-interest, best served by its traditional policies of the open door and the preservation of Chinese

sovereignty, was compatible to the championing of China a-
gainst the selfish advantages of the powers.

The onerous conditions being fostered on China, under
the loan negotiation caused the American Minister at Peking,
on February 21, 1913, to report that "it is no longer a question
of friendly international cooperation to help China but a combination of big powers with common interest to accomplish their
own selfish political aims."[30] By this time the representative
of the American group, disgusted at the delays and the conditions
demanded by the other members of the Consortium, recommended withdrawal from the negotiations.[31] However, the State
Department was convinced that American participation was vital.
When all other arguments for participation were exploited, it
asked that the bankers continue their activities until after the
inauguration of the incoming Democratic administration.[32]

The day following Wilson's inauguration, Willard Straight,
former consul at Mukden and now an agent of the American
group, telephoned Bryan to ask for the position of the administration on the Consortium loan. The Secretary indicated his
willingness for an interview. On March 10, Straight, Henry P.
Davidson and Paul M. Warburg, representing the interested
bankers, called at the Department. The three hour conference
centered around the loan, although general China policy came
in for some discussion. The pertinent facts concerning the loan
emerged. Bryan was impressed that only the four American
banks belonging to the group could participate. The same
bankers expected to control future loans in China. The loan
was to be secured by a pledge of the salt revenues. Finally, the
bankers expected the national governments concerned to furnish support, "even to the use of force," to guarantee fulfilment
of the loan terms.[33]

Four days later, Bryan made an extended report to the cabinet concerning the loan and the conditions under which the
American group would continue in the negotiations. Only
William C. Redfield, Secretary of Commerce, favored backing
it,[34] although the Secretary of Treasury, William G. McAdoo,
clandestinely opposed the President's position of issuing a state-

ment disavowing the loan. McAdoo unsuccessfully sought the aid of Colonel House to prevent the President's action.[35]

Wilson read his statement condemning the loan at the next meeting of the Cabinet on March 18. He "mentioned several nations by name and rather severely criticized them." Various members of the Cabinet suggested this unnecessary castigation be omitted, and the statement was thus modified.[36] There is no indication that the administration sought to chart a new course in Far Eastern affairs as such. It sought primarily to voice its position in relation to requesting the American group to remain in the Consortium negotiations.

A leak concerning the decision taken within the Cabinet necessitated the White House release of the complete statement directly to the press that afternoon.[37] Such a procedure was irregular, since it preceded State Department notification of the governments concerned. It also served to dramatize the whole situation. Bryan was out of the city and the State Department was uninformed concerning the changed policy. Wilson later admitted that the manner of making the release had been a mistake. The Japanese government expressed resentment at being informed through the press.[38] A representative of the American group telephoned the State Department for confirmation of the newspaper account. He was informed that the release was to be considered an official answer to the request for the administration's position.[39] A flurry of excitement occurred when Huntington Wilson, the Counselor of the State Department held over from the Taft administration and then Acting Secretary in Bryan's absence, submitted his resignation to the President. He resented being informed of a change in the loan policy through the public press when he was serving as the responsible agent of the administration. The President gave the resignation perhaps his briefest acceptance and then released the correspondence to the newspapers.[40]

The next day, the American group met in New York and decided to withdraw from the loan. They delegated their commitments under the Hukuang agreement and the currency reform loan to the International Banking Corporation in China, in which Morgan was interested. Later, the group cooperated with the administration in granting a six months extension to the Chinese government when it failed to meet its outstanding obligations under the existing loans. After the reorganization loan was concluded between China and the five remaining Consortium members, the American advances were repaid.[41]

The President's statement[42], which attracted such notice, opened with a concise account as to the purpose of the Taft administration in seeking American participation in the loan. Such participation would encourage American capital access to the development of China and thus place the United States in a position to share in the responsibilities associated with the foreign relations involved. However, the American group had declared it would continue in the loan "only if expressly requested to do so by the Government."

Wilson stated that the conditions of the loan seemed such as "to touch very nearly the administrative independence of China itself," and he did not feel that the United States should "be a party to those conditions." He further objected to the responsibilities assumed under the guise of guarantees to the bankers which could make mandatory interference in the financial and political affairs of China, "just now awakening to a consciousness of its power and of its obligations to its people." Furthermore, the conditions of the loan pledging particular taxes, and the administration of those taxes by other than Chinese nationals, he felt were contrary to American principles.

The President viewed, "The awakening of the people of China to a consciousness of their responsibilities under free government is the most significant, if not the most momentous event of our generation." With this movement the American people were in "profound sympathy." The United States earnestly desired aiding the Chinese and opening "the almost untouched and perhaps unrivaled resources of China" to her own people and to the use of the rest of the world. He believed it his duty to encourage such ends through legislation favoring the development of American trade and investment in China. Finally, he declared: "Our interests are those of the open door — a door of friendship and mutual advantage. This is the only door we care to enter."

At a later meeting of the Cabinet, Wilson explained: "I feel so keenly the desire to help China that I prefer to err in the line of helping that country than otherwise. If we had entered into the loan with [the] other powers we would have got nothing but more influence in China and lost the proud position which America secured when Sec[retary] Hay stood for the Open Door in China after the Boxer uprising." He thought the position of the United States would be stronger if it stood alone and followed an independent course in China. Then it could say to Russia and the other powers, "What are your designs?"[43] Thus in his own thinking, the President seemed to emphasize the idea of America diplomatically defending China's position against the other powers. This of course had been accepted policy within the State Department and was in no sense new.

What was new about the policy was its emphasis upon an independent course as opposed to the former administration's policy of cooperating with the powers in Asia. This too, however, was a matter of differing emphasis rather than a complete reversal of customary policy. Former administrations had frequently followed an independent course of action while emphasizing the policy of cooperation. The Wilson administration was to cooperate with the powers where and when it seemed desirable while emphasizing an independent course.[44]

Wilson's action, too, must be understood in the light of the existing domestic attitude toward the bankers. The campaign of 1912 had been waged in part against the forces of organized wealth.[45] The Pujo Committee had pointed to a possible monopoly of American finance centered in New York. The American group consisted of four banking houses, headed by the Morgan firm, an avowed enemy of the administration. Wilson confessed to his Cabinet that the statement was a rebuke to Wall Street as well as the powers,[46] although it was well understood within the administration that the bankers were indifferent and even reluctant to carry through the loan.

Press reaction generally hailed the sensational blow delivered to the old dollar diplomacy. The sentiment of the country was anti-monopoly and the action was popular since it represented an attack on the money trust. From Peking, the correspondent for the London *Daily Telegraph* hailed Wilson's action as a return to American disinterested friendship for China. The Anti-Imperialist League, President David Starr Jordan of Stanford University, Charles R. Crane, the Chicago industrialist and interested adviser to the administration in Far Eastern affairs, John R. Mott of the Y.M.C.A. international movement, all acclaimed Wilson's action.[47] The *New York World* ran a cartoon headed "Leaving The Firm." It showed Uncle Sam, constitution in hand, descending the steps of Morgan and Company. Secretary Bryan agreed enthusiastically with the President. He wrote: "I have yet to find the first man who dissents from your position . . ., and I believe you have won the lasting gratitude of China. With this nation setting such an example no other nation can force her into unfair terms. They will now become rivals for her friendship."[48] Bryan's estimate of the Chinese reception was true enough, Yuan Shih k'ai, the Chinese President, expressed himself as "very grateful to the American Government for the action in disapproving participation in the loan."[49]

Disapproval of Wilson's action was also manifest. The views of the *New York Times* correspondent in Peking correctly estimated that the United States was considered the least essential element in the negotiations, and her withdrawal would not affect the loan. He charged, however, that the Wilson statement engendered false hopes among the Chinese for independent American loans.[50] Arthur J. Brown, head of the Board of Foreign Missions of the Presbyterian Church, asserted that "if the United States would protect China, it must have a stake there."[51] Consul General Thomas Sammons of Yokohama, in a letter passed on to the President, disagreed with the changed policy. He correctly reported that China was pleased because she wished to escape the supervision of her finances. Japan welcomed the change because she desired the United States to practice a policy independent of Europe. He warned: "Japan, in fact, wishes and, in my opinion, proposes to dispose of China in her own way. China fears Japan first and Europe next. . . . Naturally, Japan does not wish any loans in China that do not serve her purpose, her destiny, her predominance in the Far East."[52] These latter words were as the voice of prophecy.

Already the administration was having Japanese difficulties concerning the California land legislation. These difficulties were to multiply in the years ahead.

The *North China Herald* saw grave danger in the false expectations of independent American loans aroused by Wilson's statement. It took issue with the President's reference to the liberal awakening within China, and said his message encouraged the opposition of the legislative forces to President Yuan's attempt at centralization of authority. The paper confessed, however, that "the operation of the Powers in the Far East have become, what they were not a year ago, entirely subordinate to European politics."[53]

American withdrawal from the Consortium loan has been looked upon as the "cause of the breakdown of the open door policy in China."[54] In the light of the wrangling of the parties and the mutual suspicions expressed during the negotiation, it is doubtful that any implementation of the open door was sought by the Consortium powers. The loan had long since assumed the appearance of a collective exploitation of China. In refusing to participate in such an arrangement, the Wilson administration achieved status as a defender of traditional friendship with China, and had escaped the odium of the exploitation embodied in the terms of the loan.

The President's action was a means of meeting an individual situation; it was not a blanket repudiation of all cooperation, but it did effectively announce that the United States would follow an independent course serving its own best interests and principles in relation to China. It was not the intent of the administration to stand aloof from the needs of the new Republic. It meant to release the market there for competitive business and finance, such as it had been its campaign promise to do domestically.[55] It tragically failed to realize that without government initiative or strong diplomatic backing, American bankers were unwilling to take the risks of advancing credits or participating in the development of a country in which bandit raids and unsettled political conditions made any investment unsafe. In the campaign Wilson had castigated this timidity of American bankers in entering foreign markets; he was now to experience the stubborn truths of the fact. He had struck a mortal blow at the American participation in the Consortium. He had announced a China policy that was benevolent, shaped as it was by American morality and political idealism. He had struck out on an independent course, although it was not a complete disavowal of the cooperative policy. Insofar as these were new, he had repudiated the Taft policy in China.

At the same time, American withdrawal from the Consortium did not prevent the remaining five international banking groups from completing the reorganization loan on April 27, 1913. Of the twenty-five million pounds advanced, half went to cover repayment of previous advances, to consolidate former loans to the provinces, and to settle claims of foreigners arising out of the revolution. Two million pounds were set aside to reorganize the salt administration. China actually received only eight and one-half million pounds to use for disbanding her troops and meeting government expenses—her most urgent needs.[56]

The American withdrawal from the Consortium caused speculation abroad as to whether or not the United States would pursue a similar independent policy in relation to the recognition of the revolution-born Chinese Republic.[57]   Wilson's sympathies for the new day in China had been well demonstrated in the Consortium statement. He was not well acquainted with the intricate forces behind either the revolution or the Republic, but the narrative of their evolution was known to him.

Spreading out of Hankow after the double ten revolt of October 10, 1911, the revolution had soon engulfed the provinces south of the Yangtze. As the southern provinces seceded and renounced the Manchu dynasty, the Assembly in Peking was encouraged to demand of the Prince Regent the establishment of a parliamentary type government with an appointed premier and cabinet. The Regent called on Yuan Shih-k'ai, former Governor of Shantung, builder of the Northern Army, and adviser to the throne, to assume power. He had hoped thereby to stem the revolutionary tide and save the dynasty. On November 2, the Regent was forced to accept the Assembly's demands.

Within the week, Yuan was elected Premier by the Assembly and confirmed in his office by the throne.[58]

Arriving in Peking, Yuan made the round of the legations. He frankly admitted that he favored a limited monarchy rather than a republic for China. Almost immediately, he left Peking to command the imperial army in the taking of Hankow and Hanyang from the revolutionary forces. No sooner was this accomplished than he returned to demand additional funds for prosecution of the war. Since none was available and a foreign loan was not forthcoming, he advised the court that it would be necessary to negotiate a peace with the insurgents.[59]

The revolutionaries demanded an armistice, withdrawal of the imperial forces, abdication of the Emperor, and the establishment of a Republic. Yuan presented their terms, and submitted his resignation. His resignation refused, he then advised the abdication of the dynasty.[60]

Meanwhile, Sun Yat-sen, leader of ten previous revolts in the South, had returned to China from the United States where he had been raising funds for a new revolutionary attempt. On January 1, 1912, he took the oath as President of the Republic in Nanking.[61] The Southern government proceeded to adopt a provisional constitution under which the Republic was to function until 1923. China was now divided with a monarchy in the North and a Republic in the South. The division was to be a familiar pattern in the troubled years that lay ahead.

The contending governments negotiated an agreement on February 7, 1912. Under its terms, the Empress Regent, in the name of the boy-Emperor, abdicated the throne to Yuan Shih-k'ai as Provisional President of the Chinese Republic. The boy-Emperor was to retain his title and receive an annual pension for the remainder of his life. Sun Yat-sen agreed to recognize the new President and resign his own office. All groups in China feared that continued division would invite foreign intervention, especially from Japan or Russia. Yuan, the military leader and old type Chinese politician, was distrusted by the republican factions; but since he possessed the most modern army in China, he seemed best able to guarantee security and stability.[62] The revolution was political in nature and aroused little interest on the part of the masses in China where government in the western sense had never existed. "Heaven is high and the Emperor far away," according to the Chinese proverb. Only now it was the Republic that existed at a distance.

As the Taft administration retired, it declared the United States was in *de facto* relations with the Republic of China. The Chinese Minister was "admitted to full relations" with the Department, and the American was similarly honored in Peking. Extension of *de jure* recognition was to be reviewed after the meeting of the newly elected Chinese Assembly, which would give the government a constitutional basis. The American government had resisted popular demand for full recognition since it desired to cooperate with the powers in such a step, and individually the other powers were attempting to secure certain concessions as a price for recognition.[63]

After Wilson's inauguration, E. T. Williams, the American Chargé in Peking, recommended early recognition of the Chinese Republic despite the disturbed state of affairs there. He thought such action was vital to the preservation of the Republic, and certainly the United States as the "Mother of Republics" should be the first to welcome the new convert. Britain would not extend recognition until some agreement was reached with Peking in her quarrel over Tibet; the other powers were making similar demands. To await their cooperation would be injurious to America's position in relation to the new Republic and could serve only to promote "the aggressive designs of others."[64] Ten days later, on March 28, the Chargé indorsed Yuan Shih k'ai's plea for recognition as a means of strengthening the Provisional President in his contest with the Assembly, which was to organize in April.[65] Williams, as did most of the foreign colony, looked upon Yuan as the best hope for Chinese stability.

Wilson was "anxious to act [on recognition] as soon as possible, because he wished to see China establish a stable government, and he was afraid that certain great powers were trying to prevent her from doing so." China's ability to operate a republic was questioned in the Cabinet, whereupon Wilson remarked that "after years of study, he had only one final conviction on government, and that was that the same sort of government was not suitable for all nations."[66]

In the Cabinet meeting of April 1, the President said he thought the United States should recognize China when her parliament met. He did not want American recognition dependent on the other powers but felt that they should be notified before the contemplated action was made public.[67] The next day, Bryan handed an *aide-mémoire* to the representatives of the nations having relations with China, informing them that it was the President's purpose to recognize the Republic on April 8, when the Constituent Assembly met. "He wishes me to say that he very earnestly desires and invites the cooperation of your government and its action to the same effect at the same time."[68] Thus a continuance of cooperation on American terms was offered the powers.

The governments of Brazil, Mexico, Peru, and Cuba instructed their diplomats to act with the American Minister on recognition. Japan dissented from joining the United States in its contemplated action. She claimed any recognition of Yuan Shih-k'ai amounted to intervention against the Southern faction of Sun Yat-sen and Huang Hsing which was already discontented with the strong methods of the Yuan.[69] The National Assembly met in Peking on April 8, possibly because of the "reported intention of the American Government to recognize the Chinese Republic."[70] Not until May 2, however, was the Assembly organized for business, thus fulfilling the conditions for American recognition. Williams then delivered Wilson's message to the Provisional President, thus making the United States the first of the major powers to extend recognition.[71]

Wilson's words of recognition carried the welcome of the United States to the "new China thus entering into the family of nations," and expressed the hope "that in perfecting a republican form of government the Chinese nation will attain to the highest degree of development and well being. . . ." The message closed with a hope that China would respect and fulfil her outstanding legal obligations.[72] Bryan, then in California working on the Japanese land legislation difficulty, wired his gratification for the recognition. He exclaimed, "It is epoch making!"[73] A national holiday was proclaimed in Peking on May 8, and a procession carried the Chinese and American flags to the legation where official thanks were expressed to the United States.[74]

Three weeks after extending recognition to the Chinese Republic, Wilson wrote the American Consul in Chefoo: "My thoughts constantly turn to the great nation now struggling to its feet as a conscious, self governing people, and it makes me very proud indeed that they should look to the United States as their friend and exemplar in the great tasks which lie ahead of them." He hoped that the United States might have the opportunity many times in the future "to show its cordial friendship for China and all those who work for her lasting benefit."[75] Certainly the President's attitude was benevolent toward the Republic.

Wilson dealt in uplift. He thought it was America's duty to help the development of the Far East, to transform it and to teach it to serve its own people. He had long looked upon trade as a major means in the process of civilization and development. China was an extant case of a government lacking representative institutions. The revolution had been due to an oligarchy which would not permit advance by conservative growth. The recognition of the Republic under Yuan was a step in the direction of stability, although he was aware of the false nature of the current republican institutions in China. Wilson was the last person to expect a change over night from a monarchic to a representative system of government. His central belief in government was that the people of a country, through their own native experience, developed the best type institutions for themselves, if allowed to do so without outside interference. This attitude was back of his "watchful waiting" in Mexico. It also loomed large in the development of his China policy in which he constantly sought to foster the forces of order and stability regardless as to whether these forces were democratic or even republican in nature. He believed it America's duty to aid the people of the Far East in finding a larger liberty.[76] Already he saw "the democratic leaven working in the Orient."[77]

Even the *Outlook* supported the recognition of China. It commented: "However much we may wish that certain conditions in China were better and more promiseful of governmental permanency, it must be admitted that China has amply shown her ability to establish a constitutional government."[78] The observation was a little premature, for only the appearance of a constitutional government had been assumed. China had long been held in public sympathy in the United States, and her recognition, especially as a newcomer in the world of republics, was a happy and popular event. On the last Sunday of April, people had prayed throughout the Christian world in their churches, at the behest of the Chinese Government, for divine aid to China in solving her problems and for the success of her new constitution, which had yet to be adopted.[79] The Chinese cause had been well advertised to the American people, and the extension of recognition was looked upon as the beginning of the hoped for progress in that distant land.

The Consortium loan and recognition had taken place in the midst of the Chinese struggle to establish a government and the contest of groups to control it. Two months before the assembly met a Kuomintang Party leader, Sung Chiao-jen, was murdered under circumstances which cast suspicion upon followers of Yuan Shih-k'ai. This murder together with the attempt of the tuchuns, or provincial war lords, to have a constitution framed by a committee instead of by the Assembly caused the members of the Kuomintang, largely composed of Sun Yat-sen's Southern followers, to suspect the good intentions of Yuan. The struggle between the two factions was transferred to the Assembly where the Kuomintang had a majority.[80] After the convening of the Assembly, the election of a speaker and organization of the body were major points of factional contention for nearly a month. Then the Sung Chiao-jen murder and the conclusion of the Consortium loan were hotly contested. When the government, in April, 1913, signed the loan without submitting it to the Assembly for approval, the Kuomintang leaders appealed to the provinces in an effort to arouse popular feeling against Yuan's action. Sun Yat-sen informed the foreign governments that consummation of the loan would precipitate a civil war.[81]

Meanwhile, Yuan Shih k'ai, who had learned intrigue as a functionary of the imperial court and as a governor in Korea, sought to establish a strong-man type of constitution dominated by the President. He appointed his own men to provincial offices until he largely controlled the North.[82] In June he dismissed two Kuomintang tuchuns on the frontier and replaced them with his own loyal followers. This led Sun to call for the resignation of Yuan. The quarrel was not over the structure or ideals of government solely; the distribution of office and the control of spending were also at stake.[83]

Out of the above differences grew the second revolution, a contest between the forces of Yuan and Sun for the control of the government. This was the July, 1913 revolution which served to distract Japan then engaged in the California land controversy with the United States. General Huang Hsing declared Nanking independent and announced a "punitive expedition" against the Provisional President. Both factions applied to the American Chargé to act as a peacemaker, but he considered that Yuan could restore order and so advised Washington. Bryan readily approved Williams' recommendation of non-interference.[84] The rebellion had little chance for success in the light of the Provisional President's modern army and his backing by the Northern war lords, who felt he was one of them.

Within two weeks after the outbreak of the July revolution, its leaders, Huang Hsing and Sun Yat-sen, were forced to flee the country. Yuan used the uprising as an excuse to dissolve rebellious provincial assemblies and to replace provincial governors, thus further consolidating his power. The recapture of Nanking, in September, 1913, brought the uprising to an end. Yuan then appointed Hsuing Hsi-ling, one of the reformers of 1898, as Premier with a carefully chosen cabinet. Finally, the articles of the constitution which were necessary to an election of a president were approved by the Assembly, and, on October 6, that body met to make the choice. Soldiers in civilian dress prevented the members from leaving. After a sit-ting of twelve hours, Yuan Shi k'ai was named the duly-elected President of the Chinese Republic.[85] When President Wilson was advised of the event, he authorized the Diplomatic Bureau to prepare a telegram of congratulations to Yuan.[86] To Wilson's message President Yuan replied: "Happily in the performance of my duties I always have the luminous example of the United States to guide and help me."[87] The major powers used the event as an occasion to extend recognition.[88]

On November 4, Yuan saw fit to dissolve the troublesome Kuomintang. The conservative Chin-pu Tang, or presidential party, became the leading political group in China's national life.[89] A committee was given the job of drawing up the constitution, and the President appointed a council of state to advise him and help in the administration.[90] Upon learning of the dissolution of the Kuomintang Party, Secretary Bryan wrote to Wilson of the "startling" news, "The President [of China] has dissolved the Nationalist Party and adopted something of Huerta's methods and given the same reasons." While it did not create the same situation as in Mexico, the Secretary observed, ". . . it may temper our expectations somewhat of rapid progress in the Orient." He also confessed, "I do not know that we are in a position to take any action."[91] At least none was taken.

Far Eastern policy by this time had been constantly before the new administration. The Consortium loan, recognition of the Republic and the Japanese-California land crisis had all taken place. Yet the United States remained without a diplomatic head in either Peking or Tokyo. Wilson now increased the tempo of his search for men to implement his policies in East Asia.

Secretary Bryan had long been in politics and felt that the foreign appointments should go to deserving Democrats. Since the clerical positions in the State Department were protected by civil service regulations, the removals were mostly from the higher branches of the service. Out of forty-odd diplomatic chiefs of missions, twenty-nine were changed within the first six months of the administration. In the more important appointments Wilson himself sought the ablest men to represent the United States abroad.[92] He favored retention of the personnel already in the diplomatic service as far as possible, but soon the problem assumed a different aspect as he explained to Charles W. Eliot:

> We find that those who have been occupying the legations and embassies have been habituated to a point of view which is very different, indeed, from the point of view of the present administration. They have had the material interests of individuals in the United States very much more in mind than the moral and public considerations which it seems to us ought to control. They have been so bred in a different school that we have found, in several instances, that it was difficult for them to comprehend our point of view and purpose. I have been genuinely distressed at the necessity of seeming to act contrary to the spirit of the merit system in any case or particular, but there are circumstances which seem to me to make a certain amount of this necessary at the opening of a new order of things.[93]

In his jurisprudence classes at Princeton, Wilson had observed that in diplomacy "A man must have that tact and address in personal intercourse, that self-possessed and self-respecting dignity, that knowledge of men and social convention, and that various knowledge of character which come, except in ordinary cases, only to men who have had wide opportunities of culture and observation and who have been trained under the influences of leisured society." Consular officers, he thought should be technical men and know commerce and economics.[94] In his earliest appointments it was to the world of academy or of letters to which the President turned. The general view and the cultured mind were ever of more importance to the former college president than was the expertness of the career diplomat.

Following the election of Wilson a movement arose under the direction of Bishop J. W. Bashford of the Methodist Church at Peking, to have Bryan sent there and at the same time raise the legation to an embassy. "The Commoner" was pleased with the compliment, for he thought a Christian should represent the United States in China. However, he had no inclination to accept the Peking post[95] nor the rumored offer of the Russian embassy.[96]

Wilson told House in January, 1913 that he thought it would be a wonderful thing for a man like former President Charles W. Eliot of Harvard to go to China and help "uplift them in their general struggle to help themselves. He express-ed a profound sympathy for the Chinese and [said that] he wished to do all that was possible to aid them."[97] In his letter urging the position on Eliot, Wilson explained: "I am very much concerned that our representatives in China and Japan should be of the best quality the country affords. I believe that there is probably nothing more nearly touches the future development of the world than what will happen in the East and it ought to happen, so far as our influence extends, under the best possible guidance."[98]

Bryan, on hearing from House of the offer to Eliot, was distressed, since the sage of Harvard was a ". . . Unitarian and did not believe in the divinity of Christ and the new Chinese civilization was founded upon the Christian movement there."[99] Since Eliot could not, for personal reasons,[100] accept the appointment, the matter passed into oblivion without any contention between Wilson and Bryan. Securing a minister for China continued to trouble the President-elect, however, and he wrote Bryan:

> The thing most prominent in my mind is that the men now most active in establishing a new government and a new regime for China are many of them members of the Y.M.C.A., and many of them also men trained in American universities. The Christian influence, direct or indirect, is very prominently at the front, and I need not say, ought to be kept there. Mr. John R. Mott, whom I know very well and who has as many of the qualities of a statesman as any man of my acquaintance, is very familiar with the situation in China, not only that, but he enjoys the confidence of men of the finest influence all over the Christian world. I am thinking of cabling to him (for he is now in China) to ask if he would be willing to remain there and represent the United States as our Minister.[101]

Again the matter arose in the correspondence with Bryan, and Wilson stated: "I want to find exceptional men, out of the common run, for all the chief posts. Men who will see and think. Mott, of whom I wrote is one of a thousand, and I have others to discuss with you."[102] Bryan endorsed the Mott appointment heartily.[103]

Wilson, meantime, sought his devoted friend and classmate Cleveland Dodge, with whom he maintained a close friendship throughout life, to bring pressure on Mott to accept the appointment.[104] So anxious was the President, for the inauguration had now taken place, to have the distinguished Christian leader accept the Chinese ministry that he offered to permit him to retain his "posts of guidance" in the Y.M.C.A. "It would be quite possible also," Wilson wrote, "to allow you in all ordinary circumstances such leaves of absence as are necessary. I have set my heart on the appointment because of all it will imply no less than because of my complete confidence in your character and ability."[105]

Despite all the pressure and imploring, Mott could not see his way clear to accept. When his refusal was made known to the President, the latter wrote Dodge: "Mott's decision was a great blow to me. I don't know when I have been so disappointed. It is a very difficult road I am traveling in trying to get the finest men in the country to serve us at foreign posts."[106] The matter of Mott's appointment was noised about in the press with approval, and Dodge observed that it had "made a great impression both here and abroad, and has announced to the world, more definitely than anything else could have done, the kind of policy which you intend to adopt in your dealings with China."[107]

Wilson talked with Dodge of the latter's suggestion of Professor Jeremiah Jenks of New York for the Peking post. He had, however, determined to go "slowly in this matter of choosing someone else for China."[108] Charles R. Crane recommended the sociology professor Edward A. Ross for the position.[109] Wilson was interested in the suggestion, and upon Mott's return from the Orient, he had the Y.M.C.A. head investigate the fitness of the University of Wisconsin professor. The President was especially concerned "with reference to his attitude toward Christianity and the church." Mott suggested the name of Professor Ernest D. Burton of the University of Chicago, who had recently spent a year in China studying mission work.[110]

It was now June, the administration had been three months in power, and Bryan thought it was "quite important that we find a minister to China as soon as it can be conveniently done." He suggested ex-Governor Joseph W. Folk of Missouri who was "identified with the religious life of the nation and would. . . be acceptable to the missionaries."[111] In attempting to impress Henry Morgenthau with the importance of the Turkish legation for which he was being considered, Wilson said he thought it and the China post the two demanding the highest abilities in the foreign service. Morgenthau expressed then a preference for China, but Wilson urged that "our Chinese interests were largely in the form of missionary activities and our minister should be an evangelical Christian."[112]

In early March, Crane, who favored Professor Ross for Peking, had suggested for a Latin American appointment Professor Paul S. Reinsch of the University of Wisconsin. Reinsch had been a member of three delegations to Pan American conferences, one of the originators of a course in world politics, an author of many articles and books, the latest of which was *Political Currents in the Far East*.[113] Crane continued to urge the appointment, saying both Senator Robert La Follette and President Charles R. Van Hise of the University of Wisconsin thought well of it.[114] Wilson knew Reinsch professionally, for both had been among the founders of the American Political Science Association. Joseph E. Davies, Chief of the Bureau of Corporations, now urged Reinsch for the China post. Wilson promised to "give earnest consideration" to it.[115] Two weeks later, when he referred his recommendations to Bryan, among them was: "Professor Reinsch, of the University of Wisconsin, a great student of world politics and particularly Oriental relationships to China. . ."[116] It was the only identification in a sizable list of recommended appointments.

On July 16, Reinsch called at the White House. It was reported that he would accept the China post. *The New York*

Times commented that "The President regards this mission as of the greatest importance and has scrutinized with extraordinary care the qualifications of all those who had been suggested for it. It was said . . . that he believed that in Prof. Reinsch he had obtained a man who was capable of handling the delicate diplomatic situation in the Far East."[117] The new Minister to China was commissioned August 15, 1913 and began his thirty day instruction period which included a week for conference with the departmental officials with reference to China.[118] On November 15, he assumed his new duties in Peking, thus relieving Chargé E. T. Williams who had acted as head of the American mission there for the past nine months of the new administration.[119]

The appointment of Reinsch to China had a far reaching effect on American activities there. Due to his position as a political scientist, he developed a great influence with the young intellectuals.[120] Reinsch himself was aware that "the rise of Japan, the great Chinese transformation, the nationalist movement throughout the Orient . . . [had] made us more generally conscious . . . that the separate existence of the East and West . . . [had] come to an end. . . ." In this drama, "upon the outcome of which depends the welfare not only of a country or section but of all mankind,"[121] Reinsch was to play a leading role. His reports and personal consultations over a period of six years kept the Chief Executive well-informed on Chinese problems. His insistence that the Chinese revolution could develop into a vast regenerative movement for its people was shared by the President.[122]

Throughout his ministry, Reinsch was able to keep his hand on the pulse of what was transpiring in China. The American consuls there were under the legation and reported to it at all times. This, previous to the Rogers Act of 1924 which consolidated the consular and diplomatic services, was an unique situation, existing only in China. Needless to say, it added much to the minister's effectiveness. With E. T. Williams coming to Washington to head the Far Eastern Division, Reinsch was assured an ear in the State Department.

In the interview previous to Reinsch leaving Washington, Wilson said that it was incumbent on the United States "to do her share independently and to give specific moral and financial assistance" to China. Reinsch declared, ". . . I received the President's assurance of active support for constructive work in China. In his conversation he dwelt, however, more on the educational side and on political example and moral encouragement, than on the matter of finance and commerce."[123]

Wilson's position in putting education, political example, and moral encouragement first as a means of serving China came naturally from his belief that these were the well springs of political life. China policy was as one with the foreign policy as a whole: America was to serve mankind by example and moral purpose. She was to aid in the development of constitutional liberty in the world. There were many means to this end. In the Orient missionary activity was one such means.

As a Presbyterian elder, the former first lay President of Princeton, the advertised son of a distinguished Presbyterian divine, a man who had all his life been thrown into the midst of missionaries and their works, Wilson was conscious of their influence. And then too, one must never forget the deep simplicity of his Christianity, his "uplift" spirit, his respect for duty and service. Wilson the man had always the greatest respect for the ability of those who toiled in the vineyard to rightly interpret the interests of the common people.[124] It must not be forgotten, however, that he had a trained mind, a wide realm of experience, and a variety of information by which he could separate the wheat from the chaff in missionary advices. At times he was not above requesting the missionaries to refrain from political interference in the countries in which they were resident, but he always respected their position of unselfish service.[125] He gave to the support of their cause.[126] Before he took public office he attended their meetings. He was keenly interested in the movement towards unity among Protestant bodies in the mission field as a means of strengthening their effectiveness.[127] Reports of the good work done by the missionaries and its cordial reception by the Chinese people inspired him to observe, "It looks indeed as if the old empire were waking to a new life."[128]

The President was always free to advise with John R. Mott as often as the Christian leader came to Washington. His admiration for Mott's work and character was unique. During the period when the Y.M.C.A. leader was being considered for the position of American Minister to China, a group of missionaries home on furlough called on Wilson to urge the appointment. "The President said he realized the influence that the missionaries had had in regenerating China and that he looked upon Mr. Mott as a man especially well fitted to serve the purposes of the administration because of his knowledge of the mission world."[129] It was true, at this time, that the investment of the United States in China was only $59,000,000 of which $10,000,-000 was in mission property and $42,000,000 in business, leaving some $7,000,000 invested in securities and government obligations.[130]

At Princeton, Wilson taught that "Christianity has [a] great unifying effect in the world. Nothing [is] more powerful in bringing about the realization of the relationships of mankind." Religion with its ideals and motives of duty was another vehicle of progress along with struggle, education, and law. In fact, "education puts man in position for progress, but religion determines the line of [that] progress." It is necessary to point out though that to Wilson, the President or the scholar, progress was never thought of so much in the realm of material aggregation as "an advance from generation to generation in [the] principles of humanity and mutual helpfulness."[131] Missionaries changed individuals; individuals changed society.[132]

Of course, it must be realized that the Professor spoke to his students and the President to a vaster world audience. His additional duty was ever to inspire and lead, to inspire support for his policies in addition to formulating them. His theological background and moral attitude had much to do with his flights of rhetoric, but his words proceeded too from a fixed realization of the basis of society in its moral principles, in the things in which it believed, rather than in its wealth or military might. Perhaps if Wilson had been more precise in developing his thesis, he would have been blamed less for being an impractical idealist. His speeches were more often than not extemporaneous; and Norman Hapwood, his liberal friend, said that Wilson often suffered from people not understanding the rapidity of his mind. But certainly it is true, as Ray Stannard Baker, his biographer wrote: "We must look at Wilson's diplomacy, therefore, as all of a piece. Whether in Latin America, or China, or the Philippines, it was a challenge to every aspect of dollar diplomacy; an effort to reassert and apply the old democratic and moral principles."[133] Once again America had become, as in Lincoln's words, "this last best hope of man on earth."

CHAPTER TWO

The California Crisis

ALTHO' THE STREAM BE SHALLOW,

YET IT WILL OVERFLOW,

IF ALL ITS WATERS ARE DAMMED UP-

THE PEOPLE'S MIND IS EVEN SO.

—Empress Dowager Shoken

On March 5, 1913, the day following Wilson's inauguration, the Japanese Ambassador Sutemi Chinda called at the White House offices to express the concern of the imperial government relating to the contemplated land legislation in California. Some 100,000 Japanese subjects had come to the West Coast of the United States. Most of these immigrants had settled in the coastal cities and rich California agricultural valleys. Since they were Asiatics, ineligible to citizenship, the proposed legislation, barring all persons not eligible to citizenship from owning land, would effectively deprive the Japanese of that privilege.

The Japanese problem, long a feature of California politics, was a compound of racial feeling and of economic competition. The frugal, industrious Japanese and the native and resident whites contested for agricultural employment and for ownership of the productive lands. Racial agitation centered largely in the San Francisco labor organizations, which were composed in large part of European immigrants. These workers had found themselves competing with the Orientals for employment, and since the great earthquake and fire they had increasingly manifested their animosity towards the Japanese. The problem had become a national issue in 1907 when President Theodore Roosevelt had seen fit to intervene in the proposed San Francisco school segregation case.[1] The flow of Japanese immigration to the United States had thereafter been controlled by the familiar Gentlemen's Agreement, in which Japan took it upon herself to restrict immigration from her own ports. Nevertheless, the Californians insisted that the Japanese continued to pour into the state, and to menace American Civilization due to their nonassimilability and different social and economic standards. From 1907 to 1913, every California legislature had considered discriminatory legislation.[2]

The race issue had remained dormant for two years as a result of an understanding between the political parties of California attempting to prevent antagonizing Japan before the San Francisco Exposition. Then in 1912 Anthony Caminetti, a Bryan Democrat of San Francisco, was elected to the state senate on an anti-Japanese platform. The legislature was Republican in both houses. When it convened, the newly elected Senator promptly introduced his program,[3] which broke the truce and brought forth a wave of anti-Japanese bills, forty such measures being introduced in January, 1913 alone. Each party now attempted to secure credit for anti-Japanese legislation,[4] since the cause was popular with the electorate.

In Washington, the California delegation in Congress defended the action being taken by the state legislature. Wilson himself had written to ex-Mayor James Phelan of San Francisco the previous October:

In the matter of Chinese and Japanese coolie immigration I stand for the national policy of exclusion. The whole question is one of assimilation of diverse races. We cannot make a homogeneous population out of a people who do not blend with the Caucasian race. Their lower standards of living as laborers will crowd out the white agriculturists and will in other fields prove a most serious industrial menace. The success of free democratic institutions demands of our people education, intelligence, patriotism [;] and the State should protect them against unjust and impossible competition. United labor is the basis of contentment.

Democracy rests in equality of the citizens. Oriental coo-
lieism will give us another race problem to solve, and surely
we have learned our lesson.[5]

It must be remembered, Wilson was a candidate in 1912. The
Democratic platform had declared in favor of an exclusion law.
Bryan too had run on an exclusion plank four years previously,
so it was nothing new in party history.

Since the Constitution defines treaties along with the laws
of Congress and the Constitution itself as the law of the land,
but does not carry any provision to prevent a state from passing
legislation contrary to national treaty obligations, the Washington authorities had no legal means of stopping the California
legislation. The danger in the passage of the bill was Japanese
resentment based on its discriminatory clause—"aliens ineligible
to citizenship."

Japan herself did not permit foreign ownership of land,
but hers was a national policy which excluded all foreign nationals. Moreover, she commonly returned Chinese laborers
entering Japan in search of employment. Thus it was the discriminatory features of the California act solely which formed
the basis for Japanese objection. She therefore demanded
equality of treatment for her nationals.

California was Japan's most important "colonization" venture. She had been granted equality with Europeans in sharing
extraterritorial privileges in China. The government of the
Netherlands Indies counted her people as European. In British
India the Japanese like the whites were "Sahib" to the natives,
and the Anglo-Japanese Alliance recognized Japan's place a-
mong the powers. The successful conclusion of the Sino-
Japanese War in 1895 and the defeat of the Russians in 1905
had established her position as a great power and had thereby
inflated her sense of national pride.[6] To be branded before
the world as an inferior people, "ineligible to citizenship," and
denied equality of treament for her nationals by another power
was an intolerable affront to this sensitive people.

More important, however, in the Japanese government's
attitude toward the California proposals was the growing sus-

picion in Japan of American ambitions in East Asia. This suspicion was magnified beyond its merits by the contemporary political situation.[7]

Japanese distrust of the United States had been of gradual growth. She had viewed with trepidation the acquisition of the Hawaiian Islands in 1898. This feeling was increased by the extension of American sovereignty over the Philippines as a result of the war with Spain. To the Japanese, American history showed that the process of pushing into a new area then incorporating it into the federal union was the standard pattern of expansion. Now the United States made stepping stones of the islands of the Pacific, had established a base in the Philippines, had missionaries in China. Through the Open Door notes, the United States had declared her position of equality in China;[8] and through her entrepreneurs, she had gained access to international loans and railway construction there.[9]

It was recalled how Averill Harriman, one of the American railroad magnates, had attempted to purchase the South Manchurian Railway from the Japanese government in 1905, and only Baron Jutaro Komura's return from Portsmouth had prevented the fulfilment of the sale.[10] Japan blamed the United States with thwarting her designs for a huge indemnity from Russia which would have paid for the 1905 war,[11] the billion dollar debt of which rested heavily upon the people and increased the popular dissatisfaction. More recently, in 1909, the Knox neutralization scheme for internationalizing the railways of Manchuria for eventual return to China[12] had scared Japan into an understanding with Russia, guaranteeing their mutual spheres of investment in the outer provinces of Northeast China. Japan looked with suspicion at American ambitions in the China market, especially in Manchuria, which by 1913 she considered of "special interest" to herself.

Unfortunately, Japan and the United States arrived simultaneously on the world stage; and mutual suspicion was bred out of conflicting interests and competition in trying for a bigger role, conscious or not, in the drama of events in the East Asia. The Taft-Katsura understanding of 1905 exchanged

Japanese disavowals of aggressive purposes in the Philippines in return for American recognition of a Japanese regency in Korea. The Root-Takahira notes of 1908 effectively gave Japan a free hand in Manchuria in exchange for renewed guarantees for the safety of the Philippines and for declarations on the open door and the independence of China. Japan's absorption of Korea in 1910, after prolonged declarations of respect for its sovereignty, had increased American suspicion. Numerous handicaps imposed on American business by the Japanese in Manchuria had aroused the resentment of the cotton textile and other business interests.[13] The language, tradition, and racial differences between the two peoples permitted the easy development of antagonism and misunderstanding.[14] American orientation was still European. Its policy in the Orient was unevenly developed, varying as it did between cooperation with the other powers and an independent course of action, but always insisting on "most favored nation" treatment.[15] From a Japanese viewpoint it seemed highly opportunistic and ambitious.

Internally, Japan was a welter of the old and the new, of the East and the West. The Japanese Constitution embodied age-old native political principles under the garb of representative institutions. The Emperor was accepted as the highest organ of the state.[16] Shintoism clothed him with a Japanese concept of divinity. Under the constitution the imperial will was paramount. By decree the Emperor could set aside any action of the two house Diet, and the Cabinet was responsible solely to him.[17] Suffrage was enjoyed by only 3,000,000 out of a population of 50,000,000 people. In the realm of social and political westernization, the initiative had come from the nation not the individual.[18] The social ethic emphasized obedience and the duty of the subject to the state, not the state's obligation to the subject. Geographically isolated, inhabited by a homogeneous people who were nationally sensitive, racial consciousness was an ever present fact of their existence.[19] California's proposed legislation was therefore a serious affront to the Japanese.

In February, before the advent of the Wilson administration in Washington, public riots, based on discontent with the current political developments, broke out in Tokyo as a result of the imperial prorogation of the Diet in an attempt to save the Katsura ministry. In December, 1912, the Cabinet of Marquis Kimmochi Saionji had floundered on its refusal to raise two additional army divisions for use in Korea as demanded by the army politicians. The army and navy factions had been an old form of political division in Japan. Saionji had favored naval expansion at the expense of the army, so the General Staff, by refusing to participate in the Cabinet, destroyed his government. In accordance with the advice of the Genro, the elder statesmen who functioned as an exofficio board of notables advising the Emperor, General Taro Katsura was called to head the new ministry. He was an arrogant and ambitious soldier who had never been popular even when serving as Japan's cabinet head during the Russo-Japanese war. He was regarded as representative of the bureaucratic spirit, and had only four months since, after being attached to the new Emperor's household, renounced all political ambitions.

No sooner had Katsura formed a government than meetings were held to denounce him. Both the Seiyukai and Kokuminto parties carried on a political campaign against the government in the name of Constitutionalism. Katsura replied by announcing his intention to organize a new party. The opposition embarrassed the ministry by asking if it would bring in a bill for the raising of the additional army divisions. The Premier resorted to an imperial decree proroguing the Diet. The opposition, through the press and public meetings, aroused the populace to a pitch of emotion so intense that the Diet was again prorogued. On February 8, 1913, disorders broke out, which were put down only after calling upon army units to assist the numerous police. Katsura resigned as a result, after only two months in office, and Admiral Count Gombei Yamamoto was called upon to form a government.[20]

Yamamoto, reportedly, by arranging the resignation of the Katsura ministry and guaranteeing the Seiyukai leaders that their party would not be dissolved by imperial edict, had gained their promised support. He then was able to assume office at the Emperor's call, but his government was not popular. The Cabinet included the old line Seiyukai leaders Marquis Kimmochi Saionji, Takashi Hara and others.[21] But the political elements were too diverse in their views to last. Marquis Saionji soon resigned as head of the Seiyukai party, the factions favoring responsible cabinet government became disaffected, and the Seiyukai found itself outvoted in the Diet. Yamamoto, while welcoming party support, attempted to stand above them. His chief problem was to find the funds to support the heavy naval building program and at the same time to raise the additional army divisions demanded without adding an extra burden on the taxpayer.[22] It was in the midst of such political and economic demands on a government in political jeopardy that the California land question was precipitated.

In the United States there was little popular understanding of the issue which had formed in California, let alone of the tenseness of the political situation in Japan. Likewise, the people of the West Coast did not comprehend the intensity of Japanese objections to the projected land legislation. The reasoned Californian attitude toward the whole matter was fairly well reflected in a letter of William Kend, a member of Congress from that state, to Secretary Bryan:

I see no reason why Japan or any other Oriental nation should object to our control, in a matter so much our own peculiar business as is tenure of land. It is not for a moment because we feel our superiority or the inferiority of the Japanese that we object to their monopolizing, as they have done, certain sections of our State. We do not ask, and especially do not demand, that Japan modify her land laws to let us in. We merely recognize in frankness what they must recognize, although they do not wish to let the fact be known, that there are such things as racial lines that cannot be crossed except with peril and irritation. The Negro problem under which this country labors is a sufficient proof of this fact. We cannot afford to have any more such problems with us. The bitterness involved in racial friction prevents the growth of domestic ideas and hampers our advancement.[23]

In the East the press was moderate on the issue, but when the legislation threatened international difficulties the tone changed to one of resentment that California would place the whole nation in difficulties with a foreign power.[24]

The international ramifications of the California land legislation soon assumed major prominence in Washington. Wilson brought it to the attention of the Cabinet on April 8, 1913. Secretary Houston sympathized with the Californians, while Secretary Lane feared that among other things political capital would be made of the situation by the local demagogues.[25] Two weeks later when considering the same matter, Bryan, always fertile in ideas, suggested the land legislation be submitted to a referendum in California.[26] This, of course, revealed his ignorance of the local situation, for the matter was popular and the extremists were threatening a referendum entailing an anti-Japanese campaign if the desired legislation were not forthcoming.[27] A referendum would certainly have increased the tension of relations with Japan. Despite this revelation of Bryan's lack of understanding, Wilson announced he had asked the Secretary of State to go to California. Bryan had agreed to undertake the mission, although he confessed that he was "far from being anxious to go." Lacking any constitutional restraints over the proposed legislation, a personal appeal seemed best to the President, who was careful to observe the niceties of federal-state relationship since the administration was in a bad public position. The Democrats had denounced Roosevelt's interference in the San Francisco school case of 1906. The present California government was Republican and in a favorable position to pass a popular anti-Japanese bill to the embarrassment of the national Democratic administration.[28]

Meanwhile, the press on April 18 carried reports of a mass meeting of 20,000 Japanese in Tokyo cheering for war rather than submit to the California insult.[29] Wilson had Bryan telegraph Governor Hiram Johnson asking consideration for the international nature of the legislation.[30] The Cabinet was not hopeful that the California situation could be improved; but it thought if Bryan went West, Japan would be convinced that the Federal government was friendly and disposed to do all that it could.[31] Wilson, too, rejected the solution offered by Professor Edward S. Corwin of Princeton for over-riding the constitutionality of the California legislation by making a treaty with Japan on the matter. The President had less confidence than Corwin in the power of the federal government to take such action.[32]

The papers of April 25 carried Bryan's parting words on leaving Washington, "I go hopefully, yet with a realization of the responsibility involved." The West was home country to Bryan, and there he had his greatest political strength. Caminetti was known as a Bryan-Democrat; and the administration hoped "the Commoner," known for his face to face political dealing, could temporize the legislation. At the time of Bryan's departure, Wilson informed the press that the Secretary's mission was "to take counsel" (How he loved that term!) with the authorities in California as to the best means of avoiding an international difficulty. He said that the attitude of Japan in protesting the contemplated legislation was proper, that the negotiations had been friendly and without antagonism.[33]

During Bryan's absence, John Bassett Moore, who had come into the State Department as counselor upon the abrupt resignation of Huntington Wilson over the Consortium affair in March,[34] became acting Secretary and drafted the diplomatic notes to Japan, which the President approved. Moore was thoroughly capable and was recognized as America's most outstanding figure in international law. Formerly a professor at Columbia, he had been a classmate of Wilson at the University of Virginia.[35] Later, Moore commented that the President was not "conversant with foreign conditions. Of international law he knew little, and of diplomatic history scarcely none."[36]

Bryan, while in Sacramento, was the guest of Governor and Mrs. Johnson. At the Capitol, he was installed in a room directly opposite the Senate chamber and there conferred with individuals and groups of local leaders. On April 28, the legislature went into executive session and invited Bryan to address the joint meeting of the houses.[37] The speech was conciliatory, without rancor, and considerate of local political opinion to the point of assuming neutrality in respect to the legislation. Bryan began by expressing a deep feeling of responsibility as a presidential representative. He asked the legislature to delay the land legislation so the matter could be dealt with through diplomatic channels. But, he conceded, "I am here to tell you that no matter what you do the President will do as best he can with any conditions you may create . . . [although] he earnestly advises against the use of any language that would offend any people that have dealings with us."

Bryan then spoke of the one hundred fifty percent increase in American exports to Japan within the preceding two years. He showed that the proposed "ineligible to citizenship" term in the bill also would affect China; and he recalled that only the day before, at the request of the new Republic, the people of the United States had prayed for the government and officials of that ancient land. China, he said, regarded the United States as her best friend because of the action of the President in disavowing the Consortium loan. In relation to the resentment aroused by the proposed measure, he warned, "You must regard the feelings of people and no matter how they may acquiesce [in what we do], we must remember that anything that disturbs the friendship between the nations is to be deplored." This was the high point of the weak challenge Bryan offered the assembled legislators.

Bryan then presented President Wilson's request that the term "ineligible for citizenship" not be employed, since it would be a declaration to the world of the inferiority of a nation. He offered as Wilson's proposals: first, the resources of diplomacy assisted by a commission to study the situation; second, the form of the non-discriminatory Illinois statute; third, the provisions of the District of Columbia statute; and fourth, avoidance of the term "ineligible for citizenship." Asked if the President were aware that "the assimilation of races and not the ownership of land is the crux of the situation?" Bryan stated, "I think he is fully advised as to the feeling in regard to immigration."

The Secretary wired Wilson concerning the questions asked, and the President concurred in the answers that had been given. Replying to the inquiry as to what he would do if the legislature passed a bill containing the words "ineligible to citizenship," Wilson could "say only that I cannot assume that the representations heretofore made to the Governor and Legislature of California [,] and which your presence in Sacramento must necessarily have greatly emphasized [,] will be disregarded and so render it necessary to consider that question."[38] The latter was an old Wilson tactic of assuming that the responsibility rested solely with the individuals entrusted to make the decision; and their obligation to their trust left them no alternative than to do as duty dictated, which usually meant to act in the manner in which Wilson desired.

Later the same day, Wilson wired Bryan that he agreed with the Secretary's plan to spend a day in San Francisco, which indicated their recognition as to the center of the anti-Japanese movement in the state. The President further directed that in the negotiations, "Our wise course seems to me to be to make it emphatically evident that we are acting just now as the Federal Government, sanctioning this nor that but as the sincere friends of California, wishing to be of such service as possible to them in a critical matter whose importance and whose critical character we are better able to advise them of then [sic] others would be." He feared sanctioning a particular bill or form of words because it might embarrass the government in diplomatic negotiations or in subsequent court action: "Our advice should be along general lines and as if we spoke as sincere and by no means unsympathetic friends of California, and yet as unmindful of our serious obligation to a friendly nation." Whatever the course pursued by the state authorities, the federal government, Wilson thought, should preserve its independence to act as it saw best under the circumstances thus created.[39]

The next day, the President protested to Governor Johnson that the Webb bill "would involve an appeal to the courts on [the] question of treaty rights and bring on what might be [a] long and delicate litigation."[40] In California, however, the legislation was still insisted upon, and Bryan wired Wilson suggesting that land ownership be restricted to "aliens whose right to hold real estate has been made a matter of treaty." Since no American treaty with Japan gave her subjects such rights, the same purposes as proposed by the legislature would be accomplished without offending the Japanese Government. Wilson heartily agreed with this positive proposal.[41]

Despite Bryan's presence and the Washington representations, the California Senate passed the Webb bill on May 2 with only two opposing votes. The following day, the Assembly similarly acted, with three persons dissenting. Two Democrats, one in either house, had stood by the national administration! Bryan made a farewell speech to the legislature, criticizing the discrimination as contained in the bill, and set out for Washington to report on the failure of his mission.[42] Meanwhile, the President, who had been conferring with Ambassador Chinda and Counselor Moore, wired the Governor for information as to how long the state executive had to consider the bill. He desired to confer with Bryan in person before the Governor acted.[43]

It is evident from the correspondence between Wilson and Bryan that the President set the policy of giving California advice without dictation. In the mission Bryan was his agent.[44] Upon his return, the Secretary explained that the Democrats in California had made a fight on the racial issue, thus forcing the Republicans to take up the matter.[45] At Wilson's behest, Bryan wired the Governor to veto the legislation and call an extra session to reconsider the measures to be taken. He promised the aid of the national administration on a diplomatic level to help solve the situation.[46]

Johnson, however, approved the Webb Act which deprived aliens "ineligible to citizenship" of the right to own land except as guaranteed by treaty, but granted them the right to lease agricultural land for three years.[47] The Californians had thus thwarted Wilson's attempt to exclude the phrase "ineligible to citizenship." As was expected by the administration, Japan resented this as an affront to her national honor.

The actual crisis in the situation was initiated on May 9, when the Japanese Ambassador handed Bryan a strongly worded protest. It expressed the "painful disappointment" of Japan in the measure and offered "their urgent and explicit protest" against the legislation. Branding the bill "unfair and discriminatory," the note pointed out that the measure was "inconsistent with the treaty of 1911 and the principles of amity and good understanding. . . . The Imperial Government . . . desire to have it made entirely clear that they attach the utmost importance to the discriminatory phase of the legislation. . . ."[48]

Bryan read the Japanese protest to the Cabinet. Its strong wording was "something of a shock, especially in view of what the government had done and was doing and of Japan's own laws against aliens." There was some doubt as to the true intent of the note. Some of the members thought it was for home consumption in Japan; others believed Japan wanted war before the Panama Canal could be opened. The bad financial plight of the island empire was evidenced against her ability to prosecute a war. To the statement that Japan could take the Philippines and land an army in California, Secretary of Agriculture Houston jokingly replied that he "would almost be willing to whip her to make her take the Philippines and . . . would eat every Jap who landed in California as part of an invading force." Showing his lack of understanding, Bryan again suggested a referendum on the matter.

Wilson called the Japanese protest unfair and stated that the bill specifically safeguarded all treaty rights. Publication of the protest was considered unwise since it might inflame public opinion. Consequently, Bryan was instructed to informally tell Chinda that the language of the communication was objectionable. Wilson suggested that Bryan take particular pains to gain some opinion from the Ambassador's personal demeanor as to how serious the protest really was. "If Japan meant what she said, it was impossible to exaggerate the situation."[49]

On May 13, the California Case was again considered. Wilson felt that it was his duty to put the matter before the Governor, and "if Johnson then preferred political stunts to statesmanship he must take the responsibility."[50] It was reported that the British Ambassador had called upon his Japanese colleague to see that something was done to allay feeling in Japan; and the revised Japanese protest, omitting the offensive language, was read. Wilson said he thought their case "very weak," and asked advice as to the answer he should make. "The possibility of war was discussed. The President thought there would be no war, and that it would be mischievous to hint that there might be, but that, of course, we should keep our eyes open." As to Japan's ability to take the Philippines, Hawaii, and Alaska, "The President said that they might do so, but they could not keep them—that eventually we would have our way." But he carefully emphasized that there would be no war.[51]

Secretary Daniels read a statement prepared by Admiral Bradley A. Fiske, naval aide for operations, on the possibility of war. While Fiske did not believe the current tension would result in hostilities, he recited the facts that Japan needed to expand, and the fertile Philippine Islands offered an outlet for her surplus population. From the Philippines, Japan could command the coast of China. Hawaii also was coveted by the Japanese, who were there already in great numbers. Fiske thought Japan might attack, occupy the Philippines and Hawaii, then, under cover of her fleet, initiate a stalemate. The United States fleet would establish a blockade, but it could not be made effective between the enemy and Korea. Japanese strategy would be to endure the blockade until such time as the Americans wearied of the effort and would be willing to cede the islands to end the struggle. The Cabinet, however, did not take such a serious view of the situation except for Secretary Redfield.[52]

The Joint Army and Navy Board, Admiral Dewey as chairman, met in New York on May 14. It viewed seriously the Japanese agitation over the California problem and recommended that the Pacific fleet, consisting of the *Saratoga* in Chinese waters and some smaller vessels on the Yangtze River, be moved to the protection of the Philippines. General Leonard Wood, who was the instigator of the Board's action, according to Daniels, said that the Japanese notes were becoming insistent and that the army quietly had been moving supplies to the Philippine and Hawaiian garrisons.[53]

Admiral Fiske's memorandum, written the same day, was more alarming than his previous communication on the situation. He now thought "war is possible." The outcome depended on whether or not Japan believed herself sufficiently prepared for the undertaking. He reminded Daniels of the Japanese tactic of attack without warning and urged that all necessary precautions be taken. Russia and Europe had thought a Japanese war impossible in 1904, yet it had come. "The disparity between Russia and Japan then was no greater than between the United States and Japan now, and the stake no greater." Near completion of the Panama Canal would greatly influence the decision of Japan, for once completed it would end her advantageous position in the Pacific; and her naval men were well aware that "the opportunity lost now is lost forever." The issue remained for Japan's decision, and Fiske believed, "war is not only possible, but even probable. . . ."[54]

At the next Cabinet meeting the President presented his draft of an answer to the Japanese protest. It defended the California legislation as explicitly recognizing the treaty rights of Japan, and explained that the courts were open for redress of any injured parties. The matter of a possible war with Japan again arose. Secretary of War Garrison, in defending the recommendations of the Joint Board, said if they were followed Manila could be held for a year. Daniels opposed any large movement of American forces or ships in the Far East as dangerous to the peaceful solution of the issue. He also explained that the ships in Chinese waters were inferior in firing range to the Japanese; and they could be destroyed before reaching Manila.[55] Garrison intimated that the Cabinet views on military matters were secondary to those of the Joint Board. "At this Bryan flared up for the first time. He got red in the face and was very emphatic. He thundered out that army and navy officers could not be trusted to say what we should or should not do, till we actually got into war. . . . " He opposed any movement of ships in the East which might excite Japan.[56] Wilson "felt strongly upon the subject, and after a warm discussion said he would take the responsibility as Commander-in-Chief of refusing to move the fleet." This view conformed with that of Secretary Daniels but opposed the professional naval and military advice.[57]

At the end of the Cabinet meeting, the President asked Garrison and Daniels to meet with him that afternoon for further discussion. Later, in the White House gardens, the President heard the views of the Secretaries and directed them to make no move on the recommendations of the Joint Board "until further notice." He said, "We must not have war except in an honorable way, and I fear the Joint Board made a mistake [in proposing war-like moves in the Pacific]."[58] News of this meeting reached the press and added to the war scare then prevailing.[59]

On May 17, learning that a leak had occurred to the press concerning the Joint Board's recommendations, Daniels had gone to the White House. The President "was greatly put out, not only about the leak, but chiefly because after he had announced his policy on the Pacific, the Joint Board had a meeting and [had] taken action relative to moving ships on the Pacific." Wilson told Daniels, ". . . I wish you would say to them that if this should occur again, there will be no General or Joint Boards; they will be abolished." He ordered that they were to hold no further deliberations until further notice. A few days later, he consented to their meeting, but warned that no action should be decided in the Pacific pending the Japanese land discussion.[60] The Board, however, ceased functioning and was not revived until the preparedness program prior to the entry of the United States into the world war.

Wilson assured the press that the Japanese tension would be "adjusted amicably."[61] In Tokyo the irresponsible war talk was condemned by speakers at a mass meeting. However, such luminaries as Professor Toru Nagai, the sociologist of Waseda University, expounded: "God made the white and colored peoples equal. Unless we claim equality we shall fail to carry out God's wishes."[62] Certainly the situation was fraught with peril, as always, when a nation identifies its national aims with those of divinity.

The *North China Herald* reported that the Japanese Government was anxious to fight the issue of inequality to a conclusion, but John R. Mott of the Y.M.C.A., just returned from Japan, told Wilson that sentiment among the Japanese was not such as to cause apprehension.[63] Nevertheless the *New York Sun* in a Sunday feature claimed that American military and naval experts recognized that Japan was better prepared for war now than she would be in the future because the military burden was growing intolerable, and that she would soon be compelled to strike.[64] The American press reported that Colonel George W. Goethals had put another shift to work on the completion of the Panama Canal so as to speed opening of the passage in case of any eventualities.[65] The American Military Attaché in Japan was urgently recalled to Tokyo for fear of hostilities. Harbors were boomed and approaches were mined in some American ports.[66]

A reassuring note was contained in the report of A. Bailey Blanchard, the Chargé in Tokyo. He cabled that the anti-American mass meeting demanding war, held April 17, was composed of a turbulent element and unrepresentative of public opinion. Bitter resentment over the California legislation was evident; and, among the ignorant classes, the possibility of war was discussed but not seriously considered. The efforts of the President and Bryan to act in behalf of Japanese interests in California were appreciated and responsible people expected a treaty solution of the matter.[67]

While the answer to the Japanese note was being drafted, Chinda asked Bryan if the reply of the United States would be final. Bryan responded, "There is nothing final between friends."[68] These words, so the British Ambassador, Spring Rice, told Moore, "had a most happy effect in Japan."[69] The attitude of the President and Bryan did much to heal the wound to Japanese pride and to work for a peaceful solution of the issue.

On May 19, the same day that Governor Johnson signed the Webb bill into law, Bryan transmitted Wilson's note to Ambassador Chinda. The views were those read previously by Wilson to the Cabinet. Pointing out the federal nature of the American structure and the inability of the Washington authorities to prevent state legislation, the note insisted that the national government had done all that it constitutionally could to modify the California legislation. It fixed the cause of California's action as economic, and stated that the terms of the Webb Act "purports to respect and preserve all rights under existing treaties." If the Japanese in California felt they were deprived of their treaty rights, the note concluded, the courts were open for redress of their grievances.[70] Technically, the administration's position was correct; but the Webb Act, as the Japanese declared, did violate the spirit of amicability of the existing 1911 treaty with Japan.[71]

The exchange of notes failed to settle the difficulties, and the Japanese sent a commission of three to Washington to confer on the California legislation. They did not see the President, but they expressed to Bryan and Moore their concern over what would occur upon the opening of the Japanese Diet in January, 1914.[72]

Meanwhile, returning by way of Asia to Britain from his post as ambassador in the United States, Lord Bryce told several of the Japanese statesmen, at the height of the tension over the California legislation, that England could never go to war with America. He advised that it was best for Japan to remain silent and wait patiently for the clamor to die down in the States.[73] Bryce wrote Wilson his views of the affair as seen in Japan,[74] and Wilson replied with his thanks for the interpretation which he found useful in dealing with the issue.

The President was very careful to prevent any disturbing element from entering the tense situation. He wrote Garrison that his judgment "halts a bit" on the regular movement of troops between the Philippines and home quarters. In approving the shipment he cautioned, "I hope that it will be made very clear, if any questions are asked, that this is pure routine."[75] The Far Eastern Division of the State Department took the same view on the movement of troops from China to the Philippines, for it feared the connection to the Japanese question that the press might make.[76]

Negotiations continued; and Bryan, Moore and Wilson, joined now with George Guthrie of Pittsburgh, newly appointed Ambassador to Japan, sought a solution. Bryan suggested that a system for purchasing the lands from the Japanese in California be devised.[77] The Secretary attempted to explain to the

Japanese the economic background of the California problem,[78] and that the facilities of the courts were open to any person injured by the Webb Act.[79] Tokyo continued to decry the clear indications of racial antagonism in the case and to insist that it was the duty of the United States to remedy the situation.[80] Chinda communicated the third Japanese protest. Bryan answered in conversations with the Ambassador rather than with a formal reply. Wilson, now fully engaged in affairs concerning the special session of Congress, asked Bryan to inform the Ambassador that he was "giving serious attention to the note from his Government and shall hope to communicate with him at an early date concerning it."[81]

There was some talk of a treaty between the United States and Japan covering land ownership, and Bryan favored undertaking such an understanding if its ratification could be secured. He sent Wilson an outline of such a treaty to serve for discussion between Chinda and the President.[82] Although Wilson favored the plan, nothing came of it. The matter of California alien land legislation was never settled in the Wilson administration. It continued throughout to aggravate the relations of the two countries and to add bitterness to the rivalry that already existed between them.

On May 20, in the midst of the California land crisis, Wilson named George Guthrie of Pittsburgh as Ambassador to Japan; but it was September 8, 1913 before he arrived in Tokyo. Meanwhile, as in China, the diplomatic duties were performed by the American Chargé.

As a Princeton professor, Wilson had taught that men were of prime importance in government. It is interesting, therefore, to note the kind of man he selected to represent the United States in Japan at a time when relations between the two countries verged on an open break. He was not completely free in the choice for A. Mitchell Palmer of Pennsylvania, whose activity on the floor of the Baltimore Convention had been influential in securing Wilson's nomination,[83] supported the appointment of Guthrie for a foreign post. Bryan and Wilson talked of the appointment in relation to Vienna or Rome.[84] On April 18, House assured Palmer that the President had

Guthrie "down for Japan."[85] Eleven days later, Wilson formally extended the offer to the candidate. Bryan was then in Sacramento, but the President promised to approach Japan on the acceptance of the new ambassador as soon as Guthrie consented.[86] Three weeks later, he named Guthrie to the post while war loomed as a thin possibility.

The new ambassador to Japan was a successful lawyer, who had become Mayor of Pittsburgh in 1906 by the largest majority polled there up to that time. A reformer with vigorous convictions, he was responsible for many improvements in the municipal life of the city. In 1912, he had been elected Chairman of the Pennsylvania Democratic Committee and had worked with Palmer in developing the campaign leading to Wilson's nomination. As a delegate at the Baltimore Convention, he had labored with Palmer for the Wilson nomination and actively supported the nominee in the succeeding election. While he had no knowledge of Japan, Guthrie had his abilities, his reform record, and his political loyalty to recommend him.[87] Wilson placed high regard on loyalty. He believed in an ambassador having general rather than specialized talents. He was pleased, as time proved, in his selection of Guthrie. In December, 1916, he wrote the ambassador of the "gratification [he felt] that we have such a representative at one of the most important posts in the disturbed world of our day."[88]

In the California crisis, Wilson had need of his best political abilities. While the mission of Bryan failed in that it did not prevent the passage of an undesirable law, in fact, did not secure elimination of the resented phrase "ineligible to citizenship," it did demonstrate the concern of the national administration for the Japanese position in the case. In a day of disturbed politics in Japan with a degree of sentiment abroad in the land for a military adventure against the United States, it was important that relations be kept from further deterioration. That war was considered a possibility inside the Cabinet is attested in the memoirs of Daniels, Houston, and Redfield. After the May 19 reply of the United States to the Japanese protest, the situation cooled somewhat, although press reports continued to see war a possibility. With the outbreak of the July revolution in China, Japan's attentions turned to opportunities in Asia; and the diversion provided the time necessary to heal the crisis with the United States.

Wilson took the initiative in California. It was his views Bryan represented. The issue was mainly one of domestic politics with foreign ramifications. The President through copies of the cables and State Department correspondence had kept abreast of reactions in Tokyo, but he seemed surprised that the Japanese protest was so violent. While he was informed on what was taking place in Japan, he had an intelligent rather than a detailed knowledge of affairs there. It is interesting to note, however, that as compared to his benevolent attitude and missionary interest in China at the time, Wilson expressed no such feelings toward Japan. He sought to do her justice, but he indulged in no flights of rhetoric in her cause. He nowhere in his correspondence made mention of the threat of Japanese retaliation for the Webb Act, but then he was very diplomatic and realized any such expression would add to the peril involved.

The California land case was thrust upon an administration unprepared to deal with it. No doubt its agitation in Japan was used as a device to divert public attention from the perilous condition of the Yamamoto ministry, for it was a minority, unpopular government. Had less good will existed in Washington, had the second wave of revolution not flared up in China to divert the more ardent Nipponese, the United States and Japan conceivably could have come to war in 1913.

CHAPTER THREE

Men and Policy
for the Philippines

ALL THE WHILE FROM ON HIGH THERE CAME THE RUSTLING
OF WINGS, ONE FELT ONE'S HEART A-THROB, AND ONE
REALIZED ONE HAD A RIGHT TO SPLENDID AMBITIONS.

—José Rizal

Woodrow Wilson was no stranger to American policy in
the Philippines. Although he made no public comment in
1898, he early entered into the debate on what should be done
in the islands and on what should be the final objectives of
American rule there. The year following the Spanish War he
reportedly opposed annexation of the Philippines.[1] In an essay
of 1901, he urged that the United States give the Filipinos a
government which, being moral itself, would moralize them,
build their character, and elevate their ideals. When they accepted the "compulsion of American character" and standards,
they would be entitled to "partnership" in the government of
the islands.[2] Thus his general belief in the gradual native development of sound institutions through moral example and
training had early rootage.

Wilson believed that during the war with Spain the United
States had "stepped forth into the arena of the world." He saw
the stern voice of duty calling to the United States to take its
place in the guidance of the movement of the nations toward
a better day. "The East is to be opened and transformed; . . .
the standards of the West are to be imposed upon it; nations

65

and peoples which have stood still ten centuries through are to be quickened. . . . It is our peculiar duty, as it is also England's to moderate the process in the interests of liberty. . . ." He saw the Philippine Islands as peopled by heterogeneous groups and not forming a community.[3] There, good leaders were needed more than charters or constitutions; and school teachers would contribute to the development of the people as much as the political governors. Wilson viewed the problem of government in the islands as essentially one of training, for to him liberty, which was the goal of government, was ever the privilege of a trained, mature society.[4]

It is clear that in the flush of new born imperialism Woodrow Wilson gloried in the new role of America as a world power; but to him it became a point of vantage from which the United States would serve the cause of liberty in the world. By 1904, however, the then Princeton President's support of the new imperialism was charged with a note of caution for he found, "We are not so anxious to behave as we should as we are able to behave as we please." The unselfish, highly moral character of the United States had become a little suspect through its exploitation of the new insular possessions.[5]

The launching of the United States into the arena of world powers had created divers schools of thought. There were questionings, both official and private, as to the American policy. In this *Zeitgeist,* Wilson did not escape fluctuation in his ideas. In a manuscript written around 1907, he committed this change in thought to paper:

> Since trade ignores national boundaries and the manu-facturer insists on having the world as a market, the flag of his nation must follow him, and the doors of the nations which are closed against him must be battered down. Con-cessions obtained by financiers must be safeguarded by minis-ters of state, even if the sovereignty of unwilling nations be outraged in the process. Colonies must be obtained or planted, in order that no useful corner of the world may be . . . left unused.[6]

Wilson was conscious that economic imperialism was a tremendous fact. Fortunate indeed for his political future, the Princeton President did not publish his views, for the Democratic Party was loud in its cries against imperialism; and its perennial son, William Jennings Bryan, was looked upon as the political leader of the anti-imperialist forces.

Wilson was thinking in terms of his place in national politics. When he left for a vacation in England, prior to the 1908 convention, he saw fit to instruct his brother-in-law, Stockton Axson, to act for him in refusing the nomination as Vice President should the convention propose him.[7] Many of the Wilson views at the time were in a flux, for the period 1908-1911 was supposedly the period of his conversion to progressivism.[8]

Wilson's lectures delivered at Columbia in 1907, and later published as his last serious book, besides showing his advocacy of Presidential leadership, instead of his earlier espousal of cabinet government, also indicated a reasoned view of Philippine matters:

> We can give the Filipino constitutional government based upon some clear and equitable understanding, intended for their good and not for our aggrandizement; but we must ourselves for the present supply that government. . . . Having ourselves gained self-government by a definite process, which can have no substitute, let us put the peoples dependent upon us in the right way to gain it also.[9]

The Democratic platform of 1912 reaffirmed the position of the party "against a policy of imperialism and exploitation in the Philippines. . .," and favored "an immediate declaration of the nation's purpose to recognize the independence of the . . . Islands as soon as a stable government can be established. . . ." Until neutralization treaties could be secured from other concerned powers, the United States was to guarantee their insular independence, and upon withdrawal, American coaling stations and naval bases were to be retained.[10] This was in line with Bryan's stand in 1906.[11]

The framing of this plank, representing the views of Bryan and the Western and Southern Democrats,[12] was in the hands of Senator John Sharp Williams from Mississippi.[13] Manuel Quezon, one of the Philippine Commissioners who since 1909 had represented the islands on the floor of the House of Representatives in Washington, had been consulted on the draft.[14] While the Democrats stood for eventual independence, Taft and the Republicans declared their policy to be "inspired by the belief that our duty toward the Filipino people is a national obligation which should remain entirely free from partisan politics." Roosevelt's Progressives, the third party in the race, failed to mention the islands.[15]

In his speech accepting the nomination for the Presidency, Wilson hedged in his concurrence on the Philippine plank saying: "It is our duty, as trustees, to make whatever arrangement of government that will be most serviceable to their freedom and development. Here, again, we are to set up the rule of justice and right."[16] His words were widely quoted in Manila.[17] There, since the American occupation, the political leaders of the Nationalist Party had carefully cultivated the cries for independence, although the word had little meaning to the greater number of the native people. Some thought it meant no more taxes. Some few thought because the rains were good independence was not needed. Independence had become "the cause" and thus the necessary cry of all factions in political life, something to cheer in speeches and to wax eloquent over in the irresponsible press columns.

William A. Jones, a Virginian member of Congress, in the 1912 session had introduced a bill providing for full and complete independence of the islands, but the measure had not come to a vote.[18] As chairman of the Insular Affairs Committee during the Wilson years, Jones, until his death in 1918, was the chief figure in House action on the Philippines, and the 1916 legislation accomplishing the administration's policy in the islands bore his name.

The Philippine Islands did not figure largely in the presidential campaign. After Wilson's election in November, the matter remained quiet. In his last annual message to Congress,

President Taft had declared for "self-government, with the power to decide eventually . . . whether such self government shall be accompanied by independence."[19] Taft's recommendation voiced the Republican position that the matter of independence was to be decided at some undetermined time in the future, with the hope that by that time the life of the islands would be so wedded to that of the United States that the natives would desire to remain under American sovereignty. The Democrats, on the other hand, were for an immediate declaration of independence to occur at some definite time in the future.

On a visit to his birthplace in Staunton, Virginia, the President-elect took occasion to remark in his address that "The Philippines are at present our frontier but I hope we presently are to deprive ourselves of that frontier."[20] This was his clearest statement on Philippine policy prior to his taking office. Already there were several persons advising him to send a representative to discover the true state of things in the islands.[21] Wilson consulted Walter Hines Page, who suggested that a private investigator be sent to the Philippines.[22] The President-elect chose Professor Henry J. Ford, a former colleague and the successor to his course work at Princeton, to proceed to the islands and to study the actual conditions there.[23] There was no official announcement of Ford's mission, but it was soon accepted in the islands that the convert-Catholic professor and his Spanish-speaking, secretary-son were there for the administration. Wilson, the professor, was at work. "Get the facts first" had long been an adage with him. Until the facts were collected he kept his own council and was as "closed-mouthed" as ever on administration policy in the islands.[24]

Following the inauguration, Wilson heard from the Philippine Governor General, William Cameron Forbes who advised that insular independence must be a matter of slow evolution achieved through a gradual increase in the native participation in the government. He desired the President to come to the islands to see conditions there for himself. Taft had planned to do so had he been re-elected.[25] The President's reply was noncommittal, thanking Forbes for his letter and documents.[26]

Commissioner Quezon, who published in Washington a small magazine *The Philippine People* in the cause of independence and other island interests, criticized the President for having been in office three months without having done anything about the islands. Even the vacancies on the American Commission had not been filled.[27] But Wilson's delay had not been utter neglect; he had collected a list of books on the islands from General H. L. Scott, and waited for more information before announcing a policy.[28] The hot summer came on and found the Chief Executive embroiled in a welter of problems with Mexico, where war threatened, and with pushing his domestic reform program through the extra session of Congress. The "new functions of America in the East"[29] also brought their problems in the form of the Japanese crisis over California, and China loan and recognition policies. The Philippines were always a central consideration in East Asian policy.

In relation to the tense situation with the Japanese over the California Webb Bill, Quezon's official organ thought it not unlikely that Japan might declare war on the United States in the not distant future. If this occurred, he ventured, the Philippines would be the first point of attack. The military were "agreed that the United States could not defend them." The Philippine Commissioner suggested that by entering upon a treaty of neutralization the United States could prevent such an attack and at the same time remove the basis of the opposition to independence — namely, that the Philippines could not defend themselves.[30]

Despite Wilson's apparent delay, Philippine policy was in the making. The new Secretary of War, Lindley M. Garrison, whom Wilson had known as the Vice Chancellor of New Jersey, finding himself in the unfamiliar environment of a new office, called for recommendations on the Philippine Islands. Since 1898 the Bureau of Insular Affairs had functioned under the War Department, handling the business of the islands and ably representing them to the American Government. Within the bureaucracy was a young law officer, Felix Frankfurter by name. On April 11, 1913, at Garrison's call, this young man drew up a

memorandum in which he reviewed the government and administration of the Philippines.

Frankfurter recommended that the administration appoint
a man of constructive leadership, who enjoyed the confidence of
the President, as Secretary of Commerce and Police in the Philippine Commission, send him to the islands for experience, and
later appoint him as the new Governor General. The Philippine Assembly should then be asked to recommend six men for
appointment to the Commission. Frankfurter believed the Assembly would suggest natives, thus giving the Filipinos control
of both branches of the legislature. This would have the effect
of putting the government in native hands without any resort
to Congressional action, and would effectively meet the demands
of the Assembly for self-government.

The memorandum further advised that the purpose of the
administration in the islands be made known at the time of the
appointment of the prospective Governor General. This announcement of purpose could be written in his instructions or
in a direct statement released to the Philippine people. In
either case, it should charge the Filipinos with working out their
own salvation and make clear to them that there was no essential
difference among political groups in the United States concerning insular policy. Frankfurter concluded his recommendations by suggesting that the policy be presented in a dramatic
way to give a "quickening impulse" to the insular service.[31]
Here was the framework, which with slight changes, was to serve
for initial administration Philippine policy.

Garrison took the Frankfurter report, made minor changes,
and sent the recommendations on to the President. The Secretary of War urged that in giving control of the legislature to the
Filipinos, the veto be retained by the Governor General, the
President, or the Secretary of War and not held in Congress. He
stated that he had discussed favorably the recommendations with
the Filipino Commissioners, Senator Gilbert H. Hitchcock, and
Congressman Jones of the Senate and House Committees dealing
with insular affairs.[32]

Meanwhile, Professor Ford made his on the spot investigation, but his report of nearly eighty typed pages did not reach

the President until early autumn.[33] Without reading it, Wilson sent the report on to the Secretary of War.[34] However, the President had been informed of its general contents in his correspondence from Ford.

As early as April, Ford had advised Wilson: "The situation in the Philippines impresses me as being very grave, and I believe that it requires radical treatment." He counseled "the remedy lies far more in a change of policy than in a change of men."[35] Before setting out for home on May 28, after completing his sixty-six days in the islands, Ford again reported to Wilson:

> There is a malevolent feeling toward you personally [in the islands] because of an expression in your Staunton speech and also because of your advocacy of free sugar; and there are many people who would be gratified if the situation here should be embroiled so as to make trouble for you. In administration circles here are evidences of a desire to discredit the Filipino Assembly and put the leaders in a hole.[36]

The Professor discovered the existence of a *cabal* attempting to embarrass the Washington administration in the islands. In addition to this partisan spirit found among the American residents, he found the Filipinos really desired independence, that secret societies supporting the Philippine revolutionary junta in Hong Kong existed throughout the provinces.

In an interview with Emilio Aguinaldo, the insurrectionary leader, Ford assured him of Wilson's favorable reaction "regarding the possibility of establishing . . . a republican form of government similar to that of Switzerland under some form of guaranty or protection." The Professor stressed the necessity of "avoiding by every means disorders and outbreaks which might enlarge and make difficult the solution of the independence problem." Aguinaldo stressed "that no fears should be entertained" as to an outbreak of violence.[37]

One-fourth of the Ford report dealt with education and showed that the high illiteracy rate was misleading since it was founded on knowledge of a western language and not native dialects. The Professor described the government in great detail and found no native newspaper favored American sovereignty.[38] The Nationalist Party, headed by the Speaker of the Assembly, Sergio Osmena, the strongest political organization in the country, reportedly composing four-fifths of the electorate. Of Taft's Federal Party there was but little following, and none at all outside of Manila. Ford spoke of the Hong Kong junta, led by Artemio Ricarte, as widely followed under the motto: "We want the immediate restoration of the Philippine Republic by whatever means in whatever form."

As to the future form of government, the Professor related that both Aguinaldo and Osmena favored a Swiss rather than American type republic, and laid great stress on the necessity for simplicity of structure. Ford thought the people were capable of carrying on their own government, and he recommended: that the electorate be expanded, the islands be given control of their own revenue and navigation laws (heretofore exercised by the American Congress), and the Commission be abolished and its powers devolved on such persons as the President might direct pending the establishment of self-government in the islands. However, there was much to praise: The administration was efficient, its accomplishments noteworthy, but the time had come when a change in the government was necessary.

The Ford report was not printed since the President thought to do so might limit his access to freely-expressed confidential studies in the future.[39] Although Ford's correspondence and the later report may have confirmed Wilson in his decision as to Philippine policy, it was the recommendation of Frankfurter's memorandum, as modified by Garrison, that was initially followed.

The Secretary of War kept urging on the President the Department's recommendation that there be no immediate change in the government structure other than granting the Filipinos a majority on the Commission. Bishop Charles H. Brent of the Philippine Protestant Episcopal Church agreed with Garrison on this recommendation and reported that Quezon also favored it "as the best thing to do at the present time."[40] Wilson, as always, was interested in the views of Garrison and the Bishop as furnishing "direct-lights on the situation," but he made no commitment as to his future policy.[41]

Meanwhile, Moorefield Storey, President of the Anti-Imperialist League and a long-term agitator for Philippine independence, observed "a very active combination aiming to influence you [Wilson] against the declared policy of the Democratic party. . . ." He sent Wilson several books he had written on Philippine independence.[42] Certain members of Congress also became restless over the delay in fulfilling the Philippine plank of the Baltimore platform.

The first necessary step in implementing the Frankfurter-Garrison program was to find a Governor General. The incumbent, William Cameron Forbes, spoke fluent Spanish and was a competent administrator. A grandson of Ralph Waldo Emerson, he was independently wealthy[43] and a crusty codger whose reports breathed his personal uprightness. He held that the Assembly, with which he was currently at odds over the budget, should never have been organized and proposed its suspension for a year. A staunch believer in education, he advocated American expenditure of a million dollars yearly on schools as the best means of improving the Filipino people.[44]

Wilson had agreed with Garrison that there was no unusual hurry about naming a new Governor General. He said "We must cover the whole field before we finally decide."[45] But the Secretary, by the latter part of April, 1913, had begun to feel that the appointment should be made immediately.[46] Various names were suggested during the summer. The President called Quezon to the White House and asked if a new Governor General should be appointed or not. Quezon later recalled that he replied:

> Mr. President, if it is your intention to disregard the Democratic platform and merely carry on the policies of the Republican administration, then you can find no better man for the job than Governor-General Forbes. If, on the contrary, you intend to take immediate steps, as in my opinion you should take, to make good the now historic commitment of your party to grant independence to the Philippines as

soon as possible, then Governor Forbes can neither be the spokesman for nor the executor of your policies in the Philippines.[47]

The summer faded without anyone being named to the Philippine position. On August 16, 1913, Bryan wrote Wilson that Congressman Jones of Virginia had a good opinion of W. Morgan Shuster for the post and also spoke highly of Francis Burton Harrison, Congressman from New York. Bryan was inclined to favor the New Yorker.[48] The same day Quezon called on Bryan, and they discussed possibilities for the appointment. The Philippine Commissioner suggested that he favored Harrison, whom he had known for the past four years in the House. That afternoon Quezon submitted this observation[49] in writing; and Bryan sent it on to Wilson, who replied that the suggestion was "thoroughly worth thinking of."[50] On August 18, Harrison himself called at Quezon's office in support of a friend for the post of Governor General. The Philippine Commissioner proposed to Harrison that he accept the position.[51] Meanwhile, Wilson was "more and more inclined to think that Mr. Harrison is the right man."[52] He telegraphed Secretary Garrison, then in Wyoming, asking if he had any objections to the Harrison appointment. The War Secretary wired that he had none if the President concluded that Harrison had the "peculiar qualifications required for what I consider a post of paramount importance."[53] Moorefield Storey, President of the Anti-Imperialist League, also recommended the appointment. Only nine days after Bryan's suggestion of Harrison, the President informed Forbes of the decision to change the Governor General and thanked him for his faithful and careful service.[54] On September 2, Wilson saw Harrison at the White House. Bryan was gratified because only one objection had been raised to the appointment and that on the grounds that Harrison was tied up with the Tammany Democrats and "interests."[55] The man had been found.

Quezon acclaimed the appointment of a man who was "young, energetic, firm in his convictions, brilliant, courteous and a stronger believer in the inherent right of every people to

govern themselves."[56] He could have added that Harrison was
the son of Jefferson Davis' private secretary, and that the elder
Harrison had left Yale to serve the Confederacy. The appointment of the thirty-nine year old, wealthy New Yorker caused a
stir in Washington; because he was known to be well in advance
of his party in advocating independence for the Philippines.

The *Brooklyn Eagle* observed that Harrison represented the
type of democracy Wilson liked to advance to authority.[57] The
Washington Post asserted that the appointment showed Wilson
wanted a man in the Philippines upon whom he could implicitly
rely.[58] The *Outlook* saw the appointment as a means of getting
rid of the young Congressman, who was in line for the Chairmanship of the Ways and Means Committee and who represented extreme views. It was virtually "a kick upstairs."[59] No
evidence supporting this latter assertion has been found in the
appointment documents. Rather, it would seem, as Harrison
asserted, the appointment was due to the recommendations of
Quezon, Bryan, and Jones,[60] all men who favored a liberal
Philippine policy, the latter two favoring early independence.

On Sunday morning, August 31, 1913, Wilson gave the
departing Harrison "in general terms his instructions as to
Philippine self-government." The Governor General later related, "I found him wonderfully well informed on Philippine
conditions, as I had previously found him a master of the intricacies of tariff revision. . . ."[61] Wilson, however, had a habit
of reviewing "the facts" in the case before he consulted on any
matter.

The new Governor General was greeted by immense crowds
upon his landing in Manila on October 6, 1913. The Wilson
election had been popularly received in the islands. The planks
of the Democratic platforms since 1900 standing for independence of the insular possession, Wilson's Staunton speech, and
the advertised statements of the various Democrats supporting
the Baltimore platform had given rise to great expectations in
the islands. The President's message had been cabled ahead
and awaited Harrison when his ship stopped at Japan. It now
supplied the words announcing the change in policy that Frank-

furter advocated. Harrison struck a dramatic note in reading them to the assembled Filipinos in the beautiful Luneta:

> We regard ourselves as trustees acting not for the advantage of the United States, but for the benefit of the people of the Philippine Islands.
>
> Every step we take will be taken with a view to the ultimate independence of the Islands and as a preparation for their independence; and we hope to move towards that end as rapidly as the safety and the permanent interests of the Island will permit. After each step taken, experience will guide us to the next.
>
> The administration will take one step at once. It will give to the native citizens of the Islands a majority in the appointive Commission and thus in the Upper as well as in the Lower House of the Legislature a majority representation will be secured to them.
>
> We do this in the confident hope and expectation that immediate proof will be given in the action of the Commission under the new arrangement of the political capacity of these native citizens who have already come forward to represent and to lead their people in affairs.[62]

The message promised ultimate independence; it gave the natives a majority in the Commission thus placing the legislature in their control; and it promised this as the beginning towards further development of independence. The Frankfurter-Garrison plan had been instituted.

Bryan, the political leader of the anti-imperialist forces, exclaimed: "It was admirable — just what they were waiting for. It is a great joy to me, Mr. President, to have this country committed to independence — it has been on my heart for fifteen years."[63]

The Republican administration, especially since 1902 when the organic act had gone into effect, manifested an attitude of stewardship in the Philippines and advocated retention of government control in American hands. After 1907, a legislature had existed, the lower house of which was elected by a restricted suffrage, while the upper house of nine men included the Governor and his commissioners were appointed by the President. While natives were represented on the Commission they were followers of Taft's Federalist and not the popular Nationalist Party. The civil servants, especially heads of bureaus, and persons in other responsible positions were largely Americans. It was an efficient but unrepresentative government. For three years the Governor General had failed to get his appropriation bills approved by the Assembly. The new Governor General found the past policies little suited to the job of training the natives for self-government.[64]

Harrison now went about implementing the Wilson program. After consulting a representative group of persons in the islands, including the two Resident Commissioners, the five native men were selected by Harrison and named by President Wilson to the Commission, thus giving majority control of the legislature into Filipino hands.[65] The three American members of the Commission were also named.[66] With Harrison they made up the four-man minority, or the American element, of the nine-man commission which functioned as the upper house.

The new Governor General, pursuing a policy of Filipinizing" the government, secured the resignation of some Americans in the civil service. He consciously sought to put the government of the islands into natives hands as rapidly as possible. Salaries were reduced in a general policy of retrenchment, and many Americans left the service. Reduction of revenues, due to the abolition of the export tax and in face of a legal five million dollar debt limitation, made this financial retrenchment necessary. But a small group in the American colony, reluctant to see the change in policy, spread rumors and press reports that Harrison was dropping Americans from the civil service indiscriminately and forcing others out by reducing their salaries.

Vice-Governor Martin wrote Garrison, in the midst of all these accusations, praising the Governor General:

> I only needed a day to discover that Harrison is absolutely disinterested in his conduct of his office. He is loyal to the Department and to the President. He is in sympathy

with the Filipinos in a manner that I am sure must be new to them and, as a consequence, he has their confidence in a manner that I am sure must be new to governors-general. He has been Filipinizing the government service, but he has not done it any faster than I should have done it.[67]

Frank McIntyre, chief of the Bureau of Insular Affairs, and a man to whom much of the success of the American administration in the Philippines was due, defended Harrison's Filipinizing, while admitting that a number of men were forced out "as a result of a necessary curtailing of government expenses and others have left for personal reasons." He added, however, that their numbers were exaggerated. In a survey of the twenty-two bureaus of the Philippine Government, only two more chiefs of divisions were Filipinos than when Harrison arrived.[68] He failed to admit that it was difficult to obtain trained Filipinos for the top-level jobs, and that the changes had been made in the lower divisions of the bureaucracy.

Meanwhile in Washington, back at his post as Commissioner from the Philippines, Manuel Quezon sought to discover the next step contemplated in the administration's insular policy. He consulted with McIntyre to explore the President's plans. The chief of the Bureau confessed that he had only the public statements of the Chief Executive for his guide. The Philippine Commissioner said there was a fear in the islands that Wilson contemplated a very early grant of independence. Quezon thought such action would be a mistake harmful to American interests, and he based his fears "largely on the conduct of Japan. He said that on his trip [home] for the first time he became convinced that the Japanese had designs on the Philippine Islands. . . ." If independence were to come soon, the Japanese would immediately begin to encourage immigration.[69]

The Commissioner's fear of independence may seem surprising in the light of his official speeches and writings on the subject. Actually, independence was a slogan proclaimed by all Filipinos in public life. Quezon sought not independence so much as self-government under American sovereignty, at least for the time being.

Now the Commissioner informed McIntyre, if the administration approved, he was prepared to advocate a new organic act for the islands that would settle relations with the United States for the next twenty-five years. He sought prior approval since its provisions were short of independence and would divorce him from his old friends, the extreme anti-imperialists. McIntyre advised him to speak to Garrison, and asked if he had the consent of Osmena, the leader of the Philippine Nationalist Party. Quezon believed Osmena would support the measure. McIntyre then asked if Quezon had spoken of the matter to Governor General Harrison, to which the Filipino replied: "My God, no! I think he believes in independence. He thinks he can turn us loose in about four years," and he repeated, "He believes it." The Insular Affairs chief said it would be difficult to obtain the administration's commitment to a policy which did not appeal to the Governor General, but Quezon maintained that he would be afraid to risk any such suggestion to Harrison. McIntyre, however, thought that Wilson, guided by the Democratic platform and his statement of taking one step and then observing its results before going on to the next, should be a source of reassurance to the Filipinos.[70]

During January, 1914, Quezon called frequently on the Chief of the Bureau of Insular Affairs, who kept Garrison informed on the interviews, and dwelt on the desire for some definite legislation that would allay talk of immediate independence. He spoke of the Southern Democratic block in Congress as simply wanting "to get rid of the Philippine Islands and that they did not care what happened to them." He thought this had originally been the view of Congressman Jones, though now the Virginian seemed more sympathetic to the Philippine people; but it remained, Quezon thought, the main reason for the Virginian's sponsoring Philippine independence. On his part, Jones thought it strange that Quezon opposed a Philippine independence bill.[71]

Quezon left notes with McIntyre containing the desirable contents for a Philippine bill and asked for the assistance of the Bureau of Insular Affairs in preparing them for submission to Garrison and to Wilson. Briefly, his plan permitted the appointment of a Governor General with final veto powers retained by the American President. A native two-house legislature would exercise all law-making functions, except for tariff and trade relations with the United States. The President would be given power to negotiate trade treaties solely affecting the Philippines. In the main, the island officials would be appointed by the Governor General with the consent of the local Senate. The plan also provided that when seventy-five per cent of the adult males were literate in any language, or when sixty per cent were literate in English, a condition of peace existing throughout the islands, and the insular revenues sufficient to support the government, an election was to be held to determine whether or not independence was desired by the Filipinos. If the election favored independence, a convention would adopt a constitution, and the President of the United States would then proclaim the independence of the Philippines.[72]

The Commissioner confided to McIntyre that the section of his bill calling for independence was not to his liking, "but that he believed it would appeal to the President in view of his expression in favor of ultimate independence and would appeal to the more extreme Filipinos, as well as to those people in the United States who had taken so strong a position in favor of independence." Quezon, though, was aware that under his literacy qualifying conditions "the matter was almost indefinitely postponed."[73] This memorandum was sent on to Wilson by Garrison,[74] and the Chief Executive was thus fully aware that the eloquent Quezon was playing independence as a necessary political expedient while privately fearing that it might be granted.

Quezon and Manuel Earnshaw, his fellow commissioner, completed a draft of the proposed bill along the lines discussed in the talks with McIntyre. In summarizing the bill, the Bureau of Insular Affairs observed that it "apparently intended to provide for a permanent relationship of the Philippine Islands to the United States."[75]

At the same time, Congressman Jones prepared his bill for submission to the House. In addition to a preamble promising independence when a stable government was established, the

bill made two basic changes in the organic law of the islands.
It increased the powers vested in the Philippine Government by
confering upon the Filipinos general legislative powers and by
specifically authorizing them to enact land, timber, mining,
coinage and tariff laws with the approval of the President.
Secondly, it substituted for the system of government responsible
to the President of the United States, a government responsible
to the Filipino people by providing that both branches of the
legislature should be subject to insular Senate confirmation.[76]

When the Democratic caucus failed to include the Philippine bill on its list of legislation for the session, Quezon, who
had agreed with Jones on the proposal, thus giving up his own
measure, called McIntyre to learn the cause. He said the President had favored the legislation subject to the approval of the
Secretary of War. The Commissioner, thinking Garrison had
held up the measure, expressed a fear that any delay in legislation would only increase the demands of the islands for a greater
degree of independence. He favored the Jones bill, but he dis-
liked its provision giving the Governor General an absolute
veto. According to Quezon, Jones had favored a more extreme
measure, but he was convinced that the bill as written was "as
radical as the President wanted."[77]

Garrison disclaimed holding up the Philippine bill. He
had sent the proposed measure to the President, but there had
been no reply. He thought perhaps Wilson was too busy to give
it his attention.[78] Informed of the source of delay, Quezon then
called on President Wilson to warn him that as time passed
it would be increasingly difficult to gain acceptance of a moderate measure in the Philippines. The President blamed the administration's inaction on Congress. He declared that he had
talked with Jones and outlined the legislation favored. Quezon
informed him that the Jones bill was ready and promised the
Chief Executive a copy as soon as it was printed. Wilson said
he would gladly see the bill, but that he would have to advise
with the Secretary of War concerning it before committing
himself.[79]

After the bill came into his hands, Wilson consulted with
Jones,[80] and recommended support of Quezon's proposal grant-

ing final veto power to the President. It was the item he had "been thinking most about."[81] He later submitted the bill for the comment and criticism of his friend Professor Ford of Princeton. Meanwhile, Quezon showed the bill to Osmena,[82] and the Secretary of War cabled a skeleton of the measure to the insular Commissioners.[83] The bill had the full backing of the War Department, many of its provisions having been written by McIntyre himself. Garrison informed Harrison that Congressman Jones was very willing to accept changes, within limits, and he thought it was possible to make it an excellent piece of legislation. The Secretary, in the light of the Quezon and Harrison representations on uneasy conditions in the islands, favored introducing a bill stating America's promise of eventual independence, although he thought it unlikely the bill would get past the house calendar during the crowded session.[84] At the same time, he recommended to Wilson that the Jones bill be supported "because of the natural pressure that is being brought to bear upon us from various sources. . . ."[85] Wilson agreed that it should be backed and told Garrison to consult with Gilbert Hitchcock of the Senate Committee on the Philippines.[86]

Meanwhile, in the islands, all was not peaceful. The American community opposed Harrison violently and abused the administration for its policy of Filipinizing the government. Still more, they feared what Wilson might do toward further independence. Judge James J. Ross, the titular head of the American Democratic Party in the Philippines, protested to Clinton T. Riggs, the Secretary of Commerce and Police in the insular government, that all political factions realized that independence would be disastrous. Independence, he said, was agitated for political purposes, but the agitators were not actually for it. Ross opposed any extension of the legislative authority and believed that the appointment of all high offices in the insular government should be kept in the hands of the President.[87] Riggs added his protest to that of Ross and sent both to Garrison. He hoped the Secretary of War could visit the islands before the enactment of any policy legislation in Washington.[88] There was thus a division in the views of Riggs and Harrison that made for trouble, only Riggs' illness and consequent return home kept it from becoming an open break.

On July 11, 1914, the Jones bill was introduced in the House. Secretary of State Bryan was decidedly for the bill. He urged Quezon to press for its popular acceptance by the Filipinos and vowed that although it did not fix a definite date for independence, it was not a backward step from the Jones bill of 1912.[89] The bill was backed by Wilson. Harrison also cabled his approval.

The preamble of the new bill expressed "the purpose of the people of the United States to withdraw their sovereignty over the Philippine Islands and to recognize their independence as soon as a stable government can be established therein. . . ." This promise became the basis for contention between the parties, the Republicans charging the Democrats with insincerity in the proposal as a desire to fulfil their Baltimore platform with words only.

In reviewing the Democratic position concerning Philippine independence during the 1913 session, Representative George F. Burgess of Texas had emphasized that the continuance of America in the islands weakened the Monroe Doctrine because it invaded a sphere of interest outside the western hemisphere. "For myself, I am frank to say that if the Japanese Government were to intimate even that they would like to have the Philippine Islands, I would offer them to them as a Christmas present, provided they would enter into a treaty to protect certain rights of life and liberty and property there."[90] Fear of provoking the enmity of Japan was very real as an argument favoring withdrawing from the islands.

The outbreak of the European war in 1914 increased the load of legislation to be undertaken by the Congress, but towards the end of September serious debate was held on the Philippine measure. Jones and Quezon argued for the bill on the grounds that island trade was disrupted by the war and the United States must give the Filipinos a status which would allow them some freedom in raising their own revenues; otherwise, Congress would be forced to grant relief through the federal treasury. Simeon D. Fess of Ohio opposed this contention, claiming it was but an expedient to pass the measure. He said to grant the natives more self-government in the midst of a war was to weaken the Philippines at a time when other nations might take advantage of them. When asked what he meant by the statement, Fess said he could explain it, but there were things the President did not want talked about. However, if the Democrats pressed him, he could be specific. No one pressed for further elaborations, but it was clearly evident he had Japanese ambitions in mind. Then on suggestion of Representative James R. Mann, the Republican leader of the House, that a discussion of the bill should also include a review of relations with Japan and the control of the Pacific, the House went into a Committee of the Whole to discuss the matter.[91]

In the debate that followed, some members viewed the retention of the islands as perpetuating military weakness and involving the United States in "the dangerous maelstrom of Oriental politics."[92] Mann declared that within the next century "a conflict will come between the Far East and the Far West across the Pacific Ocean." He saw the islands as a necessary link in our command of the Pacific and was irrevocably set against releasing them.[93] Representative Horace Towner, the ranking minority leader on the Committee of Insular Affairs, gave Wilson credit for restraining the Democratic Party on the independence issue.[94] William Murray of Oklahoma feared losing the Philippines to the Japanese, who would use the islands as a means of involving the United States in a war. Jones answered that once a stable government was achieved under the bill, he would oppose any further assumption of responsibility on the part of the United States for the Philippines.[95] James W. Bryan of Washington related the Philippines to a possible Japanese-American war and advocated fortifying the islands to hold them indefinitely. Although favoring a greater degree of freedom for the people of the islands, he opposed "the meaningless promises" of the preamble.[96] Representative Towner explained that while there were differences of opinion on the preamble and independence, all agreed that there should be a greater measure of self-government in the islands. He wanted to make of the Philippines a commonwealth like Canada.[97]

In September, 1914, McIntyre had informed Governor-General Harrison that the war legislation in addition to the two conservation bills, the shipping bill, and the emergency revenue bill would "leave but little time for consideration of the Jones Bill."[98] But the prolonged debates in the Senate on the emergency tax bill allowed the House leaders to bring up the Philippine legislation as unfinished business; and, after general debate for eight hours, it proceeded under the five minute rule to pass the legislation on October 14, 1914. Congress adjourned ten days later, and the Senate failed to act on the measure.[99]

The President hoped to get the bill through the Senate during the coming short session,[100] and management of it was given to Senator Gilbert M. Hitchcock, Chairman of the Committee on the Philippines.[101] Governor Harrison was pleased at Hitchcock's active leadership in the legislation and hoped for its early passage, including the preamble, which he considered "vitally essential."[102] Vice President Thomas R. Marshall anounced his backing of the bill.[103] Between December 14, 1914 and January 9, 1915, the Senate Committee heard eighteen witnesses on the Philippines. The Bureau of Insular Affairs put its resources at the command of Hitchcock, and the administration strove to obtain the Senate's approval of the bill. Harrison called for passage of the legislation to allay political and financial uncertainty and to bolster the conservative legislative influence in the islands.[104] Quezon requested Wilson and Garrison to lend their assistance to its passage.[105] Wilson complied to this request, saying:

> I feel it is my duty to urge the passage, if it is at all possible at this session of the Senate, of the Philippine bill, because, deeply important as the general power and the conservation bills are, they do not touch, as the Philippine bill does, the general world situation, from which I think it is our duty to remove every element of doubt or disturbance which can possibly be removed. Such communication as that we have received from the Governor General of the Philippines shows that a very important element of disturbance indeed will be removed if we can get the Philippine bill through.

If it must be a choice, therefore, among the three bills, I must give my preference to the Philippine bill. I do not see how it is possible to pass all three of them.[106]

Garrison talked with Senators F. M. Simmons and Hitchcock on the possibility of passing the bill as the President desired. The Republicans had assured Simmons that the bill could be passed if a slight change were made in the preamble. Garrison favored sticking to the preamble although it might mean the bill would not be passed. He sought Wilson's views;[107] and the President, after conferring with Jones, agreed there should be no omission of it. Senator Hitchcock agreed, and it was decided to press the administrative side of the bill which all factions generally favored and leave the preamble promise of eventual independence, over which there was so much difference, until later.[108]

Senate debate on the Jones bill began on March 3, 1915, but differences developed, with the Republicans generally attacking the preamble's commitment on independence. The short session adjourned without Senate passage of the measure,[109] whereupon Garrison cabled Governor General Harrison: "The President and I did everything which we consistently could do in an endeavor to get the bill through the Senate, but there was such a rush of other matters, mostly appropriation bills which had to be passed, that it was impossible to bring up the bill."[110] Garrison was, of course, in error for the bill had been brought up; it was the difference of views on the preamble and lack of time which prevented action on it. The Secretary of War felt, nevertheless, that if the Filipino people would continue to act "politely and wisely" the next session would see passage of the bill. [111]

Wilson confirmed his interest in the measure to Harrison: "It was constantly pressed by the administration, loyally supported by the full force of the party, and will be pressed to passage when the next Congress meets in December. It failed only because [it was] blocked by [the] Republican leaders who were opposed to the legislation and who would yield only if we withdrew the assurance of ultimate independence contained in the preamble. That we would not do."[112] The President assured the Filipino people of his "deep and abiding interest in their welfare and my purpose to serve them in every possible way."[113] He expressed his appreciation "for the self-respecting behavior of the people of the Philippines in the midst of agitations which intimately affect their whole political future."[114]

During the summer of 1915, McIntyre went to the Philippines on a tour of inspection and to confer with Harrison, who habitually spent his vacations in the Orient, not returning to the States until 1919. At a conference held in Manila, the two men discussed the Jones bill with the Filipino leaders. McIntyre brought their suggestions back with him and fed them into the legislative hopper in the new session opening in December, 1915, in which the Philippine bill was the first measure introduced. Jones was then in poor health, but he managed to work with Hitchcock toward getting the legislation passed.[115]

William A. Kincaid, a native Texan and now a Manila lawyer representing many wealthy enterprises, including the Catholic Church in the Philippines, came to Washington to lobby for what his retainers thought an acceptable bill. He was particularly interested in obtaining the right of the Philippine government to acquire utilities and issue bonds on the utilities so acquired and to take over the Cebu branch of the Philippine Railroad. He opposed any radical movement toward granting the islands their independence. During the Christmas recess, he introduced Representative Richard W. Austin to members of the firm of C. J. White and Company, who were retainers of Kincaid in seeking to get rid of their interests in the Philippine Railroad. As a result of the trip, Austin attempted to convince Congressman Mann, the Republican minority leader, to support the Senate bill. Of this arrangement, McIntyre was fully informed by Kincaid.[116]

After the holidays, the Philippine bill was taking its natural course through the Senate when, on January 11, 1916, an unexpected development occurred. Senator James P. Clarke of Arkansas, finding a number of his colleagues in the cloakroom agreeing with his views on American withdrawal from the islands, walked back on the floor; and, on his own initiative, in-

troduced an amendment to the Senate bill.[117] The Clarke
Amendment authorized the President to recognize the independence of the islands within two years and to withdraw from
the Philippines, retaining only naval bases and coaling stations
there. Meanwhile, the President was to attempt negotiation of
agreements with interested powers for the neutralization of the
islands. If such agreements were not forthcoming, the United
States alone would give such guarantees and then withdraw.[118]

The bill had indeed taken a strange course, unplanned by
the administration! Wilson called at Clarke's hotel room late
at night after the amendment was proposed and talked over the
matter. The hotel music disturbed them, and the Senator went
at another time to the White House for further discussion.[119]
As a result of representations by the President, Clarke changed
his amendment. In its new form, all danger was removed from
the proposal by extending the time in which the United States
was to leave the islands from two to four years, and by providing
that American sovereignty should be relinquished only if the
President at the end of four years found the internal and external
affairs of the island of a stable nature. If these conditions were
not met, the President could recommend extension of American
occupancy; but he was not to nullify the act by unnecessary extension. For five years after formal withdrawal, the United
States would guarantee the independence of the islands, meanwhile attempting to arrange guarantees for their neutralization
with other interested powers.[120]

On a week end cruise down the Potomac, such as he often
took to get away from Washington, Wilson radioed Secretary
Tumulty: "Please say to Senator Clarke, of Arkansas, that the
amendment as he has worked it out is satisfactory to me. If the
Senate thinks it necessary to take definite action at this time
the amendment in this shape is excellently worked out and
satisfactory."[121] All doubt of the administration's position was
now removed, and the following day, Clarke proposed the above
changes as Wilson desired.[122]

Quezon, who privately feared independence, and Osmena,
the two leaders of Philippine political life, publicly acclaimed
the Clarke amendment.[123] Harrison rejoiced over the new pro-

posal, but he asked for the private views of the President so that he would not embarrass the administration by any statements.[124] Wilson, on his own typewriter, wrote his private reaction to Garrison, who had expressed opposition to the amendment that afternoon in the Cabinet. The Chief Executive asked the Secretary to inform the Governor General: "It is the President's judgment that it would be best to pass the Philippine Bill in the shape in which it was originally proposed but, being convinced that some action such as is proposed in the Clarke Amendment is desired by a majority of the Senate, he has consented to the Clarke Amendment as the best form of action to that end."[125] Privately, Quezon too was much troubled over the turn of affairs, particularly after the failure of his attempt to have Senator Hitchcock refer the Clarke Amendment to the Committee on Foreign Affairs.[126]

Clarke frankly admitted that he stood for withdrawal from the Philippines on the basis that it was an extension of American occupation into Asian spheres, produced racial antagonism, and bred misunderstanding with Japan. He maintained that the United States could not exclude the Japanese and at the same time invade their hemisphere without creating ill will. It was best for the United States to withdraw. Although a Democrat, he had offered the amendment in opposition to the preamble, which promised eventual independence, because it had to be done.[127]

Senator Willard Salisbury of Delaware supported the Clarke stand as opposing American encroachment on Japan's proper sphere. He saw "much reason" in what Japan might term the "White peril" in the Orient. The speeches of various Senators favoring American dominance of the Pacific, Salisbury thought, had not added to Japanese respect for America's ambitions in Asia.[128] Senator Robert L. Owen of Oklahoma also supported the amendment on the basis of the incompatibility of American and Oriental races to exist side by side.[129] Senator Thomas J. Walsh of Montana pointed out that there was a real struggle for the control of China in the Orient, that American-Japanese relations could deteriorate into a struggle for power.[130] While Senator William J. Stone objected to any rapid move toward independence as being unfaithful to America's mission in the Philippines, he thought any sudden withdrawal would be disastrous to the islands.[131] Charges of "scuttling" the islands and pulling down the American flag were hurled at the Democrats by Senator William A. Smith of Michigan.[132] But the bill passed on February 4, 1916, with the Clarke Amendment intact.[133]

Representative Jones, having opposed the Clarke Amendment, called in McIntyre to learn the attitude of the War Department on the amended legislation. McIntyre pointed out that the amendment was contrary to the announced policy as stated by the Secretary during the Senate hearings.

Upon passage of the measure, Jones saw Wilson and expressed a desire to propose the original Senate bill in the House rather than the Senate measure containing the Clarke Amendment. "The President said that he, unfortunately, had not formed a very definite opinion as to what ought to be done and, therefore, he could not outline a measure which he would support to the end, and that he would like to have a decision as to this matter deferred until he could better form an opinion." When Jones suggested that Wilson send for Clarke and get the Senator's consent to some plan which would be adopted by the House (for it was generally understood the amendment could not pass the House), the President said he had committed himself to Clarke.[134]

Secretary of War Henry Breckenridge, meanwhile, asked Wilson to withhold any commitment to Jones on the bill until Secretary Garrison, who opposed the Clarke Amendment, returned to Washington.[135] Since the War Department was charged with the responsibility for insular affairs, the request was normal enough. Garrison and Wilson, however, were at odds over the means of raising an army under the new preparedness program.[136] Garrison, returning to the capital, protested against "the Clarke Amendment [as] an abandonment of the duty of this nation and a breach of trust toward the Filipinos; so believing, I can not accept it or acquiesce in its acceptance. . . ." The Secretary also considered "reliance upon the militia for national defense an unjustifiable imperiling of the nation's safety."[137]

Wilson replied to the disgruntled Secretary that he too viewed the Clarke Amendment as "unwise at this time." However, for him to take a dissenting position from such action, should it meet with the approval of both Houses, would be "unadvisable." He could not forecast what he would do after the action of Congress on the measure. For the time being, he was consulting with Jones and others as to what action should be taken in the House, and he thought it necessary to act calmly and deliberately in the matter, taking into consideration differing views on the problem. Of great importance to Garrison was the President's refusal to force Congressional acceptance of the War Department's views on preparedness. The Chief Executive said he was working on a solution of the whole preparedness program, and he urged Garrison to express himself on the matter.[138]

It surprised Wilson when on the same day, February 10, 1916, he received Garrison's terse letter of resignation. The Secretary of War wrote: "It is evident that we hopelessly disagree upon what I conceive to be fundamental principles. This makes manifest the impropriety of my longer remaining your seeming representative with respect to these matters." Henry Breckenridge, the Assistant Secretary loyally followed his chief in resigning.[139]

In accepting Garrison's resignation, Wilson said no action had been taken in either the Philippine bill or the preparedness program. The matters were in the stage of debate only. He consented to the resignation with expressions of appreciation for the past services of the Secretary.[140] McIntyre informed Governor Harrison that the "cause of his resignation was the controversy with reference to military legislation, rather than disagreement as to the Philippines."[141]

During the agitation of the Clarke Amendment, in February, 1916, the Democratic Party was split over the President's position opposing the warning of Americans from traveling on belligerent ships. Advocating that the warning be issued were the outstanding members of the Congress. Presidential leadership was being tested within the party, and Congressman Jones thought it placed Wilson in a weak position to aid the unpopular Clarke Amendment in the House. Privately, Jones continued disgusted at the injection of the amendment into the insular legislation.[142] He was not alone in his opposition for the Southern cotton manufacturers and other business interests of the country with markets or investments in the islands resented the action of the Senate.[143]

For the time being, until a new Secretary of War was named, General McIntyre was out of touch with administration plans for the Philippine bill. He mistakenly thought the whole situation of the amendment was caused by too frequent cables between Quezon and Osmena, which had stirred up the independence movement in the islands with the consequent reaction in the Senate favoring it. The General observed, however, that the Clarke Amendment had so upset Quezon that he had found it necessary to take to bed.[144]

On March 5, 1916, Wilson requested Secretary of the Navy Daniels to offer Newton D. Baker, the reform mayor of Cleveland, the post as Secretary of War. Baker had been from the beginning a friend of the administration. A Wilson man at the Baltimore Convention, he had been offered the cabinet post in the Interior Department, and the position of White House Secretary, but he had refused the appointments in favor of continuing his work in Cleveland.[145] In many respects Wilson and Baker were much alike as devoted reformers, and the President was greatly pleased when the Cleveland attorney accepted the Secretary of War post.

At the time of the new Secretary's appointment, McIntyre drafted a memorandum to be used as background for a conference between Baker and Jones on the Senate Philippine bill. The Chief of the Bureau of Insular Affairs thought the Clarke Amendment and other changes of the Senate bill so unwise that it would be better to have no legislation.[146] On the other hand, Baker, who himself favored Philippine independence, learned from Governor General Harrison that although the "Filipino people would prefer [a] temporary guarantee of independence as at first proposed, the great majority, including all classes, are

in favor of [the] Clarke Amendment as it passed the Senate and
desire [the] immediate settlement of [the] Philippine question."[147]

After considering the situation fully, the administration
prepared to go ahead with the Senate bill, containing the Clarke
Amendment and to seek its approval in the House, where the
Jones bill on the Philippines had passed in 1914, nearly two
years previously. The President "sincerely hope[d] for its early
adoption. . . ."[148] Acting Governor General Martin informed
the President, "The Filipino people have such unbounded confidence that your administration will reward their hopes that
the entire failure of the pending legislation would be deplor-
able."[149] Already the House Democratic Caucus in Washington
had included the Philippine bill in its legislative program for
the session.[150]

Opposition to the bill was now more manifest. *The New York
Sun* observed that the religious and business interests of the
islands finally were making their sentiments known. It revealed
that Kincaid, the Manila lawyer, had been in Washington for
two months working against the legislation.[151] Actually Kincaid
had been active in opposition to the bill as it came from the
Senate. He wrote Wilson that it was "a threat to every Christian
Church in the Philippine Islands and is a violation of the
promises under which they entered the field. It is violative of
the implied considerations which led to the investment of American capital in the Islands. It is violative of our obligations to
the Filipino people and to the nations interested in the Far East
who acquiesced in our assuming a government of the Philippine
Islands."[152] The opposition did not have a free field, however,
for the bill gained some strength from the Republicans when
Theodore Roosevelt endorsed American withdrawal.[153]

When the Senate bill came up for a vote in the House, on
May 1, 1916, although loyally supported by Jones and the Democratic organization, twenty-eight members, led by the Tammany
Democrats who opposed the Clarke Amendment, bolted the
party to defeat the measure. By clever amendment, they substituted for it a reconsideration of the Jones bill of 1914.[154] Explaining the House defeat of the bill, *The Boston Herald* stated,

"Out of the 30 Democrats who voted against independence thereby insuring its defeat, all but one or two were Catholics, whereas
of 164 Democrats voting for the bill only two or three were
Catholics." It reported that one member who voted against the
bill, in an indiscreet moment, said the Church wanted the bill
killed.[155] Harrison understood that the bolting members were
Catholic, and "that their attitude was the result of intervention
by James Cardinal Gibbons of Baltimore, acting, it is supposed,
at the instigation of the ecclesiastical authorities in the Philippines."[156]

The administration showed little concern with the House
substitution of the Jones bill and looked to a joint committee
of the two houses to adjust the differences. Secretary of War
Baker urged the President "to bring about a prompt agreement
and the early passage of the bill."[157] Wilson, in reply, promised
"to do everything possible," adding "I feel the importance of it
very profoundly."[158]

On August 15, 1916 the joint conference report on the
Philippine bill was submitted by Senator Hitchcock to the Senate.
He explained that the Conference had made four changes in the
bill. The House members of the Joint Committee, by instructions
from the Chamber, had been forbidden to consider any such
proposal as the Clarke Amendment so it was struck out. The
Senate accepted the House preamble of the original Jones bill
and an amendment involving some minor changes.[159] The
chief changes made by the joint committee consisted of omitting the Clarke amendment and dropping the proposed prohibition amendments contained in the Senate bill.

The Philippine bill emerged slightly in the presidential
election of 1916. The Democratic platform for the campaign,
written mostly by Wilson, endorsed the bill as passed by the
House and reiterated "our endorsement of the purpose of ultimate independence for the Philippine Islands, expressed in the
preamble of the measure."[160] In an address at Topeka, Kansas,
Wilson spoke of the United States as being trustees for the Filipino people, "and just as soon as we feel that they can take care
of their own affairs without our direct interference and protection, the flag of the United States will again be honored by

the fulfilment of a promise."[161] Although the Republican platform condemned the administration's threatened abandonment of the islands, Hughes made no major issue of the matter.[162] To Harrison's cable of congratulations on his re-election, Wilson replied, "I rejoice that what we have begun in the Philippines under your administration is to be continued."[163]

In the House, meanwhile, Congressman Clarence B. Miller, Republican of Minnesota and a bitter critic of the Harrison regime, made much of the Philippines as a base for American interests in the Far East, warning that even if the United States were not "other nations are interested in the Orient." He accused Japan of ambitions for an empire to the South. The war had disrupted the direction of her growth by offering an opportunity for expansion on the continent of Asia and in the North Pacific islands. He predicted if the United States withdrew from the Philippines "it is as certain as both death and taxes . . . that Japan will seize an early pretext to acquire the islands."[164]

No more difficulty was encountered, the conference bill passed both the House and Senate[165] and Wilson signed the bill into law, on August 29, 1916. The vote in the Senate was perfunctory. In the House, it brought forth a moving speech by Quezon, who praised the House on the legislation, thanked the American people, the Congress, and President Wilson for the law, and particularly praised Jones for his part in the legislation. Quezon also used the occasion to announce his retirement as Philippine Commissioner after eight years in Washington.[166]

From the Philippines, Governor Harrison reported great rejoicing over the success of the legislation. Wilson, replying to the resolutions of gratitude from the insular Assembly, acknowledged their courtesy and expressed the gratification he felt that he "should have been privileged to take part in doing justice to the people of the islands."[167]

What did the Jones Law[168] accomplish? In the much discussed preamble it provided for independence of the islands whenever a stable government was established. A popularly-elected legislature of two houses was authorized in which the

Governor General appointed representatives for the non-Christian tribes. Full law making powers were vested in the legislature, save for certain matters of international concern. The trade relations between the United States and the Philippines remained under the exclusive control of Congress, while legislation affecting lands, mining, forestry, currency, coinage, and immigration was subject to the supervision of the President of the United States. The Governor General, Vice Governor, Justices of the Supreme Court, and auditor were appointed by the President. The Governor General had a veto on legislative action. If a bill were passed over his veto, the President had the final veto power. Executive heads of departments were selected by the Governor General and confirmed by the Island Senate. A Bill of Rights and other constitutional guarantees were also granted.[169] The new law, popularly called the Jones Law, had been formed in the United States. It was a forward-looking piece of legislation, but in some particular details it was unreal to insular conditions.

As the first legislature prepared to meet under the new act, President Wilson asked Governor Harrison to convey his greetings to the members and to express his hope that the "confidence that has been reposed in them by the people and government of the United States will be abundantly vindicated by their whole course of action and policy. For myself, I look forward with confidence to the growth of self-government in the Philippines under this new and happier order of things and am glad to have had a part in taking the great step in advance which has now been taken."[170]

Baker wrote a statement on the new law for the guidance of the insular authorities. He warned Harrison against permitting any encroachment by the legislature on the vastly extended powers of the Governor General. The Secretary promised to be ever vigilant in Washington to prevent Congress from invading the new powers of self-government extended to the islands.[171] William Jennings Bryan, for over a year a private citizen, cabled Osmena: "Urge your people to show their appreciation of our nation's action by proving their wisdom, their self-restraint and their unselfish devotion to order, progress, and the prosperity of the masses."[172]

Seldom has a law been so liberally interpreted as was the Jones Act by Governor General Harrison. The Nationalist Party, since the beginning of the Harrison administration, had held the majority in the Philippine Commission; and the Governor consulted Speaker Osmena, the party leader, upon every question of government, thus bringing the executive branch under informal yet effective party control. Harrison had constantly worked with Osmena to place control more and more in the hands of the native leaders. When the Jones Act came into force, the fact of party government and leadership had thus already been established. The complication of an elective Senate, and the subsequent election of Manuel Quezon, the second politico of the Nationalist Party, as its President introduced a note of trouble into the harmonious arrangement for now Osmena and Quezon contested for control of affairs. Osmena solved the contest for control by creating a joint caucus of both houses, which established him as the leader in both legislative and executive branches of the government. Not until 1918 did he regularize his position by securing an executive order from Harrison creating a Council of State, composed of the Governor, the members of the Cabinet, and the presiding officers of the two houses of the legislature. Originally designed to function as an advisory council, it came more and more to center control of Philippine affairs in Osmena who thus became an extra-legal Premier of the government. All general policies were decided in the Governor's cabinet and gradually certain legislative functions such as distribution of appropriations were given over to it, but the actual political control lodged in the Osmena dominated Council of State.[173]

In the prolonged agitation over the Jones Law many aspects of American policy in the Philippines were brought to light. The Republican and the Democratic administrations differed in their final objectives. Taft and his followers, at least, had come to the view that they would like to remain in the islands, and make a dominion of them if possible. Although opposed to an overnight relinquishment of American control, Wilson seems never to have wavered from his position favoring eventual independence. The Southern and Western representatives of the Democratic party stood for rapid withdrawal of the United States and so bent were they on absolving America from responsibilities in the islands that their policy took on the appearance of "scuttling" American interests there. When this move came to a focus in the Clarke Amendment, in February, 1916, Wilson reluctantly consented to their program but only after having Clarke change the amendment to place the future of American policy under the Presidential control. It was general knowledge that the bill with the Clarke Amendment had little chance of getting through the House, and the President perhaps was being politically astute in not fighting the Senate on an issue which so certainly would solve itself in the normal course of legislative consideration, or even if enacted into law still gave him control of the situation.

While the rise of Japan was often cited as an argument in Congress for America abandoning the Philippines, the President made no mention of a fear of conflict. It was understood though that he wished the threat of Japan talked about as little as possible. His concern was ever for the welfare and progress of the Filipino people. Yet, in conformity with his usual procedure in administration, he interfered very little in affairs in the islands. He had confidence in the Governor General and expected him to carry out the general policy of training the islanders for self-government. For general policy and the details of administration, Wilson leaned heavily on the War Department, or more directly, the Bureau of Insular Affairs in that Department, where the able abilities of Colonel, later General, Frank McIntyre were ever at his command. From the first, the President sought the advice of men who were expected to know the conditions of the islands. Even his initial policy came through the bureaucracy from Felix Frankfurter, the young law officer in the War Department. Wilson viewed his job as one of coordinating and conciliating the legislative process. His was the responsibility for leadership toward the administration goals. In relation to the Philippines the principal goal was self-government for the native people.

Wilson's major task in the Philippines was completed with the passage of the Jones Law, although the islands, as will be subesquently shown, were to engage his attention at infrequent intervals thereafter. The entry of the United States into the World War in 1917 permitted the Filipinos to develop their own political institutions. Their loyalty and patriotism to the American cause were a source of great satisfaction to the war-harassed President.

CHAPTER FOUR

War and Consequences

Yuan Shih k'ai, the President of China, was "an able and interesting man, with a good deal of personal charm. . . ."[1] He was generous to his friends and remorseless to his enemies.[2] Minister Paul S. Reinsch compared him to Georges Clemenceau in appearance and declared him an autocrat at heart. Yuan told the newly-arrived American Minister; "Our traditions are very different from your Western ones and our affairs are very complex. We cannot safely apply your abstract ideas of policy."[3] He "recognized that representative institutions had by the revolution been imposed on a people having no comprehension of them." In an address he declared the word ". . . Republic is a beautiful term; but it only implies that the people have the right to know about the affairs of the State, not that everybody can have a hand in it." Trained in the old Manchu court, he confused political opposition with disloyalty, or even with treason to the state itself.[4] In control of the army and experienced in management of affairs, Yuan was looked upon as a stable factor in Chinese politics, and as such he enjoyed the trust of the business interests and of the foreign powers. This then was the man upon whom the fate of the Chinese Republic depended.

Yuan's dissolution of the Kuomintang Party on November 4, 1913, in part had been forced on him by its opposition precipitating the July revolution. This having failed, it then tried to force through a constitution which would weaken the President's control over the central government. The dissolution of the party, however, only drove the movement underground; and from Japan and other foreign countries, the Kuomintang carried on activities and plots against the Peking regime.

When former Chargé Williams returned to Washington in December, 1913 to become Chief of the Division of Far Eastern Affairs, he brought President Wilson a red silk covered greeting with an autographed photograph from Yuan. Wilson used the occasion of the courtesy to return his thanks and express the interest of the American people in "the development of representative government in China," and their rejoicing "in all that tends to promote the strength and permanency of the new republic and the prosperity and happiness of its citizens."[6] While this message was sent upon a ceremonial occasion, it actually represented Wilson's constant benevolent regard for China.

Meanwhile, Yuan continued to strengthen his position. In January, 1914, he proclaimed the dissolution of the Assembly, and promptly nominated a committee to revise the constitution so as to vest the governmental strength in his hands. The changes were accomplished in May, 1914.[7] Hopes now rose that Yuan could bring the divergent forces within China into a unified, stabilized nation.

Concurrently in Japan, Admiral Yamamoto, who had succeeded Katsura as Premier, found the California land issue and the Chinese civil war an advantage in distracting public interest from his unpopular ministry. The national debt was excessive and taxes high. Yamamoto was able to push the budget through the Diet, but only with the smallest possible majority. Chinese disunity contained attractive opportunities, and the sacking of Nanking by revolutionaries led to the murder of several Japanese shopkeepers.

The director of political affairs in the Japanese Foreign Office was assassinated as a protest to the weak China policy of the government. Tokyo then made representations to Peking. Chinese troops in Nanking were paraded to salute the

Japanese flag, and Yuan's government paid an indemnity of 800,000 yen by way of apology.[8]

When the Japanese Diet met in January, 1914, excitement arose over revelations implicating Japanese naval officers in foreign bribes concerning foreign sales of telegraph equipment and armaments in Japan.[9] These revelations occasioned widespread public protests; and, within the next few days, troops were called upon to put down the attending demonstrations. The scandal was thrown into the Diet debate on reduction of the naval budget, and the resulting confusion forced the resignation of the Yamamoto Cabinet.[10]

The Genro canvassed the opportunities for forming a government and reluctantly came to call in Marquis Shigenobu Okuma,[11] who led the factions in opposition to the Seiyukai Party. The new Premier, who accepted office on April 16, 1914, was seventy-six. His cabinet experience dated back to 1881 when as Minister of Finance he had resigned upon rejection of his memorial asking that true representative government be instituted. In 1888, as Minister of Foreign Affairs, he had revised the extraterritorial treaties with the powers.[12] Okuma was known as the "tribune of the people,"[13] and after the scandal of the past two ministries, the Genro felt that he was necessary to restore popular confidence in the government. As founder of Waseda University, whence so many journalists graduated, the new Premier enjoyed a friendly press.[14]

From Peking, Minister Reinsch saw the accession of the new government in Japan as heralding a new day in the relations between that country and China. He had talked to Okuma in Japan the previous autumn and thought the new ministry desired the friendship of China and cooperation for Asia's common advancement.[15]

Okuma's much acclaimed liberalism, however, was typically Japanese and something quite aside from the understanding of the term in the West. It is best revealed in his refusal to join the Genro upon leaving office in October, 1916. Between his accession in April, 1914 and his resignation, two important events were to occur in Japanese history: her entry into the

World War in September, 1914 and the presentation of the twenty-one demands to China during the following January.[16]

The war of 1914 broke over Washington while Mrs. Wilson lay dying. She was the President's invaluable helpmate and adviser; with her death the world had a bleakness it had never worn before.[17] Wilson had extended his good offices to the nations of Europe during her last days. He thought the war an incredible catastrophe.[18]

Developments in Europe during late July had assumed great importance in Japan. The Foreign Minister Baron (later Viscount) Takaakira Kato had been Ambassador to the Court of St. James, and Prime Minister Okuma had strong sympathies for the Japanese ties with England, which had been reaffirmed in 1911. Sir Edward Grey, the British Foreign Minister, informed Sir Conynham Greene, the Ambassador in Tokyo, on August 1, that the situation in Europe was grave. England might find it necessary to intervene on the Entente side, but she did not see any likelihood of calling on Japan under the alliance.[19] Greene in turn told Grey that Kato would await the British decision before deciding upon Japanese policy. Although she claimed no interest in the European conflict, Japan offered to come to Britain's assistance in case of German aggression against British property or subjects in the Far East.[20] Meanwhile, Grey asked Sir William Tyrrell of the Foreign Office if Britain's declaration of war on August 5 affected Japan under the Alliance. Sir William thought it did only if the war should spread to the Far East. He advised the Foreign Office to warn Japan that in case of German attack there, Britain would ask aid of them.[21] When this expectation on the part of Britain was communicated to the Japanese, it was considered before the Cabinet by Kato, who then informed the British Ambassador that the second battle fleet was ready for immediate action.[22] Sir Edward thanked the Japanese for their assurances, but said Britain would attempt not to involve Japan.[23]

London was finding the Japanese Alliance a source of embarrassment since the "prospect of unlimited Japanese action was repugnant to Australia and New Zealand." American public opinion also had to be considered. Sir Edward Grey confessed, "To explain to an Ally that her help will be welcome, but that you hope it will not be made inconvenient, is a proceeding that is neither agreeable nor gracious." By August 6, however, the naval situation in the Pacific, where the German Asiatic fleet was at large, forced Britain to ask Japanese assistance in the destruction of the enemy in Chinese waters. Grey realized it was asking Japan to go to war; but he confessed ". . . we do not see how this is to be avoided."[24] After receiving the British request, the Japanese Cabinet met at Okuma's residence. Certain members, representing the strong pro-German influence among the military, hinted that Britain might not win the conflict; but Okuma and Kato, after four hours of discussion, won the day. Japan would act with Britain against Germany.[25]

As early as August 3, the Chinese Minister of Foreign Affairs had approached John V. A. MacMurray, the American Chargé, asking the good offices of Washington in neutralizing China and her marginal waters for the duration of the war.[26] The State Department informally undertook to "sound out" opinion on such an arrangement, meanwhile authorizing MacMurray to participate in discussions with the diplomatic body in Peking concerning the neutralization of the foreign settlement.[27] In Washington, Bryan talked with Sir Cecil Spring-Rice, while American Ambassador Walter H. Page saw Sir Edward Grey in London, and Ambassador James Gerard sought the German views in Berlin. Sir Edward favored the American proposal for an agreement among the belligerents to maintain the status quo in China, but he felt neutralization of the Pacific as Washington proposed, included too vast an area for consideration.[28] When the German answer arrived on August 13, it agreed to neutralize the Far East if Britain would reciprocate, and it further proposed a mutual withdrawal of warships in Eastern waters. The note referred equally to Britain and Japan and stated that Germany did not seek war with the latter.[29]

Britain agreed on August 13 for Japan to enter the war on condition that she confine her operations to the west and south of the China Sea, the Pacific, and the German leased territory in China. A Council before the Throne was held in Tokyo, and Japan decided to send an ultimatum to Germany.[30] The document asked Germany to withdraw or disarm her ships in Chinese and Japanese waters and to deliver to the Japanese authorities, by September 15, 1914, the German leasehold of Kiaochow in Shantung with a view to its eventual restoration to China. Upon presenting Ambassador Guthrie with a copy of the ultimatum, Foreign Minister Kato asked that the State Department be advised that the Imperial government "was not animated by any selfish purpose" but acting in pursuance of the alliance with Great Britain in entering the war.[31]

In transmitting the ultimatum to Wilson, Secretary Bryan noted, "It contains a definite statement of purpose and a disclaimer of value." The Secretary asked to talk to the President over their private wire after he had read the ultimatum.[32] As a result of their conference, the American answer was sent Guthrie. The United States, in strict neutrality, expressed no opinion concerning the difference between Germany and Japan; but it noted with satisfaction that in demanding the surrender of Kiaochow by Germany, Japan proposed to restore it to China, "and that Japan is seeking no territorial aggrandizement in China in the movement now contemplated," but acted only out of compliance to its obligations under the Anglo-Japanese Alliance. The Secretary noted that one of the terms of the Alliance was preservation of the common interest of all powers in China by insuring the independence and integrity of China and the principle of equal opportunities for the commerce and industry of all nations in China." The note ended by suggesting that should disturbances in China require action, Japan would consult with the United States in accordance with the Root-Takahira note of 1908.[33] Wilson reviewed the communication and thought it should be sent. He wrote Bryan, ". . . I think it wise for us to be on the safe side in letting the Japanese Government know what our own understanding of the situation is."[34] With the Japanese, the administration had learned it was best to keep the record straight.

The day previous, on August 18, the British had reassured Washington that Japanese activities would not extend beyond the China Seas, except for the protection of Japanese shipping, "nor beyond Asiatic waters westward of the China Sea, or to any foreign territory in German occupation on the Continent of Eastern Asia." Bryan scrawled across the bottom of the document: "A reassuring telegram submitted to the President for his consideration."[35] In the light of Britain's August 13 acquiescence to Japanese operations on the Asian continent, their assurances to the United States were not completely accurate.

The Japanese ultimatum reached Berlin on August 17 and was made public the following day. The *North China Herald* commented that despite the necessity of the ultimatum, Japan had made cynical use of her alliance with Britain. It criticized Japan's intervention in the war as unnecessary. British and French vessels could blockade Tsingtau until troops were sent from Vladivostok to take the German port. The whole idea of Japanese intervention was suspect as a German plot, for Japan would not willingly leave once in Tsingtau, and the whole matter could lead to a rift in the Anglo-Japanese Alliance.[36]

MacMurray informed the Department that the German Chargé had been talking of retroceding Kiaochow to China, but the Chinese had been warned by Japan to discontinue the talks.[37] The British Minister, too, had informed Peking that his Government could not recognize any German retrocession of Kiaochow. The Chinese Minister of Communications informed the American legation that in transmitting to China a copy of their ultimatum to Germany, Japan had advised the Chinese Government that the matter did not concern them and they were expected to remain passive. If internal disturbances broke out in China, Japan threatened that both Britain and the United States would help in suppressing them. Japan privately objected to Peking's seeking American good offices in neutralizing the Far East, although the same request had been later made of Tokyo. Now with a German-Japanese war materializing, the Chinese suggested that the United States approach Japan and Britain to have the German leasehold of Kiaochow ceded to the American Government for restoration to China,[38] but to this suggestion Bryan immediately replied, "The Department feels sure that such a course would do more to provoke than to avert war."[39]

On August 23, 1914, Tokyo time, Japan issued an Imperial rescript declaring war against Germany and commanding the "Army and Navy to carry on hostilities against that Empire with all their strength. . ."[40]

Colonel House, upon learning of the declaration, wrote Wilson that he was sorry Japan had "injected herself into the general melee for it will place an additional strain upon us not to become involved."[41] Later the same day, while House was dining with a group including William Phillips, the Third Assistant Secretary of State, who was then in general charge of Far Eastern Affairs, and W. W. Rockhill, who had been John Hay's chief adviser on the area, word came from England "that she did not wish Japan to declare war against Germany, but Japan did it for her own purposes which were primarily to throw Germany out of the Eastern Seas." England, the report said, had tried to keep Japan from taking Samoa and thus becoming a close neighbor of the United States there; but House thought if Japan wanted to seize the German colony in Samoa, the United States should not protest since, "Japan was no more dangerous to us than Germany. . ."[42]

Japan, however, was plainly suspect, her ambitions in Asia were suspect, her willingness to fulfil her treaty obligations under the open door were suspect. Suspicion of Japan's motives and ambitions, of her every action in Asia, then was in the background throughout the war years.

Despite China's protest, Japan, on September 3, invaded Shantung Province at Lunghow on the north coast, far from their objectives at Tsingtau. Three weeks later, a token force of nine hundred ten British troops joined the Japanese. China defined a war zone, but Japan paid little attention to its limits. Despite the understanding concerning the policing of the Shantung Railway by Chinese troops, the Japanese found military necessity obliged them to take over the railway as far west as Tsinan, the provincial capital located some two hundred odd miles in the interior. This action, according to Japan, did not extend the belligerent zone.[43]

The Japanese invasion aroused the Chinese press. Said the *Shanpao*, ". . . those who wish to know the future fate of Shantung have only to look at the present condition of Manchuria and Liaotung." The *Eastern Times* commented: "It is not easy to keep one's ground when standing upright unless one is firm in the leg." China was the scapegoat of the belligerents. Remarking on the fact that Germany protested to China for permitting the Japanese landings, the *Sinwanpoa* exclaimed: "Oh! how difficult it is for a daughter-in-law to please two mothers-in-law."[44]

On November 6, 1914, two months after the Japanese landings, the German Governor, Admiral Meyer Waldeck surrendered his combatant force of 4,500 men to the Japanese, and the "rising sun" went up over the forts of Tsingtau. The victory had cost the Japanese 1,968 killed and wounded, one destroyer and one torpedo boat lost.[45]

The American Minster, Paul S. Reinsch, at the outbreak of hostilities was vacationing in Europe. Upon his return to Peking, he found the Chinese more upset over the extension of the Japanese occupation of Shantung along the railway than over the original invasion. They assumed, and correctly, that Tsingtau was to be merely a base for spreading Japanese domination throughout the province. Such beginnings could lead to a Japanese annexation similar to her action in Korea. They also believed, and rightly, that the revolutionary intrigues in China were backed by the Japanese in an attempt to create a situation which would permit their intervention in Chinese affairs while the western powers were distracted by the European war.[46]

By October, 1914, the Japanese had taken over the Marshall Archipelago in the Pacific. The Japanese press itself was pleasantly surprised by the action, since the Government had announced that its activities would be restricted to Chinese and Japanese waters. The *Yamoto Shimbun* believed that the war would result in the recognition of the open door and equal opportunity of commerce in the South Seas. The sensational antigovernmental journal, the *Yorozu Choho*, explained that the seizure of the Marshalls counteracted the American bases in Hawaii, Guam and the Philippines, which formerly had checked Japanese interests and weakened her in the South Pacific. The *Niroku Shimbun* expressed similar opinions and proclaimed the future of Japanese expansion lay in the South Seas.[47]

Just preceding the German surrender at Tsingtau, Lansing informed Reinsch that the United States would keep its troop strength in China at a maximum and increase its number of naval vessels in Chinese waters in view of possible internal disorders. While the American government desired to protect American rights and interest in China, it was anxious that its aims be not misunderstood by the Chinese. Lansing declared: "The United States desires China to feel that American friendship is sincere and to be assured that this Government will be glad to exert any influence which it possesses, to further, by peaceful methods, the welfare of the Chinese people, but the Department realizes that it would be quixotic in the extreme to allow the question of China's territorial integrity to entangle the United States in international difficulties."[48] America's attention was riveted on Europe as the main theatre; side shows must not be permitted to distract from the main event. American interests in China were limited and certainly not worth a war. Herein lies much of the weakness of the American-China policy.

By mid-December, the Japanese were demanding the right to appoint custom officials at Tsingtau.[49] This directly involved the rights of the treaty powers, for Chinese customs had been collected by the Maritime Customs Service under an agreed international arrangement. Only reluctantly and with some adjustments did Japan alter her plans to take over the service.[50] But her ambitions were showing.

Yuan Shih k'ai, meanwhile, was confronted with the multiple problems of establishing his authority. The plottings of the outlawed Kuomintang, the loss of revenues due to the hostilities together with its weakening effect on his power to resist Japanese encroachments added to the task.[51] Despite these complications, however, the opening of 1915 appeared propitious for a period

of quiet under the strong leadership of Yuan. Then suddenly
the Twenty-one Demands were privately handed the Chinese
President by the Japanese Minister at an interview on January
18, 1915.

There were many complicating factors in the presentation
of the Twenty-one Demands at this time. Kato's immediate
excuse was the Chinese abrogation of the war zone erected in
Shantung during 1914. Tokyo, however, had grown increasingly
irritated over the Chinese tendency to enlist American diplomatic aid. Japan too had no desire to see a successful republic
established in China, especially one under the leadership of
Yuan Shih k'ai, who had so consistently opposed Japanese ambitions on the Asian continent. Above all, the European war
provided a golden opportunity for Japan to secure a dominant
position, especially in northeast Asia.

Personal ambitions were also present in the presentation of
the Demands at this time. Foreign Minister Kato had come
home from London to take office under Katsura in 1913, only
to find the government dissolved in two months, thus giving
him no time to settle the problem of relations with China. He
had talked of the matter with Sir Edward Grey before leaving
London. Once out of office, Kato worked for his scheme and
consulted with various officials of the Yamamoto government
concerning it. Now with Okuma in power and Kato again the
Foreign Minister, he was once more in a position to deal with
Sino-Japanese relations. What he planned is not exactly clear.
"With pardonable pride he thought himself the greatest expert
in the art of diplomacy that Japan could show. It was his
fourth term at the Foreign Office: he would crown his career
with a signal triumph by solving the most difficult problem
of the day."[52]

But even Kato was not free to carry out his plans in his
own way, nor was the popular Prime Minister Okuma free
from influences. The Elder Statesmen and their satellites were
still of vast importance in Japan, and they had decided now was
the opportunity to establish the dominance of Japan in China.[53]
The Twenty-one Demands were the means. Too, the Ministry
lacked the support of the lower house in the Diet, and it was

thought a strong policy toward China would win popular approval in the March elections.[54] Whether due to the success in the elections or not, it is a fact that once they were over the Demands were somewhat moderated. The opposition and the Japanese liberals attacked the Demands as a diplomatic blunder rather than upon any essential unjustness.[55] On Japan's ambitions in China there was general agreement. Difference arose over the means to be employed.

In handing President Yuan the Demands, the Japanese Minister, Eki Hioki, admonished him to keep them secret or suffer undefined consequences.[56] The following day, January 19, a Japanese press reporter called at the American legation to inquire why Hioki had called on Yuan; evidently his intent was to discover if anything had been communicated to the American Embassy. It was not until three days later, on January 22, 1915, however, that Minister Reinsch learned of the Demands from a Chinese official.[57]

The Demands were divided into five groups: In Group one, China was to assent to any agreement of Japan with Germany over rights in Shantung, to cede or lease no territory to a third party, to grant Japan railway building rights, and to open additional ports in the province to foreign commerce. Group two established Japan's paramount interest in South Manchuria and Eastern Inner Mongolia, extended her leases of Port Arthur and Dairen as well as her control of the South Manchurian and Ontung-Mukden Railways to ninety-nine years, and granted Japanese the right to own and lease land and engage in mining in these regions. China was to consult Japan first if she needed advisers in these areas, and the railway of the region was given into Japanese control. Group three required China to agree in establishing the Hanyehping iron mines as a joint Sino-Japanese Company with monopoly mining rights in the Yangtze Valley. Group four engaged China not to cede or lease to any other power any harbor, bay or island along the China coast. Group five consisted of a miscellaneous collection[58] that the Japanese later called "requests," which will be discussed in their pertinent place below.

Reinsch informed the State Department of these Demands as they became known to him. He admonished Washington of the secret nature of the negotiations. This fiction of secrecy as to the exact nature of the Demands, especially group five, was maintained until February 17, and strictly limited the action of the State Department in the whole affair.[59] Although no official communication of the full nature of the Demands was forthcoming for nearly a month, they were being discussed within a week of their presentation by the public press and confidentially by the diplomatic corps in Peking. From January 25 on, high Chinese officials advised frankly with the American Minister on the negotiations;[60] and he kept the State Department fully informed.

In Washington, Colonel House, State Department Counselor Robert Lansing, who succeeded as Counselor upon the resignation of John Basset Moore the year previous, and President Wilson talked about the new Chinese difficulties. The Colonel confining his diary comments of the meeting to his own views said: "Trouble may grow out of this and I advised great caution. We are not at present in a position to war with Japan over the 'open door' in China."[61] The attention of the administration was riveted to the European War. Its first reaction to the Asiatic crisis was to keep it from developing into an open conflict.

Edward T. Williams, the former American Chargé in Peking, was relied on heavily for advice in the situation. Counselor Lansing's desk diary for the period shows daily interviews with him and frequent consultations with Frank Lockhart, the Assistant Chief of the Far Eastern Division. Bryan and Lansing worked closely on the matter, with the latter drawing up the notes and gathering information for the Secretary.[62] Wilson consulted both Lansing and Bryan, reviewed the notes, and from time to time, as will be shown, gave new direction to the course of the diplomacy. In its general policy, the administration followed along the general lines outlined by Minister Reinsch, although it was not as active in China's behalf as he persistently advocated.

The first reaction within the State Department to the Twenty-one Demands came in a memorandum of E. T. Williams, Chief of the Far Eastern Division. It recommended that Japan should be asked for a statement and an explanation of the Demands. Averring that an independent China was to the best interest of the United States, Williams recommended sympathetic support of her in the controversy. He warned that despite Japan's commitments on the open door, where her self-interests were involved, she could not be expected to live up to her agreements, especially after the shameless way she had violated all her pledges in relation to Korea.[63]

Wilson was seriously disturbed at the turn of events in Asia. Replying to a current suggestion of Bryan for settling the continued controversy relating to the California land case by a treaty with Japan on the matter, he observed:

> This is, of course, something that (or, at least, something like what) we must at the opportune time seek to do for Japan, whose friendship we so-desire and to whom we so sincerely desire to do justice.

> But there are many things to consider first: among the rest her present attitude and intentions in China and her willingness or unwillingness to live up to the open door in the East.

> I would be very much obliged if you would ask Mr. Lansing to prepare for our discussion a memorandum explicitly setting forth just what obligations in this sense she did undertake.[64]

Wilson was viewing the new developments in relation to the traditional American policy of the defense of Chinese sovereignty and the open door. Professorial like, he was gathering his facts of Japan's commitments in relation to that policy.

At this time, so little credence was placed in the rumors of the Demands that the press in both Britain and the United States refused to print stories of their correspondents concerning them.[65] This attitude was encouraged by the Japanese official denials that any such developments had taken place. The pall of secrecy surrounding the negotiations caused Reinsch to suggest that the Department urge the Chinese to disregard the Japanese warnings and make the facts known.

Reinsch felt that Britain was the key to doing anything with Tokyo since Japan would back down rather than face any break in the Anglo-Japanese Alliance.[66] This tendency to rely on British cooperation against Japan dominated every crisis in Asia throughout the Wilson years. It was the "will-o'-the-wisp" of the State Department as well as the foreign service personnel. Insofar as British and American interests corresponded in China, the cooperation was somewhat natural, and it was true that Britain was the leading foreign power in Asia. The Anglo-Japanese Alliance also strengthened her position in relation to the challenging power in the Pacific.

Bryan followed the course suggested by Reinsch. He asked Ambassador Page in London to determine the nature of the Demands which Bryan felt were "probably exaggerated," for if they actually were as reported they would violate the sovereignty of China as well as the commitments under the open door.[67] On February 3, the day following Bryan's inquiries in London, the Japanese assured the United States that the negotiations in no way threatened the integrity of China or the open door policy. Premier Okuma himself took pains to reiterate these assurances to the American Ambassador.[68]

On February 5, the Chinese government declined to accept the Twenty-one Demands on the grounds that they were in violation of her sovereignty. Japan insisted that China comment on each demand rather than submit a blanket rejection. The war had caused such an upset in the Asian power relationships as to leave a weakened China at the mercy of a determined Japan. China therefore agreed to continue the negotiations.[69] Meanwhile, the Demands were so generally known that the Japanese saw fit on February 8, to issue an incomplete list of them to the powers. In this list she did not include any mention of group five, which contained the most noxious demands.[70]

Wilson, most anxious to aid China in the crisis, wrote Reinsch:

> I have thought a great deal about the present situation in China, in view of the Japanese demands, and have been doing what I could indirectly to work in the interests of China. I have had this feeling, that any direct advice to China or direct intervention on her behalf in the present negotiations would really do her more harm than good, inasmuch as it would very likely provoke the jealousy and excite the hostility of Japan, which would first be manifested against China herself. I have been trying to play the part of prudent friend by making sure that the representatives of Great Britain realized the gravity of the situation and just what was being attempted. For the present, I am watching the situation very carefully indeed, ready to step in at any point where it is wise to do so.[71]

The policy of the "prudent friend" for the time being then required watchful waiting and full advisement with Britain as to the action of her Japanese ally. The President seemingly realized that a strong American stand without the necessary national will or power to implement it could only serve to antagonize Japan.

Even after publication of the full Demands by the Chinese on February 17, Bryan made a conscious effort to consider the Japanese position. In his memorandum to the President in which he considered group five as interfering with the political integrity of China and the commitments under the open door, he revealed a sympathy for the Japanese position. While he thought it unlikely, he admitted, "I am not sure but that it would be worth — while for China to agree to the cession of Manchuria if, by so doing, she could secure freedom as to the rest of the country."[72] Oddly enough appreciation for this attitude was also shown by Williams and Lansing. Williams saw, "The diversion of the tide of Japanese migration toward Manchuria may somewhat relieve the situation on our own Pacific Coast." He thought the "special rights" of Japan should be recognized in that area.[73] Lansing also suggested that an understanding should be worked out with Japan in which the United States would refrain from urging its treaty rights in South Manchuria and Shantung in return for Japan agreeing to make no further complaint regarding land tenure legislation in the United States. In addition Japan should affirm her adherence to the open door.[74] Thus Bryan, Williams, and Lansing, the three most important figures on Far Eastern policy within the State Department, had come to see that an "arrangement" must be made with Japan permitting her expansion on the Asian continent. This was not so new as it seemed for Theodore Roosevelt had done the same thing in the Taft-Katsura Agreement of 1905, recognizing Japan's "suzerainty over" Korea.

The provisions of group five of the Demands, as revealed by the Chinese on February 17, contained five items. First, China was to employ influential Japanese subjects as advisers for conducting administrative, financial, and military affairs. Second, China and Japan were to jointly police important points in China, or China was to employ a majority of Japanese in her police departments. Third, China was to purchase at least half her arms in Japan or establish joint arsenals in China. Fourth, China should permit Japan to build certain railroads around Manchang. Fifth, in case the province of Fukien, across from Japanese held Formosa, needed foreign capital, Tokyo was to be first consulted.[75]

Wilson felt that the American disapproval of group five should be "very frankly" submitted to Japan. "I think those views can be made very weighty and conclusive. We shall not have uttered a more important state paper."[76] The Far Eastern Division differed with the decision to lodge objections in Tokyo only in relation to group five and not the rest of the Demands. It suggested a *quid pro quo* arrangement if a surrender of valuable treaty rights were to be made, especially in Manchuria and Eastern Mongolia.[77]

Reinsch, considerably irritated over seemingly American inaction in the crisis was reassured by Bryan: "The President is consulted on all international questions. All your recommendations are laid before him as received." Bryan further explained, "Owing to [the] injunction of secrecy, we have endeavored to avoid embarrassing the Chinese Government here or in Peking."[78]

Upon learning that Japan, displeased at the slow progress of the negotiations, had set March 13 as the date for certain concessions to be granted, or means other than diplomatic would be employed, Wilson urged that the American note on group five be hurried.[79] In China it was rumored that the second squadron had sailed from Japan with 30,000 men. Japanese garrisons in Tsingtau, Tientsin, and Manchuria had been doubled.[80] But the deadline passed without incident.

The State Department drafted the note and dispatched its contents to Tokyo. It followed Bryan's strategy in preserving the Japanese fiction that the "demands" were merely "requests," which permitted the United States to discuss them frankly. It maintained America's interest in the independence, integrity and commercial freedom of China and the preservation of the legitimate American rights and interests there. The "requests" were held to be in violation of these rights and policies. However, two important concessions were made to Japan in the note: The United States raised no objections to the demands relative to Shantung, South Manchuria, and East Mongolia, and it declared "the United States frankly recognizes that territorial contiguity creates special relations between Japan and these districts."[81] These were major concessions, loosely made, the interpretation of which was to haunt future American-Japanese diplomacy.

Wilson instructed that the note be "communicated in strict confidence to the Governments of Great Britain and France and perhaps the Government of the Netherlands." He asked that it be sent to Reinsch so that he could let the Chinese see "what we are attempting to do in their support."[82] Despite the precautions to keep the American note secret, the newspapers of March 17 reported that the United States had voiced its objections to Japan.

Ambassador Guthrie had an interview with Foreign Minister Kato who read him the Japanese answer to the Bryan note. Kato dwelt especially on Japanese fears, ever since the days of John Hay, of American ambitions to establish a coaling station in Fukien province. These fears had been revived as a result of the negotiations of the Bethlehem Steel Company with the

Chinese Government for the improvement of the harbor. Kato, therefore, asked the United States to agree with Japan on foreign rights in Fukien.[83]

In reviewing the Japanese note, Bryan was appreciative of Japan's concern over Fukien province since it was within sight of Formosa; but the United States had no desire for such a station as Kato suggested. The Secretary thought that any agreement over the rights in the province should be between China and Japan, and so worded that China would then be able to prevent any nation from gaining a foothold there. The Secretary confessed surprise on learning that Great Britain, France, and Germany had secured agreements, since the establishment of the open door policy, which were identical with the Demands now asked by Japan. Bryan stated he had no objections to the employment of Japanese advisers by China since Kato's note said it was only a suggestive proposal. On the question of armaments, the Japanese note said it was only seeking an estimate from China so Japanese military production could be planned, that the republic purchased much of its military needs from them. The policy proposal, Bryan gladly noted, was confined to Manchuria and Mongolia.[84] Japan had not neglected to note the Secretary's recognition of her "special position in South Manchuria, Eastern Mongolia and Shantung. . ." Japan made the point that commercial and industrial undertakings in China became factors of international policies, "even are very often conceived at the very inception particularly on the part of China, and are so engineered as to add still a more disquieting element to the situation."[85] Certainly the Secretary was making every attempt to see the Japanese view.

Wilson's reply, to Bryan, agreed that the fear of an American coaling station in Fukien could best be solved, as Bryan suggested, by Japan and China forbidding it as a matter of treaty. The President was somewhat more suspicious than Bryan of the Japanese position.

Frankly, I do not think that the explanation of the other "requests" which are offered in Ambassador Chin [d] a's note are convincing, and I hope that a candid discussion of them by the two governments may result in putting them in a more satisfactory light. I quite understand the motives disclosed. I do not feel like criticising the Japanese government in regard to them. But I think that the remedies and safeguards proposed in the "requests" go too far. Whatever the intention, they do, in effect constitute a serious limitation upon China's independence of action, and a very definite preference of Japan before other nations, to whom the door was to be kept open.[86]

At this time the President publicly stated that the United States neither approved nor disapproved the Demands of Japan on China.[87] It is evident that Wilson had acknowledged the population pressure argument for Japan's expansion, but he was unwilling to see the Japanese go so far as to interfere with the treaty rights of the powers in China or of China's independence. Bryan prepared the telegram on Fukien to go forward to Guthrie and submitted another in regard to advisers, arms and police supervision to Wilson. The Secretary observed: that in the interests of understanding Japan should not demand too much, nor China concede too little. Distrust and suspicion of one another, already present, made negotiation difficult. In the matter of advisers, he thought that the agreement should be that Japan should not be discriminated against; he would apply the same solution to the matter of armaments. In the matter of police, the difficulty was that there was no specific limitation to Manchuria and Eastern Mongolia in writing, but only in verbal understanding. Williams and Lansing approved of this plan, as they did the telegram on Fukien.[88]

Again fear of Japanese military measures emerged in Peking, and Reinsch reported reinforcements to the Japanese garrisons throughout Manchuria and Shantung where ordinary traffic on the railways had been stopped in favor of military transport. This threat of force precipitated a boycott of Japanese goods in China, despite the stringent attempts of Peking to prevent all such public demonstrations.[89] Reinsch from the first saw the Demands as an invasion of China's sovereignty. He sought more active resistance on the part of the United States, but the administration's cautious policy of "prudent friend" to

China prevailed. Reinsch, at the same time, realized that in manifesting friendship for China, care had to be exerted not to give the impression that the United States would intervene as a matter of international justice.[90]

John V. A. MacMurray, who acted as Chargé in Peking during Reinsch's absence, had been a former student of Wilson's at Princeton. At this time, he wrote the President a private letter which came into the Chief Executive's hands somewhat later. MacMurray suggested the crisis in Asia had been caused by China's weakness at the outbreak of the World War. The current Japanese claims that the Demands were only the settlement of problems long in discussion were false, for only two of the Demands had formerly formed any part of a discussion between the two governments. Anti-American feeling among the Japanese was strong; and, because of the friendship of Wellington Koo for the United States, the Japanese refused to recognize him as a Chinese representative in the negotiations. It seemed to MacMurray that the danger of Japan making war on the United States was conditioned by two factors: the possession of the material resources necessary, and the psychological factor that the United States was used by the Japanese politicians to frighten the electorate "to vote right," and the belief of these same factions that the United States would always placate the Japanese. Already, Japan was beginning an Anti-American campaign in China as a means of solidifying Sino-Japanese relations. The United States was pictured as hypocritically asserting friendship for both Oriental powers while denying them immigration rights. He thought the Japanese policy extremely dangerous to the good relations of Japan, China and United States. Wilson directed that the letter should be acknowledged and a statement made "that I have followed the Japan-Chinese affair with the greatest solicitude and am sincerely obliged to him for the light he throws on it."[91]

On April 8, 1915, the Peking petition signed by Charles F. Hubbard, Minister of Union Foreign Church, H. H. Loary, President of Peking University, and others, asked that the United States demand of China representation in the negotiations. It stated, "By every consideration of honor and self interest the greatest republic of the western world ought to stand by the great republic of the East to the extent of seeing that it gets justice at this critical time."[92] Wilson asked Bryan if he had seen the message and what he thought of it.[93] Bryan did not think it wise to give out a document which criticized the Japanese Government and at the same time emphasized American material interests in opposing its program. He thought such a protest as the missionaries presented would put their activities in Japan and China under suspicion, and hurt rather than aid China's cause.[94] It was later revealed that the telegraph charges of the missionary protest, something over $7,000, and the news concerning it from Peking sent out by the United Press, were paid for by the Chinese Government.[95] In her weakness China pitted one power against another, relied on the activities of friendly pressure groups, and sympathetic foreigners. This strategy was recognized within the Wilson administration, but it was difficult to determine to what extent it was being used.

The Japanese attempted to undermine Chinese confidence in American backing. They cited every concession by the State Department as evidence of American support for Japan's position in China. The *Tientsin Times* quoted a prominent Japanese as saying it was useless to hope for any American action, since the Secretary of State was "so much under the influence of Baron Chinda that he is not saying a word against the wishes of Japan. . . ." The paper commented bitterly that this seemed to be true since the United States was no longer championing the open door policy. So vigorously did Japan carry out this program of undermining American support of China that Reinsch asked permission to wage a counter campaign showing that the United States had not abandoned its obligation or interest there.[96]

Wilson was increasingly uneasy concerning Reinsch's reports. He frankly admitted that he did not credit the assurances given by the Japanese. On April 14, he asked Bryan to see Ambassador Chinda and to express to him the American concern over the information that Japan was still insisting upon group five of the Demands, even though they were "so clearly incompatible with the administrative independence and autonomy of the Chinese Empire [sic] and with the maintenance of the policy of an open door to the world." The President strongly added, "In short, I feel that we should be as active as the circumstances permit in showing ourselves to be champions of the sovereign rights of China, now as always, though with no thought of seeking any special advantage or privilege for ourselves." He sought to know if the American Minister in Peking had been told that we had not acquiesced in any of the Japanese demands, although Count Okuma had been quoted in the newspapers as saying that we had.[97]

As a result of these representations, Bryan informed the Chinese Minister to consult the State Department for its attitude rather than accept any Japanese interpretations of American policy.[98] On the same day, he cabled Reinsch permission to give out informal assurances of the continued interest of the United States in maintaining its obligations and treaty rights in China.[99]

Now that his information on the Demands was more complete, Wilson was "convinced that we shall have to try in every practicable way to defend China." He thought the Chinese resistance to the demand concerning the Hanyehping iron mines was justified, and he thought Bryan should talk to the Japanese Ambassador about it. The Secretary would be justified in showing Chinda that such demands contained "a very decided infringement of the principle of China's administrative and economic integrity." He warned: "We shall have to be very chary hereafter about seeming to concede the reasonableness of any of Japan's demands or requests either, until we get the whole of the situation in our minds by hearing from Peking as well as Tokyo."[100]

Reinsch now suggested that it might be possible for the United States to obtain in advance from Great Britain and her allies an assurance that they would accept a circular invitation to renew adhesion to the China policies of the open door and equal opportunity.[101] Wilson accepted the suggestion, and instructed Bryan to say to Chinda that the American position "has been so generally misunderstood and so misleadingly speculated about that we feel that it may become immediately necessary to make our views public, *perhaps* in conjunction with the other nations whose interests and sympathies are equally involved. . ." It was the only means he saw of reassuring "China, our own people, and other governments less free than we to protest." He also thought that Reinsch should be instructed "to assure the Chinese government that it has our sympathy in resisting any demands which too seriously impinge upon its sovereignty, its administrative independence, or its territorial integrity."[102] The President had shifted to the offensive.

Bryan drew up the memorandum for Chinda's perusal, but he made no mention of any invitation to the powers.[103] He justified this omission on the grounds that "None of the Allies are in a position to join us in anything that we say or do and of course we could not invite Germany to join us in view of the relations existing between Japan and Germany."[104] Wilson then suggested that instead of an invitation, Bryan might take the occasion of presenting the American views to the Ambassador to say orally that "it might become our duty to make our position clear (and invite comment) by means of a circular note. I mean, just to intimate this to him as something we had in mind as possible."[105] Threat of a circular note reiterating the open door then became the instrument to coerce Japan into dropping the more noxious items of group five.

Chargé Post Wheeler informed the Secretary that the Japanese Foreign Office was determined on Eastern Mongolian rights, munitions control, and joint ownership of the Hanyehping mines, but had about decided to abandon the joint police demands, and let the railroad south of the Yangtze await the end of the war for discussion. Wheeler said the press in Japan was denouncing Kato's methods of negotiation, and it was suggested that the Diet would severely criticize the government for its China policy when it convened on May 17.[106]

On the last of April, Count Chinda handed the Secretary of State a memorandum revealing the status of negotiation on the Demands and listing the Japanese proposals for an early decision. Bryan gave the President a copy of the memorandum at the cabinet meeting. Three days later, the Secretary wrote a commentary on the document in which he interpreted the mild changes made in the Demands by Japan as representing her desire for a settlement.[107]

At this time, Reinsch sent a recently obtained copy of the notes on the remarks made by Dr. Hioki, the Japanese Minister, to President Yuan when presenting the Demands in January, and another of the Japanese Dragon Society program, recommending that Japan take advantage of China's weakness and the preoccupation of the powers to incite revolution in China, impose a friendly monarchy, and then form a defensive alliance with her as a protectorate of Japan. On the latter document, Reinsch commented that its authenticity was unquestioned by the Chinese authorities.[108]

The newspapers of May 4 stated that Japan was contemplating an ultimatum to China. The State Department drafted a release to the press and a letter to Chinda concerning the threatened action. Bryan informed the President that he would, at the same time, say to the Japanese Ambassador that he hoped that Japan was not considering such action. Wilson agreed with the Secretary's procedure.[109]

The press release stated that Japan had given assurances to the United States that the Demands would not interfere with the political or territorial integrity of China, discriminate against other treaty powers, or interfere with the open door. It also reiterated the American position of protecting its treaty rights in China, and expressed the hope that the present negotiations would benefit both nations.[110]

In the face of the threatened ultimatum, Wilson thought it wise that Reinsch be kept informed as to what the United States was doing for the Chinese government. At the same time, he instructed the American Minister to advise conciliation in Peking as Chargé Wheeler was doing in Japan.[111]

Bryan's message to the Japanese Premier was unofficial and placed upon an intimate friendship basis. It deplored any threat of war between China and Japan, and called on Okuma, as a known advocate of world peace, to work for a continuation of peaceful negotiations.[112] With Wilson's approval, the Secretary also sent out telegrams to the American representatives in London, Paris, and Petrograd, asking them to inform the respective Foreign Offices of the American alarm and distress at the news concerning the ultimatum, and to ask if the governments would join the United States in an appeal for continuance of negotiations between the two countries.[113]

The same day, Reinsch cabled that the ultimatum had been received in Peking and was to be presented the next day. To prevent its delivery the Chinese had offered concessions accepting nearly all the revised demands, but Japan refused to reconsider the ultimatum, which materialized in the form of revised demands. While not admitted as part of the Demands, discussion of the items under group five was postponed.[114] Reinsch thought the Chinese Government would comply with the ultimatum.

While awaiting reply to the proposal for joint representations by the powers, Lansing proposed that if the governments consulted failed to agree in asking continuation of the negotiations, the United States should notify both Japan and China that it could not recognize any agreement or understanding impairing American treaty rights, the political or territorial integrity of the Republic of China, or the open door policy. This action would constitute a complete reservation of all possible rights of the United States, and it would protect China from a forced agreement. The agreement could then properly become the subject of discussion in the future when conditions were more propitious.[115]

As a result of the American appeal, Foreign Secretary Grey handed a memorandum to the Japanese Ambassador in London which expressed concern over the prospect of war between Japan and China. The memorandum stated that such action might imperil the independence of China, which was the object of the British-Japanese Alliance. Britain trusted Japan would agree with China and not close the door on negotiations without consulting London and permitting the government an opportunity to aid in a friendly settlement.[116]

Colonel House, who was then in London, talked with Grey concerning the Twenty-one Demands. The British Foreign Secretary confessed that Japan had kept them uninformed on the negotiations. Sir Edward had finally sent for the Japanese Ambassador and had a frank talk with him. The Ambassador had then informed the British "rather well" concerning the negotiations. Grey said that after getting at the bottom of the business, China seemed to be acting very stupidly. At first she accepted the conditions, save group five, then she recanted her acceptance and introduced a lot of minor objections to prolong the discussions. House commented that the feeling in London was that Japan was using the war to further her own ends while Europe could not object. Grey also expressed appreciation for Japan's desire for expansion in Manchuria, since the white world was closed to her citizens.[117] In this latter view he agreed with the State Department's attitude.

On May 8, 1915, China submitted to Japan's ultimatum on the Twenty-one Demands. Between May 3 and 7 daily conferences had been held by the Chinese leaders with President Yuan on the subject of the anticipated action of the Japanese. At a diplomatic reception on May 5, Reinsch had been informed of the contemplated ultimatum. The ministers of Great Britain, France, and Russia, had taken the occasion to express to the Chinese Minister of Foreign Affairs that it would be wise for China not to attempt armed resistance to the Demands. The ultimatum had been delivered on May 7, and the violent military party had then agreed to accept the Japanese Demands. Group five was reserved as items of future discussion.[118]

After receiving the news of China's submission to Japan, Bryan wrote Wilson, "Our dispatches from there indicate that the matter is now settled, which is a great relief at such a time as this." There was no expression of regret as to the acceptance of the Demands by China. Wilson, in returning papers concerned with the affair, replied, "This needs no comment now, since the whole suspicious business has lost for the time being its critical character." The President thought Sir Edward had acted well in making his representations to Japan for a peaceful solution.[119]

Two days later, Wilson suggested that in view of the world situation, it would be wise to file the *caveat* as Lansing proposed, withholding recognition of any agreement between China and Japan affecting American rights. He affirmed: "It would not do to leave any of our rights indefinite or to seem to acquiesce in any part of the Japanese plan which violates the solemn understandings of the nations with regard to China. Such a statement might favourably affect the Japanese official mind with regard to the wisdom of postponing the discussion of Group V for a very long time indeed."[120]

The American disclaimer went forth to the two Oriental powers on May 11, 1915, three days after the Chinese had agreed to the Japanese terms. It followed the line advocated by Lansing in much the same language, stating that the United States could not "recognize any agreement or understanding which has been entered into or which may be entered into between the governments of Japan and China, impairing the treaty rights of the United States and its citizens in China, the political or territorial integrity of the Republic of China, or the international policy relative to China commonly known as the open door policy."[121] The reservation was to serve as a precedent for the later Stimson policy of nonrecognition of Japan's conquest in Manchuria.

The treaties arising from the Twenty-one Demands were exchanged between China and Japan on May 25, 1915. A wave of anti-Japanese boycotts spread over China, despite a Presidential telegram to the provinces forbidding such retaliatory action.[122]

The Japanese took advantage of their opportunities under the treaties so rapidly that Reinsch feared they would soon become the sole influence in China. The problem now was would the United States give enough backing to the other interested powers to preserve international rights and Chinese sovereignty until the end of the war?[123] Wilson told Bryan to have a talk with the Japanese Ambassador and to let him know exactly where the United States stood on any change in the political suzerainty of China.[124]

Throughout the Twenty-one Demands, Wilson was active in guarding traditional American policy which also, under the open door, seemed to protect the treaty rights of the Western powers then engaged in the war. He was a prudent friend of China, desiring to maintain her territorial and political independence by diplomatic means. The President respected the Japanese need for expansion but he thought she went too far in her demands. He, however, approved the Bryan note which agreed that the United States should not insist on the treaty rights in South Manchuria, East Mongolia, or Shantung—and these were regions of considerable American interest. He also permitted recognition of Japan's "special interests" in these regions. Once the negotiations were concluded, the President had approved the caveat reserving full American rights in China. He waited the end of the war for their fuller discussion.

Since the diplomacy had to be carried on without the strong support of the European powers engaged in the war, and in face of American lack of force, and her unwillingness to commit such force as she did have for her objectives in the O-rient, it was singularly successful in preventing an open war and in helping to achieve the cancellation of group five. What Lansing had said in 1914, however, continued true as far as the United States was concerned, ". . . it would be quixotic in the extreme to allow the question of China's territorial integrity to entangle the United States in international difficulties."[125]

CHAPTER FIVE

Minor Conflicts of
Japanese-American Relations

WHO IS THERE THAT CAN TAKE THE TURBID WATER, AND BY
STILLNESS MAKE IT GRADUALLY CLEAR?

—Lao-Tzu

Japanese-American relations were complicated by a diversity
of national interests, and punctuated by periodic crises such as
the California lands question of 1913 and the Twenty-one Demands two years later. But these were only major episodes in a
story of increasingly bad relations encouraged seemingly by every
point of contact.

Even in 1913, before the outbreak of the war in Europe, the
Japanese shipment of arms to General Victoriano Huerta in
Mexico had increased tensions between the two countries.[1]
United States policy sought a stable solution of the problem in
the revolution-torn country south of the Rio Grande, and the
State Department protested the Japanese shipments as aiding
the turmoil. Foreign Minister Nobuaki Makino replied that the
arms contracts had been made in open competition and he did
not feel "he had the power to forbid delivery, but he was using
pressure and he hoped to prevail [against the shipments]." At
the same time, the United States expressed regret that Japanese
naval officers accepted entertainment by the Mexican revolutionary government.[2] The shipment of arms continued; and, as late
as February, 1917, according to British Ambassador Cecil Spring-
Rice, his Japanese colleague in Washington, Aimaro Sato, ad-

131

mitted that the activities of his countrymen in Mexico embarrassed the home government. The arms supplied Mexico, Sato claimed, were so outmoded that they could not be sold to the Russians who bought the major portion of Japanese military production. Spring-Rice cautioned the Japanese that Britain desired to be kept abreast of its ally's relations with America.[3]

John Lind, the President's special representative in Mexico, had found the British not so concerned about Tokyo's relations with Washington in 1914 and had accused her minister, Lionel Carden, of using the American fear of Japan for Britain's own purposes.[4] During the war, German agents in the United States did not overlook opportunities to emphasize the Japanese threat to America, and the Zimmerman note served to confirm American suspicion of Germany in this effort.

Various elements within Mexico made use of the American suspicion of Japan to seek favor with Washington. In February, 1915, with the Twenty-one Demands thrown into the maelstrom of diplomacy between the two Pacific powers, G. C. Carruthers, a special agent in Mexico, reported to Secretary Bryan that General Pancho Villa had been approached by a Japanese naval commander, who confided that for the past three years Japan had been prepared for war with the United States. The Commander desired to know Villa's position in event of a Pacific war. The General, according to his own testimony, had declared that in any conflict between Japan and the United States, Mexico would make her resources available to her northern neighbor.[5] Thus buffeted between British, German, and factional self-interest, the relations of the United States and Japan in Mexico served to provide but another sphere of suspicion.

Eight thousand miles away across the Pacific, the Philippine Islands supplied a second area for American-Japanese tension. Japan had reluctantly welcomed the United States into the islands in 1898. She did so realizing that American occupation was no grave danger, since militarily the United States could not hold the Philippines.[6] Theodore Roosevelt had feared Japanese ambitions in the islands. The Taft-Katsura understanding had grown out of this fear and permitted Japan her own way in Korea in exchange for assurances to respect America's position in the Philippines. Nevertheless, the Japanese press from time to time cried out against America standing astride Japan's expansion to the south.

Throughout 1913-1916 agitation of the Philippine bill in Congress, Japan was used as the *bete noire* of the Pacific by some members of both houses. To them the Philippines were either the key to American defenses in the Pacific to be held at all cost or released at once as a preventive of certain war. Some shared Bryan's admiration for the Japanese and were prone to think the resources of the islands could best be developed by these frugal, hard-working, oriental people. Suspicion of Japanese policy in the Pacific became more and more obvious in the Wilson administration as time passed. The presentation of the Twenty-One Demands of January, 1915 marks a turning point in any understanding American attitude toward Japan. By 1917 the administration was openly resentful, and in 1918 it was at work to oppose Japan as a rival, especially in China.[7] This growing suspicion for Japanese motives is reflected in an increased American distrust for her activities in the Philippines.

Professor Ford's supplementary report to Wilson on the islands, submitted on January 17, 1914, pointed to the strategic weakness of the Philippines, stating: "It is a common belief throughout the East that sooner or later, the Philippines will belong to Japan. The Filipino leaders—and indeed the mass of people as well—are aware of the danger and would like to prepare for it." Ford recommended military training on the Swiss model and in the schools for the security of the islands,[8] but the Wilson administration took no such defensive measures. The military expenses of the islands were often agitated in Congress as a reason for granting independence, but the whole matter was stubbornly contested.[9]

With the American ultimatum to Mexico in late April of 1914 and the resultant Vera Cruz incident wherein American lives were lost, Governor General Harrison of the Philippines reported "that the Japanese residents of the islands were rather active and greatly interested when the first news of hostilities with Mexico came to us. . . ."[10] No overt acts occurred, however, and although native animosity utilized anti-Japanese stories,

Japanese population in the islands continued to increase without encountering serious difficulties. After the outbreak of the World War, due to the profits to be had in the growing of hemp, a colony of some 10,000 settled in Davao, Mindanao, to develop plantations there.[11]

As the preamble of the Jones bill, promising eventual independence to the Philippines, came up for Congressional consideration in the autumn of 1914, Wilfred T. Denison, the Secretary of Interior in the Philippine Commission, informed the War Department that while Japan might not fight for the possession of the islands, it was foolish to imagine that she would permit the Philippines to remain free and independent. He cited Japanese ousting of the Germans from Tsingtau and absorption of the "trifling and relatively valueless islands of the Pacific" as indicating their expansionist tendencies. American withdrawal from the islands would serve as the best means for "removing precisely the causes which are most likely to make friction." According to the army and navy men whom Denison had consulted, the islands were "a point of strategic weakness which we should have to abandon at the outbreak of any hostilities." Retention of the islands as a base for American enterprise in the Orient at the risk of a possible war with Japan he felt was indefensible, especially so if it were based on generosity to the Philippine people.[12]

The military and naval authorities had long been urging adequate facilities and strength for the protection of American interests in the East Asian theatre. Soon after the fall of Tsingtau and the taking of the German islands by Japan, the General Board demanded a navy second to none in order to protect the Panama Canal and American national policy in the Orient. One of its members, Rear Admiral Charles E. Vreeland, informed the Naval Affairs Committee of the House of Representatives that Japan could take the Philippines, and that strategy must be planned to counter an attack made without warning.[13] This testimony gained such notoriety that Wilson felt it necessary to assure Japan that American intentions in the Pacific were not aggressive, as the Admiral's words seemed to indicate.[14]

The defenselessness of the islands was aired not only on the floors of Congress and in private reports but also in the popular press. The *Illustrated Buffalo Express* contended that "When Japan begins its war with the United States, some persons declare, the Philippines will fall at the crack of the first gun."[15] Hudson Maxim, in his plea for stronger American defenses, argued that the Japanese were a far-seeing and patient people. "They know how to wait, but know also when to strike, and how to strike with the force of a Jovian thunderbolt."[16] Contending that Japan could land a quarter of a million men on the Pacific Coast faster than the United States could get thirty thousand regulars there to receive the enemy,[17] Maxim urged America to awaken to her military weakness. The popular Homer Lea's *Valor of Ignorance* predicted as early as 1909: "This Republic and Japan are approaching, careless on the one hand and predetermined on the other, that point of contact which is war."[17] Even James F. Abbott, who taught in the Japanese naval academy and who professed he did not think a war likely, confessed: "If we were all wrong in smiling away the predictions of the European debacle, are we all right in disregarding those of a coming American-Japanese conflict?"[18] On such miscellaneous evidence was American fear of a Japanese threat in the Pacific encouraged.

In answer to these fears, Dr. Toyikichi Iyenaga, a former Japanese minister, in a New York symposium on "How We Can Keep Peace With Japan," declared that his country "would not take the Philippines as a gift, unless the United States accompanied the gift with $1,000,000,000. . . ." He explained that although no bar to Japanese immigration existed in the Philippines, there had been no mass immigration there because the tropical islands were unsuitable for colonization by his countrymen.[19] This was also the contention of Judge Charles B. Elliot of Minneapolis, a former member of the Philippine Commission; but although Japan did not want the island, the Judge thought, "the islands might fall on Japan."[20]

The editor of the *Kobe Yushin Nippo* asked Manuel Quezon, then Philippine Resident Commissioner, for comment on Filipino fears of Japan in relation to the independence of the islands should it be granted. Although privately confessing his fear to the American authorities, Quezon found it expedient to reply that "the people of the Philippine Islands do not share the view that Japan intends to seize the Philippines either now or after they shall have been granted independence by the United States."[21]

The suggestion of Mississippi Senator John Sharp Williams that the United States sell the islands to Japan was branded by the *Consalidacion' Nacional* in Manila as "infamous." The paper declared, "Japan might annihilate us, but never impose her sovereignty upon us."[22] The same paper saw the position of the Phillippines as analogous to that of Belgium or Tsingtau in case of an American-Japanese war. Only in independence, so that they might "go along unnoticed among the strong nations," was security possible.[23] Of course the war menace was twisted to argue for the early independence of the islands. To one seeking reasons for announced desires, reasons are usually under every headline.

After the Clarke Amendment, granting independence within four years, passed the Senate in February of 1916, *La Democracia* remarked: "It was even said that the behavior of certain members of the Upper House in the United States was the result of fear [of Japan], just as if there was something in the world calculated to alter the serenity of these almighty gentlemen." The paper declared the Philippines were being sacrificed to settle the Japanese land problem in California and to rid America of the military liability imposed by the islands. The arrival of a Japanese Mission in Manila caused the press to warn: that Japan's "need for expansion is a fact. This is pursuant to inflexible economic reasons, just as our future and the independence of our country are essentially economic problems demanding the study and attention of our best men."[24]

The Japanese official announcement to occupy the North Pacific islands for the duration of the war seemed to cause no concern among the American public.[25] The Navy, however, viewed the Japanese encroachment on the Caroline-Marshall group as making the American Pacific position untenable in case of future trouble. It sent fuel and ammunition to its bases in Hawaii and the Philippines, which seemed to indicate that the fleet might be dispatched to keep Japan in check. Both the Army and Navy at this time were of the opinion that enough territory should be seized in the Far East as was needed for the maintenance of American interests there.[26]

British Ambassador Spring-Rice advised Lansing in 1916 that Japan would retain possession of the German islands north of the equator at the end of the war. Later, Viscount Ishii gave Lansing similar information.[27] This knowledge was not passed on to Breckenridge Long, who in January, 1917 became the Third Assistant Secretary in charge of Far Eastern Affairs, and there is no evidence that Wilson knew of the arrangement. In an interview, years later, Long stated that the Far Eastern Division believed Japan to be in the war for purposes of territorial expansion and considered the Pacific islands arrangement from a viewpoint of a possible war with Japan. Not until the Bolshevik documents were published in December of 1917 did the State Department personnel, aside from Lansing, learn of the islands arrangement; and, according to Long, they were stunned.[28] The islands were to emerge again as a complication at the Versailles Conference in 1919.

Another source of distrust in American-Japanese relations arose out of the suspicion that Japan was not to be trusted as an ally. It was known that she had modeled her constitutional empire after that of Germany.[29] Her military were largely German-trained and many were of German sympathy. As early as April 26, 1915, Bryan reported to Wilson a confidential communication made a few days previously by the Japanese Ambassador. "It was to the effect that the Japanese Minister in Stockholm was approached by the Austrian representative on the subject of Japan entering into a treaty of peace with Germany." The Japanese reportedly replied that they could not consider the matter independently of their allies. After making this report to Bryan, Ambassador Chinda asked if the Allies had indicated any desire for a cessation of hostilities, to which Bryan could answer only in the negative.[30] Wilson thought the Chinda report "significant," and expressed himself generally on the expectation of peace, declaring: "Reasonableness has not yet been burned into them [the warring powers] and what they are thinking of is, not the peace and prosperity of Europe, but their own aggrandizement, an impossible modern basis (it might be well for Japan to reflect) for peace."[31] No suspicion had to be expressed that Japan might be using the Austrian proposal as a means to encourage the United States to view her Twenty-one Demands, then in negotiation, with more tolerance.

In December of 1915, Counselor Polk saw fit to inquire of the British Ambassador if it were true that many German cables were going through Japan. The Ambassador confessed to British knowledge of the strong pro-German sentiment in Japan, even Chinda acknowledged this, but Britain thought the present Tokyo government would continue to honor the Anglo-Japanese Alliance.[32] When Colonel House went abroad in January of 1916, in an attempt to feel out a basis for peace, he suggested to David Lloyd George, the British Prime Minister, that Germany might be given a free hand in Asia while Britain looked to Africa as her proper sphere at the end of the war.[33] Apparently, the Colonel felt that the world could be so easily arranged, despite the inroads Japan had already made on Occidental control of Asia.

At the same time, Ambassador George T. Marye reported from Petrograd that the Russian papers were carrying a translation from the Japanese sources of a proposed Russo-Japanese Alliance.[34] Wilson sent the information on to Secretary of State Lansing with the terse comment: "Here is an unexpectedly interesting and important letter from Petrograd, which I wish you would read. It gives us something more to think about, for fear our minds should be unoccupied."[35]

The treaty as actually concluded, July 3, 1916, contained a positive pledge to prevent a third power from acquiring political influence in China that would be hostile to Russia or Japan. The two powers were to mutually aid each other. Japan, however, would not be asked to assist in any war against her British ally.[36] It was, without directly stating so, directed at the United States. Sazonov said the treaty would prevent Germany from competing with America, England and France for Chinese trade, and it was not injurious to American rights or interests. In

Japan, Prime Minister Okuma defended it as an expansion of the Anglo-Japanese Alliance.[37]

Four days after its conclusion, the treaty was made known to President Wilson by the new American Ambassador in Petrograd, David R. Francis.[38] There was some fear in the United States of secret articles in the treaty; and William Phillips, in formal charge of Far Eastern affairs at this time, asked Polk to consult with the Japanese Chargé and express the hope that the interests of the United States were not affected.[39] Guthrie cabled that he found no evidence of secret clauses. Both Japan and Russia, after State Department inquiry, assured the United States that in no way was the territorial integrity or independence of China or the open door policy involved.[40] The facts contradicted this assertion however, for the treaty attempted to exclude the United States from the North China spheres of Japan and Russia.

By the news reports reaching him from the States concerning the Russo-Japanese convention, allegations of Japanese designs on Mexico and in China, Ambassador Guthrie judged that suspicions of Japanese motives in America were rife and equalled those entertained by Japan of American motives in East Asia. In his prophetic opinion "the danger, or possibility, of war between Japan and America lies in China," therefore, he believed the two powers must come to an agreement on the issues there.[41] This suspicion of Japan was further amplified in Colonel House's letter to Wilson informing him that Ambassador Jules Jusserand of France had reported in June, 1916, a month before the Russo-Japanese Treaty was negotiated, that such an "alliance" had been signed by the two nations in Washington. Jusserand "seemed to think that Germany might later drift into that alliance and if so, the balance of us would have a strong combination to reckon with." The United States in particular, he thought, should be concerned, for Germany and Japan had "an unforgivable grievance against us. He hinted we would have no sympathizers in our troubles unless we more actively took the part of the Allies."[42] Jusserand's purposes were certainly obvious. The Russo-Japanese treaty was thus an additional note in the cultivation of the distrust growing between the

United States and Japan. In the complexity of rumored and realized treaties, getting at the factual was difficult. The secret treaties which were to be of such concern to the United States, arranged in the winter and early spring of 1917 among the Allies, were at the time unknown to Washington. In January, negotiations were opened by Japan with Russia and Great Britain for an agreement whereby these powers would give assurances of support to Japan's position in Shantung and her retention of the German islands north of the equator. In return, the British empire was to acquire those islands south of the equator.[43] On February 16, Britain agreed to the terms. Four days later Russia accepted. Later Italy and France acquiesced. Japan promised Britain assistance in the form of naval-convoys for the Mediterranean waters; to Russia and France she engaged her influence in bringing China into the war.

The Bolsheviks published the documents concerning the secret Japanese treaties on December 14, 1917. This publication in reference to assurances on the islands and Shantung consisted only of the Russian Ambassador's telegrams to his government containing the clause of such a proposed treaty, and it was not certain anything had been agreed between Russia and Japan. When the documents were discussed in the State Department, in February, 1918, the Far Eastern Division pointed out that there was no evidence of Russian assent to the terms.[44] As has been indicated, Lansing alone knew of the treaties, but he saw fit to inform no one in the Department. These treaties were to again arise at Paris during the peace conference.

A continuing source of conflict between the United States and Japan was the problem of state legislation over oriental immigration and land ownership. Wilson was on record against Asiatic immigration.[45] In the California case of 1913, he made no objection on principle to racial discrimination, but he sought to be clear of any accusation that the United States had transgressed her treaty guarantees to Japan. When Japan appealed for a treaty that would assure her subjects equal rights to those of other aliens, the President did not see how the United States could deny her such an understanding.[46] But nothing came of such a treaty; in fact, with the national temper opposing Japan, it is certain that there would have been difficulty obtaining Senate approval for such an arrangement.

California labor leaders continued to agitate for additional land restrictions after the outbreak of war. This time they sought an amendment to eliminate the right of aliens ineligible to citizenship to lease land, permissible under existing law for a three year period. This was to be but the beginning of an effort to bar orientals from the United States. Charles K. McIntosh of the City Bank of San Francisco suggested that Wilson speak a word to Samuel Gompers, President of the American Federation of Labor, about preventing the legislation.[47] Tumulty, Wilson's White House Secretary, explained to the labor leader how the legislation might embitter relations with Japan, and Gompers got in touch with union chiefs on the Coast. No bill was passed, and Wilson expressed appreciation for Gomper's activity on behalf of the administration's policy.[48] Meanwhile, Ambassador Guthrie reported popular feeling in Japan so intense concerning the California legislation that its passage would probably cause the downfall of the Okuma ministry.[49] The Episcopal missionaries there protested the proposed legislation as creative of discord and suspicion in American-Japanese relations.[50]

James D. Phelan, candidate for the Senate from California, found Wilson's popularity very high during the 1914 elections despite the administration's stand on the anti-Japanese legislation. Phelan, campaigning on the slogan "With Wilson for California," received a 30,000 plurality which so he wrote the President, "was meant by the people as an endorsement of your administration."[51]

During the war, the issue of Japanese immigration lay dormant, but it was always a potential source of trouble. Under date of January 23, 1915, Bryan wrote Wilson that he had had several talks with Ambassador Chinda, who was anxious to end the Japanese immigration and land problems in the United States. The Secretary recalled that the United States had promised to secure a treaty guaranteeing equality of treatment for the Japanese so as to prevent any state difficulties. Simultaneously, Chinda suggested that Japan and the United States sign a conciliation treaty such as Bryan had negotiated with other countries. The Secretary advised Wilson that "such a treaty would go a long way toward answering the 'jingoes' who are always insisting upon our getting into war with Japan."[52]

Negotiations for a treaty settlement of Japanese land rights continued; and in March, 1915, while the Twenty-one Demands engaged American attention, Bryan brought the matter once again before the President. This time the fertile-minded Secretary estimated that the question of Japanese immigration was economic rather than racial, since trouble occurred only when they settled in large numbers in a community. As a solution he suggested that the United States undertake scattering the Japanese throughout the union, thus reducing their numbers in California by one-half. There should be no more than one thousand Japanese to a state, one hundred to a county, and no more than five per cent of the population in any city or voting precinct. Bryan said that he had talked of the matter with Chinda and thought it was a way of securing repeal of the anti-Japanese laws in California.[53] Wilson quietly took the suggestions into "consideration" and diplomatically mentioned that there might be danger of producing alarm in the states to which the Japanese were induced to emigrate, which might lead to popular clamor and widespread legislation on the matter — the very thing the government was attempting to avoid.[54] This was a familiar method used by the President in soothing the enthusiasms of his Secretary of State.

The whole matter arose again in an unexpected manner when Tumulty received correspondence suggesting that some large landowners of Louisiana were intending to bring Japanese colonists there from California.[55] The President asked his Secretary to arrange for Walter Parker, General Manager of the Association of Commerce in New Orleans, and Senator Joseph E. Ransdell of Louisiana to see Bryan on the matter. Wilson warned "It is a matter of the greatest consequence that we should head this thing off."[56] He did not wish to repeat the perilous days of 1913 again, certainly not during a diplomatic crisis of the proportions of the Twenty-one Demands.

During February, 1917, the state legislatures in Idaho and Oregon were considering anti-Japanese legislation. Counselor Frank Polk declared the bills "entirely contrary to the spirit of the administration. . . ." He saw the Japanese Ambassador and then went to the Capitol to see Senators George E. Chamberlain, and William E. Borah and Secretary of Interior Franklin K. Lane to get them to intercede in the states concerned to prevent embarrassment to the administration.[57] Of the pending measures Wilson wrote, "It would be not only a great, but perhaps a tragical, mistake to pass such legislation at this time. . . ."[58] Clifton N. McArthur, Congressman from the Third Oregon District, telegraphed his State Senate of Washington's concern over the proposed bills and urged, "While there may be need for legislation of this kind it is not so imperative that it cannot be postponed until [the] present grave crisis is passed."[59] The same day Oregon dropped its proposed legislation. Idaho also thought better of her proposals, and administration interposition thus succeeded in 1917 where it had failed four years earlier.

Not only in preventing state discriminatory legislation but in small matters of cultural provocation of Japan, President Wilson sought to prevent irritation. In June of 1917, busy at the organization of the war, he nevertheless wrote J. A. Berst of Pathe Productions that while attending Keiths' Theatre in Washington he had seen portions of a film entitled "Patria," which depicted a Japanese invasion of the United States. The President said he found the story "extremely unfair to the Japanese" and feared "it is calculated to stir up a great deal of hostility which will be far from beneficial to the country, particularly in the present circumstances, be extremely hurtful." He asked for the withdrawal of the film from exhibition. Berst replied that the film had since been revised and that it was not now objectionable.[60] Not satisfied, Wilson sought the advice of the Attorney General as to the legal right of the government to interfere with the showing of the film. He found that the government could in no way prevent it.[61] A representative from the State Department and one from the Japanese Embassy reviewed the revised film and found it objectionable. Again the

President wrote Berst protesting that the invaders were depicted in Japanese uniforms and Japanese households were shown. Unless further modification were made, he would have to insist on the removal of "Patria" from circulation.[62] After many changes in the production as a result of Wilson's interference the State Department, in October, 1917, finally approved its showing.[63]

Conflict there was in the relations of the United States and Japan in Mexico, the Philippines, and over land rights in the American west, but the center of tension remained China. There can be no understanding of this period of diplomatic mistrust unless one realizes the extent to which each nation suspected the other's aims and objectives there. This rivalry was in large measure commercial and financial. With the coming of the war the advantage shifted to Japan, for war profits gave her surplus capital seeking investment throughout Asia while American investors were prone to place their surplus capital at home.

Americans had been ever reluctant to invest heavily in China. The tale of their financial adventures there was strewn with uncomplete projects. One of the earliest proposals brought to President Wilson's attention after he took office by Mabel T. Boardman of the National Board of the American Red Cross was the Huai River project. In many respects it is representative of the higher purpose and failure of fulfilment which characterized American aid in China throughout the Wilson years.

In the provinces of Anhui and Kiangsu, the Huai River runs midway between the greater Yellow and the Yangtze rivers. For over two thousand years flood and famine had devastated the river valley region. The disasters there had come into notice of the western nations through the influence of foreign missions; and millions of dollars, three-fourths of it from the United States, had gone into the region for relief of the victims. During the summer of 1911, the National Committee of the American Red Cross in conjunction with the Department of State sent an engineer to survey the region for possible flood control action. The survey, submitted in April, 1913, recommended an undertaking costing 3,000,000 Mexican dollars and requiring six years for completion. In addition to flood relief, the project was to reclaim 6,000,000 Chinese mau of land, and dredge the Grand Canal for the improvement of transportation.[64] The latter was a most important phase of the project, since transport in the area was largely by water and the canals had silted and deteriorated over the past decade of China's troubled history.

Miss Boardman described the project to President Wilson early in July. She suggested that the American Chargé, E. T. Williams, be granted authority to proceed with the matter of making arrangements, since the Red Cross was ready to send its engineer.[65] Wilson received the letters just as news of the July revolt in China came to his notice. He replied that he "should like to take a hand in the matter in some proper way, but my judgment is that the present is not the favorable time."[66] Miss Boardman, who was considerably informed on China, explained that the fighting would touch only a few thousand of China's countless millions, and she insisted that Chargé Williams, who had been twenty years there, should be trusted to judge the internal situation and present the President's approval of the work to the Chinese at the propitious moment.[67]

The next day, when the State Department notified Miss Boardman that the work had been placed in the hands of a Chinese, Chang Chuen by name, she wrote Wilson that she feared any Chinese control of funds because of the graft it would occasion, especially if they obtained unregulated financial assistance from Belgium. The undertaking would result only in debt, and no useful work for the Chinese people would be accomplished. Wilson consulted with Tumulty about this tangle of Chinese complications.[68] The negotiations accomplished little until January, 1914, when, with the revolt put down, Yuan Shih k'ai offered to give the American Red Cross exclusive right to undertake the project. John Bassett Moore then Counselor of the State Department and Chairman of the International Relief Board of the Red Cross, drew Wilson's attention to the proposal and informed him that the engineering company and bankers "who would take the bonds which they would receive in payment for their work require the assurance by this Government that they [it?] will lend its good offices and diplomatic support to them."[69]

Asking for such assurances after its denial to the Consortium bankers on March 18, 1913, appeared as seeking a reversal of the administration's policy; but Wilson asured Moore: ". . . I hasten to write not only to express my gratification [of China entrusting the project to the Red Cross] but to say that, with the concurrence of the Secretary of State, I shall be glad indeed to have it understood that the Government of the United States will give assurance of good offices and diplomatic support in behalf of the American contractors should he [Moore] be able to agree with the Chinese Government on fair and equitable terms."[70] However, he explained these good offices would not go to the extent which some governments had gone to enforce the rights of their nationals in the matter of contracts. Wilson, as always, was willing to serve American enterprise abroad so long as the objectives were good and the means did not violate native sovereignty nor work harm upon the people involved. He had withdrawn support from the Consortium, because he thought it did not serve the Chinese people but transgressed upon the sovereignty of China and placed the United States under guarantees which obligated it to intervene in Chinese internal affairs to protect Consortium interests.

After receiving Wilson's assurances, Miss Boardman reported that the new Chinese Minister was to proceed to Washington for purposes of negotiating the final agreement.[71] At her suggestion, Wilson had Congress release an officer from the army engineers to assist the Red Cross, "a disinterested body in serving a great nation just awakening. . . ."[72] He wished to aid in every way "the admirable work the Red Cross is doing for conservation in China." As a result, an American party set forth to examine the Huai River region.[73]

All went well with the project. Then interposed the great cataclysm of August, 1914, the First World War. On the last of October, the Red Cross informed the Chinese Minister that it was now impossible to float the necessary loan on the American market.[74] Although the society sought aid of the Rockefeller Foundation and similar organizations, it found no benefactors.[75] However, it was willing to continue partial support of the necessary preliminary engineering studies of the job.[76] President Yuan by rescript extended for another year the Red Cross option on the project.[77] Another extension of four months was arranged by Reinsch, the American Minister, during January, 1916.

Meantime, the American International Corporation studied methods of improving the Grand Canal in Kiangsu and Shantung provinces, and then turned the project over to its subsidiary the Siems-Carey Company.[78] The provincial authorities of Shantung signed agreements with the corporation in April authorizing issue of a loan for $1,300,000 to be used in improving the canal and reclaiming the land areas in Shantung. A similar agreement was signed with the Peking government for improvement of the Kiangsu section of the canal.[79] Details of the loan, however, continued in negotiation through the Autumn of 1916.

The Japanese government, claiming the German privileges in Shantung and Chinese recognition of the rights under the agreements growing out of the Twenty-one Demands, took the position that it should have priority on the loans.[80] The American International Corporation agreed to accept Japanese cooperation in the loan, subject to the approval of the Chinese government.[81] China, seeking restoration of the canal, finally consented to Japan taking $2,500,000 of the total $6,000,000 loan.[82] Straight explained the agreement was absolutely necessary in the light of American inability to float the loan as long as there was Japanese opposition to the project.[83] Delay now followed delay until America entered the war, and the project was sacrificed. The agreement with the Japanese was reached without the consent or aid of the State Department and was bitterly resented in Washington.

The Siems-Carey Company, meanwhile, had concluded an agreement on May 17, 1916 with China granting the right to build 1,500 miles of railway. Five lines were proposed, but should any line meet with obstacles in its construction, an equal mileage elsewhere was to be granted.[84] The Entente powers objected to the proposed lines on the grounds of conflicting prior commitments to their nationals[85] and the American International Corporation, as a partner of Siems-Carey, refused to undertake the financing so long as a dispute over claims existed.

Throughout the canal and railway negotiations of the Siems-Carey Company, Wilson and his administration supported the efforts of the American concern. Although the company surveyed a number of possible routes, no construction was undertaken. It was the general fate of American industrial development in China throughout the period.

Upon his withdrawal of official backing to the First Consortium in 1913, Wilson had made it clear that he would support legitimate means for aiding American investment in foreign countries. He had practiced this policy in assurances to the interested contractors in the Huai River loan. Under the new Glass Banking Act provision was made for the establishment of American branch banks abroad. In September, 1913, Bryan had reassured the American Chargé of Washington's interest in maintaining equal investment opportunities for its citizens in China with the limitation that "This Government is not the endorser of the American competitor, and is not an accountable party to the undertaking."[86] In other words, the United States would not serve as a collecting agent or use force to collect bad debts. The President's attitude was well known and played no small part in discouraging American investment in China, but given the circumstances of unstable political conditions there, Japanese opposition, Consortium claims, and the welter of difficulties to be overcome in every venture, there seems little reason to think the story of American development of China would have been much changed had the President's attitude been different.

China's finances meanwhile went from bad to worse, and despite the Consortium loan, the war precipitated a crisis forcing the government to declare a moratorium on certain of its debts. The United States arranged to return the unused funds of the China Boxer Indemnity payments to help the internal financial situation of President Yuan's government.[87] China's ability to borrow was handicapped by the Consortium terms of 1912 which for five years limited her seeking administrative loans from any but Consortium sources. With the United States withdrawn, and the European states at war, Japan alone was left as a source of funds. But in 1914 Japan staggered under a national debt, and her trade was dislocated by the war. Official Washington was cognizant of the situation. The State Department now forsook its policy discouraging all but industrial loans and sought to have American bankers individually make direct loans to the Chinese Government. Reinsch argued against the apprehension of the American bankers that the internal political conditions interfered with foreign investments. He represented China as presenting "all the elements favorable to a sound establishment of American business interests" there.[88]

Wilson, personally in particular instances, did what he could in encouraging American banking interests to participate in Chinese investments, although it appears doubtful if he quite realized the extent to which the government would have to intervene in order to make such investments attractive. In the spring of 1915, President Goodnow of Johns Hopkins, who had been constitutional adviser to the Peking government, received a letter from Westel W. Willoughby who succeeded him in China. Willoughby inquired as to the possibility of China loosing her severe financial straits by placing a loan of one to two hundred million dollars in the United States. The purpose of the loan was to reform the banking and currency system and offered the income from the land tax as security. Goodnow turned to B. Howell Griswold, a graduate of Hopkins and the head of Alexander Brown and Sons, bankers of Baltimore. Griswold, repeating Willoughby's admonition for discretion concerning the proposal, wrote of the plan directly to President Wilson. The banker confessed: "My interest in the matter, however, as a banker, is secondary to my desire to be of service to the Government." He stated that where the Consortium loan of 1913 required the government to become a party to an agreement with foreign nations, the new proposal would not need the sanction of the American Government and would at the same time permit the bankers to reform China's land tax. However, Griswold did not wish to undertake any negotiation that might embarrass the State Department. Wilson made an appointment to see both Goodnow and Griswold the following week.[89]

During their interview, Wilson agreed that Griswold should draw up a private letter for his approval and signature recommending participation in the loan to as large a number of banking houses as possible. The banker saw Bryan on May 3 and asked to have the decision as to when and where the loan should be announced so as to test out the Japanese attitude.[90] A month later, the Baltimore banker again broached the matter of the loan to Bryan and urged action. Griswold appreciated the diplomatic problem of floating a loan to China while the Twenty-one Demands were being pressed by Japan, but he felt the loan was of great consequence to American as well as Chinese interests, and he pressed for action in the matter.[91] The bankers had drafted for the President what they considered a suitable letter for his approval of the loan and left it with Bryan on May 3. When Bryan wrote Wilson of the urgency for action, Wilson replied that he had just found the letter and would "try to revise it at once for use."[92]

The Wilson revision of the letter cut out all reference to the former Consortium loan; otherwise the changes were in form only.[93] As sent to Griswold over the President's signature, the communication stated the loan was not objectionable. The administration "will always seek to support citizens of the United States in all legitimate enterprises abroad; and it would welcome action by American bankers which would be of benefit to the Chinese people and tend to increase the friendly relations with the two peoples." The suggestion was made: "If the loan is agreed upon, the offering should be so arranged that an opportunity to participate in the underwriting will be given, as far as practical, to American bankers of credit and standing generally, and the loan made in effect a popular one." The offering on a wide basis of participation presented difficulties, "but it may be explained to bankers that the offer has been made in this way at the request of the Government." It was contrary to administration policy to make the government a collector of debts, "and we must not be understood as committing the government to the use of physical force for this purpose; but legitimate assistance will be rendered." The letter was personal and confidential, but the President stated he had no objections to Griswold mentioning it in his negotiations with other bankers.[94] The attitude expressed in the letter, while drafted by the bankers and approved by the President, in reality represented the latter's attitude throughout his administration when dealing with Chinese finances.

But the Griswold negotiations were all for naught, and the year 1916 saw intensification of the Chinese need for funds due to inflation caused by the profitable heavy export of silver from the country. The condition became a permanent condition of the economy throughout the war and the immediate post-war periods, but by 1919 silver values declined and trade improved. During these years, 1916 to 1920, the silver exchange was China's outstanding financial problem.[95] The disorganization of the Chinese government, corruption, foreign intrigue, and unwise official borrowing beggared the government. Individual Chinese refused to invest in government bonds, and the inefficient tax system yielded inadequate revenues.

In the early spring of 1916, Chinese government finances were further imperiled when the Japanese withheld payment of the gabelle tax collections pledged to them under the involved loans. European and American banking firms came to the assistance of the native bankers during the crisis.[96] Wilson was gravely disturbed at this manifestation of the hegemony of Japan over the internal affairs of China, but he confessed "I do not see what is to be done."[97] Peking without avail appealed directly to the State Department for financial aid. Reinsch supported the appeal for an American loan thinking it necessary as a means to protect the independence of China against Japan. The State Department relayed the appeal to Straight of the Morgan firm and to Lee, Higginson and Company of Boston,[98] the latter being the fiscal agent for China in the United States.

Lee, Higginson meanwhile had completed arrangements for a $5,000,000 loan to China.[99] Of this sum only $1,000,000 was actually transferred for when Yuan Shih k'ai's monarchial ambitions raised the banner of revolt Reinsch opposed further advances.[100] Once Yuan renounced his imperial ambitions, Reinsch again supported the loan, but the Boston firm found it impossible to complete it without aid from the New York bankers.[101]

Lansing reported to Wilson that the American group in cooperation with their Entente colleagues favored America's reentry into the Consortium as a means of floating a loan to prevent Japanese monopoly of Chinese finances. The American bankers would carry their European colleagues and join the Japanese in the loan. The Secretary felt that such an arrangement would have the advantage of giving "Japan participation but keep her controlled by her European associates and in this way probably check her encroachment in China." Lee, Higginson, however, was desirous of joining the American group, and Lansing felt that while it was desirable, it might delay the loan and result in Japan securing the prize.[102]

Attempts to revive American participation in the Consortium failed, however, and the State Department then again attempted to secure the independent cooperation of the bankers in an American loan without consultation of the other banking powers in the international group. Morgan, however, felt bound to the terms of the agreement of 1912 which denied any but Consortium administrative loans to China. If the loan was to be other than administrative, the bankers desired to know the security of the loan and to what extent the government would guarantee its collection.[103] The Wilson administration was unwilling to give guarantees encouraging any particular enterprise, and the independent loan attempt failed.

When it became known that the attempted resurrection of the old American group had failed, F. E. Howe of the Department of Labor Immigration Office suggested that the United States make a direct loan to China. Wilson replied: "I wish with all my heart that we could act upon the suggestion of your letter of August fifth about China. I am afraid that in the present need for money and piling on of new taxes the Congress would back off from the thing, but I am going to discuss it at least with some of the men on the Hill to see if it is by any chance feasible."[104]   Again nothing came of the matter.

On November 16, 1916, the Continental and Commercial Trust and Savings Bank of Chicago made an independent loan of $5,000,000 to China for purposes of industrial and internal development, including bank stabilization. As a result, it was given first option on a contemplated further loan of $25,000,000 to be sought in America. French and British bankers objected to the loan as a violation of their rights under the Consortium. At the same time, the Japanese inferred that the Chicago bank had a strong German bias which accounted for the loan.[105] Upon being informed of the objections being raised, Wilson dropped Lansing a note, saying: "This interference on the part of the Entente bankers annoys me intensely, and I think we ought to put our protest into pretty plain terms."[106] Lansing advised that the protest await developments, but Wilson instructed that Reinsch should make known to the legations "that any strained construction of existing agreements between the Chinese government and their banks would meet with very decided resistance from this government. . . ."[107] China hoped for an American loan and argued that the inability of the national banking groups to arrange for funds under the Consortium released her from previous commitments.

As a result of the two independent loans in 1916, and the increasing dominance of Japan over Chinese finances, the Entente members of the Consortium deemed it desirable to invite the return of the American group to participate. On their part, the Japanese feared competition with American banks for loan opportunities in China.[108] When the Chinese government requested the bankers for a supplementary loan of from ten to twenty million pounds in January, 1917, Japan proposed, the other groups concurring, an invitation for American participation.[109] In making this proposal Japan, of course, visualized America joining the old Consortium which Japanese bankers had come to dominate. She saw this as a means of getting around a competitive struggle for Chinese investment opportunities. Ambassador Sato called on Lansing to present the invitation. The Secretary said that the United States was not opposed to cooperative financing, but where cooperation was used "to promote political objects it tended to arouse suspicion rather than friendship." The United States could not participate because the terms of the Consortium interfered with the sovereign rights of China.[110] However, the American group manifested some interest in the proposal as an "exceptional opportunity again to promote the legitimate commercial aspiration of our country in the Far East," but if it undertook to supply the funds on an equality with Japan "there would have to be no doubt either then or at any future time of our Government's sympathetic interest in and support of the project."[111] Before negotiations had proceeded further, the United States was at war with Germany. The Japanese Ambassador inquired concerning the American plans, and Polk said that nothing had come of the attempt at reviving American group participation.[112]

In the meantime, Japanese bankers accumulating investment capital through their mounting war profits, loaned funds promiscuously to China. From 1915, the year of the Twenty-one Demands, to October of 1918, these loans totaled as much as 391,430,000 yen on reported loans only, and many investments were not reported. Japan thus gained her economic ascendency in China, due to the Allied and American failure to give China the financial assistance she needed.[113]

Wilson consistently advocated American private investment in Chinese loans and enterprises. He was willing to go to any legitimate length, short of interference in the affairs of a sovereign people, to obtain such participation. As early as 1915, he had been willing to back the Griswold group in a loan to China. He had expressed himself as friendly to the idea of a governmental loan direct to the Chinese when private bankers failed to provide the necessary funds; but despite all this activity, he lacked realization as to what extent government leadership was necessary in making these loans an actuality. In 1917 he came to see its necessity.

Not all the American suspicion of Japan was confined to the economic field however. In September of 1916 there was a flurry of excitement over news of the killing of several Japanese soldiers at Chengchiatun, while inspiring the Mongols to restore a monarchy in Mongolia and thus offset Russian hegemony there. The Japanese made demands on China that extended their privilege in Manchuria and Eastern Mongolia. As in 1915, the strictest secrecy was imposed on the negotiations.[114] The State Department had Ambassador Guthrie bring reports of the secret demands to the attention of the Japanese Foreign Office, express American concern, and ask for the facts in the case.[115]

E. T. Williams, Chief of the Division of Far Eastern Affairs, gave his opinion of Japanese activity in China at this juncture. He pointed to the promises of Japan concerning Korean independence and then noted its fate. Japan's pretenses of friendship for China he thought were a "lie." He cited the Shantung seizure of 1914, the Twenty-one Demands in which Japan "lied" to the United States as to their contents, the part of Japan in fomenting revolutions in the Southern provinces and her present aid to the Manchu loyalists in Mongolia as evidence of her insincerity. The United States, Williams said, did not desire to hinder the legitimate development of China by Japan, but cooperation between the two Asian powers was not aided by General Terauchi, the former Governor of Korea, becoming Premier in Tokyo. Williams added, "Perhaps it is well for the white race that so much antagonism exists between China and Japan. A union there with universal military service might terrify the world."[116] The report completely failed at anything constructive and demonstrated the chief reason for subsequent failure of American policy with Japan — where there is little understanding there can be no real solution.

The Japanese Minister said there was nothing conflicting with the Root-Takahira notes in the Chengchiatun demands, and he could not recognize the American right to interfere, but he was willing to discuss the matter with Guthrie informally.[117] Lansing, however, saw that the extension of police jurisdiction of Japan in Mongolia affected the *status quo* and thus gave the United States the right for consultation under the Root-Takahira Convention.[118] Negotiations continued between China and Japan until January 31, 1917, when an agreement was reached in which the most stringent provision was that ". . . Chinese soldiers and civilians in the districts where there is mixed residence [were] to accord considerate treatment to Japanese soldiers and civilians."[119]

Not only financially but also politically, in every area of contact, whether in China or elsewhere, the United States and Japan differed. The Wilson administration, conscious of its possession of the Philippines, looked upon itself as the guardian of China's territorial and political integrity and the open door policy. Although at times able only to file protests and put off decisions for the future, it ardently defended these traditional policies as imperative to American interest. Japan's initiative in seizing the opportunities to promote her own national interests created suspicions which were firmly established in the official American mind in 1915; by 1917 they mounted to an anti-Japanese point of view in evolving our East Asian policy.

CHAPTER SIX

War and Adjustment

Wilson had an "understanding heart," so British Ambassador Spring-Rice put it, for the Allied cause in Europe.[1] Much of his preaching for neutrality "in spirit and feeling" was done to keep emotions under control and the people united. He hated war as a principle, and thought America could best serve herself and the world by remaining out of the conflict.[2] With the resumption of the German submarine campaign in February, 1917 and the March revolution in Russia, the President altered his views on American participation.[3] When he went to war, he went reluctantly and with a solemn sense of the awful responsibility which America took unto herself in doing so.[4]

The opening episode in the final chain of events leading to war took place on January 31, 1917, when the German Ambassador, Count Johann von Bernstorff, delivered the German announcement renewing unrestricted submarine warfare, thus renouncing the assurances given the American government on the subject the previous May. Lansing was aware of the serious note this introduced into German-American relations. That evening he discussed the situation with Wilson and urged a break in relations.

The President, though deeply incensed at Germany's insolent notice, said that he was not yet sure what course we must pursue and must think it over; that he had been more and more impressed with the idea that "white civilization" and its domination over the world rested largely on our ability to keep this country intact, as we would have to build up the nations ravaged by war. He said as this idea had grown upon him he had come to the feeling that he was willing to go to any lengths rather than to have the nation actually involved in the conflict.[5]

The whole matter of American action on the German declaration was discussed in the Cabinet on February 2. Secretary of Agriculture Houston recorded:

As we sat down the President asked what we thought should be done. "Shall I break off diplomatic relations with Germany?" He immediately followed this question with a somewhat startling statement. He would say frankly that, if he felt that, in order to keep the white race or part of it strong to meet the yellow race — Japan for instance, in alliance with Russia, dominating China — it was wise to do nothing, he would do nothing, and would submit to anything and any imputation of weakness or cowardice. This was a novel and unexpected angle.[6]

Wilson's statement was not so startling in the light of the gradual deterioration in American-Japanese relations that had been taking place, the known Russo-Japanese Treaty aimed at the United States, and the chaotic state of affairs in China. Japan had expeditiously seized a dominant position in Asia during the preoccupation of the West with the European war. America's benevolent China policy had been shattered in conflict with the realities of Japanese imperialism there. Any involvement in the conflict would serve to increase Japan's opportunity to expand her hegemony in Asia. It was a matter which statesmanship was forced to take into account. The Cabinet decision was unanimous for breaking relations with Germany. The next day Wilson announced the break to the Congress.

On the same day that Wilson spoke to the Congress, Secretary of State Lansing sent to the American diplomatic representatives in all neutral countries notice of America's break in relations with Germany. The note stated that the President believed it would "make for the peace of the world if the other neutral powers . . . [could] find it possible to take similar action to that taken by this Government."[7] It was the President's intent to thus censure the German action by gaining additional neutral representations to Berlin.

Since 1915 China had been disposed to join the Allies, but Japan had twice opposed the step. China's leaders realized that by becoming a belligerent she would assure herself a place at the peace conference where her grievances, especially with Japan over Shantung, could be redressed. The situation in China was complicated by a diversity of views and by self-seeking to further their own interests among the various political factions.[8] When Reinsch informed the Peking authorities of the American break in relations with Germany and of Wilson's desire that the other neutral powers should associate themselves with the United States in this action, the invitation was looked upon as a renewal of China's opportunity to join the Allies.[9] Li, the Chinese President, inquired of the American Minister if the United States would support his country in undertaking the proposed step. The Premier confessed that if China were to follow the United States, she would need financial and other assistance. Unfortunately, cable communications were cut off, and Reinsch, taking the American invitation most seriously and in face of a Chinese cabinet meeting, seized the moment to suggest that "in the event of the Chinese Government associating itself with the President's suggestion, the Government of the United States should take measures to put at its disposal funds immediately required . . ., and should take steps to fund the Chinese indemnity." He, however, hedged his promise by emphasizing that such measures would have to be determined through consultation with administrative organs of the American Government and perhaps Congress itself. He confessed himself in no position to "make in behalf of my Government any definite commitments . . . [such] as China desired."[10] Despite the evasiveness of the note, the Chinese Cabinet decided that should the United States, as a result of provocation, go to war with Germany, China would at least break diplomatic relations.[11]

Lansing, although informed of Reinsch's previous action, cabled him to avoid giving any promises and assurances and take no action, that the whole matter was under consideration.[12] Wilson typed a letter to Lansing suggesting:

> I think it would be well to let Reinsch tell the Government of China how sincerely we desire to help China and that we are constantly trying to shield her against the selfishness of her neighbor. I do not want them to get the idea that we are unappreciative of their present willingness to stand with us, which is singularly generous and enlightened.[13]

Three hours after Lansing's first cable to Reinsch, he sent a second containing the gist of the President's views. Regretting the inability of the United States to give any assurances to China, the message pointed out that other important neutrals were unwilling to follow American example, and China should prudently consider this in avoiding isolated action.[14] Reinsch asked for reconsideration of this Washington policy in view of China's confidence in the aims of the American Government and its willingness to act upon them.[15] Meanwhile, China protested Germany's resumption of submarine warfare and threatened to break relations. She took the action serving her own best interests and in confidence that she would gain in associating herself with the United States.[16]

In Japan, the American attempts to induce China to take action with the neutral powers against Germany were greeted with concern. It seemingly deprived Japan of her leadership and isolated her from the advantages which would arise from securing China's consent to war with Germany. As the American notes were being considered in Peking, Japan unknown to Washington, was urging the Allies to give assurances on Shantung and the North Pacific German Islands in return for which Tokyo would bring China into the war.[17]

The State Department continued to employ its policy of placing Chinese stability above her participation in the war. Lansing urged the Chinese Government to the utmost secrecy for the time being concerning Reinsch's proposals, and asked that Peking, if she took action, should do no more than break diplomatic relations.[18] Nine days later, after due consideration, Lansing informed Reinsch that the United States could not give China any assurances of financial assistance "if serious opposition should be offered to such assistance," and any attempt "to override that opposition might precipitate the very aggression which China fears. . . ." The Secretary thought China should await developments concerning her desire to be heard at a peace conference and cautioned against American encouragement "lest China through our advice should become involved in difficulties from which we shall be unable to extricate it."[19] The State Department was well aware that they could do little in China without the risk of difficulty unless Japan were agreeable.

On February 16, Japan received the British assurances of support at the peace conference regarding rights in Shantung and possession of the German Islands; and, in return, Japan sent destroyers to convoy shipping in the Mediterranean. On February 20, Russia accepted the Japanese terms. France and Italy also agreed to support the Japanese claims. Thus before America entered the war, Japan secured the assurance of the Allies to back her war gains at the peace conference.[20] Japan had in these negotiations promised to do what she could to bring China and her vast manpower reserves into the war. Now Japan no longer opposed but sought China's war entry. Tokyo sent a representative to Peking with a confidential memorandum proposing an agreement among the legations to postpone the Boxer indemnity payments for three years, to guarantee cancellation of the German share of the indemnity if China would abolish the internal tax, or *likin,* and to raise the tariff to an effectual seven and one-half percent. It asked the Entente powers to use their good offices in securing these provisions.[21] In return for these favors, China was to declare war against the Central Powers.

President Li favored cautious action, but Vice President Feng, the Premier, and other leaders, in fear of Japan and also in hope of advancing their own ambitions, were disposed to

accept the proposals. Reinsch thought that without some assurances from the United States, the Chinese President would
be unable to maintain his resistance and would be forced into
war as a protege of Japan.[22] Lansing, however, continued to
voice Wilson's decision and to insist that "China will lose
nothing by waiting."[23]

On March 14, 1917, diplomatic relations between Germany
and China were severed by the latter's action. The declaration
of war was used as an issue through which the Premier-General
Tuan Chi-jui, Vice President Feng, and a number of other
officials, some undoubtedly helped by Japanese money, attempted to wrest political control from parliament. As this
pro-Japanese party grew in influence, Minister Reinsch reassured the Chinese Foreign Minister that the United States
maintained its interest in China, and would continue to exert
itself "to protect the independent position of China, to encourage sound laws, and to assist China in obtaining representatives at the peace conference."[24]

Counselor Polk believed "that China was taking this opportunity to play a little international politics with a view to
making friends here and in Europe who would be useful in
its relations with Japan." He thought assurances to China
should not be categorically denied, since it would result in a
loss of American influence there.[25]

When these assurances in the form of the Entente proposals,
initiated by Japan, concerning possible Boxer indemnity post-
ponement arose, Lansing sought a guarantee that China should
continue to support Tsing Hua College, the Chinese students,
and the educational missions resident in the United States. He
also sought assurances from China that her military forces,
equipment, arsenals, and munition factories would not be placed
under foreign control.[26]

On January 16, 1917, during the Congressional debates on
the bill authorizing the arming of merchant ships, the German
Chancellor Alfred Zimmerman wired Ambassador Johann Bernstorff in Washington that despite the risk of American entry
into the conflict, Germany would renew unrestricted submarine
warfare in February. In event war resulted, the Ambassador

was instructed to negotiate an alliance with Mexico, assuring that revolution-torn republic that she should regain "the formerly held territory in Texas, New Mexico, [and] Arizona." The President of Mexico was to "invite Japan to immediate [,] spontaneous [,] concurrent effort and at the same time use his good offices between us and Japan." Zimmerman was to inform Mexico that Germany expected the renewed submarine campaign to force England to sue for peace within a few months.[27]

Germany used four channels to transmit the note from Zimmerman to Herr von Eckhardt in Mexico, but every one was blocked by the British.[28] Admiral William R. Hall, Chief of the British Admiralty Intelligence, gave the information to the American authorities in London. It was passed on to Washington and Counselor Polk showed Wilson the note on February 26, 1917. The President was for publishing it immediately, but Polk prevailed on him to await the return of Secretary Lansing,[29] then at White Sulphur Springs.

Lansing returned the next day, on February 27. Already the original coded message had been secured from the telegraph company and transmitted to Britain with a request that a member of the American Embassy sit in on the decoding of the original message. The releasing of such an explosive matter was closely considered. It was thought it might be misconstrued as an attempt of the administration to influence Congress to vote favorably for the arming of merchant ships bill then under consideration. To avoid such an interpretation, Lansing devised the scheme of unofficially giving the telegram to the United Press for publication.[30]

Counselor Polk, at Lansing's instruction, informed the Japanese Ambassador of the telegram on February 28. During the interview, Sato "expressed great amusement" at the suggestion of Japan adhering to a German-Mexican alliance, and said it was too absurd to take seriously. Polk told the Ambassador that the note might create some feeling in the country when it was published. The Ambassador "again stated that there was no possibility of Japan being party to any alliance with Mexico against the United States."[31]

On March 1, the papers all over the country carried the story of the Zimmerman note. Under press questioning, the President admitted that he was informed of the telegram. Incidentally, the American government released confirmation of the authenticity of the note before the London authorities finished deciphering the original telegram. When the German Ambassador confirmed its authenticity, however, there was no longer any room for doubt.[32] Lansing wrote in his private diary of March 4, 1917: ". . . the message and Zimmerman's unexpected admission have caused a tremendous sensation; the people all over the country are extremely enraged at the perfidy of the German Government in talking peace and friendship with this country and at the same time plotting a hostile coalition against it."[33]

Meanwhile from his command along the Mexican border, General John Pershing reported that Alvaro Obregón had taken precautions against Germany organizing any movement in Mexico. Both Mexican principals, Venustians Carranza and Obregón, decided that it was best to look to the United States for their future welfare. Pershing's information was that no Japanese-Mexican Alliance existed.[34]

Wilson's biographer, Ray Stannard Baker, says the Zimmerman note "convinced the President, then and there, that the German leaders could not in any circumstance be trusted." Following so closely upon their declaration of unrestricted submarine warfare, with a seemingly underhand plot to assist Mexico in invading the United States, the Zimmerman note disillusioned the President. "No single, more devastating blow was delivered against Wilson's resistance to entering the war."[35]

Wilson reluctantly came to the decision for war. As late as March 19, 1917, Lansing found him opposed to a special session of Congress to consider the recent submarine sinkings of American vessels, and he urged Colonel House:

> I suggested that he [Wilson] might call them [Congress] to consider declaring war, and urged the present was the psychological moment in view of the Russian revolution and the anti-Prussian spirit in Germany, and that to throw our

moral influence in the scale at this time would aid the Russian liberals and might even cause revolution in Germany. He indicated to me the fear he had of the queries and investigations of a Congress which could not be depended upon because of the out and out pacifists and the other groups of men like Senator Stone.

If you agree with me that we should act now, will you not please put your shoulder to the wheel?[36]

On March 20, the Cabinet, in a session lasting two and one-half hours, indicated its unanimous decision for war. The President at this meeting "was disinclined to the final break." He spoke of "the glorious act of the Russians" in overthrowing the Czar. It had changed conditions "but he could not give that as a reason for war."[37] On the following day, the Chief Executive called the Congress into special session for April 2.[38] Wilson's address to the Congress was solemn; he declared:

But there are things more precious than peace, and we shall fight for the things which we have always carried nearest our hearts, — for democracy, for the right of those who submit to authority to have a voice in their own Governments, for the rights and liberties of small nations, for a universal dominion of right by such a concert of free peoples as shall bring peace and safety to all nations and make the world at last free.[39]

There were forms to accomplish, and on April 6 the United States and Germany were at war. The President was satisfied that the issue was joined and that a united nation was back of him. He wrote, ". . . there is a certain relief in having the task made concrete and definite."[40] It was an European war upon which the nation had embarked, but like a stone thrown into a still pool, its repercussions were felt afar.

Upon American's declaration of war, Japan ceased her insistence for Chinese participation in the conflict, whereupon the pro-Japanese elements in Peking became discouraged. Reinsch continued to call for China's belligerency to strengthen the position of the United States in the war and to offer China an opportunity for badly needed financial assistance.[41] On April 23 Lansing told Minister Koo that if China went to war, "she might have some reason to expect such financial assistance from the United States."[42] Congress was then voting funds for Allied loans, so this was a natural assumption. When the Chinese Minister put the question of loans to Polk, the Counselor thought that China might post date her declaration of war to become eligible under the loan provisions of the seven billion dollar bill Congress had meanwhile passed.[43]

China's entering the war unfortunately forced a showdown between the President and Parliament as opposed to the military tuchuns. Hired mobs assailed the Parliament which with President Li held out against Premier Tuan Chi-jui, representing the tuchuns. Li relieved him of office and appointed Wu Ting-fong, as Premier.[44] Then the Military Governors of Honan, Shantung, Manchuria, and the Governor of Anhui declared their intention of severing relations with the Peking government unless it dissolved Parliament.[45]

In the midst of all this disorder in China, with the entire northern military party opposing the President and a division of the country threatening,[46] Washington saw fit to appeal to the Chinese government for the re-establishment of tranquility and political coordination. Wilson continued to look upon internal stability as his primary policy in China. The note said: "The entry of China into war with Germany, or the continuance of the *status quo* of her relations with that Government, are matters of secondary consideration. The principal necessity for China is to resume and continue her political entity and to proceed along the road of national development on which she has made such marked progress." The United States expressed an interest in the form or personnel of the Chinese government only insofar as friendship impelled it to be of service. "But with the maintenance by China of one central, united and responsible Government the United States is deeply interested, . . ." and it hoped all factions would work "for the re-establishment of a coordinate government. . . ." A similar message went to all the Entente powers for their information.[47] Sun Yat-sen expressed his deepest gratitude to Wilson for this "foresight and timely warning."[48] Japan viewed the advice with "grave displeasure." When Sato called concerning the communication, Lansing "told him frankly that the United States had as much right as Japan to express its opinion to the Chinese Government. . . ."[49]

Conditions in Peking offered little hope of stability. The author, Richard Washburn Child, had put them very luridly in a letter to House, which the latter passed on to the President:

> Three members of the Ministry were under indictment or in jail, the Vice President had just accepted a bribe from the Jewish opium dealers, the Minister of Justice had been caught smuggling opium, the Minister of Finance was involved in a railway equipment graft, the Premier was accused, probably justly, of making an equipment contract for the telegraph and telephone system to Japan. The real ultimate power was in the hands of the military governors of the provinces and their soldiers, who are more than half a million bandit horde.[50]

The military governors of Fengtien and Anhui provinces declared their independence in June. President Li called for General Chang Hsun and his forces to come to Peking and mediate the situation between the Parliament and Premier factions. Chang's idea of mediation was to dissolve Parliament. When President Li refused, the General made himself dictator on June 14 and brought the boy Emperor out of retirement as a constitutional monarch. The Emperor appointed his all-reactionary cabinet with Chang Hsun as Premier. President Li left Peking,[51] where once again the Manchus were in visible power.

The United States, concerned for its nationals in China, consulted with the Japanese as to the measures to be taken should the necessity for protection arise.[52] The republican government of China, now firmly in the hands of the militarists, removed to Nanking and named Vice President Feng Kuo-chang as President and reinstated Tuan as Premier.[53] The tuchuns had been betrayed by General Chang's restoration of the monarchy, but by July 12 with 50,000 troops they were back in Peking and the monarchy was overthrown. Chang fled to the legation quarter for refuge.[54] President Feng offered Li his office once again, but the former President refused it, and Tuan, continuing as Premier, set out to form a Cabinet dominated by the military. Japan advanced ten million yen for the new administration.[55] Thus did the military come into open domination of the Republic.

There was considerable dissatisfaction with the new government within China, and a military government of disaffected parties was established in Canton. China, which had been unified in the person of President Li was once again divided politically. Wilson's goal of internal political stability seemed lost. The government at Peking was recognized by the powers as the legal government of China; and on August 14, 1917, it was this government that declared war on Germany.[56] A week later, the military governors of the six Southern provinces refusing to recognize the Peking government took similar action. Reinsch was disappointed that China did not make more definite terms with the Allies regarding respect for her future rights as a condition for entering the war.[57]

The Southern leaders, Sun Yat-sen and T'ang Shao-yi, discredited by their extreme political views, found the military leaders in Canton unwilling to follow them.[58] President Feng desired an understanding with the South, but Premier Tuan was opposed. Meanwhile, the Japanese supported Tuan whose cabinet contained several friends of Japan. At the same time, the American Consul General at Canton reported that Japan was also probably giving financial assistance to the Southern government.[59] Such was the complex of internal politics and forces in the divided Republic.

From Shanghai, Samuel Woodbridge wrote to Woodrow Wilson, his cousin-in-law, that China was "upside down . . . in these unhalcyon days. . . ."[60] From Abu Bekr, Professor of the Mosque in Peking, came a magnificent scroll saying:

But as for the present condition of China, it is like the man who is suffering with terrible pains time after time, who desires to flee from his own internal malady, and finds it impossible; or like that of a village troubled with highway robbers and complaining from day to day to the authorities and to the soldiers, but the soldiers themselves have fled away. Verily, the hearts of the rulers of China are divided so that there is constant change, and there is no permanent responsibility.[61]

These were sad words for Wilson who saw the failure of his China policy at a time when the war weakened his ability to curb Japanese advances there.

Colonel House, inspired by reading several reports on China in early September, wrote Wilson that her backwardness, her "lack of sanitation, disease, near-slavery, infanticide, and other brutal and degenerate practices make the nation as a whole a menace to civilization." There was no administration of justice and 800,000 mercenaries controlled by those who could pay them wreaked their wills on the people. He enclosed a report of Richard Washburn Child, just back from the Orient, proposing that the administration of China be given over to three trustees, one each from China, Japan, and a third power to be chosen by the other powers subscribing to the plan. House thought Child's comments might be of some help in view of the Japanese Mission then ariving.[62] At this time, also, Wilson received Charles E. Scott's book, *China from Within*. The President hoped soon to read what his former student had written "about a country which engages my interest, I think, as much as any country in the world."[63] The existing situation, however, strictly limited the possibilities of American initiative in the Orient.

When Reinsch sought authorization to travel out of Peking to get the views of various sections of China on events, Lansing refused his permission for fear of the suspicion it might arouse in Japan. The Secretary informed the Minister of the Japanese complaints of his undue influence in Peking. Reinsch admitted his close relationship with "the most reliable members of the Government and with his colleagues, particularly the British Minister." Through such associations, he was able to exercise some influence in behalf of American national interests in China.[64]

The Japanese claimed that the multiple activities of the American Minister in China's behalf made renunciation of an aggressive policy difficult for Premier Terauchi.[65] In June, 1917, as the struggle of political factions in China reached a divisional state, Chargé Wheeler, in Tokyo, reported that ever since the question of China's entry into the war had arisen, Japan found American interest in China affairs increasingly menacing to her own position. Wheeler thought Japan would utilize any American activity in Peking as an excuse to open opportunities to secure recognition of her paramount position in China.[66]

The resentment of Reinsch's activities was expressed in Ambassador Sato's oral reply to the American note of June 4, requesting the powers to call for Chinese unity. Having confidence in the assurance that America's interests in China were non-political, his government ignored the reports of the American Minister's recent political action in Peking. It did not doubt the recent appeal made by the United States asking for unity within the country; but the Ambassador went on to suggest American recognition of Japan's special position in China, citing the familiar concessions of the Bryan note of March 13, 1915 for a precedent. The Japanese people were sensitive concerning China, and he suggested that it would make a good impression in Japan "if the United States Government sees its way by some appropriate means to confirming the statement of Mr. Bryan and clearly reasserting its friendly attitude toward Japan in respect of Chinese problems."[67]

In answer to Sato's oral statement and the Japanese claim of paramount interest in China, Lansing took issue with the viewpoint that Bryan had recognized Japan's "special and close relations, political as well as economic, with China. . . ." He claimed that Bryan merely stated "that territorial contiguity created special relations between Japan and the districts of Shangtung, Southern Manchuria and East Mongolia, but he did not admit even there that the United States gave up its right to express its views in Sino-Japanese relations." He made it perfectly clear that he did not accept Japan's claim of "paramount" interest in China. The Secretary asserted that while the United States had no political ambitions in China, "its historic interest in the welfare of the Chinese people and the territorial and administrative integrity of the Republic, its treaty relations and extensive commerce with China, render it impossible for the United States to be indifferent to matters affecting these interests, which the civil dissension in China . . . threatened to do."[68] The ambiguity of the Bryan statement which Lansing had originally helped with was now arising to haunt the administration.

Wilson telephoned the Secretary, after going over the preliminary draft of the note, to say that he "entirely" approved. He hoped the Secretary would "reread the latter portion of it, however, with a view to making the idea of Japan's *political* influence over China a little more prominent as the thing we have *not* assented to in the sense she evidently has in mind."[69]

The undercurrent of distrust in American-Japanese relations was continuously fed. As America entered the war, Wilson was frankly concerned as to Japan's future activities. Breckenridge Long, Third Assistant Secretary of State, said that after January, 1917, suspicion of Japan was a vital part of the background on which American policy was formulated.[70] America's war effort called for negotiations to adjust differences and arrange for a living arrangement in the Pacific. Suitable terms were difficult to achieve in the face of Japan's determined power and America's relative weakness and public unconcern.

With the stepping up of the submarine campaign in the late spring and early summer of 1917, the United States found it necessary to shift its shipbuilding program to anti-submarine and merchant vessels. This meant that the fleet power visualized for the Pacific was drastically reduced. Colonel House proposed that Great Britain, in return for this shift in the American program, should give the United States an option on the purchase of capital ships at the end of the war so as to compensate for the sacrifice.[71] The negotiations for such an understanding were carried on between Foreign Secretary Arthur James Balfour through Sir William Wiseman, his representative in the United States, who had direct recourse to Colonel House representing Wilson. American suspicion of Japan was primarily instrumental in broadening the negotiations to consideration of a general Anglo-American naval agreement.

On July 6, 1917, Balfour informed the Colonel that he had taken up the matter with the War Cabinet which was attracted to the idea of an agreement with America. "They were clear that, with or without guarantees, popular opinion in this country would undoubtedly force us to go to the assistance of the United States if she were attacked by Japan." The Cabinet realized though that an informal understanding on the matter would be insufficient to permit the United States to forego the building of capital ships, "in view of the widespread popular mistrust of Japan's intentions. . . ."[72]

The main difficulty, Balfour believed, in any naval understanding, guaranteeing British aid to America in event of a possible war, lay in the Anglo-Japanese Alliance as amended in 1911. This made it incumbent upon each power to inform the other of negotiations for any such agreement as House suggested. Any announcement of consideration for an Anglo-American agreement might throw Japan into a German agreement, out of a feeling that the English-speaking nations were blocking Japanese aims in the Far East.

In the face of the difficulties of an Anglo-American understanding, London suggested broadening the understanding to include Japan and the other major allies. Balfour suggested the agreement might read:

> That, in view of diverting Government shipbuilding in naval yards of the United States from construction of capital ships to that of vessels suitable for anti-submarine warfare, the Governments of the United States, Great Britain, France, Italy, Russia and Japan engage singly and severally to assist each other against any maritime attack for a period of four years after conclusion of the present war.[73]

The Foreign Secretary expressed his willingness to find alternatives and make amendments as the President might suggest.

House sent Balfour's cable and his own comments to Wilson by Breckenridge Long.[74] The Colonel said that British Ambassador Spring-Rice knew nothing of the negotiations. House could not see that Balfour's solution would be of much service, "excepting that it would prevent Japan from falling into the hands of Germany and forming a combination against us." It would force the other powers to be neutral in case of a war between the United States and Japan, or between any of the signatory powers. The Colonel could see no reason why Japan should object, and wished to know the President's conclusions on the matter. He thought the British wished negotiations to be kept unofficial so that treaty obligations to Japan would not call for London to inform Tokyo of the matter.[75]

President Wilson saw Sir William Wiseman concerning the negotiations. The Chief Executive felt little inclined to seek an Allied naval understanding. "With regard to Japan, Wilson said that in his opinion a successful attack on the Pacific Coast was absurd owing to the long distance from the Japanese base and the difficulty they would have in obtaining any suitable base on the Pacific Coast." On the other hand, the President thought an attack on "the Philippines or some outlying possession was . . . quite another matter, and presented a possibility which could not be overlooked."[76] The President informed Wiseman that he had "no fear of attack from Japan at any early time after peace is declared," and that the House proposal was unnecessary.

The British Foreign Secretary confessed that he shared in the President's conclusion and, according to Page, stated, "there is not a shadow of a doubt but, if such an attack shd be made, Great Britain wd come to our rescue." The Ambassador informed Wilson that the Prime Minister wished to send a telegram direct on the subject, but that his associates preferred to have the matter handled in the "most informal way possible, at first."[77]

In the course of his interview with Wiseman, Wilson expressed a poor opinion of the value of capital ships. When Sir William informed House of this the Colonel thought the President had been misunderstood for "the present control of the seas is solely due to the superiority of the British Fleet in capital ships." House advised the President he had talked the whole matter over with the British Admiralty when he was in England, and they had no objection to the post-war arrangement for purchasing capital ships. The Colonel hoped Wilson would make some arrangement on the matter with the British before the end of the war since the President did not approve of the recent proposals.[78] The negotiations revealed the tenseness of feeling on the part of the United States, and in part help to explain the administration's determination to seek a *modus vivendi* with Japan in the Pacific. House seems to have exceeded the Presidential thinking on the threat of Japan. Wilson without hesitation, called the matter back to a more reasonable view as to what was feasible under the circumstances. For the time being, negotiation seemed the more realistic method of achieving American policy in East Asia.

Special missions were not unusual in the summer of 1917. The State Department was overtaxed with entertaining and conferring with the representative of the allied countries. Notice of a mission from Japan headed by the former Foreign Minister Viscount Kikujiro Ishii appeared in the press as early as June, 1917. As Far Eastern relations drifted from bad to worse, this mission assumed increased importance. While Lansing complained of the time and expense the various missions were taking, he thought the Department might as well resign itself to the task since "we have two far more important commissions yet to arrive — the Russian and Japanese. In their case political expediency requires us to show them every possible attention, especially the Japanese. The expenditure of money in entertaining them will be very worth while."[79]

Before the mission was officially suggested, Ambassador Sato, early in May, had approached House, as did many foreign representatives, on the subject of differences with the United States. Sato lunched with the Colonel and talked of the immigration and land questions. He said he was led to open the subject because of a recent public statement by Wilson that all international difficulties should be settled in the spirit of justice. House suggested that any early attempt at an undertaking on these problems might be misconstrued by the public as Japan taking advantage of America's recent entrance into the war.

The Colonel asked the Ambassador for a written statement, since he thought any settlement should be approached formally.[80]

The later memorandum on differences between the United States and Japan, as covered by Ambassador Sato, suggested that the treatment of Japanese in the United States be made a matter of treaty, guaranteeing them most favored nation status. Although realizing it was not a matter for international discussion, Sato proposed the United States by constitutional amendment restrain the states in their action in such matters. He thought the Gentleman's Agreement adequately solved the problem of Japanese labor immigration.[81] House promised to take up these matters with Washington when it seemed opportune, but he did not think the time propitious for the calm consideration the matter demanded. He, nevertheless, promised to do all he could for the maintenance of good relations between the two countries.[82]

In the covering letter of his and Sato's correspondence, House informed Wilson that Walter Rogers, an expert on Far Eastern news service, had just returned from the Orient. Rogers reported that the news of America's armament program had gotten abroad in Japan and had worked to somewhat alleviate the openly-expressed antagonism toward the United States. The belief in both Japan and China, said House, was that the United States was as unwilling to fight as China. He suggested this stereotype of America could be changed with little cost, and he offered to undertake such a program if the President desired.[83]

The news of the coming Japanese mission caused some concern on the part of the Chinese Minister. On June 16, he called on Counselor Polk to sound out State Department plans. He desired to know if the United States intended to recognize Japan's paramount influence in China. Polk informed him that nothing of the sort was under consideration.[84]

The Far Eastern Division worked out two-copies of a varied information memorandum for the attention of Lansing in preparation for the coming Japanese talks. After Polk read the document, Long, who with Williams drew it up, sent one copy on to House, so that he might know what discussions were contemplated. As third Assistant Secretary of State and in charge of Far Eastern Affairs, Long was delegated to meet the Japanese Mission in San Francisco and accompany them East.[85]

In the Polk papers there is a report on the various members of the Japanese mission. It describes Ishii as a delightful gentleman of the Kensekai Party, friendly to the United States, and an authority on the Chinese situation and thoroughly familiar with the California question. As a pupil of Kato, he had succeeded his mentor in the foreign office in 1916.[86] When Ambassador William G. Sharp in Paris read of the Japanese Mission, he wrote Wilson that Ishii was "a frank, friendly man, possessed of good sense and the most cordial feeling toward the United States." While Ambassador to France, Ishii had "manifested not only the greatest admiration for the United States but deprecated any possibility of any future trouble between the two countries."[87]

America's entry into the war had disturbed Tokyo. "The Japanese statesmen were apprehensive lest the military and naval forces being organized in the United States were to be used to check Japan's designs in regard to China." Lansing said Japanese psychology could not understand America's altruistic purpose of "fighting for liberty and democracy in Europe."[88] The activities of Reinsch in encouraging China to enter the conflict, and the independent advice rendered China by Washington only served to intensify Japanese suspicions. Tokyo had concluded her secret treaties with the other Allies for support of her claims to the Pacific islands and the German rights in Shantung; it remained to commit the United States to the objectives. Viscount Ishii admitted only that the purpose of the mission was to express Japan's gratitude for American entry into the war and to use the opportunity "to exchange with responsible American officials frank views concerning problems in China and reach some form of understanding and settlement." He claimed to have only the "bare outlines of what he might discuss," and no detailed instructions.[89] On its part Washington sought an understanding with Japan which would assure peace and the *status quo* in the

Pacific, thus freeing the United States to concentrate on an all out effort to defeat Germany on the Western Front.[90]

For two weeks following the arrival of the Mission on September 1, 1917, the official entertainment kept the delegation from any serious negotiations. They were officially received in San Francisco, at the White House, in both houses of Congress, at Admiral Perry's grave in Newport, in Boston and New York. Long pressed every available soldier into a parade in California and conducted Ishii on a review of the fleet off the East Coast in an attempt to impress him with America's growing military might. He said the mission was well but not popularly received for Japan was not in good repute with the public.[91] The tour afforded Viscount Ishii an opportunity to explain the position of Japan in the war and her attitude towards common international problems to the American public.[92] At one point of the program, during a parade in Washington, Long suggested that the Japanese be given a place in the reviewing stand with the President. Wilson replied that he thought it not wise, "preferring the Japanese representative to those of the other Allies might lead to misunderstanding."[93]

In conversing with Ishii at the White House, the President declared that America desired nothing more than the preservation of the open door and equal opportunity in China. He regretted that spheres of influence had been created there by the powers. Ishii agreed with the President, saying that his country had never failed to uphold those principles. At the conclusion of the conference, Wilson expressed his interest in the conversation and asked Ishii to talk the matter over with Lansing. Thus were the Lansing-Ishii talks arranged. While they took place the various other members of the Mission held discussions with army, navy and war boards.[94]

Ishii relates that following the conversation with Wilson he communicated with his government the President's views on spheres of influence, adding that if Wilson "could be satisfied on this point . . . [they] might induce him to agree with Japan on other issues." Tokyo failed to reply to the Viscount, since the Foreign Affairs Council differed concerning abolition of the spheres of influence in China. Without instructions then, Ishii avers, he opened discussions at his own discretion with Secretary Lansing.[95] Beginning September 6 and ending November 2, 1917, there were in all thirteen conferences between the two men. The President was kept fully informed through Lansing's memoranda concerning the negotiations.[96]

In the first conference, Ishii talked of the difficulty in Japanese shipbuilding caused by the American embargo on iron. Since Japan was aiding the Allies in the Mediterranean, he thought such an embargo directly hindered Japan's war contribution. Lansing thought some arrangement could be made on the matter. The Viscount talked of the industrial situation in Japan which seemed much on his mind. (There were strikes and a nascent socialist movement causing the Japanese leaders much concern.) Ishii told of his talks with Viscount Grey in London in 1915 when he told the British Minister that Japan would return Kiaochow but keep some of the German North Pacific Islands. He told Lansing that Grey in 1915 had practically consented to Japan retaining the islands north of the equator while Britain took those to the south. Lansing expressed his appreciation at learning this, but made no comment.[97] (The Secretary could have told Ishii that Ambassador Spring-Rice had told him of the island arrangement in 1916.) There was no mention of the 1917 secret treaties.

Lansing suggested: "That the co-belligerents re-declare the 'Open Door' policy in a statement which would have a very beneficial effect upon China, and . . . upon the world at large, as it was in accord with the principles of commerce to which we all agreed." Ishii thought there would be opposition to such a declaration without some mention of Japan's special interest. At last the matter for discussion was before them! Lansing said the United States recognized Japan's "peculiar" interest in China; but since it was geographic and not political, it seemed foolish to make it a matter of declaration. Japan, Ishii said, favored the open door; but he was not sure they would see the advantage of reaffirming it. Lansing then pointed out the threat of the growth of spheres of interest to the natural geographic location Japan enjoyed in respect to Chinese trade.[98]

In this first conference, Ishii revealed "that through various channels the German Government had three times sought to persuade Japan to withdraw from the Allies and to remain neutral, but that in every case his Government had firmly rejected the suggestion." Lansing reassured the Viscount that the American Government felt no concern as to the loyalty of Japan as an Ally and "her reputation for good was too well established to be even suspected."[99]

The conversations of the negotiators were not continuous and Ishii went to New York to fulfill several speaking engagements. In New York, the Viscount explained that Japan favored the open door and equality of opportunity in China as a benefit to Japanese trade. He also explained the Japanese Monroe Doctrine for Asia to a seemingly appreciative audience. Upon his return to Washington, he found Wilson friendlier than ever. The President complimented him on his addresses, stating they had removed much misunderstanding in the minds of the American people.[100]

By the time of the third meeting, September 22, Ishii had heard from his government on the subject of the open door. He said "that they did not wish to do anything to affect the *status quo* in China and that it would be hard to explain to the Japanese people why a declaration was made at this time if the suggestion was adopted." Lansing protested that if the creation of new spheres of influence in China, which seemed to be going on, were allowed to continue, the Allies would look on Japan and the United States as seeking to use the war to monopolize the opportunities in China. A redeclaration of the open door would be the best kind of a reassurance to them. Ishii agreed, but he added something must be said within the declaration concerning the special interests of Japan in order to avoid an attack on the government by the opposition in the Diet. Lansing replied "if he meant by 'special interest' [to say] 'paramount interest', I could not see my way clear to discuss the matter further; but if he meant a special interest based upon geographical position, I was not unwilling to take the matter into consideration." Ishii seemed pleased and asked the Secretary to submit such a formula for his consideration.[101]

Lansing explained Japan's misunderstanding of the Monroe Doctrine, of which Ishii had talked in New York, claiming Japan's similar doctrine for Asia. The Doctrine was not as Ishii believed it "an assertion of primacy or paramount interest by the United States in its relations to other American Republics. . . . " It was rather to prevent foreign interference and preserve the power of self-development to each country—the United States claimed no special privileges. Lansing said he thought the same policy should be applied to China. He expressed appreciation for Japan's population pressure and need for industrial expansion, and that the occupation of Korea and the development of Manchuria had been chiefly of this "unavoidable necessity." Ishii spoke of Japan's desire for the open door in Manchuria; in fact, he said his government would refuse cession of the region to Japan. Lansing expressed appreciation of this viewpoint and hoped that they agreed on the application of the term "open door." Lansing said his view of the open door "was that in China foreign commerce and trade should be entirely unhampered." The Viscount agreed with this view. When Lansing expressed further that if a railroad or canal were built in China, all nationals should receive equal treatment in its use, Ishii agreed with hesitation; and Lansing thought he "seemed desirous to avoid a discussion of the application of the principle of the 'Open Door'."[102]

Wilson followed "the negotiations carefully and gave his full consent to every step. The conversations concerned the same subject: agreement upon the principle to be observed with regard to China."[103] In the next few days following the second session of the talks, the President spent a half hour with Ishii. Wilson confessed to doing "most of the talking (to let him see my *full* thought) and he seemed to agree throughout in *principle*."[104]

The negotiations were now largely concerned over the phrasing of the declaration. On November 2, the notes were finally exchanged. After both governments recognizing that "territorial propinquity creates special relations between countries, and consequently, the Government of the United States recognizes that Japan has special interests in China, particularly in the part to which her possessions are contiguous," the note declared, "The territorial sovereignty of China . . . remains unimpaired. . . . " Both Governments agreed not to infringe the independence of territorial integrity of China and to adhere to the principle of the so-called 'open door' or equal opportunity for commerce and industry in China." Moreover, they mutually declared their opposition to the acquisition of special rights or privileges by any government that would affect Chinese independence or territorial integrity.[105]

During the course of negotiations a discussion arose over the clause, "they [the Governments of Japan and the United States] will not take advantage of the present condition to seek special rights or privileges in China which would abridge the rights of the subjects or citizens of other friendly states." The negotiations agreed to suppress this clause as it was "liable to create [an] erroneous impression in the minds of the public. . . ." But, in a secret protocol, signed along with the agreement and unpublished at the time, it was understood that the statement "was in perfect accord with the declared policy of the two Governments in regard to China."[106]

Lansing looked upon the negotiations as successfully recommitting Japan to the Root-Takahira understanding of 1908 in a "more far reaching and vital [way] to the preservation of China's sovereignty than the previous agreement had done." The central thought of the Lansing-Ishii Agreement, the Secretary believed, was its declaration preserving the independence and territorial integrity of China, although it also re-declared the open door.[107]

Concurrent with the conclusion of the Lansing-Ishii negotiations on November 2, 1917 a "complete and satisfactory understanding upon the matter of naval co-operation . . ." was reached between the naval representatives of the two governments.[108]

Minister Reinsch telgraphed from China on November 4 that the Japanese Minister in Peking had shown him the Ishii note in which the United States recognized the special interest of Japan in China. Reinsch asked, "While I understand that the reasons which prompted this momentous decision are confidential," should not an explanation to China be made of the action, "which so profoundly affects their interests and which at first sight appears a reversal of American policy in China?"[109] Wilson was swift to urge the Secretary of State: "I hope that the proper reassurances have gone, or will go at once, to Reinsch." The President declared, "There has not only been no [sic] change of policy but there has been a distinct gain for China, of course, and I hope that you will be kind enough to send Reinsch such a message as will serve to put the whole thing in the right light at Peking and throughout China."[110]

On November 5, the notes were sent to the American representatives in Tokyo and Peking.[111] The following day they were reported to the interested European governments.[112] The agreement was to be released simultaneously in the United States and Japan on November 6, but Tokyo transmitted the notes to the Japanese Minister in Peking, who delivered them to the Chinese Government, and used for the term "special interest" the objectionable "paramount interest," which Lansing had denied throughout the negotiations. The American Secretary saw this action of Japan as a deliberate attempt to make China believe the United States had abandoned her. The Japanese press and diplomats abroad also gave circulation to this position.[113] In the light of this interpretation, upon Reinsch's advice, the Chinese Government delivered a memorandum to the United States, declaring it was not bound by the agreement.[114]

The same day as the arrival of the Chinese reservation, Lansing saw Minister Koo and assured him that the memorandum was unnecessary, since it had not been the intent of the negotiators to bind China in any way. Lansing explained that he had consciously refrained from mentioning the negotiations to the Chinese in order to avoid any question of China giving her assent to the notes. He had not wanted anyone to have grounds to say that China had relinquished any right by not dissenting during the negotiations. The Secretary assured Koo that China's interests were in his mind throughout the negotiations. He urged this viewpoint as the reason for the agreement: Japan and the United States were the only two countries with surplus investment capital. Because of the war, the American financiers could find ready markets at home for their investments, and if they dropped out of the China field, Japan would be left in control. The Secretary said that the United States was anxious to aid China financially, but the only way she could do so at present was by cooperating with Japan. As to the "special rights" issue, Lansing explained that it was a geographic axiom that territorial propinquity created special interests and by conceding this axiom the United States had obtained "a declaration of policy which restrained the other party. . . ."[115]

The new American Ambassador, Roland Morris, who had been named just prior to the Lansing-Ishii negotiations, now reported from Tokyo that the Japanese newspapers were most favorable in their coverage of the arrangement. It placed the chief emphasis on the definite concessions to Japan's special interests, which unofficially were very broadly interpreted. Only the opposition press was critical. Business interests and official circles as well as resident Americans seemed satisfied. It was expected, however, that stronger opposition would develop in December, when the Diet convened.[116] From London, Rome, and Paris congratulations came from the American Ambassadors on what each considered an achievement of American diplomacy.[117] The Copenhagen legation reported that with events in Russia, the offensive in Italy and a political crisis, Germany had found no time for comment on the new Japanese-American arrangement.[118]

The then Russian Ambassador to the United States, Boris A. Bakhmeteff, later told MacMurray that he had protested to Lansing at the time of the negotiations that Japan had her own peculiar interpretation of "special interests," but the American Secretary had replied that there was no reason to doubt Viscount Ishii's understanding of the way the United States employed the term. Lansing observed that if the interpretation were disputed the United States would be compelled to address a note explaining its position to Japan.[119]

The ambiguity of the Lansing-Ishii Agreement was intentional with both parties, according to A. Whitney Griswold. The negotiations, he claims, were forced on the administration out of expediency and made necessary by the circumstances in which the United States was preparing an offensive against Japanese expansion in Asia. The agreement then was "a stop-gap measure, a temporization, a grudging concession to the threat of Japanese imperialism when the United States was girding itself to destroy the dragon of German autocracy."[120] La Fargue prefers to look to the agreement as growing out of an attempt to prevent Japan absorbing China through investments. He concludes that the Agreement was "an unfortunate episode in American diplomacy" because of the ambiguity of the term "special interest."[121]

The Lansing-Ishii Agreement was sought by the United States while considerable friction existed in the relations of the two countries, largely over China. It was an attempt on the part of the United States to maintain the *status quo* in China while getting on with the war. In the light of Lansing's explicitness on the meaning of "special" as differentiated from "paramount" interest and subsequent protests to Japan maintaining his position, it is evident that the United States had no thought of sacrificing China's interest. Viscount Ishii, as he confesses, did not represent entirely the views of the Japanese Foreign Office. In a period when opportunity motivated the action, leaving the manufacturing of excuses to the diplomats, Japan acted. There is little surprise that confusion arose as to what was done behind closed doors in Washington.

Ishii confessed, "There is no doubt that the negotiations would have ended in disappointing disagreement had it not been for Mr. Wilson's moderation."[122] The Japanese emissary felt he was dealing directly with the President, though Wilson intervened but once in the negotiations to show Ishii his full mind. Lansing was the President's agent, and the Lansing-Ishii Agreement was in a very real sense representative of the Chief Executive's policy of protecting the territorial integrity and independence of China and guaranteeing the open door. In exchange America ambiguously recognized Japan's special position in relation to contiguous territory in China. As a document reiterating American policy in China to which Japan consented, it was a real victory. In reality the interpretation given "special" by Japan served her own purposes. Perhaps the greatest gain of the agreement was in somewhat alleviating the tensions which had developed for a short time thereby preventing any disruption over Asian policy between the two powers.

A month previous to the arrival of Ishii in the United States, Roland Morris of Philadelphia had been appointed as Ambassador to Japan, filling the vacancy left at the death of Ambassador Guthrie on March 9, five months earlier.[123] House was very anxious that Morris understand Wilson's mind on Japanese affairs and he wrote the President:

> I had a talk with Roland Morris today. I hope you will see him for ten or fifteen minutes before he leaves for Japan next Tuesday, in order to give him your viewpoints as to Far Eastern questions. I think he has the right view himself and, if you agree with it he will understand in what direction to proceed.
> We cannot meet Japan in her desires as to land and immigration, and unless we make some concessions in regard to her sphere of influence in the East, trouble is sure, sooner or later to come. Japan is barred from all the undeveloped places of the earth, and if her influence in the East is not recognized as in some degree superior to that of the Western powers, there will be a reckoning.
> A policy can be formulated which will leave the door open, rehabilitate China, and satisfy Japan. Morris sees this clearly but needs your sanction, if, indeed, such a policy has your sanction.[124]

A week later, Wilson saw Morris, who was ready to leave for Japan. The President dryly advised the Ambassador, "Don't write me too many letters."[125] He always complained about long, useless correspondence that took much of his time and added so little to his knowledge.

Morris took the President at his word and his letters were infrequent; but the course of events in Asia kept him constantly on the cable after his arrival in Tokyo on November 6, 1917. He had the duty of reporting the ineffectiveness of the Lansing-Ishii Agreement, the further conquests of Japan on the continent of Asia, the delays in securing Japanese consent to the Second Consortium, and the Siberian adventure. In the latter instance, Morris indeed became one of the chief actors in the drama.

CHAPTER SEVEN

The New Consortium and Troubles

MONEY ANSWERETH ALL THINGS

—Ecclesiastes

EVEN THE BLIND CAN SEE MONEY.

—Chinese Proverb

MONEY HAS NO EARS, BUT IT HEARS.

—Japanese Proverb

American policy motives in Eastern Asia were complex, but essentially they stemmed from an attempt to bolster the open door, which demanded an independent China, a balance of power in Asia, and opposition to Japanese hegemony over any sector of China's national life. This gave American policy the appearance of defending helpless China against a predatory Japan, but in actuality it was the best means of achieving the long range objective of a stable Eastern Asia in which American interests would be safe.[1] Both Japan and the United States looked upon one another's policy as motivated primarily by ambition rather than as proceeding out of deep national interest. The very spirit of Wilsonian diplomacy was incompatible with Japanese practices, however, and the President was looked upon as entering the lists against Nippon. The United States thoroughly suspected Japanese ambitions in East Asia, although on a policy level there was some sympathy for Japan's need of expansion. This latter attitude was certainly evident, as we have seen, in the modus vivendi negotiated by the two powers in 1917—the Lansing-Ishii Agreement. It was again evident during discussion of the Japanese reservation of South Manchuria, Eastern Inner Mongolia, and Shantung in relation to the formation of the Second Consortium.

American participation in the Consortium as a means of relieving the financial burdens and the Japanese pressures on the Peking regime was not suddenly born. The Wilson administration, it will be recalled, had encouraged the bankers to reactivate the American group in the Spring of 1916 to no avail. When this failed, the President encouraged, as he did in 1915 under the Griswold plan, a direct loan by the American bankers outside the Consortium; but this too was unsuccessful, since the old American group members adhered to the 1912 principle of looking upon administrative loans as strictly Consortium business. Meanwhile, Japan had fastened her hold on Shantung, South Manchuria, and Eastern Mongolia, and seemed bent on establishing her hegemony over China through a multitude of loans, demands, and investments. The Entente bankers, increasingly concerned, sought American participation in the Consortium as a means of destroying the near-monopoly condition that Japan had achieved over Chinese finances.[2]

The opportunity for inviting American participation occurred in January, 1917, when the Chinese government sought a loan of ten to twenty million pounds for administrative purposes from the Consortium bankers. The Entente groups, busy with war financing, could not participate; and this left Japan to make the loan. The Entente bankers once again suggested a revival of American participation in the Consortium. Japan was not unwilling to hear their suggestion, since the amount of the loan was more than she could possibly manage. The Japanese were attracted to the loan since it offered the land tax as part security which would admirably serve Japanese purposes. In addition, the completion of the Lee, Higginson and the Continental and Commercial Trust loans to China in 1916, together with the increased concern of the American government threatened competition of independent American banks for financing the needs of China. Such competition was all the more feasible since the 1912 Consortium agreement expired in June, 1917, and the American banks need no longer feel under its restraint.

Japan visualized American participation under the organization of the existing Consortium which she controlled, and she therefore had no fears in inviting reactivation of the American group.[3]

As the United States readied itself for war in Europe, the State Department policy matured of associating the United States with Japan as the best means of protecting the open door and Chinese sovereignty.[4] This meant, of course, an understanding with her on basic China policy, such as was attempted in the Lansing-Ishii Agreement, and participation by a revived American group in the Consortium. Lansing frankly admitted that the war had changed many things and that membership in the Consortium was being carefully considered "from the standpoint of expediency."[5]

The entrance of the United States into the war, following an invitation to the neutrals to break relations with Germany, had precipitated a political crisis between the pro-war Parliament and the President in China. General Chang Hsun, called to mediate the difference between Cabinet and Parliament, overthrew the Republic and called the young Manchu Emperor to assume his full function. The Chinese Minister in Washington, V. K. Wellington Koo, implied that the destruction of the republic was a plot of Chang Hsun in cooperation with the Japanese.[6] The reestablished monarchy received a $5,000,000 loan from Japan, but it was to little avail for in July the republic was reestablished. The military dominated the new government, headed by President Feng,[7] and certain members of the cabinet were suspected of serving Japanese interests. These events were carefully followed in Washington by the Wilson administration.

The Root Mission returned to Washington from Russia where it had been sent by Wilson following the March revolution, the Allied missions arrived, China entered the war, and the Lansing-Ishii talks began on September 6. It was a hurried time in which Lansing consulted often with Wilson, Phillips, Williams, and Long on the progress of the loan to China. During these talks the administration decided to revive the American group and to participate with Japan in the offered administrative loan.[8] The expiration of the 1912 Consortium agreement in June gave the Department an opportunity it did not formerly possess, for now the American bankers could freely engage in administrative loans to China. However, the task remained of deciding the feasibility of such loans and then interesting the bankers in their issuance.

On November 9, 1917, a week after the signing of the Lansing-Ishii Agreement, the Secretary of State cabled Reinsch that the United States was considering American participation in the Consortium and would probably undertake to organize a new American group at once.[9] Meanwhile, the Chinese applied for an advance of two million pounds on the proposed loan. Japan looked with favor on the request, while Britain was reluctant to make the advance,[10] and the French took the occasion to urge the prompt organization of an American group.[11]

Reinsch reported from Peking, where negotiations were in progress, that the advance would be carried by Japan alone, since the Entente groups were unable to participate. The Chinese Minister of Foreign Affairs "feared advantage may be taken by the Japanese of [the] existing disorganization of China to make such [an] advance upon terms which might hereafter restrict the financial independence of China." The Wilson administration sought to have the French group participate in the advance and have the American group, once organized, carry their further obligations in the loan. It urged similar participation on the part of the British.[12]

Secretary of Commerce Redfield, consulting Lansing about the possibility of reassuring the foreign service personnel that the Lansing-Ishii Agreement did not mean the abandoning of China to Japan, inquired as to the possibility of American participation in the proposed China loan.[13] Lansing responded that the Department for some time had been considering participation, since it was politically desirable. He had recommended the formation of a new American group "in no uncertain terms," to the President, who had approved it "in principle." The matter had then been referred to McAdoo who had opposed floating a loan in competition with the second liberty loan drive of November, 1917. The Secretary averred that current American policy was not to compete with Japan or to desert China but to join Japan on a China policy.[14] The independent policy was being replaced by cautious cooperation with the imperial power of the Pacific. This had been the temper of the Lansing-Ishii Agreement, and followed the popular admonition of joining the opposition and working from within, when other resistance proved unsuccessful.

Certainly Japan had established herself in a position of financial dominance in China. By 1918, she had made over eighty Chinese loans aggregating hundreds of millions of dollars. Only fractions of these loans had actually been expended, for her policy was to grant a loan, make a token advance on it, and then exact other concessions from the supine Peking or provincial authorities before advancing further funds. Under this system she had gained valuable maritime rights, territorial concessions, strategic railway lines, and projected railway rights into the very heart of China, Manchuria, Eastern Mongolia. Shantung had thus been brought under her control, and Japanese money in Peking had subordinated various departments of the government to her interests. Breckenridge Long, surveying the situation, wrote of China, "Only time was needed for the financial rope to hang the giant."[15]

The international bankers agreement of 1912 had expired, German and Russian banks had long been inactive in the arrangement, the Entente bankers had been unable to participate, and Japan had come to dominate and use the Consortium for her own purposes. The German offensive in France was fierce, and the Allies favored China loans to increase her war effort for the benefit of the Allied cause. The time was opportune for the exercise of an American initiative.

After a conference with Assistant Secretary Long, Lansing, on June 20, 1918, proposed to President Wilson that the United States sponsor the organization of a New International Consortium. Conditions had changed since the first of the year, and the Treasury now approved going ahead with the China loans. He suggested calling the bankers together to see what could be done.[16]

Three new investment developments in China made early organization of an American group advisable. The Continental Trust and Savings Bank of Chicago, whose November, 1916 loan was secured by the income from the wine and tobacco tax, had sixty days to take up its option on the additional $25,000,-000 loan offered. Japanese interests were already negotiating to advance loans on the same security, which would, if completed, liquidate the former Chicago loan and place "the organization and control of the whole tobacco and wine industry of China — its manufacture, production, and sale" in Japanese hands.[17]

Lansing failed to mention that certain business interests were considerably disturbed over the situation. Senator Lee S. Overman of North Carolina had called on him five days earlier concerning the Japanese attempt to secure a tobacco monopoly in China. The same afternoon, he had brought several of his Senate colleagues along with James B. Duke and three other gentlemen representing the tobacco interests to the Department for consultation about the Japanese threat.[18] These businessmen saw a real difficulty for American interests if the present loan opportunity were neglected.

The remaining two projects, in which Lansing thought it important for the United States to share financially, were the completion of the projected Canton to Hankow Railroad and the much discussed loan for currency reform purposes. The financing of the line which had been begun by the British, would enable "American interests to control a very important railroad." British and French groups also promised to withdraw their claims to spheres of influence in the region affected if the Americans financed the project. The currency reform loan was committed to the Consortium from which America had withdrawn, and in which the French and British groups were now financially unable to participate. Under the present arrangements, it left only Japan to carry a loan amounting to between one and two hundred million. The Japanese, in January, 1917, had requested, Lansing explained, American participation; and while the loan was not imminent, it would become an active factor in the next few months.[19]

Finally, so Lansing informed Wilson, China had entered the war "at our invitation . . ., and it is to us that she is looking for some financial help to guard against possibilities now that the scenes of war are nearing her borders."[20] He thought if the United States were to give permission to the American banks to make the loans, based on the security of the tobacco tax and the railroad, and to join Japan in the currency reform loan, it would serve the interests of all concerned. The Secretary, therefore, requested Presidential approval for the organization of a new American banking group to take advantage of the current opportunities.[21]

Wilson consented to the formation of a New Consortium, but with reservations:

> I approve of the course proposed in this letter. I take it for granted that everything necessary would be done to protect the Chinese Government against such unconscionable arrangements as were contemplated by the former consortium, because I am afraid it is not less but rather more likely that the Chinese Government would permit unfair advantage to be taken of it at the present time of stress than formerly.[22]

Wilson was still the prudent friend, concerned with the welfare of China, and unwilling to be a partner in any arrangement that would weaken her further or place her in a disadvantageous position in relation to Japan or the other powers.

With the President approving, Lansing called a meeting of the bankers in Washington on June 26, 1918 for the purposes of "making a loan or loans by private banking institutions to the Government of China."[23] The four former members of the American Group and three other large banks were asked to send their representatives. On the day appointed, all the agents of these banks gathered with the government representatives in the Diplomatic Reception Room at the State Department. After calling the meeting to order, Lansing turned the group over to Assistant Secretary Long, who had been acting, and was to act, as the agent of the government throughout the negotiations.[24]

Long found some antagonism between the original American group and advocates of a New Consortium, which the State Department supported; but the meeting was a success. The plan to form a new group and then invite members from England, France, and Japan to join gained the day. Wilson's decision as to the objectionable features of monopoly and the guarantees to be given were final and respected. Long confessed that his problem was to conciliate the ideas of the government and bankers and at the same time to overcome their antipathies to the administration. He later wrote of the meeting: "We discussed around the table the undeveloped plan, or rather discussed the principles which might be incorporated in a plan — but no mention was made of *the ultimate objective, to drive Japan out of China.* This could not have been done, even in so select and judicious a company, and it is quite doubtful if, even under the influence of the prevailing psychology the bankers would have lent themselves to a scheme which was at heart political." He admitted that his job was "to present to them a legitimate banking proposition. Concurrently it was necessary to keep out of the discussion the political character of the ultimate objective."[25] Long thus confessed that the administration had decided to take the offensive and to offer an American structured Consortium as a challenge to Japan in China.

Later, on July 1, Long met with a larger representation of twelve to fifteen bankers in New York. Morgan acted as chairman of the meeting. The bankers presented a written statement of principles to be embodied in the New Consortium and their plan of government cooperation which they considered essential.[26] Long reported to Lansing by phone on the negotiations[27] and then returned to Washington where he revamped the bankers' recommendations into letter form. One letter appeared as from the old American group to the Department of State, suggesting the formation of a new group. The other contained the Department's reply accepting the suggestion and outlining the procedure to be followed. These drafts were submitted through Lansing to President Wilson, who approved the letters.[28] Long picked up the approved letters at the Department and took them to Lansing's home. The two men went over the papers together, and the Assistant Secretary took the midnight train to New York. The bankers were still there, and the administration desired to strike while the "iron was hot."[29]

The next morning, Long telephoned Morgan and agreed to meet him in the latter's library. The Department's representative later confessed that he was convinced if Morgan could be won over, the other bankers would follow out of deference. He therefore did his best to present the proposed Consortium as something entirely new and of a larger scope, in which Morgan would be the leader of a larger number of banks than in the old arrangement. For two hours, both men talked and pored over the documents. Morgan called the other gentlemen on the committee to meet with them at noon. He then recommended adoption of Long's report and letters. The Committee authorized the financial magnate to sign for them.[30]

The banker's letter, as drafted by Long and approved by Wilson, mentioned that during the conference in Washington, American-Japanese cooperation in a Chinese loan had been suggested; but a broader basis in international cooperation was felt advisable.

> We suggest therefore that this can best be accomplished in a four-power group consisting of financial members to be recognized by the respective Governments of Great Britain, France, Japan, and the United States; our Government to recognize as their member of such group the American banks or firms which may become associated for this purpose, and which we should hope to have representative of the whole country.

Under the present circumstances it was expected that Japan and the United States would carry England and France for the time being.[31]

The distinctive innovation of the New Consortium, and the means by which the United States hoped to offset the gains made by Japan in China, was embedded in the condition of membership. It required the "relinquishment by the members of the group either to China or to the group of any options to make loans which they now hold, and all loans to China by any of them should be considered as four-power group business." Such cooperation among the four powers would work for the maintenance of Chinese sovereignty and the preservation of the open door; it might also aid in developing the large potential revenue resources in China. The letter sought recognition of the change in America's "international relations, both diplomatic and commercial, brought about by the war." At the same time, it called upon the administration "at the time of issue to make it clear to the public that the loan is made at the suggestion of the Government. . . ."[32]

The reply, also framed by Long and bearing Wilson's approval, stated that the war had brought Great Britain, France, Japan and the United States into a state of "cooperation in matters relating to their interests abroad." All four powers were now interested in loans to strengthen China and fit her for a more active part in the war against the Central Powers. Since the proposed loans thus touched French and British interests, the American Government felt it best to form a four power group as suggested in the bankers' communication. It hoped that the whole of Chinese finance could ultimately be treated under the Consortium in which all loans would be submitted to and approved by China and each of the cooperating governments. But the stubborn Wilson reservation was made "that this Government would be opposed to any terms or conditions of a loan which sought to impair the political control of China or lessened the sovereign rights of that Republic."[33]

The Wilson administration would announce that the loan was made at its suggestion. It favored the relinquishment of existing options to make loans to China, now held by various bankers of the United States and other countries. It sought such a provision as a condition of membership in the new American group and would use its good offices abroad to bring about a similar agreement within the other groups. The United States, on its part, undertook to assure the bankers of its intent "to aid in every proper way and to make prompt and vigorous representations to take every possible step to insure the execution of equitable contracts made in good faith by its citizens in foreign lands." It also approved the suggestion of widespread participation among American banks in the loan.[34]

The provision to have the New Consortium given a retroactive and current option on all business in China was the chief weapon to be used against Japanese dominance. Through this means, the international group, of which the American banks were to be the most important element, would share in all the business.[35] This, of course, meant the base of the new international group was being widened to include all types of loans rather than those solely administrative, which had come to be looked upon in the past as of Consortium concern. All loans would require unanimous approval of the participating groups. This was a positive position which gave the United States, supported by France and Britain, a really determining position in relation to China's finances. The Wilson administration, like that of Taft was using its bankers as a political instrument rather than serving any expressed need of American business for investment opportunities in China.[36] Faced seemingly with two possibilities in its policy on China loans: independent action, or reentering the Consortium, the United States created a third way out through organization of a New Consortium, excluding Russia and Germany, and structured on American principles.

On July 10, 1918, with the completion of the formation of a new American group, identical notes were sent to the Japanese, British, and French governments advising them of the organization and inviting their participation in the New Consortium. The correspondence carrying the terms of agreement was inclosed for the information of the governments concerned.[37]

Although the Department attempted to keep formation of the American group a secret, the New York papers released the story.[38] Since the notices did not truthfully represent the situation, Counselor Polk drafted a press statement, which Wilson approved for publication.[39] It followed closely the Long letters to and from the bankers. A loan of fifty million dollars, roughly the sum America spent each day in the war, was initially contemplated. The money was to be used to build up the defenses of China along the Siberian border and to aid her preparations for more active participation in the European war.[40] News of the American sponsored Consortium was welcomed in

China as ending the period of frenzied finance and as cancelling Japan's financial domination there.[41]

During the formation of the new American group, the State Department and President, in turn, conferred with Minister Reinsch who had been called home to advise on the China loan.[42] Lansing was glad to have the memorandum of the American Minister's conversation with the President on Chinese finances and to discover "Reinsch's views in complete accord with those of the Department as set forth in the plans already formed and in process of execution. . . ." Wilson desired to discuss the memorandum with Lansing.[43] Reinsch thought it of the greatest importance that a favorable reply come from the Allies, particularly Japan, on the proposed cooperation. The Minister hoped the United States would move to make funds available for the completion of the Hukuang Railway, since it would be a trunk line binding the sections and would aid China to mobilize her resources for war.[44] The stress on China's participation in the war resulted from the Siberian situation currently provoking Allied schemes for intervention which the United States was resisting. China wished to participate in the venture, although under the September, 1918 treaties she had placed her armed forces at the disposal of Japan against any Russo-German troops operating in Siberia.[45]

On October 8, 1918, Lansing reported to the Allied ambassadors in Washington that thirty-one banks from all sections of the country had joined the American group. These banks agreed that members of the group should subscribe to the policy, that all preferences and options for loans held by any member should be shared by the whole American Group, and that all future loans in China having any governmental guarantee should be conducted as a common undertaking. The administration felt the best interests of China would be served if this same policy were adopted in each of national groups and then carried over to the International Consortium.[46]

So much confusion had resulted from the American invitation that the Secretary enclosed a clarifying memorandum on the plan. First, the United States did not intend to rejoin the old Consortium but to create a new organization so broad as to include the old group banks. It proposed dealing with no specific loan, but desired to create an organization that could deal with all types of Chinese loans. The American group was willing to share with Japan in carrying the Entente bankers for the present in the currency reform loan. Secondly, while it did not propose making relinquishment of the private options on Chinese loans a qualification for international membership, it felt that American banks should do so upon joining the group; and it "submitted that it is possible properly to conduct the business of the international group only by similar relinquishment to the respective national groups by the individual banks forming these groups, without distinction as to the nature of the options held." Thirdly, the United States proposed to include industrial and administrative loans under the new arrangement; because demarcation was difficult, and both should be removed from unsound speculation. Fourthly, the United States in objecting to loans impairing the political control or sovereign rights of China did not mean to call into question the propriety of any existing arrangements, but it referred solely to the future activities of the American group. Neither did it mean to imply that foreign control of the collection of revenues nor the appointment of advisers would be objectionable. Lastly, while the United States made no objection to the adherence of Belgian or Russian groups, it felt the present proposal should be addressed to those who could most actively be associated in the proposed loans to China.[47]

The climax of victory on the Western Front in the Autumn of 1918, the armistice of November 11, and the Paris Conference were not events to increase the priority for consideration of East Asian affairs, but the Consortium continued to be a matter of continuing concern to the four governments. Not only the thunderous tread of European events, but divergent views and interests also kept it from becoming a realized fact. For instance, the British bankers resented the encouragement for an increased number of participating banks, since it would reduce the share of each banking house in the loans. Already, under the old Consortium, the Hongkong and Shanghai Banking Corporation had its China loans reduced two-thirds of what they would have been under an independent arrangement. A compromise on admission of more bankers emerged, with the British group taking in some new members but fewer than the Foreign Office desired. Since the bankers agreed to seek government support only for those banks within the Consortium, official London wished to make the representation as broad as possible. The banks did not respond in sufficient numbers, and the British joined the French to seek exception to the "exclusive support" clause.[48]

These Paris meetings, at which Hugh D. Marshall represented the State Department and Thomas W. Lamont the American bankers, produced another controversy over the provision to require equality of participation in existing and future loans. This, it will be recalled, was the central part of the Wilson administration plan to free China from Japanese financial domination. While the Japanese bankers agreed, their government would not consent to include the rights and options of Japan in Manchuria and Mongolia within the arrangement for Consortium business.[49]

Long confessed that the Japanese objection came as no surprise. Lamont protested to the Japanese bankers that these regions were important parts of China and could not be excluded, so he referred the matter to the State Department. This raised the point whether or not China's seeming surrender, through the 1915 and 1918 treaties, of political supremacy in these regions should be recognized. The Department, consistently opposed to such recognition, took the position that it could not agree to the Japanese reservations, since they would limit the effectiveness of the Consortium to serve China. The Diplomatic Advisory Council, meanwhile, met in Tokyo and approved the decision of the Cabinet to participate in the New Consortium under the condition of excluding Manchurian and Mongolian loans. Thus the government flatly opposed the agreement of the Japanese bankers. "These matters were brought to the attention of Mr. Wilson and he suggested the possibility of proceeding with a 'Three Power Group,' composed of the United States, England, and France to the exclusion of Japan and as an incitement to the Japanese bankers to exert their influence in opposition to their colleagues of the military party."[50] Already at Paris, during the Shantung Settlement, the President had confessed that he had lost his trust in Japan.[51] This threat of forming a Consortium without her was the strongest diplomatic device America possessed to gain Japanese agreement, and Wilson used it for all it was worth.

The State Department undertook to carry out the President's suggestions, understanding that the threat was a diplomatic gesture only to be implemented as a last resort, since it was well known that financial circles would not welcome competing with Japan for financing China. Discussions were held with England, France, and China concerning a smaller consortium, with the expectation that Japan would hear of the talks; but the Department "sincerely thought the best interests of all would be served by cooperation with all the powers, including particularly Japan." Negotiations took place between Tokyo and Washington, with the latter urging that the sharing of loans apply only to projects in which no considerable progress had been made.[52]

Early in February, 1920, Thomas Lamont, as a representative of the American group, left for Tokyo to confer with the Japanese bankers.[53] The State Department gave him all but the most private of information in their files on Eastern Asia matters and facilitated his trip in every way possible.[54] American policy averred that in case Japan remained reluctant to join the Consortium, the United States would "revert to the old form of national and individual action in spite of all its disadvantages of competition and conflict, giving our support to every proper financial concern in the United States which should wish to do business on an independent basis with China."[55]

Japan now urged the exception of South Manchuria and Eastern Inner Mongolia from the Consortium terms on the grounds that these regions were vital to her economy and national defense. Tokyo submitted a formula which permitted her to undertake such arrangements and investments in the disputed region as would guarantee Japanese security and exclude from Consortium business certain railway rights in the region.[56] The United States and Britain viewed these exclusions as "superfluous and potentially dangerous."[57] When it appeared that the other groups would not submit to its views, the Japanese introduced additional reservations to the operation of the Consortium[58] whereupon Lamont, Morris, and the British Ambassador in Tokyo concluded that if suitable arrangements could not be made the formation of the three power consortium should be undertaken.[59]

Lamont and Morris recognized that some consideration should be given Japan's interest in safeguarding her lines of communication to raw materials and foodstuffs on the Asian continent, but it was difficult to determine the extent of such a concession. Meanwhile, the Japanese bankers seemed ready to join the international group, but there was "a feeling of suspicion and distrust among strong elements in the Government," and public sentiment was also strongly set against the proposals.[60]

The American group now decided that it was not feasible to grant Lamont the alternative of presenting Japan with either accepting the current proposals or facing the Wilson alternative of a three power consortium in which she would be excluded.[61] This limited Lamont's ability to deal with Japan, and he was forced to agree to her conditions excepting the railroads together with the multiple rights of exploitation in the disputed regions. Both the British and American governments protested the arrangement without beneficial result.[62]

Breckenridge Long explained to the Japanese Ambassador that the railroad reservations had no place in an agreement "which attempted to lay down general principles of cooperation."[63] If Japan failed to approve any individual loan in relation to the disputed region, the other bankers would find it impossible to sell the bonds. This adequately protected them in all enterprises. Long urged that Japan view the Consortium as a cooperative rather than a competitive enterprise.[64]

Lamont concluded his negotiations with the Japanese bankers on May 11, 1920,[65] and Japan entered the Consortium on the same basis as the other governments, except for the desired railroad reservations.[66] Thus the questionable Japanese economic monopoly of Northeastern Asia acquired under the 1915 and

1918 treaties, the war time loans, and secret-dealings were believed to be nullified by transfer to the control of the international group. On October 15 the final signatures were obtained and the Consortium was officially a fact.[67] Rejoicing was premature, however, for only the underlying principles and policies were agreed; the practical details of its operations were to be equally difficult in negotiation.

Breckenridge Long confessed that the Wilson administration did not intend to deprive Japan "of the dominating position she naturally enjoys in regard to the Far Eastern matters. That position is due to her geographical location, to the stamina of her race and to the strong government which has been developed there." The Consortium, however, was an attempt to divest her of the political control over China gained through investment in industrial enterprise and the use of monetary corruption. Long felt the cooperation manifested by the powers during the negotiations pointed to the future abandonment of the spheres of influence in China, except in those areas reserved as necessary to Japan's defense. If such were the case (which it was not), the Third Assistant Secretary thought the open door had been realized through the Consortium negotiations under Woodrow Wilson.[68]

The New Consortium was hailed by the administration as supplying the death blow to Japanese hegemony in China; but while it did stop the indiscriminate lending to irresponsible military adventurers, it made no loans and was to that extent a negative factor in America's East Asian accomplishments.[69] Insofar as disagreements among the powers prevented China from securing financial aid from the Consortium, it worked to throw the post-war Republic into seeking aid of the Soviet government, and thus encouraging Communist opportunity in China.

The New Consortium grew out of culminating circumstances, the war in Europe, American fear of the increased domination of Japan over China's finances and national life, the desperate state of Chinese finances, and the request of Peking for additional loans to further her war effort; but chiefly it was a device to implement the Wilson's East Asian policy.

indeed in a "high-handed manner" against the Chinese in Shantung:

> They widened the scope of their operations without apparent military necessity until they were in control of practically the whole Province, and then proceeded, under the screen of military occupation to dig themselves in; both commercially and otherwise with apparent confidence in the permanent control of the principal resources and transportation facilities. Complaints have been made of trade discriminations, in practice, and of injustice done to individual Chinese in matters of property rights. Brigandage has been prevalent in the Province and while it might be difficult to prove that the cases of brigandage were instigated and led by Japanese, as believed by Mr. Scott, it is stated that the Japanese have done little to discourage these outrages and have interfered with Chinese troops attempting to do so. Questionable practices, such as dealing in opium, establishing brothels, export of copper cash, forced sales of property, and maltreatment of Chinese are reported not uncommon.[76]

Reinsch, also sought out for comment on the Scott letter, affirmed that the Japanese abuses were "unfortunately borne out by every report received. . . ."[77]

Wilson's suggestion to President Hsu encouraging Chinese unity was followed two weeks later by a Japanese proposal that the Allied governments and the United States make a "joint representation" to the North and South factions in China to compose their differences.[78] Although somewhat skeptical, Miller favored the proposal, meanwhile confessing, "I have been looking for the 'joker' but do not find it." Trusting Reinsch's approval of the step, he thought the Department might act as Japan proposed.[79]

Lansing admitted to the President "I can see no harm in this action at the present time, and it undoubtedly offers the possibility of impressing the antagonistic elements in China with the idea that neither can gain independent support from this or that Power."[80] Wilson then, in an interview with the Japanese Ambassador, agreed as to the form of the proposal for unity in China and sent the Ambassador to Lansing.[81] With Wilson's approval, the United States joined, on December 2, 1918, in the Allied representations to China asking that the various factions compose their differences. The European war was now over. Already a truce between the two factions in China had been declared in November, and delegates were appointed to the internal peace conference to meet in Shanghai in February, 1919.[82]

Among the first acts of conciliation between North and South China was the appointment of C. T. Wang and C. C. Wu, both of Southern sympathies, as Paris delegates on the Chinese Peace Commission.[83] But any realization of unification seemed hopeless. The Canton, or Kuomintang Party, was under the influence of its military tuchuns as much as the Anfu, or Peking faction. However, the Anfu leaders were more closely connected with the Japanese, although public opinion curtailed the open manifestation of their outright cooperation. "The native press and the student class, buoyed up by the hope that President Wilson and Wilsonian idealism would enable the Chinese nation to escape paying for the misdeeds of the corrupt rulers who had claimed to represent China from 1914 to 1919, vociferously demanded that Japan be defied at the Paris Peace Conference."[84] This was then the policy of China at Paris, while in Shanghai discussions took place on internal differences. Unfortunately, China was to fail in both conferences.

In Japan, the war years brought great changes. New industries and commercial developments spotted the face of the country as a result of the war activities, for until the downfall of Russia, Japan was her chief source of outside supplies, and sales abroad brought a new class of industrialists into being. The new business magnates resented their exclusion from governmental influence and attempted to gain a place for themselves, thereby upsetting the old political alignments and introducing new forces into Japanese politics. At the same time, there was a blossoming forth of the labor movement; and Japan experienced her first big strikes.[85] The students and intellectuals opposed the militarists. Count Terauchi, the Premier, while immune from party affiliation, was a protege of Yamagata and inclined to the Seiyukai. He was opposed by the press and suspect of foreigners because of his rank as a field marshal. The prosaic advance of the cost of living, however, caused his downfall.[86]

In the Autumn of 1918, rice riots followed by mine and industrial strikes broke out in many of the larger cities. Ambassador Morris viewed them as significant:

> . . . because they revealed extended popular unrest due, in my judgment, more to resentment against the unequal distribution of recently acquired wealth and vulgar display by the newly rich than the rising price list. The action of the Government in suppressing all newspaper reports of the riots only served to increase excitement and to give credence to [the] wildest rumors. In spite of this blunder riots have entirely ceased but the present ministry has lost the confidence of all classes and a change in the near future appears inevitable.[87]

He thought the people uneasy, but there were no signs of social revolution. "Politically, too, the riots have given a stimulus to the advocacy of liberalism and freedom of speech, while the extension of the franchise is being extensively discussed."[88]

The Terauchi ministry gave way in September, 1918 to that of Takashi Hara, the leader of the Seiyukai. Hara was a controversial figure, stubborn and obstinate, a demagogue of good intent who had fought his way up through the party to become the first commoner ever to head a Japanese ministry.[89] It was his government which assumed responsibility for the Paris negotiations seeking recognition of Japan's privileged position in Asia, an objective favored by all factions despite party lines. With Siberia, China, the Consortium, and the peace conditions as breeding ground for difference, Japanese-American relations deteriorated to a new low.[90]

In 1914, Japan had been laboring under the enormous burden of debt, which had been increased four-fold by the Russo-Japanese War, and an adverse balance of trade, increased in 1914 by the war readjustments. But with the removal of European competition during the war years, she increased her markets and expanded her industries. Exports to the United States alone increased from 180 to 530 million yen between 1913 and 1918, and she doubled her merchant marine in addition to supplying vessels for sale to other nations. Only in 1916, with Germany's peace offer, and in 1918, with war's end, were there interruptions in her prosperity; but with the advent of the period of readjustment in 1920, a serious business depression set in and was not abated until two years later.[91]

While the domestic political situation and the unparalleled opportunity of the European war freeing her hand in China explain much of Japanese foreign policy during these years,[92] the irresponsible chauvinism of the press greatly abetted popular support for its implementation. Sales rather than advertising supported the newspapers, and the journalism of the day played up the popular and sensational. In both Japan and the United States little was published concerning a serious attempt to appreciate the diversities of views on any of their conflicts. Cable charges ran nearly one dollar a word, hence only the most sensational items appeared in the press of either country. In addition, German propaganda stories given the Japanese news agencies helped to embitter public opinion against the United States.[93]

Walter S. Rogers, one of Charles Crane's business agents, went to the Far East in 1917 to acquaint himself with the methods of the Oriental press. He found that the American story was not being presented, although the German, Japanese, and British had their news services established in China. Rogers returned to America and sought out Colonel House who sent him on to the State Department. Finally, with George Creel, he saw the President. The interview was not entirely satisfactory, since the conversation went off into details that Rogers thought should have been left for experts, and Wilson seemed tired.[94]

Roger's story of the need for communications in the Far East did impress the Chief Executive, however; and on October 9, 1917, he wrote Lansing suggesting that it was an opportune time to negotiate with the Japanese for improving existing radio and cable communication in the Pacific, which entailed expansion of the communication facilities and the establishment of reasonable rates. Wilson pointed to Japan's control of her own domestic internal telegraph and wireless stations and of her ownership of a vital leg of the trans-Pacific cable as realities in the picture, and he asked Lansing to consult with Rogers and the Japanese Ambassador on what might be done.[95] This, as shall be shown, was only the initiation of the administration's attempt to bring international regulation into the field of world communications.

George Creel's War Information Service, in an attempt to put the American war effort before the world, later established a branch office in San Francisco, which prepared a daily news service to China, Japan, the Philippines, and Hawaii. The naval wireless flashed news from San Diego to Pearl Harbor, and from there it was radioed to the Philippines. From Manila the news went to Tokyo and Shanghai by cable. In China, Carl Crow sent it to a chain of newspapers while in Japan two news services, the *Kokusai* and *Nippon Dempo*, took care of its distribution. Later, as Siberia developed into a region of American activity, Crow relayed the news from Shanghai to Vladivostok. Films were also sent to the Far East by the Creel agency.[96]

Despite these arrangements, anti-Americanism in the Japanese press was at no time more rampant than during the immediate post war period, when the outstanding differences over Shantung, Siberia, and the New Consortium embittered relations.[97] The occasion for unleashing the full attack, however, occurred with the declaration of independence on the part of the Korean nationalists in Seoul on March 1, 1919.[98] Japan had absorbed the Hermit Kingdom in 1912, and had learned to supress nationalist pretensions with a heavy hand. Numerous arrests were made, to which the natives retaliated with a nationwide strike. This occurred at the time Japan was attempting a settlement of the Shantung issue at Paris, and it was thus highly embarrassing to Tokyo. The Koreans, believing the Hara government liberal in a Western sense, appealed for relief from the heavy hand of suppression, only to find itself disappointed. Meanwhile the Japanese press saw American inspiration in the revolt.[99]

It is true that Wilson's words concerning national self-determination of peoples had been spread by the Y.M.C.A.

agencies and through the American missionaries,[100] numbering some 3,800 in Korea. The revolt centered around the cities with mission centers and was led by native Christians. It was well known that the missionaries were very close to the Korean people, that perhaps ninety per cent of them "while recognizing the material benefits of Japanese rule are at heart antagonistic to the Japanese method of military government in Korea."[101] This, of course, furnished fuel for the anti-American press campaign.

The American Consul in Seoul, Leo Bergholtz, had earlier warned the missionaries to refrain from political opinion, advice, or action during the uprising.[102] Some arrests of missionaries were made after the revolt, but Ambassador Morris in Tokyo thought that they had not "directly inspired or supported the present movement of passive resistance to Japanese authority."[103]

The United States was most anxious to abstain from any action which would encourage Korean nationalism. When the Korean National Association of San Francisco had appealed to Wilson for his good offices in securing self government for the Korean people at the peace conference, the Chief Executive had made no reply.[104] In February, 1919, when Syngman Rhee, propagandist for Korean nationalism and a Princeton graduate, sought a passport from the State Department to represent Korea at the Conference, it was denied.[105] Two delegations did arrive in Paris representing the Korean people, but they were given no encouragement.[106] The United States made no acknowledgement of the insurgent declaration of a Republic of Korea,[107] and instructed the Consul at Seoul to refrain from doing "anything which may cause the Japanese authorities to suspect [the] American Government sympathizes with the Korean nationalist movement."[108]

By the end of April, 1919, the revolt had been ruthlessly suppressed, and thousands of Koreans fled across the border into Manchuria and Siberia to await their future rendezvous with history.[109] A junta was organized in China to work for Korean independence, and Syngman Rhee continued his propaganda activities in behalf of Korean nationalism in the United States.[110] Meanwhile, the Japanese head of the Department of Domestic

Affairs in Korea circulated a statement that President Wilson was to blame for the uprising. He explained that when the Koreans had requested the President to sponsor Korean independence at the Paris Conference, Wilson had replied that there was little opportunity for a hearing on the subject as long as things were quiet in Korea.[111] The revolt had been the answer. Of course, such rationalizations of causation may appear foolish in the light of the present, but of such insidious innunendoes are suspicions fed and misunderstandings engendered. Throughout the Wilson years, there was no famine of such statements encouraging bad relations in either the United States or Japan.

CHAPTER EIGHT

The Siberian Fracas

WRONGS MUST FIRST BE RIGHTED, AND THEN ADEQUATE
SAFEGUARDS MUST BE CREATED TO PREVENT THEIR BEING
COMMITTED AGAIN. WE OUGHT NOT TO CONSIDER REMEDIES
MERELY BECAUSE THEY HAVE A PLEASANT AND SONOROUS
SOUND. PRACTICAL QUESTIONS CAN BE SETTLED ONLY BY
PRACTICAL MEANS. PHRASES WILL NOT ACCOMPLISH THE
RESULT. EFFECTIVE READJUSTMENTS WILL; AND WHATEVER
READJUSTMENTS ARE NECESSARY MUST BE MADE.
　　　　—Wilson's Address to the Russian People.

In March, 1917, the Russian revolution threw over the rule
of the Czar for a moderate liberal government first under Prince
George Lvov and then under Alexander Kerensky. It was
hailed throughout more liberal circles of the democratic world
as a forward step in the direction of self government for the
Russian people. Woodrow Wilson was especially pleased. Ever
since his teaching days, Russia and czardom had been his
classic example of autocracy and backward government.[1] The
United States was the first nation to recognize the new government.[2] America had already broken with Germany. It was
easier to fight alongside a democratic rather than an autocratic
Russia. In his war message to Congress, the President found
the revolution "heartening,"[3] and expressed himself privately
as having "the greatest sympathy" with what had occurred
there.[4]

David R. Francis, a former Governor of Missouri, a banker
nearing seventy, a colorful figure well known for his ability at
poker and sure-aim at his brass cuspidor which always accompanied him, was the American Ambassador in Petrograd.[5]

Francis had been joined by a number of American aid groups such as the railroad mission under John F. Stevens which was sent by Wilson to assist the provisional government in rehabilitating the Russian transportation system,[6] the Elihu Root diplomatic mission to bolster resistance to the German enemy,[7] the American Red Cross mission to relieve distress among the Russian people, the Young Men's Christian Association to help the Russian soldiers, and the Committee of Public Information to tell the story of America's war aims to the revolution-torn country. By these means Wilson sought to place the United States in a position of disinterested service to Russia, and to prevent any outside interference in her internal political affairs.[8]

With the coming of the Bolshevik revolution, on November 7, 1917, a new element was added to the Russian situation. In Wilson's view this was social revolution and a departure from the Western liberal tradition. The President would have nothing to do with the new regime which aroused antipathies and divided world opinion. There was a widespread belief that the Bolshevik leaders were in the control of the German militarists.[9] When the Bolsheviks took overt measures to withdraw Russia from the war, grave concern was manifest over the possibility of German legions being transferred to the Western Front, where the Allies were already war-weary and committed to their fullest strength. In Britain and France discussions took place within government circles on how the Eastern Front could be maintained. In addition, the Bolshevik disavowal of all Czarist financial obligations struck deep in Allied financial circles, especially in France. A welter of forces, both public and private, in which the ideological always appeared, were thus unleashed, resulting in foreign opposition to the new Bolshevik government.

There had been talk of using Japanese troops on the Russian front at the beginning of the war, but nothing came of the suggestion. With the March revolution of 1917, the proposal was revived as a means of bolstering the demoralized Russian armies. At the same time, there were moves among the Allies to request Japanese troops for use in France. To all these suggestions Wilson was unfriendly,[10] although Colonel House in midsummer of 1917, suggested that American troops be sent to Russia to assist on the Eastern front.[11] Similar proposals were widely discussed in official circles; but the President thought, "There are very many reasons why it would be unwise even if it were practicable."[12]

By August, 1917 Colonel House thought the welding of Russia "into a virile republic" was more important to the world than beating Germany "to her knees." He shared the somewhat general apprehension that continued disorder under the provisional government would lead the more stable elements of Russian society to welcome German intervention.[13] The President and House agreed that a powerful Germany on the border of a weakened Russia boded ill for the future of Europe.[14]

From that day in April when the United States entered the war against Germany, the President fully committed his energies to victory over German militarism. No policies were to be undertaken to weaken the American contribution to the Western front. His East Asian policy was directly influenced by this resolve, and it was to show itself most clearly in his resistance to Siberian intervention.

During December, 1917, Bolshevik elements in the zone of the Chinese Eastern Railroad, where Russia since 1896 had exercised a "crown-colony sovereignty," attempted to secure control of the road from its manager, General Dimitri L. Horvat. Thereupon the Allied ministers in Peking, Reinsch abstaining, requested Chinese intervention to prevent the Communist seizure of the road, and Chinese troops proceeded to disarm and deport the Bolshevik troops in the area.[15]

Horvat, encouraged by various anti-Communist elements, then undertook organization of a resistance movement to the Bolsheviks. Refusing the Japanese offer of support in exchange for certain concessions,[16] he secured the promise of aid from the European Allied diplomats in Peking. The Cossack Captain, Gregory Semenov, heading one of Horvat's detachments, secured French, British, and especially Japanese backing, to establish a base astride the Trans-Siberian Railroad in Trans-Baikal, where independent of Horvat he carried on a campaign of attrition and butchery beyond description.[17] Other war lords sprang up in Eastern Siberia subsequently to fade away. Only in Admiral Alexander Kolchak, who with British backing was set up as head of a government at Omsk in November, 1918, and remained a power until January, 1920, was there real Siberian resistance to Bolshevism.[18]

The penetration of the Germans into Southern Russia and the Semenov defeat and retreat into Manchuria spread the alarm that the Sino-Siberian border might become an active war theatre. This state of affairs initiated a series of military and naval agreements between Japan and China during March and May, 1918, under which the Japanese came to control the Chinese forces operating in Siberia, and to occupy the Chinese Eastern Railway zone. This served to intensify American suspicion of Japan's ambitions on the Asian continent.[19]

With Soviet approval, allied intervention first came at Murmansk in April, 1918 as an effort to resist the German threat in the region. On June, 1, the Supreme War Council in Paris decided to reenforce their forces there, and Wilson assented to American participation. General Bliss conferred with Foch on the matter and recommended to Washington the use of three battalions of troops for the venture. Wilson approved the policy on July 6, and the venture got underway without delay. These troops were placed under the British, who also transported and provisioned them.[20] The movement became in a short time anti-Bolshevik in nature; and American troops, some 4,500 in number, were used actively against the Reds in the area. While this intervention occurred simultaneously with the Siberian venture, its motives were more European and were of passing concern to East Asian affairs.

The Bolshevik armistice of December, 1917 aroused France and Britain to propose Japanese intervention as a means of protecting allied interests there. The Russian Ambassador, Boris Bakhmeteff, representing the American-recognized, defunct provisional government, first voiced the proposal to Lansing who considered such a course "unwise." The proposal was supported by the British Ambassador, but his Japanese colleague agreed with Lansing's opposition to intervention.[21]

British Ambassador Spring-Rice followed the rebuff of his proposal with a memorandum for President Wilson concerning an interview with Japanese Ambassador Sato concerning Siberia. Sato declared the situation was no threat to Japan unless Germany succeeded in dominating Russia. Meanwhile, his government would act as the developing situation demanded. Sato confessed to Japanese suspicion of the Allied interests, especially of the United States, in Eastern Asia, and thought it necessary that Japan be reassured against sole American intervention in Siberia should Germany gain control there. He stated that his country had certain geographic advantages in the Far East of which she proposed to take full advantage and would resent any interference. Japan was willing to accept the position as "outpost of the free nations of the Western Pacific," he somewhat ambiguously admitted, "but the free nations should accept the comradeship of Japan on a basis of mutual respect, mutual confidence and entire and perfect equality."[22]

The Bolsheviks signed an armistice with Germany in December, and the Eastern Front ceased to exist.[23] Meanwhile, in Britain the War Cabinet discussed the possible Bolshevik seizure of the reportedly 648,000 tons of military stores at Vladivostok. It was feared these supplies would find their way into German hands. The War Cabinet decided that an Allied protective force, mainly consisting of Japanese troops, should be landed there. Sir Robert Cecil, Balfour's assistant in the Foreign Office, proposed the intervention to the Japanese Ambassador, who expressed the hope that the local Siberian government would be able to protect the stores.[24] John K. Caldwell, the American Consul in Vladivostok, reported that fighting was certain between the local factions there unless a show of force was made by the West. The Japanese Consul was asking for ships to protect national interests, and Caldwell recommended that this naval force be joined by one or more ships from the other Allies. The U.S.S. Brooklyn was immediately ordered to the scene.[25]

Realizing the diversity of propaganda and misinformation in the revolution torn country, George Creel advised the President of the need for a brief statement of America's war aims to bolster belief in the Allied cause within Russia. This was one of the reasons for the short form of the Fourteen Points, which Wilson gave to the world on January 8, 1918.[26] In the sixth of these points, the President called for the evacuation of Russian territory and cooperation of the powers to obtain for her "an unhampered and unembarrassed opportunity for the independent determination of her own political development and national policy. . . ." He proclaimed, "The treatment accorded Russia by her sister nations in the months to come will be the acid test of their good will, of their comprehension of her needs as distinguished from their own interests, and of their intelligent and unselfish sympathy."[27] He later confessed, ". . . you may be sure that I wrote the passages about Russia in my recent address to Congress from my heart. I wish most earnestly that it were possible to find some way to help, but as soon as we have thought out a working plan there is a new dissolution of the few crystals that had formed there."[28]

The day following Wilson's address, the Chinese Minister called on Counselor Polk and said he thought Japan would welcome the opportunity to land troops in Siberia. When the Russian Ambassador inquired of the Counselor as to American action if Japan, threatened by German control in Siberia, sent troops there, Polk replied that the United States had ships in Japan that would go to Vladivostok to protect American life and property. At this point, the State Department also was anxious that the Russian people should not feel abandoned; supplies continued to be shipped to them, but munitions were stopped.[29]

As an answer to the diplomatic feelers favoring Japanese intervention in Siberia, Ambassador Morris was instructed to call at the Japanese Foreign Office to make clear the President's views of sympathy for the Russian people in their current troubles. He expressed American rejection of the proposal to occupy Vladivostok, and to send a military mission on the grounds that it would be considered hostile by the Russian people and would encourage German propaganda efforts against the Allies.[30]

Britain now frankly informed Wilson that she was urging her allies to ask Japan to act as their mandatory in occupying the Siberian railroad. Foreign Minister Balfour explained that this move was not prompted by anti-Bolshevik motives, but that Britain did not consider the Bolsheviks any more representative of the Russian people than the autonomous bodies in South East Russia which she sought to assist. While it might prove difficult to dislodge Japan from the maritime provinces of Siberia once in occupation, the situation made Japanese intervention inevitable. He thought: "The very fact that Japan will be obliged to come out in the open against Germany and that the respective interests of both countries will come into open conflict, will almost certainly do much to lessen Japanese pressure in other directions." The War Cabinet considered the suggestion requesting Japanese action of urgent military importance.[31]

Colonel House believed "it would be a great political mistake to send Japanese troops into Siberia." There was no military advantage to be gained, and it might arouse the Slavs throughout Europe against the Allied cause.[32] As the situation in Siberia and European Russia changed according to the Peking, Tokyo, and Stockholm cables, his listening posts on the Russian situation, Wilson felt "that information and advice are futile until there is something definite to plan with as well as for."[33] He did not know when he had "ever had a more tiresome struggle with quicksand than . . . in trying to do the right thing in respect of our dealings with Russia."[34]

Information of Japan's willingness to undertake the independent occupation of Vladivostok and the operation of the Chinese Eastern and Amur railways came from Ambassador Morris.[35] On February 8, 1918, he reported serious discussion in Tokyo concerning immediate intervention. The Japanese Foreign Minister, Viscount Motono, doubted the wisdom of leaving the moderate Russian element without support, or failing to evolve some plan to prevent the spread of German influence in Siberia. He proposed the occupation of the Trans-Siberian up to its junction with the Amur railway.[36]

A week later, President Wilson saw Wiseman and suggested that Japan could not consider intervention since such a program might throw the Russian moderates into the arms of Germany. He opposed Japanese intervention either with or without allies. It was clear to Sir William that if Japan landed troops at Vladivostok, she would do so on her own initiative and not by invitation as far as the President was concerned.[37]

But the British were not to be deterred; they now brought the proposal for Japanese occupation of the Trans-Siberian from Vladivostok to Cheliabinsk before the Supreme War Council in Paris. Although Japan would be asked to give guarantees as to the scope and intention of her intervention General Tasker H. Bliss, the American member, opposed the proposal. The British and French represented that it was the only way to consolidate the strong pro-Allied sentiment in Russia. Bliss said that preventing the stores at Vladivostok from being captured by the Bolsheviks and "sold" to Germany would be the lone military advantage as he saw it. The British argued that occupation of the railroad was the last chance to save Russia for the Allied cause and to prevent collapse of the Eastern Front with the consequent shift of enemy troops to the West.[38] Japan Britain posed, was ready for the expedition and could seize the Siberian maritime provinces at will if she so wished, although American armament was now somewhat of a deterrent to such freedom of action. The British also suggested the possibility of a Japanese-German domination of the world should Russia fall to Germany and the latter come to an agreement with Japan. Bliss, however, continued to oppose any intervention as a danger to the Allied position in Russia.[39] The decisions of the Supreme War Council required unanimity. Bliss did not feel he could bear the responsibility of opposing the otherwise unanimous decision of the Allies for intervention, so he referred the matter to Washington.[40]

The Allies now considered the decision on Siberian intervention up to Wilson. The British doubted if Japan, irritated at the suspicion of her motives, would now accept a policy of joint intervention, and she proposed that the United States join the Allies in requesting Japanese occupation of the Trans-

Siberian Railway as far as Chilianbinsk or perhaps Omsk. The occupation was to be accompanied by a declaration of its temporary nature. That same afternoon, February 26, 1918, Balfour again cabled that he had learned that enemy prisoners in Siberia were organizing for cutting the railroad, thus making intervention of extreme urgency.[41] London also relayed a cable from the French Ambassador at Tokyo in which Foreign Minister Motono stated his willingness to promise Japan's disinterestedness in Siberia "and even to say so publicly. He also declared that he was ready to pledge his country to act so far as the Ural Mountains."[42] Lansing, fearing the arming of the prisoners and believing that the Japanese assurances changed the situation, urged reconsideration of the British proposal.[43]

On March 1, Lansing and Wilson agreed on the policy to be pursued. The Secretary then conferred with the British Ambassador and informed him that while the United States Government could not join in the request to Japan, it would doubtless raise no objection. At noon, the President handed Lansing a draft telegram of the American position, which stated that while the United States desired to cooperate with the Allies, it desired whenever possible to "leave itself diplomatically free." For this reason it had "not thought it wise" to join in the Allied request for Japan to act in Siberia. The United States declared:

It has no objection to the request being made, and it wishes to assure the Japanese government that it has entire confidence that in putting an armed force into Siberia it is doing so as an ally of Russia, with no purpose but to save Siberia from the invasion of the armies and the intrigues of Germany and with entire willingness to leave the determination of all questions that may affect the permanent fortunes of Siberia to the Council of Peace.[44]

Lansing showed the draft telegram of America's consent to the British,[45] French, and Italian ambassadors.

That afternoon, Counselor Polk talked over the American attitude with the French and later the Russian ambassadors. The latter now protested Japanese intervention, saying it would have a fatal effect on the Russian people.[46] The following day, Bakhmeteff repeated the warning to House who did not disagree.[47] That same day, March 2, the Colonel had Polk[48] send the President a memorandum prepared by William C. Bullitt, a young man of subsequent fame in the Division of European Affairs, charging that the United States had assented "tacitly to Japan's invasion of Siberia . . . because we fear that if we oppose Japan, she will switch to the side of Germany. We believe that Japan will take this step because of her desire to annex eastern Siberia, which she covets so intensely that if she can not obtain it with the consent of the Allies she will take it with the assistance of Germany." Bullitt proposed that the President refuse to make the request. He believed, "If Japan should throw herself into Germany's arms, then a line of autocratic and democratic powers would be formed, and the war would really be one for democracy." He concluded dramatically: "We cannot wash our hands on the matter. Unless we oppose, we assent. Pontius Pilate washed his hands. The World has never forgiven him."[49]

Colonel House was now convinced that the decision for tacit consent to Japanese intervention had been a mistake, and for this reason he undertook to change Wilson's decision. He informed the President that Senator Root, who had headed the Russian Mission, agreed "with you and me as to the danger of the proposed Japanese intervention in Siberia." Root believed the Japanese action would throw Russia into the arms of Germany. House warned, "We are treading upon exceedingly delicate and dangerous ground, and are likely to lose that fine moral position you have given the Entente cause." The Colonel could understand the Allied insistence for Japanese intervention only in the light of the intense hatred of the French for the Russians and of the English for Germany.[50] He gave his son-in-law, Gordon Auchincloss, Assistant Counselor of the State Department, a memorandum to telephone the President. It contained information similar to the letter and advised Wilson to call the Allied ambassadors together, point out where intervention might lead, and suggest that Japan, at the time consent was granted, should make a statement as to her objectives in Siberia.[51] These communications were but an extension of the House-Wilson talks of the previous week on Siberian intervention.[52]

The total effect of these representations[53] seemed to bolster Wilson's distrust of Japanese intervention. Although the French and British Ambassadors had seen his own typed draft consenting to intervention, and the press was frankly discussing the expected action,[54] Wilson called in Polk and told him to hold up the consent cable to Japan. The following day, on March 5, he handed a revised position on intervention to the Counselor[55] for the Japanese Ambassador.

The new Wilson message was an about face of the consent policy. It deemed Siberian intervention unwise, as it might play into the hands of Germany and "of the enemies of the Russian revolution, for which the Government of the United States entertains the greatest sympathy, in spite of all the unhappiness and misfortune which has for the time being sprung out of it."[56] On March 3, 1918, Russia had signed the Treaty of Brest-Litovsk and was technically out of the war; this no doubt influenced the statement of friendship for the revolution made in the message.[57] Commenting later in his diary on Wilson's changed position on intervention, House wrote: "Neither of us, I think, was altogether fit last week to solve the problems which confronted us. There was never a more critical week in our history, and the fact that it found us both at rather low ebb was unfortunate to say the least."[58]

When the Japanese Foreign Office was informed of America's refusal to consent on intervention, Motono told the British that the attitude of the United States made it impossible to obtain steel, or financial and material backing, and it would be difficult for Japan to act. He suggested that the whole matter be delayed.[59] Balfour, on learning of Wilson's reconsidered action professed fear of its effect upon Japanese opinion, especially among the pro-German party.[60]

At this time, Polk informed Wilson that Lansing had been working on an accounting of the war materials at Vladivostok, practically all of which had been purchased by the Russians on British credits. He recalled that the President had made funds available to the American military attaché in Petrograd for safeguarding and purchasing the supplies. The French and British had done likewise, but it was difficult to prove title to much of the goods. Admiral Knight, Commander of the Pacific fleet, had reached Vladivostok on March 1 and would shortly report on conditions there.[61]

A week later came the curious request of Commissar Leon Trotsky asking American aid against what he deemed was a German-Japanese plot to seize Vladivostok and the railroad. Trotsky suggested that the recent treaty with Germany did not mean Russia was absolutely out of the war; he thought hostilities would be resumed.[62] House suggested that Wilson use the opportunity to send a message to the Congress of the Soviets, meeting on March 12, "to clear up the Far Eastern situation but without mentioning it or Japan in any way."[63] Wilson, accepting the suggestion, used the message to proclaim America's determination "to secure for Russia once more complete sovereignty and independence in her own affairs and restoration to her great role in the life of Europe and the modern world." He reiterated, "The whole heart of the people of the United States is with the people of Russia in the attempt to free themselves forever from autocratic government and become the masters of their own life."[64]

The Allies were not so easily daunted in their attempt to secure American consent to Siberian intervention, and at a meeting of the prime ministers and their foreign secretaries held in London on March 15, Lord Balfour was officially deputed to lay the expedience of Allied intervention before Wilson once again.[65] In renewing his appeal to the President, Balfour stressed the weakness of Russia and the possible seizure of her food and stores by Germany, thus prolonging the war.[66] Once more the matter was brought before the Supreme War Council, which again recommended intervention. The French and Italian ambassadors supported the necessity of the policy in calls at the State Department. Polk warned the latter that the Japanese would need money and supplies for the intervention, and America could not possibly furnish either without diversion from her obligations to the Western Front.[67]

Under date of March 18, Lansing confided to his diary his views on the Siberian intervention, with which, he stated, Wilson agreed. The situation had both moral and military aspects. Reliable opinion said any intervention would be received by disfavor and probably armed resistance, and there was no military advantage to be gained.[68] Meanwhile, Lord Reading talked the matter over with Wilson.[69] Vance McCormick, the close friend of the President, called on Polk and insisted some action be taken in Russia.[70] Lansing received a number of protests against intervention, mostly from Russian and Socialist groups, which he sent to the White House.[71] The same day the Secretary conferred with the President on Siberian matters and saw Secretary of the Navy Daniels to oppose Admiral Knight's suggestion for proclaiming an independent government in Siberia.[72]

Japan, on March 19, replied to the American refusal of consent to her Siberian intervention. The note stated that the government would refrain from any action until there was an understanding with the United States. It reassured that any Japanese action in Russia would "be wholly uninfluenced by any aggressive motives or tendencies. . . ."[73] Lansing's reply professed that the United States did not suspect Japanese motives, but it opposed intervention because of the bad effect on the Russian people. The proposal lacked sufficient military justification to compensate for the moral loss entailed.[74]

At this time, Wilson was convinced that Semenov was rapidly changing the situation in Siberia and asked Lansing to follow his activities to see "Whether there is any legitimate way in which we can assist." It was clear to General Peyton C. March, Chief of Staff who opposed Siberian intervention throughout[75] that "there is no sufficient military force, in Japan or elsewhere, to do anything effective in Siberia." As to the representations of the Allies for an expedition to Murmansk, also then being agitated, the President stated it was clear to the military that any such venture must be subtracted from the American contribution to the Western Front.[76]

After seeing the President on Siberia, Lansing confided to his diary of March 21 his alarm at the press reports of the arming of German and Austrian prisoners in Siberia by the Reds. If true, German domination of the railway and thus of the situation was a real threat. The report of 80,000 prisoners occupying Irkutsk he thought exaggerated, but if these prisoners were organized, it posed a German threat to China as well as Russia, which would force a change in American policy. Sending troops into Siberia as far west as Irkutsk seemed a necessity. A cooperative expedition, he believed, would best accomplish the purpose; and Japan could be brought to agree by giving her command of the forces. The Secretary thought the problem now changed from the effect of intervention on the Russian people to what must be done to obtain Japanese agreement for joint intervention.[77]

On March 21, 1918, some four thousand German cannon along the Western Front heralded the opening of the "Spring Drive." By nightfall the offensive had inundated the British front; within a week it had reached a depth of forty miles. Succeeding weeks of the Spring offensive saw the Allied cause reach its lowest ebb.[78] These events increased the demand for revival of the Eastern Front as a diversion to prevent the transfer of German troops from Russia.

Ambassador Jusserand warned Lansing concerning the arming of German and Austrian prisoners by the Reds in Siberia. Major Stephen Pichon, just returned from Siberia, reported that order there would be restored by Germany or the Allies.[79] Lansing instructed Morris in Tokyo to see Jan Masaryk concerning the possibility of organizing within Russia an effective resistance to the Central Powers.[80] By April 4, no confirmation of the arming of the prisoners of war having been received, Wilson wrote Lansing concerning the recent appeals, "I must say that none of these memoranda has anything in it that is at all persuasive with me. I hope that you feel the same way."[81] The Secretary reversed his position to agree with the President.[82]

On April 5, after three of her nationals were murdered in Vladivostok, the Japanese landed an armed force from the naval patrol.[83] That afternoon, the British also landed fifty sailors to protect the British consulate, but the Americans refused to take similar action.[84] The landings did not affect Washington policy, which continued to oppose intervention by the Japanese; although Third Assistant Secretary Breckenridge Long, Russian expert Basil Miles, and Far Eastern Chief Ransford S. Miller[85] now favored intervention contrary to the continued opposition of the Secretary and Wilson.[86]

The war persisted in going badly for the Allies, and by the last of April, Balfour renewed his campaign for intervention by informing the American government that the Germans were in the process of transferring forty divisions from the Eastern to the Western Front. If Russian food resources fell into German hands, the war would be indefinitely prolonged. The Foreign Secretary urged the United States to insist upon Russian consent to a joint American-Japanese intervention.[87] House thought the new proposal would meet with Wilson's approval since it was for a joint intervention undertaken with Russian consent.[88] Wilson suggested a conference on the matter between Reading, Ishii, Baker, and Lansing. The Secretary of State promised Reading to have a preliminary conversation with Ishii on the new proposal.[89]

The following Sunday, Ishii called at Lansing's home to discuss the matter of joint intervention.[90] Lansing reminded the Japanese Ambassador of the three previous German attempts to separate Japan from the Allied cause and expressed the thought that a fourth attempt would perhaps be made "on the basis of a division of Siberia between them." Ishii protested that Japan could not trust German offers. He affirmed Wilson's position that while there were rumors of German activity in Siberia, there was no evidence. Japan favored a waiting policy. As to Lansing's suggestion of joint intervention, the Ambassador replied that personally he would welcome it and thought his government would be of similar opinion. Japan could put 250,000 men into Siberia immediately. He thought they need not be sent west of Irkutsk. Lansing very carefully made it clear that America's interest in intervention was only to keep German troops from being transferred to the West.[91]

Minister Reinsch, in Peking, thought the Siberian situation favorable for joint action under American initiative. He suggested that a commission having financial support would be able to reconstruct Siberia as an Allied factor in the war. Wilson was interested, as always, in Reinsch's views and asked Lansing's comment.[92] The Secretary disagreed with the Minister, submitting as proof the recent Siberian report of Basil Miles, in charge of Russian Affairs.[93]

The Miles report stated that Semenov had 2,500 men, was able to maintain himself in the field even after defeat, and had seized the junction of the Amur and Trans-Siberian Railroad. The British, French, and Japanese were contributing to his support as the most stable government in Siberia. If Semenov were to be supported, Masaryk's Czech troops would be most useful. Reports stated that 6,000 of them were in Vladivostok, 40,000 preparing to go to Archangel, and 50,000 in the process of organization.[94]

The Foreign Office informed Wilson of a threatened break in Bolshevik-German relations. Bruce Lockhart, the British agent in Moscow, reported that Trotsky would welcome intervention, although for political reasons he could not extend an invitation for it.[95] With these views before him and the titanic struggle on the Western Front in mind, Wilson reconsidered intervention and consulted with Sir William Wiseman on Siberia.

Sir William said Japan sought to recreate an Eastern Front and help the Russian people. Wilson stated that his military advisers believed revival of an Eastern Front impossible. "He remarked that he would go as far as intervening against the wishes of the Russian people — knowing that it was eventually for their good — providing he thought the scheme had any practical chance of success." But nothing seemed practical; even Japan said she could not go beyond Omsk. "They were," he thought, "anxious enough to have an invitation from us so that they might occupy the maritime province, but [they] had no intention of engaging on a vast military enterprise sufficient to reach even the Ural Mountains." If Britain and the United States could put a force along the Trans-Siberia, they might rally the Russians to defend the country, but to use the Japanese would be no advantage except to rally "a small reactionary body who would join anybody to destroy the Bolsheviki." Wiseman said the matter could not be made worse. Wilson observed that it could be made worse by putting Germany in a position where she could organize a Russian national movement against Japan. Wiseman asked, "Are we to do nothing at all?" Wilson replied, "No, we must watch the situation carefully and sympathetically, and be ready to move whenever the right time arrived." The President favored, however, an Allied commission to organize the railroads, food, and trade at Vladivostok and Murmansk. If an open invitation for intervention came from Russia, it should be taken advantage of; but any oral or secret agreement with Trotsky for intervention was not to be trusted for it would only lead to repudiation. Wilson confessed awareness of the importance of his decision, since Japan would not intervene without American sanction.[96]

The President's position now came under additional pressure. General Pershing cabled that the United States would fight Russians in France if the Allies did not create an Eastern Front.[97] Jusserand called on the President with a special message from Clemenceau urging intervention.[98] From Rome, Ambassador Thomas Nelson Page reported it was believed that "there is something in the Germanization of Russia unless some aid is forthcoming by the allies."[99] Ambassador Pleasant A. Stovall reported that thousands of former Russian officers in Switzerland were waiting to join an expedition against the Bolsheviks.[100] The report of the Russian Ambassador to France on the Russian hopes of intervention was transmitted to the President.[101]

The State Department now gradually came to view intervention with favor while the War Department continued to oppose it. On June 19, Secretary Baker wrote Wilson, "If I had my own way about Russia and had the power to have my own way, I would like to take everybody out of Russia except the Russians, . . . and let the Russians settle down and settle their own affairs."[102] Chief of Staff General March supported Baker's position;[103] Bliss also agreed.[104]

General Foch now came forward in advocating intervention. He informed the President: "I learn from certain sources that the Germans have called back from Russia a certain number of divisions during the last weeks. This appears to be a decisive military argument in favor of the Allied intervention in Siberia, since those divisions are destined for the Western Front."[105]

The United States had 1,000,000 men in France. Wilson was consistent in placing everything secondary to winning the war. On military matters he sought military advice. Foch headed the Allied armies. His advice was for intervention. Wilson said, "I was very anxious to get a direct expression from General Foch about this perplexing matter. . . ." He sought Jusserand to see if Foch thought the United States would be justified in sending troops to Russia "if there were involved in doing so a subtraction of that number of men from those whom we could send to France."[106] The President thus seemed to sense the French offensive against his opposition to intervention,[107] and he made the choice difficult — Siberian intervention or all-out aid on the Western Front. It could not be both.

In addition to the Foch representations, the report of the Bolshevik attack on the Czech forces at Irkutsk also influenced the decision to break with the policy of watchful waiting. These forces, desiring to make their way to the front in France, were supposedly withdrawing from Russia, where they had been the last effective troops opposing the Germans. Some 70,000 strong, they represented the most immediate military potential for Allied purposes within Russia and thus became a pawn in the great game of policy and power. Caldwell, the American Consul in Vladivostok, reported that Trotsky had ordered the disarmament of these Czech forces, their arrest, and imprisonment. The 15,000 Czech troops in Vladivostok went to the aid of their comrades imperiled by the war prisoner and Bolshevik forces along the Trans-Siberian.[108] They sought allied munitions and armed aid through the Allied consuls in Vladivostok. Consul Caldwell believed aid to the Czechs demanded intervention. The Czechs estimated that adequate aid consisting of 50,000 troops would serve to reestablish the Eastern Front but that it must come within three weeks.[109] Lansing confessed that intervention was a necessity in the light of the threatened position of the

Czechs. He thought Japan would have to furnish "considerable" of the troops, supplemented by Allied and American units.

Britain's Lockhart warned that time was all important, that the Czechs were the "last chance"; Siberian intervention not Murmansk was "the real factor of importance."[110] Meanwhile, Reading informed Wilson that the British would lay their plans for intervention before the Supreme War Council on July 2.[111] The same day, Balfour warned Reading that the Czech forces were in danger as a result of Red and war prisoner forces forming at Irkutsk.[112]

At the meeting of the Supreme War Council on July 2, Foch and the military advisers of the three governments concurred in the resolution that as a result of the Reds arming prisoners of war and cutting off the Czech forces at Irkutsk, a "complete change" had been made in the Russian situation. It was the duty of the Allies to save the Czechs as their comrades in arms. Much sympathy existed in Russia for Allied intervention, and it was necessary to win the war and prevent Germany from dominating Russia. Japan agreed to undertake intervention and at the same time to give guarantees concerning Siberia. American and Czech forces could join her to present an Allied intervention. The Supreme War Council estimated 100,000 troops would be necessary, most of which would be Japanese.[113]

The War Council decision for intervention was a fact, the threat to the Czech forces seemed a reality, Japan would undertake intervention. In the light of the new situation presented, Wilson changed his policy and called a conference of Secretaries Lansing, Baker, and Daniels, representing the Cabinet, Admiral Benson, Chief of Naval Operations, and General March, Chief of Staff, the services; and to them he announced his decision to go into Siberia.[114] After reviewing the situation, the group decided that establishment of the Eastern Front was impossible. The situation of the Czech troops required the United States and the Allies to aid them in forming a junction between the forces in the West and at Vladivostok. They agreed that Japan should furnish the small arms and ammunition, the United States sharing the cost. A force of 7,000 men each was to be dispatched by Japan and America with the declared mission to guard the line of communications. Japan was to send her troops at once. Allied forces, meanwhile, were to be landed from the naval vessels to take Vladivostok and to cooperate with the Czechs in holding the city.[115]

Only Japan's acceptance was now needed for undertaking the Siberian intervention. Ishii arrived back in town the day following the American decision, and Lansing took up the proposal with him.[116] Wilson wrote House that he had "been sweating blood over the question what is right and feasible (possible) to do in Russia. It goes to pieces like quicksilver under my touch, but I hope I see and can report some progress presently, along the line of economic assistance and aid to the Czecho-Slovacs."[117]

In his interview with Wiseman, the Chief Executive expressed concern lest Japanese dependence on America for supplies and equipment subtract from the American contribution to the front in France. He was at his canny best and refused to inform Wiseman of his new policy favoring joint intervention, although the decision was already made and the Chinese informed.[118] He said his decision awaited the reports of his experts and the outcome of the Lansing-Japanese talks.[119] House understood this secrecy as an attempt on Wilson's part to expedite a decision and to avoid long discussions.[120]

The President was attempting a belated arrangement with Japan. He was persisting in his course of "the lone hand." When Reading, after being informed of the proposal for intervention, talked with Lansing of the contemplated American arrangement, he asked if the Allies were to participate. The Secretary said Wilson had not informed him concerning it, and everything would have to await Japan's decision accepting the joint intervention. Lansing believed the British felt they had been ignored, although the French and Italian ambassadors seemed to approve the American position.[121]

On July 9, the British, French, and Italian ambassadors called on Lansing to clarify the confusion resulting from individual interviews with him on intervention policy. The Secretary frankly outlined the American program of limited joint intervention with the Japanese and stated it did not include the presence of other troops. Informing the Foreign Office of the American action, the British Ambassador found satisfaction in that the project would be a military means of testing Russian reaction to intervention,[122] that "must mean so much for the future. . . ."[123]

Meanwhile, Lansing was finding his negotiations with Japan a little embarrassing. Ishii had cabled the American proposal to his government, yet day succeeded day with no reply. Finally, the Ambassador suggested that it might "expedite a decision if some arrangement could be made as to the Chief Command of the combined forces."[124] At this juncture in the negotiations, the Secretary left Washington for a month's vacation; and the negotiations devolved to Polk, who thought the question of command in Siberia had a lot to do with Japanese hesitancy.[125] The Acting Secretary saw Wilson on the matter; and they decided, while no official statement was to be given out, the Japanese were to send the ranking general. It would be understood that the American forces would be under his command, so Polk informed Ishii the next day. At the Cabinet on July 16, Wilson announced that the Japanese would have command, and that American participation was to help the Czechs at Vladivostok and did not contemplate a military intervention such as the Allies had in mind.[126]

While the British were extremely anxious to do nothing that would make the President of the United States think that they were "forcing his hand," the movement of Empire troops from Hong Kong aroused the suspicion of the President.[127] Admiral Knight, aboard the *Brooklyn* at Vladivostok, in the meantime, was ordered to keep the port open as a base for the Czechs and "to afford them all sympathy and support consistent with avoiding political entanglements."[128]

Finally, on July 24, the Japanese Ambassador called at the Department with an oral communication. Tokyo for political reasons could not give assurances to limit troop strength to 7,000 men, since the opposition would say the demand for such assurance showed American lack of confidence in Japan.[129] This was the very situation Wilson had feared. How to maintain a limited intervention already posed a problem! Ishii said Japan would send around 12,000 men, with the understanding that any increase in strength would depend on the amount of resistance met. In communicating the matter to Wilson, Polk inclosed the statement Japan proposed making respecting the territorial integrity and abstaining from all internal political interference in Siberia.[130]

The next day, Wilson, Polk, and Baker met at the State Department and decided on an oral answer to Japan. The United States would not object to their sending 10,000 to 12,000 men, but the actual number must be limited.[131] House thought the difficulty arose because there were two Japans — the civil government, which wished to cooperate, and the military, which saw no advantage in a limited intervention. The Colonel simplified the intervention tale in this way: "It is the old story one meets everywhere and the one met since the beginning of the world; what is there in it for me!"[132]

Polk then informed the Japanese that the United States would agree to Japan sending a division without objection; this would give them the major force as well as command. Later, if the force were not adequate, an increase could be discussed. Polk hinted at American reluctance in the intervention; if difficulties were created, she would withdraw her plans for participation.[133]

Wilson informed the British, who deemed the proposed forces inadequate, that a larger expedition was impossible, even if composed of Japanese troops; because they would rely in part on American supplies, which could only be supplied at the expense of the Western Front commitments.[134] The French Ambassador, alarmed lest the contention over the strength of the intervention forces might cause Wilson to withdraw his proposal, suggested nothing be said concerning the number of troops.[135] But this was a vital matter to the President.

Alarm over the delayed intervention was increased by Admiral Knight's cable that armed war prisoners and Red Guards now endangered Czech forces in the West. The Eastern Czechs felt it necessary to go to the rescue of their comrades and could leave only 1,500 troops in Eastern Siberia. If this were done, there was danger of the enemy moving in on Vladivostok and the supplies there. He advised if Allied forces were to be sent that they be dispatched immediately. The British had 800 men arriving August 2 from Hong Kong, and the *U. S. S. Brooklyn* had landed 250 men to guard munitions and the American consulate. At the request of the Czechs the Japanese were sending gunboats to the Amur river.[136]

Wilson was exceedingly disturbed by the new situation, but he did not know what answer he could make Knight on intervention for "unhappily the Japanese Government is trying to alter the whole plan in a way to which we cannot consent, and for the time at any rate the whole matter is in suspense."[137] Polk called in the Japanese Ambassador and read him the Knight cable. The Ambassador said a cable was just arriving and he thought it might contain agreement to the American conditions on troop strength.[138] The Ambassador later returned to advise Polk that Japan accepted the American proposal, "reserving the question as to sending of additional troops to Vladivostok or elsewhere until circumstances should arise which might make it necessary." To Polk's question as to whether Japan planned to send 10,000 or 12,000 troops, Ishii made no statement other than there was no question on that point. Japan had already released her consent to the press.[139]

Polk consulted with Wilson and Baker. When Ishii returned to the State Department, the Acting Secretary said there were three points on which the President was anxious: (1) He did not want over 10,000 troops sent by Japan. Ishii assured Polk on this. (2) Was Japan sending troops elsewhere than to Vladivostok? Ishii said he understood they would not without consultation. (3) *When* would it be necessary in the Japanese interpretation to consult other governments before increasing their troop strength? Ishii said consultation would be made whenever the military situation demanded an increase.[140] With these assurances from Japan, the United States was now ready to embark on the joint Siberian intervention.

On August 3, Secretary Baker met Major General William S. Graves in the station at Kansas City, informed him he was to go to Siberia, handed him the *aide memoire*, saying: "This contains the policy of the United States in Russia which you are to follow. Watch your step; you will be walking on eggs loaded with dynamite. God bless you and goodby."[141]

The *memoire,* written by Wilson, reiterated the conclusion of the United States that intervention in Russia was unwise and admissible "only to help the Czecho-Slovaks consolidate their forces and get into successful cooperation with their Slavic kinsmen and to steady any efforts at self-government or self defense in which the Russians themselves may be willing to accept assistance." The only legitimate object for employment of Allied troops was "to guard military stores. . . ." There was no expectation that the United States would take part in any organized intervention in adequate force from either Vladivostok or Murmansk and Archangel. Troops would be used only for the stated purposes, and to safe-guard the rear of the Czechs.[142]

The General arrived in Siberia on September 1, 1918, and found that he was expected to serve in a subordinate capacity to the Japanese commander. Having no orders on the subject, he refused a subordinate status and busied himself with initiating a separate command.[143] Oddly enough, Graves was never informed of the Wilson-Polk agreement with Ishii granting Japanese Command of the expedition, although Polk had informed General March of the commitment on August 13.[144]

The British sought an enlargement of the forces committed, and Polk took pains that they should understand that the United States was not intervening in the British sense in Siberia.[145] The Embassy warned London that the whole situation was very delicate, and it must be careful not to overdo "even by official communication through the State Department the pressure on the President."[146]

Polk talked to the Japanese Ambassador of the size of the American forces being sent. It was now understood the United States was sending 8,000 men.[147] This is important in the light of the fact that Ishii later in talking to Long claimed the United States by sending 9,000 men had abrogated the agreement as to numbers. On August 14, after Lansing's return to duty, Long conferred with Lansing on increasing the American strength to 9,000 men.[148] This too is interesting, because Long later was stunned to learn this very thing had been done by the War Department.[149] Since both Polk and the President had left Washington for much-needed rests,[150] there is some reason to believe that the fine details of their arrangements, since they were oral in nature, were not passed on to others in the official family. On August 27, the Japanese informed Lansing they were sending 10,000 more troops.[151] The same day, the War Department informed Wilson that the Japanese had ordered troops of her Third Division to help the Czechs in the Trans-Baikal region and the Twelfth Division to Vladivostok. On inquiry, the Japanese Military Attache said a division numbered 28,000 men.[152] Such information proved startling to the administration.

Meanwhile, the American forces in Archangel had arrived quietly and were placed under command of the British General Arthur J. Poole. Early in September Poole instructed the Czechs to take Perm and effect a junction with his forces, which Consul Harris said would be impossible unless the Allies hastened their advance in Siberia. On learning of this, Wilson was upset and declared: "This illustrates in the most striking way the utter disregard of General Poole and of all the Allied Governments (at any rate of all who are acting for them) of the policy to which we expressly confined ourselves in our statement about our action in Siberia."[153] From Vladivostok the Japanese had struck out with such rapidity that Wilson observed they were letting the Czech forces "tag along instead of acting themselves as a supporting force."[154]

Once intervention was undertaken the European Allies pressed for a rehabilitation of the Eastern Front. The Wilson administration consistently opposed the project but continued to seek advice on the matter. Masaryk agreed on its impossibility.[155] On September 25, Lansing, March, and Wilson went over the Czech situation and decided it was impossible to get troops to the Volga, and that the Czechs should be withdrawn beyond the Urals.[156] The British were reluctant to abandon the forces in Russia loyal to the Allies and refused to give up the idea of reestablishing an Eastern Front. They hoped if the United States would not join the project it would at least not discourage the plan to the other Allies.[157]

During an inspection of the troops north of Vladisvostok, General Graves found all the towns and villages occupied by "ten times as many Japanese troops as necessary." The same condition existed along the Trans-Siberian and Chinese Eastern railways, which led him to estimate the Japanese forces at around 60,000 men.[158] Wilson found the report "exceedingly disturbing, if true" and asked that it be probed thoroughly.[159] Graves continued to find the Japanese extending themselves and reiterated his former estimate of their strength. General Ivonoff-Rinoff, Minister of War for the Omsk Government, said Japan was establishing herself permanently in Siberia and was encouraging factions among the Russian people. In addition Graves found the junior officers and soldiers of the Japanese army "most-highhanded."[160]

Basil Miles, the Russian Area man of the State Department, reported that Japan had leaped ahead in Manchuria by this time and practically had absorbed the Chinese Eastern Railway. Stevens found the divided operation of the railroad impossible. Japan's action was at variance with the President's purposes in Siberia, and Miles proposed some sort of commitment on the part of Tokyo "to prevent any separate action."[161] By the last of October, the Japanese were bringing in such a preponderant number of troops that Graves doubted the usefulness of the few Americans in Eastern Siberia.[162]

On November 6, Graves reported a complexity of factions in Siberia. General Semenov was now clearly in the pay of the Japanese. Horvat was reported to be also. General M. K. Diederichs, one of the best of the Russian officers, was in the pay of the French. Graves thought the Siberian people trusted America more than any other power, but he feared American association with Japan would lead to confused identification of the two forces in the Siberian mind. Secretary Baker was so discouraged by Graves' report that he wrote Wilson, "I heartily wish it were possible for us to arrange affairs in such a way as to withdraw entirely from that expedition."[163] The same day Wilson talked with Ishii concerning Japanese mistreatment of the American Railway Commission. Vance McCormick reported the President was prepared to send troops along the Trans-

Siberian, but he could not see how it was possible with the Japanese in the way.[164]

The First World War ended on November 11, 1918. The long struggle over the stated reasons for American intervention in Siberia ceased. Baker wrote Wilson that there were now two reasons given for remaining in Siberia: the United States could not withdraw and leave Japan there. Secondly, American relief groups needed protection. He believed, however, that the United States had no right to compel reception of its relief agencies. Baker thought America, although disliking Bolshevism, had no right to assist in its overthrow in Russia. Japan's strength in Siberia grew daily, and he dreaded "to think how we should all feel if we are rudely awakened some day to a realization that Japan has gone in under our wing and so completely mastered the country that she cannot be either induced out or forced out by any action either of Russia or of the Allies." If he had his way the United States would withdraw, after asserting she would henceforth limit her Russian aid to economic measures.[165]

Since September, unsuccessful attempts had been made to create a new national anti-Bolshevik government. Finally, on November 18, 1918, Admiral Kolchak, with British and Czech support, became the "Supreme Governor." Semenov defied the new ruler and the picture was puzzling. In late December, as the Peace Conference delegates gathered in Paris, a widespread revolt against Kolchak in Omsk was so brutally suppressed that the Czech forces refused to participate thereafter in the struggle.[166] Their morale deteriorated while awaiting Allied ships to transport them home.[167] The Soviets, meanwhile, appealed to Wilson to negotiate a peace in Russia, but the President made no replies. Anti-Bolshevik leaders flocked to Paris to plead for Allied support of Kolchak and General Denikin in South Russia.[168]

From Japan, Morris reported that public opinion favored a strong Siberian policy. He believed the Hara Ministry favored Japanese cooperation with the United States; but lacking popular support, they could not overcome the military. An understanding on Far Eastern policy between the European powers and the United States, he thought, might serve to strengthen the Hara liberals. Polk too approved this course.[169]

After the Armistice, control of the Siberian railroads became the chief argument for retaining American forces in Russia;[170] and from Paris, Lansing directed that in all representations to Japan, Russian rights in the roads must be emphasized as well as the Russian desire to place Stevens in control. As to the railway guard, he felt it could be equally divided between the interested powers.[171] When it was learned in Paris that General March was contemplating withdrawal of American forces in Siberia,[172] Lansing cabled Polk, "The President wished me to say that he trusts nothing of the sort would be done until he had been fully consulted about the matter."[173] The Acting Secretary assured Lansing that the War Department would do nothing without Wilson's consent.[174] Meanwhile, the Senate argued American-Siberian policy, and there was mixed sentiment for both withdrawal and further commitment of force against Bolshevism.

On January 16, 1919, the Japanese Ambassador informed Polk that the Stevens arrangement for the control of the railroads had been accepted by Japan.[175] Since the preceding March, Stevens had had units of his corps along the Chinese Eastern Railway and had found Japan opposing him constantly in her effort to establish control of Manchurian transportation.[176] When the Japanese had planned to place the Chinese Eastern under military control, the State Department had gained the support of France and Italy in resisting her, although Britain had proved unwilling to approve.[177]

Morris had negotiated an informal agreement in October, 1918, with the Allied, Russian, and Japanese representatives at Vladivostok providing for the operation of the Siberian and Chinese Eastern Railways under the protection of the Allied military forces in Siberia and the general management of Stevens and the Russian Railway Service corps.[178] The Japanese military in Tokyo refused to recognize the agreement, and it was only after much negotiation that a new arrangement was put into effect in March, 1919, which placed the railroads under an Inter-Allied committee with Technical and Military

Transportation Boards. Stevens was made President of the Technical Board. The whole arrangement was to cease upon the withdrawal of the Allied forces.[179]

The matter of Siberian intervention was hopelessly intertwined with the ever-present Red threat discussed in January at the Paris Conference. Wilson said he could see no advantage to be derived from words and public statements on Bolshevism. "What I am at present keenly interested in is in finding the interior of their minds." He thought, "The real thing with which to stop Bolshevism is food."[180] He felt the employment of force unwise "before the Powers were agreed upon a course of action for checking Bolshevism as a social and political danger."[181]

Bolshevism, according to Bliss occupied the governments at Paris "day and night."[182] The British were for treating with the Reds, but the French would have none of it. The Prinkipo Conference with the Russian factions was an enterprise backed by Wilson that never came off. Lansing exclaimed, "I hate the idea of even investigating those assassins."[183] When House informed Wilson of Winston Churchill's plan of intervention to put down the Bolshevist terror, presented during the President's absence in Washington, Wilson expressed strong dissent. He favored the earliest withdrawal of the forces already there and said, "It would be fatal to be led further into the present chaos."[184] Ambassador Francis, after an operation in England, returned with Wilson aboard the *George Washington*. He too favored strong intervention,[185] but it made little impression on Wilson's mind.

Meanwhile in Siberia, Graves held rigidly to his instructions and found himself resisting the Japanese in local incidents involving troop relations and interpretation of the intent of intervention. Polk, in Washington, thought the General should be instructed to throw his influence behind support for a policy of political moderation in Russia. He privately believed the situation beyond the ability of Graves who interpreted instructions very conservatively and refused to show initiative.[186] Meantime Graves, in compliance with the President's instructions to support Stevens, had moved one company of American troops to Harbin and two companies to Irkutsk.

Lansing wrote Wilson about changing Graves' instructions and the situation in Siberia. The next day he forwarded Admiral King's recommendations that strong units of the fleet be moved to the Pacific to increase American strength there. Lansing feared any such movement of the navy would be viewed with suspicion by Japan.[187] According to naval intelligence, Prime Minister Hara was attempting to carry out a moderate policy in Japan, but the military in Siberia disregarded him.[188] Meanwhile, Graves' attempts to remain neutral brought charges of his favoring the Bolsheviks. According to General A. W. F. Knox, the British commander in Siberia, the Russians contrasted the American attitude with the Japanese to the latter's advantage, for where there were disorders the Japanese sent troops to suppress them.[189] Wilson saw the whole story from a different viewpoint in Graves' letter, which explained that Japanese policy in Siberia was to support anyone willing to serve their own purpose.[190]

William Phillips, who in late March, 1919 took over for Polk as Acting Secretary, added his backing for additional instructions to Graves defining American participation in the suppression of disorder and support of more moderate elements in Siberia.[191] He endorsed the recommendation of Consul Harris for the recognition of Kolchak and protection of his rear in Siberia against Semenov, Kalmykov, and Japanese intrigue. An American independent policy in Siberia, he thought, was no longer possible.[192]

The persistent representations of the State Department for increased American instructions bore fruit. On April 2, Lansing cabled Phillips that the President, pending approval of Secretary Baker, consented to Graves being instructed that the United States favored the economic rehabilitation of Siberia and felt a policy of political moderation among the several Russian factions necessary. The American mission in Siberia was to insure the operation of the railroads, and Graves' forces should be limited to a three mile zone "on either side of the railways; within which zone he should exercise definite police power and prevent any disturbances that might interfere with the operation of the railways."[193] General March thought the President's plan for guarding the railroad and the adjacent six mile strip through which it ran "ridiculous." Baker also disapproved the plan since it would require 500,000 men.[194] Upon these advices being received, Wilson instructed Lansing to adopt the Baker policy of limiting the use of military forces to the preservation of order in the immediate vicinity of the railroad and its property.[195]

In Paris, the French especially were urging the strong support and recognition of Kolchak.[196] Consul Harris agreed with this policy; but Ambassador Morris, who was more nearly Wilson's agent in Siberian affairs, had doubts as to the permanency of the Kolchak government.[197] However, Polk thought if the United States failed to recognize or give open support to the Omsk government, Graves would be unable to function in Siberia. He believed that the United States must come to an understanding with Britain on Siberia and so strengthen the situation, else the whole Siberian policy would fail just when there was hope for success.[198] Finding the Japanese were considering recognition of Kolchak, Morris advised it would be difficult for the United States to abstain from doing so.[199] Graves thought Kolchak unfriendly to American occupation of the railroad, because the neutrality of the United States was a source of weakness to him. He said the Siberian people were not back of Kolchak, but the British and French were determined to force the use of American troops against any armed forces not supporting the Omsk leader. So preponderantly favorable were these representations concerning Kolchak's recognition that even Baker, the crusader for neutrality in Siberia, thought Graves should be directed to cooperate with the Omsk leader or be withdrawn.[200]

Greatly disturbed by the Siberian problem and Kolchak's place in it, Wilson presented the whole matter to the Council of Four at the peace conference. Favoring a neutral policy within Siberia, the President said he did not wish to withdraw leaving Japan in control. The present situation demanded that either the United States send stronger forces to Siberia and take sides with Kolchak or withdraw.[201] After discussing the situation, the Council of Four drafted a letter to Kolchak, stating the conditions under which they would continue aiding him. The communication asked pledges for a freely elected assembly to be convoked upon Kolchak arriving in Moscow, guarantees against any attempt to restore the class privileges of the Czarist regime, assurances that national obligations were to be recognized, and promises that the new democratic Russia would join the League and cooperate in settlement of border states and limitation of armaments problems.[202] On June 4, 1919, Kolchak made an affirmative reply to the conditions.[203]

Meanwhile, Wilson privately ordered Morris to undertake a mission to obtain "official and definite assurances" from Kolchak regarding his plans for a future Russian government, land tenure, extension of suffrage, and the establishment of a constituent assembly. He also desired to know "the influences that Kolchak is under."[204] The recall of Ivanov-Rinov, the paragon of reaction in Eastern Siberia, at this time Wilson viewed as a move by Kolchak in the right direction.[205]

Not until August 4 was the Morris report on Kolchak filed.[206] It found the Siberian leader a courageous but conservative patriot of limited administrative ability who was controlled by his council of ministers. His government had failed miserably. Although the only alternative to Bolshevism in Siberia,[207] Kolchak, despite Allied aid, was unequal to the task of opposing the Reds.[208] In a subsequent report, Morris reversed himself and recommended formal recognition of Kolchak, granting him loans, and sending 25,000 American troops to assist in guarding the railway. To do less was to be forced to abandon Eastern Siberia to Japan.[209]

In Washington, the State Department discussed a loan for Kolchak.[210] The Department was having its troubles. Miles was leaving the Russian Division and DeWitt C. Poole who had been long a Siberian interventionist was preparing to take over. There was a great deal of intra-Department suspicion and division. Polk, one of the leading Siberian interventionists, was now representing the United States at the concluding conferences in Paris. Tumulty was spreading the news of Wilson's

loss of faith in House and dislike of Auchincloss. Lansing had
been at odds with Presidential policy since the early spring in
Paris. There were many resignations at home and overseas,
Minister Reinsch of the China post among them. A general
let down in the high purpose of the country had occurred during the Paris Conference. The surrender on Shantung had been
widely disapproved, and the Senate was making political advantage out of the Versailles terms. Lansing believed the rumors that House wanted to take diplomacy out of control of the
State Department and give it to the League. The Bullitt testimony on Russia and Lansing's statement before the Senate
Committee in regard to Shantung had widened the breach between Wilson and his Secretary of State. Wilson undertook to
take the Versailles settlement to the people. On September 25
he was forced to abandon his western tour because of illness.
Lansing commented, "Looks like [a] nervous breakdown."[211]

The Secretary of State was out of Washington when Wilson's
breakdown occurred. William Phillips was acting Secretary. In
reporting to Polk at the time, Phillips said nothing desperate had
happened in the affairs of the Department,

"... with one exception: the act of General Graves with
the Omsk Government. It ought to cost the General his
head, and I am doing my best to make it so. At a moment
when Kolchak has begun a general advance, just after the
President had given specific instructions to me by telegram
that we should sell to Kolchak on credit such army supplies
as were available — boots, clothing, etc., when the British
and French were doing rather successfully their part of assistance in the South, lo and behold General Graves addresses
the Omsk Foreign Office directly over the head of Harris,
refusing to deliver one million dollars' worth of American
rifles which had been bought and partially paid for by Kolchak and which are now lying at Vladivostok."

The action by Graves caused the Omsk authorities to inquire
if the American government had decided to desert Kolchak.
Phillips knew Baker and March would back the General as

always, but he believed "the President will be with us in this instance."[212] No one knew the President was so desperately ill.

Not until October did Wilson come actively into the Siberian picture again, when he approved sale by the Grain Corporation of wheat flour for the relief of the civil population of regions freed from Bolshevik control. His approval stated, "It is the announced policy of this Government to relieve in every possible way the material distress of the Russian people."[213] On November 3, Wilson disapproved Lloyd George's proposal for a conference of the Allies with the Bolsheviks and stated that he felt the Russian situation would have worked itself out long ago if it had been left alone.[214]

In November, Kolchak suffered defeat at the hands of the Red troops, Baker had disturbing news from Graves of Red threats to American troops, and took the matter up with the President through Admiral Cary Grayson, who during the illness cleared things for the President's approval. Wilson said before any change in policy was made, we must insist on a statement from Japan on her intentions in Siberia.[215]

Friction with the Japanese over operation of the inter-Allied Railway Agreement caused the State Department to threaten Japan with American withdrawal from Siberia unless these differences were resolved.[216] The differences continued, and at the prompting of Secretary of War Baker, the State Department requested a reply to its note. Japan's reply was mildly conciliatory while reasserting the independence of the Japanese military from civil control in Siberia.[217] On December 8, the Japanese frankly asked for a statement of policy in relation to Siberia. Did the United States propose to maintain the *status quo*, withdraw, or send reenforcements in case of need?[218]

Lansing sent the President a letter on December 23, recommending withdrawal from Siberia. The Kolchak government had collapsed, the Bolshevik armies were advancing in Eastern Siberia and approaching the American sectors[219] where contact with them would lead to open hostilities. America must either withdraw or wage war against the Bolsheviks.[220]

Wilson had had no direct communication with Lansing in months. When important business had to be transacted a note would come from Mrs. Wilson stating "the President directs" that a certain action be taken. The break between the White House and State Department was open, with Wilson seemingly attempting to force Lansing into resigning and the Secretary holding on. In the light of the threatened engagement of American forces with the Bolsheviks in Siberia, Breckenridge Long went to the Secretary and urged withdrawal of the troops. Lansing confessed he had sent such a recommendation to the President, but there had been no reply. Long went back to his office and made the decision to appeal to the White House. He saw Tumulty and explained the seriousness of the situation. Tumulty told Long to go back and prepare a statement on the situation, and he would show it to the President. This Long did. Scarcely two hours after delivery of Long's statement, the directive came from the White House to withdraw the American forces.[221]

On January 9, 1920, Lansing handed a memorandum to Ambassador Kijuro Shidehara stating the American decision to withdraw from Siberia.[222] The American announcement created ill will in Japan, although the State Department tempered the abrupt change of policy by pretending its decision was but the answer to Japan's *Aide Memoire* of December 8 inquiring of future American policy.[223]

On All Fool's Day, April, 1920, General Graves left Siberia with the last echelon of American troops. General Oi, the Japanese Commander, came down with a band to see the Americans leave. The band struck up the popular tune "Hard Times Come Again No More." America's Siberian fracas was over.[224] Japan remained until 1922 when she consented to withdraw as part of the agreements stemming from the Washington Conference.

The whole course of intervention in Siberia had been counter to the President's wisdom, but once entered upon it had brought forth its own events and necessary expedients of action. So far as America's purpose was to prevent Japanese seizure of the Siberian maritime provinces, it was a success. The President had never looked upon the intervention as a means for overthrowing Bolshevism; he did, however, give serious thought to support of Siberian unity, even to the extent of considering recognition of the Kolchak regime.

Wilson throughout the venture was limited in his commitment in Siberia; because he, like the War Department, was a "Western Frontier." He was conscious of the expanded purposes of the European Allies in Siberia, but he did not share in their purposes. Japan's violation of what Wilson considered an agreement on the limitation of troops to be sent to Siberia alienated him further from that country, while the excesses and lack of principle of the Bolsheviks completely divided him from the Russian leaders.[225]

CHAPTER NINE

Paris, Peace, and East Asia

YOU ARE AWARE, AS I AM AWARE, THAT THE AIRS OF AN
OLDER DAY ARE BEGINNING TO STIR AGAIN, THAT THE STAND-
ARDS OF AN OLD ORDER ARE TRYING TO ASSERT THEMSELVES
AGAIN.

—Wilson at Suresnes Cemetery

Paris in 1919 had only recently been relieved of bombard-
ment from German guns. She put out her flags and welcomed
the gathering delegates to the peace conference with a warm
fervor of emotion. Georges Clemenceau, the French Premier,
looking upon the Fourteen Points as a joke on history, and,
believing in force, planned well his strategy for the meeting.
In a world of potential war, France would seek security through
a hard peace. David Lloyd George, the British Prime Minister,
brought to Paris an expeditious view of obtaining what he
could for England and the Empire, but he was not without
idealism, and hoped for the achievement of some form of a
better world order. He had only recently won the "khaki election" which, while keeping him in power also returned a vindi-
cative Commons, demanding that Germany be made to pay.
Vittorio Orlando of Italy, a quiet believer in Wilson's principles,
a professor himself, understood the stringent peace demands of
his parliament.[1] All three men were cognizant of the secret
treaties of 1915 concerning Europe and of 1917 concerning the
Far East, yet, they had agreed to the Armistice provisions of a
peace based on the Fourteen Points and their extensions. The
glow of victory had brought hope for a better world.

Wilson was conscious of the forces he was to confront in Paris. He told his experts aboard the *George Washington* that their mission was a battle of the new with the old order.[2] These experts were in all fields and were mostly young men, many being professors in the areas for which they were engaged. They were largely continued from the Inquiry, organized in 1918 by Colonel House under the general direction of his brother-in-law, Dr. Sidney A. Menzes, for a study of possible terms and information concerning the items likely to arise on the agenda of the conference.

The American Mission had an unusual degree of experience in Far Eastern affairs. Lansing, now nearly five years in the State Department, had as Counselor and Secretary a background of experience in dealing with oriental matters. Henry White was an old friend of former Secretary John Hay; and, according to Patrick Gallagher of the *New York Herald*, "His heart beats for the open door." General Tasker H. Bliss, the American representative on the Allied Military Council, had been a former army commander of the Department of Luzon and a past Governor of Moro Province in the Philippines. Reportedly, the General "had a high sense of our national duty in Asia."[3] Colonel House, whose Texas honorific title and lack of military bearing baffled the Japanese, had kept informed on events in the Far East through his close connection with diplomatic personnel. His information through the State Department, where his influence was paramount, was so complete that he knew, though he possibly did not understand fully, the current of the times in Asian affairs.[4] Then there was Wilson himself, an avowed friend of China and cognizant of the Japanese position in relation to expansion on the Asiatic continent. For six years his mind had been facing the problems of the world. If he knew little of diplomacy and the Far East when he entered upon his duties in 1913, it could not be asserted that the Wilson departing aboard the *George Washington* on December 4, 1918 was inexperienced and uninformed concerning events there. Across his desk had come the flimsies of State Department telegrams and special reports bearing intimate observations from representatives and governments all over the world. His leadership was now an admitted fact throughout that same world.[5]

Far Eastern technical experts of the American Mission were Edward T. Williams, the former head of the Far Eastern Division, called back from his professorial duties at Berkeley to advise the American peace delegation, along with Captain Stanley K. Hornbeck, a former Rhodes scholar and author of *Contemporary Politics in the Far East.*[6] David Hunter Miller served as the legal officer of the delegation and kept the record of what transpired at the Conference.

The Japanese delegation at Paris consisted of Marquis Kimmochi Saionji, a Genro and twice Prime Minister who headed the mission; Viscount Sutemi Chinda, now the Ambassador to England, formerly in the same capacity at Washington; Viscount Nobuaki Makino, and the Japanese Ambassadors to France and Italy. Marquis Saionji did not appear at conference sessions, in fact there was some doubt as to whether he was really in Paris; but in oriental fashion he lived luxuriously in his hotel, manipulating his delegates from behind the scene. Viscounts Chinda and Makino became his chief spokesmen. The former, a proper, grey-mustached little man, was very much in the stereotype of an elderly professor of aesthetics, while Makino appeared as a somewhat larger, stern, bold figure with a military bearing.[7] Among the American delegation they were known as "the two Mikados."

China was represented by a coalition delegation headed by Lou Tseng-tsiang, the Foreign Minister in Peking. He was the only member of the Chinese Mission educated in the old classical manner and unable to speak English. Like Saionji, he appeared little on the scene, and the members of the delegation representing Young China carried the burden of negotiations and decisions. C. T. Wang, a Yale graduate, dominated the commission, although with S. T. Wei he represented South China.[8] The chief spokesman was the oval-faced, young V. K. Wellington Koo, Minister to the United States, fated to be the perennial figure in Chinese politics. A graduate of Columbia, Koo in his years there had achieved Phi Beta Kappa and the varsity debating squad. His graduate work had been in international law under the idealistic and legalistic John Basset Moore. He had also been a student of James T. Shotwell, the historian of the American delegation. The last member of the group was Alfred Sze, Minister to Britain, a former Cornell man. As the Chinese delegation passed through the United States on their way to Paris in early January, 1919, they declared they "would stand for the principles enunciated by President Wilson."[9]

The American and Chinese delegations from the first were on very friendly terms with the former advising the latter quite frankly. Shotwell was consulted by Wang concerning China's program at the conference. Seymour took Wang to talk with Hunter Miller, the American legal Adviser, and Captain Stanley K. Hornbeck. Together they planned the procedure to present China's case at the conference.[10]

On January 6, Minister Reinsch from Peking sent a last urgent appeal to Wilson for support of China at Paris:

> I feel in duty bound to call your attention to the imperious necessity of including a thorough-going and permanent settlement of the Chinese question among the arrangements to be made for the establishment of peace. I appeal to you directly . . . because you have become to the people of China the embodiment of their best hopes and aspirations. . . . Never before have the words of a foreign statesman entered so deeply and directly into the hearts of the Chinese people. . . .

> . . . I have been forced through the experience of five years to the conclusion that the methods applied by the Japanese military masters can lead only to evil and destruction and they will not be stopped by any consideration of fairness and justice but only by the definite knowledge that such action will not be tolerated.

> * * *

> . . . China must be freed from all foreign political influences exercised within her borders, railways controlled by foreign nations and preferential arrangements supported by political power.[11]

Hornbeck thought the Minister's suggestions of utmost importance and agreed with the conclusions, and he made a précis of the contents for the American delegation.[12] In a general way, the Reinsch report represented the American delegation's pro-Chinese and anti-Japanese point of view. Williams' comment on it left no room for doubt as to where he stood: "The spirit of Japan is that of Prussia, whom Japanese leaders openly admire and whose government they deliberately chose for a model." From the beginning of her history, so the idea ran, the militarists had bought unity at home by war abroad. They aimed, said Williams, at the hegemony of Asia. The present Hara government in Japan was no more liberal than the former ministries. "Japan must be restrained if justice is to prevail or liberty survive in the Far East."[13]

The Peace Conference was organized formally on January 18, 1919; a week later the first general or plenary session was held and the Council of Ten created. It was in this Council, upon which Japan, like the other major powers, had two representatives and China had none, that the island empire brought forth her claims to Kiaochow and the German rights in Shantung, as well as to possession of the North Pacific islands formerly belonging to Germany. In addition to Shantung, Japan also sought equality of position among the powers and recognition of her paramount position in Eastern Asia as a result of her war time treaties with China. When discussion of the Shantung claims was delayed by the mandates debate, Japan shifted to agitation of racial equality.[14] This was to be her strategy throughout the Conference; if blocked on any one of her objectives, she pressed her other points.

The day following the opening session of the League of Nations Commission under the chairmanship of Wilson, Makino and Chinda came to solicit the good offices of Colonel House for support of their project to include guarantees of racial equality in the Covenant. The Colonel advised them to prepare two resolutions: one containing their full desires and another comprising the minimum they would accept. The following day, they brought the resolutions to House who showed them to Wilson. After discussing the two resolutions, the President made some changes in the acceptable proposal and said he wished to discuss the matter with his colleagues. Chinda then brought a new draft on the race question, since the Japanese legal adviser said the former proposals were innocuous.[15] Birdsall suggests that they had learned that Prime Minister William H. Hughes of Australia had resolved to resist unalterably any provision suggesting racial equality in the treaty, and thereupon realized the inability of the United States to stand for the desired clause. They then decided to advance an unacceptable demand on the point so as to gain respect at home.[16] Hunter Miller thought the Japanese refused the House-Wilson draft because it was but a stated principle and had no legal effect. He observed that any draft on racial equality having a real legal obligation had no chance of approval.[17] Lord Robert Cecil, the House of the British delegation, told the Colonel that the "British would not agree to it at all, probably not in any form."[18]

The Japanese on February 13, attempted to amend Article 19 of the original draft of the League Covenant containing the statement: "The High Contracting Parties agree that they will make no law prohibiting or interfering with the free exercise of religion, and that they will in no way discriminate either in law or in fact [against any religion]. . . ." To this the Japanese desired to insert also racial equality.[19] This was a reasonable request, but they were persuaded to drop it. The following day the League Covenant was presented at the plenary session, and immediately thereafter Wilson left for Washington to sign bills and take care of administrative affairs at the end of session.

On the day Wilson left Washington to return to Paris, March 4, 1919, Japanese Ambassador Ishii handed Breckenridge Long a memorandum for the President concerning racial equality. Long managed to get it to the White House within the hour of Wilson's leaving.[20] In the memorandum the Japanese Government expressed its appreciation for the President's "sympathy and support" in abolishing racial discrimination. Japan regarded it as a basic principle and should it "fail of general recognition the Japanese Government do not see how a perpetual friction and discontent among nations and races could possibly be eliminated." Therefore, their representatives at Paris would continue to agitate for its adoption and Tokyo hoped the President would support them in the matter. "As for the form and wording of the proposition, the Japanese Government have no intention to insist on the adoption of the original draft and any suggestion from the President on this point will be intertained [sic] with great pleasure."[21]

The Japanese appeal for the President's support of racial equality was followed on March 14 by an address of Ambassador Ishii at a dinner of the Japan Society in New York. Ishii attempted to allay the public fear that such a provision in the League would interfere with American immigration policy.[22] Telegrams from the Japanese residents of Hawaii and from thirty-seven Japanese Associations in Tokyo petitioning for racial equality were presented to the Council session.[23] In late March, Marquis Okuma, "the grand old man of Japanese politics," prepared a discourse on racial equality which was read at a mass meeting in Tokyo. While he indorsed Wilson's idea of the League, he stated the solution of the racial question was essential "in order to avoid future strife among nations arising out of the present unequal distribution of natural riches."[24]

General Jan Christian Smuts of South Africa and Baron Makino, on March 29, came to the room of Stephen Bonsal, House's erstwhile Secretary, interpreter, and adviser on Balkan affairs, for a long talk on the racial equality issue. Smuts expressed his intent to oppose the Japanese proposal on equality if it came up before the whole Conference. The General charged Makino, "Your position is incontestable and so is the status of Japan — so why raise the question?" After the General departed, Bonsal showed Makino newspaper clippings in which the impression was definitely made that the United States was preventing adoption of the racial equality declaration. Makino promised to see the press and straighten out the facts.[25] House also complained to him about abuse of the United States in the Japanese press, and Makino admitted it was due to popular belief in Japan that the United States had held up the adoption of racial equality provisions.[26]

Meanwhile, Wilson's reservation on the Monroe Doctrine, which he had brought back from Washington in early March along with other suggested Congressional changes, was gladly supported by the Japanese. The Amendment as finally approved stated that nothing in the Covenant should affect the validity of the Doctrine. The American delegation was not overly pleased by the Japanese cooperation in securing the amendment, since they thought it was due to the reservation being also a tacit recognition of the Okuma-Ishii Doctrine of an Asian Monroeism for Japan.[27]

The Tokyo Embassy informed Washington that Marquis Okuma, in a press interview, stated the issue of racial equality was vital to Japan and though she might wait for a considerable time, "if not finally conceded by the Powers Japan should resolve to withdraw from the League of Nations."[28] At this time, Benjamin Fleisher, a correspondent in Tokyo, found the race equality question the leading topic of discussion there. The Japanese Government through *Kokusai,* the leading news service, and other channels was "disseminating [the] race equality discussion broadly through many countries in Asia." The *Nippon Dempo* agency was circulating to the local and country press ridiculous statements of American arms shipments to China.[29] Meanwhile, fearing that racial equality would be written into the League, the San Francisco Board of Supervisors sent resolutions to Washington and to Paris opposing any such action.[30]

The racial equality issue came to a decision on April 11, when Baron Makino proposed an insertion in the preamble endorsing "the principle of equality of nations and just treatment of their nationals."[31] This was a mild statement, and Wilson was willing to agree with it; but House passed the President a note, "The trouble is that if this Commission should pass it, it would surely raise the race issue throughout the world."[32] Cecil, the British representative, under instructions from his government, shamefacedly objected to it. Hughes had threatened to make an issue of any such concession to the Japanese.[33] Wilson realized the Hughes threat was no idle one; he had learned much of the strength of the opposition in Washington during his return trip in February; he possibly recalled the racial issue in California in 1913; it was not a problem foreign to American politics; the British were unalterably opposed. House was right. The President, who was chairman of the body, then spoke[34] opposing the proposal as unnecessary, maintaining that controversies outside the Commission would be entailed in the amendment, and that equality need not be mentioned since it was a fundamental principle of the League — the very spirit of its Covenant.[35] Makino insisted on a vote, and eleven of the seventeen members favored the Japanese proposal. Since the order of the Commission on the League called for unanimous consent, the amendment was rejected. No contrary vote was taken. British and American abstinence from voting had defeated one of the strongly-held objectives of the Japanese mission — racial equality.

There was no basis for the cry that the proposal of the Japanese would interfere with domestic immigration policies in the United States and the various dominions, since Article XV of the Covenant provided, "The Council is to make no recommendation in cases affecting a member's domestic jurisdiction." The Japanese were bitterly disappointed at the outcome. House admired the manner in which Makino took the rejection; but he did not fail to tell him that it was impossible to include the provision, since the Senate would not ratify any treaty containing it.[36] Bonsal thought the Japanese defeat was not a total one. The Monroe Doctrine Amendment soothed them, which seemed to indicate that they thought of it in relation to their Greater Asia plans.

Makino reiterated his position on racial equality in the plenary session of April 28. He said, "We will not, however, press for adoption of our proposal at this moment."[37] The mildness of his statement, as shall be shown, was due to an understanding by which Japan captured her major objective in Shantung for abandoning the controversial issue of racial equality. By such small maneuvers is diplomacy accomplished! The loss of racial equality made the Shantung settlement inevitable.[38]

The disposition of the German North Pacific islands was another item on the agenda for international settlement. They had surrendered in October of 1914 to the Japanese fleet. Soon after, the islands were closed to foreign trade. American ships were precluded from landing in all but two islands set aside for gathering the copra of the region. This was an impractical arrangement, since the natives would not inconvenience themselves to the extent of transporting their products for sale. Even in normal times, with the schooners calling locally, the natives worked only under the greatest of enticements. The Japanese arrangement thus served to ruin the trade of several American companies interested in the area. This, of course, had added to the bad feeling and suspicion in America regarding Japan's ambitions in the Pacific.[39] In December, 1918, it was rumored that Japan had fortified some of the islands. Her possession of Yap, where the cables to China, Southeast Asia and Australia crossed, was viewed as a communications threat.

It was known when the conference opened that the British Empire would claim the South Pacific and Japan the North Pacific German islands. The American Naval Planning Committee, realizing the threat of Japanese possession, yet aware of the impossibility of forcing Japan to release the islands, suggested that "A possible solution might be to give Japan a free hand in Eastern Asia." They posed the problem: "Will it not be better to provide for the future expansion of Japan at the Peace Conference, rather than exclude it, and thereby leave in existence an immediate cause of future war in which Japan might attempt to expand in a direction opposed to the interests of the United States?" The Navy advised, "It must be borne in mind that it is of vital interest to the United States to turn Japan towards the continent of Asia." It recommended that the Marshalls, the Carolines, German New Guinea, and Samoa be internationalized.[40]

The General Board made recommendations along the same line, but advised that unless the United States was willing to fortify any islands taken by her, it would be better to support neutral supervision of them. The islands were potential submarine bases. Guam in its undeveloped condition could be occupied by Japan at will in case of a war; and with Guam in Japanese hands, she could undertake operations in the Philippines with little fear of interference from the United States. Therefore, the General Board favored the acquisition of the Caroline and Marshall islands for strategic reasons.[41]

The Far Eastern Division of the State Department, under the direction of Third Assistant Secretary Breckenridge Long, undertook a study of the Pacific Ocean area, especially with a viewpoint of establishing American ownership to certain insular areas, including the German islands. President Wilson, however, through Lansing, had given a basic directive that no part of the German islands would be claimed by the United States, since this would be in contravention of the American policy of "no material gain" from the war. Lansing had taken little interest in the Pacific area in the days prior to the peace conference, but Long and the Far Eastern Division worked out a plan for the United States to support return of the islands to Germany. At a later date, but not during the Conference, the United States would then arrange to accept certain of the islands from Germany as partial payment on the expected indemnity.[42]

The whole matter of the islands was brought up in the mandates discussion on January 27, when Japan presented her claims to the German possessions north of the equator and the Kiaochow concession in China. Wilson explained that the idea of a mandate was to enable the more advanced nations to serve the people in undeveloped regions and to aid them in their development under League supervision.[43] Hughes of Australia, throughout these discussions, was for outright cession of the islands south of the equator to his dominion. He was strongly backed in his contention by New Zealand, France, and Japan. While Wiseman and Cecil agreed in a private meeting with House that the islands should be given to Australia and New Zealand under a mandate, Lloyd-George was arguing for the Hughes principle of outright annexation.[44]

Colonel House wrote Wilson on the day following the above meeting that he believed the British delegation, including its dominion members, opposed the claim for annexation rather than the mandate that Hughes was demanding. House was skeptical of Australian public opinion being behind Hughes and suggested that if he persisted in his position, "the best solution would be to tell him that the whole arguments on both sides must be published in order that the world may judge Australia's claims, but so far as the Conference is concerned his proposal strikes at the whole idea of the League of Nations and cannot be accepted."[45]

The idea of mandating the German colonies had been clearly in Wilson's mind as early as December 10, 1918. Even then he favored the mandate being exercised by the small nations and the resources being made "available to all members of the League."[46] While Wilson thus held out against annexation, House in conference with Cecil and Smuts, sought to find a compromise. Smuts finally drafted an article defining different types of mandates, and giving the mandatory varying degrees of authority in the region under its control. This eventually became the solution for the islands,[47] providing they "be administered under the laws of the mandatory state as if they were integral portions thereof," subject to certain safeguards.[48] Wilson was troubled over the plan, because the islands could be made naval bases by Japan. "The President said that he did not trust the Japanese; that he had trusted them before, — in fact they had broken their agreement about Siberia. . . . and that he would not trust them again."[49] Wilson here referred to the fact that Japan had sent more troops into Siberia than provided by the agreement with the United States.

In making his decision on the Pacific islands, Wilson followed the recommendation of the Intelligence Section rather than that advocated by the Far Eastern Division or the Navy Department. The Intelligence Section's "Black Book" recommendation favored mandating the islands to Japan under strict limitations as to their fortification. It asserted that the strategic advantages of possession were practically nullified by the creation of the League and the contemplated abolition of the submarine. The United States had no legitimate claim to the region, and to assert such a claim would undermine her strong moral position at the conference. On May 6, the President agreed Japan should receive the mandate for certain of the Pacific islands north of the equator.[50] Even this concession of a mandate Wilson distrusted,[51] because the numerous islands were across the path from Hawaii to the Philippines and could be developed as Japanese naval bases, while the United States had only Guam in the area.[52]

The solution did not represent Wilson's desires. Japan was already in occupation, and she had allied treaty guarantees of her rights there. Although, under the mandate principle the League had strong supervisory powers, the concurrent aggressive policy of Japan in Siberia, Manchuria, and China proper did not bode well for the future. Wilson was receiving constant reports of Japanese activities in these regions from the State Department; his experts were convinced of her ambitions in the Far East; public sentiment in the United States was anti-Japanese. The President had gone through the whole struggle concerning Japanese objectives in the Pacific area many times since 1913; suspicion of her ambitions had been a primary consideration in his sending the Siberian expedition and organizing the New Consortium.[53] It now served to bolster his strong defense of China's case in the issue of the German rights in Shantung, which was the major decision taken in relation to Eastern Asia at the conference.

A glance at the map reveals the Shantung Peninsula, about the size of Iowa, jutting into the Yellow Sea and occupying a commanding position as a keystone in the densely-populated coastal provinces of China. Germany had seized slightly over one hundred square miles of the coastal region of Shantung, known as Kiaochow, in 1898. Following the murder of three German missionaries there, the Kaiser had joined in the movement with France, Britain, and Russia for carving up China into spheres of influence. In addition to Kiaochow, where they built the model port of Tsingtau, the Germans also received certain mining and economic rights within the province of Shantung. Possession of the port and control of the railroad from it to the capital at Tsinan, a distance of two hundred fifty miles, gave to the possessor a strategic advantage in shutting off North to South communications and the ability to menace Peking itself. In addition it was among the richest of China's northern provinces.[54]

The Japanese, after capturing Tsingtau in November, 1914, set about their occupation duties, retained the German concessions, and replaced the German officials on the Kiaochow-Tsinan Railroad. They scattered troops along the entire line and established a garrison in the provincial capital at Tsinan, where the road joined railways going north to Peking. Japanese officials soon opened the German mines and settled down to production. As the Chinese saw stone and concrete barracks erected in the interior, General Kamio appointed Governor General at Tsingtau, and Japanese police and tax collectors on duty, even outside the former German leased area, their suspicions were confirmed. It was another Korea! Japan had come to stay.[55] Their certainty was assured when Japan forced Peking, during the Twenty-One Demands of 1915, to "assent to all matters upon which the Japanese Government may hereafter agree with the German Government relating to the disposition of all rights, interests, and concessions, which Germany by virtue of treaties or otherwise, possesses in relation to the Province of Shantung."[56]

The American Government refused to recognize the binding force of the agreements growing out of the Twenty-One Demands and their subsequent extension in the 1918 treaties. From the Japanese point of view, their commanding position in Asia established during the war years rested upon these agreements. It therefore became of primary importance in Japanese policy at the Conference to secure American and foreign recognition of these agreements with China.[57]

At the opening of the Conference, the State Department was of the opinion: "With respect to Shantung the German rights there lapsed with all Sino-German treaties upon the declaration of war. A succession of treaty rights from Germany to Japan is therefore not possible. . . ."[58] This was also the position taken by the Chinese on the matter.[59] Wilson's advices were unanimous on the question of the German rights in Shantung. They must be returned to China! The Naval Advisory Staff,[60] the Intelligence Section, [61] the State Department and advisers[62] were as one in the matter.

The "pass the button who is to get Shantung game" began on January 27 in the Council of Ten, when Baron Makino made claim to the former Kiaochow leased territory, to the railroad and other rights possessed by Germany there, and to all the former German islands north of the equator. He justified these claims as only just and fair in the light of Japan's contributions in destroying the German bases in the Orient and safeguarding the Pacific, Indian, and Mediterranean trade routes.[63]

On the day following, Wellington Koo made an eloquent defense of the Chinese position. Koo asked for the restoration of the leased territory of Kiaochow, the railroad, and other former German rights in Shantung to China. He pointed to the historic role of the province as the cradle of Chinese civilization, as the birthplace of Confucius and Mencius — the "holy land" of China. The enormous population of 36,000,000 in an area of 35,000 square miles made it worthless for purposes of colonization, while its strategic location gave it command of the North China gateway. China, he said, felt indebted to Japan and Britain for having freed the territory from Germany, but now she looked to the Conference to see that justice was done to her in return of the province. On the basis of nationality and the preservation of territorial integrity, it could not do less. Koo's statement contained a misleading assumption which was to carry through the whole of the Shantung controversy. Sovereignty over the whole province was not technically in question, as the Conference and the general public were led to assume, but only over the area comprising Kiaochow. Of course, if the Japanese claims under the 1915 and 1917-1918 treaties were met, Japan assumed extensive economic and political rights in the province which virtually reduced it to vassalage. In this respect only was the sovereignty of all Shantung involved.

Makino replied to the Koo statement by reading from the Japanese war ultimatum to Germany, in which Japan asked for the surrender of the province for its eventual restoration to China. Since the victory at Tsingtau, he said, Japan had been in possession of the area and had entered into friendly understandings with China under the Twenty-One Demands and the 1918 agreements, which governed the question. Wilson thereupon interrupted to ask that the notes constituting the understanding be laid before the Council. This was exactly what

Japan wished to avoid. She did not want these war-time arrangements called into question but hoped for their recognition as governing the Shantung question. Such recognition, of course, would constitute a claim for the validity of her whole system of war-time arrangements with China,[64] upon which rested her new position in East Asia. Makino protested Wilson's proposal, saying he would have to have his government's permission before submitting the agreements in question. Koo, however, readily agreed to submit them. It was at this point Clemenceau revealed that there were certain secret treaties of the Allies with Japan regarding her claims in the Orient. This seemed to cause no special excitement and indicates that the treaties were better known than Wilson later admitted.[65] Makino continued to insist that if Japan were to make good its agreement to return the territory to China, it must first have recognition of the rights ceded by Germany.[66]

Koo maintained that the war had abrogated the German claims and superseded the Sino-Japanese agreements.[67] This was the position outlined by the American Minister from Peking and adopted as the American view, although Koo did not mention it.[68] The position was on questionable legal grounds since the understanding of 1915 had preceded China's entry into the war and came after the surrender of the German forces in Shantung, while the 1918 agreement had followed after China's declaration of war. Only if a new moral order, which outlawed force as a means of bringing about international agreements, were established could China hope for success in redressing her position. The Chinese delegates had counted heavily on this new Wilsonian order of international relations, for Koo maintained that all the previous arrangements made with Japan were provisional and subject to revision by the Conference in the light of this new era of justice being established.[69]

Secretary Lansing thought that Koo "simply overwhelmed the Japanese with his argument."[70] Even the Japanese were so impressed at the success of Koo's presentation that Viscount Chinda called on Lansing the next day to say that if Japan failed to obtain the German rights, she would hold the United States responsible. Lansing countered ". . . we need an open mind [,] but [we] must see the treaties and agreements on China."[71] At the same time in Peking, the Japanese reportedly exerted pressure on the Chinese to discredit Koo and the delegation, to temper their claims, and to obtain the promise of China to withhold the war-time agreements from the Conference, unless Japan gave consent to their release.[72] Wilson, when informed of these moves on the part of Japan instructed Lansing:

> I recognize the seriousness of this matter and think that it might be well for you to send a message to Reinsch, telling him to advise the Chinese Government to stand firm, and a message to Morris in Tokyo instructing him to have a friendly conversation with the Minister of Foreign Affairs about this matter and disclose our knowledge of what is going on in Peking, and express our distress that there should be these indications that the Japanese Government is not willing to trust to the fairness and justness of the Peace Conference.
>
> Koo might be advised in the meantime to follow the course that he thinks right.[73]

Wilson was still the prudent friend of China. After his continued insistence, the treaties and agreements were laid before the Conference.

The tone of the meetings was changing, Lansing confided to his private diary: "As I see it, the dominant spirit in the Peace Conference is selfish materialism tinctured with a cynical disregard of manifest rights. What will be the outcome? Will American idealism have to succumb to this evil spirit of a past era? Will principle or expediency control the work of the Conference?" He thought the President's relaxation in pushing for principles meant the loss of them entirely.[74]

On February 14, the President returned to Washington, taking with him the completed Covenant as he had presented it to the Plenary session on the day of his departure. He left Colonel House to take his place with Lansing in the Council of Ten. It was understood that House would go ahead with the program on arms reduction, reparations, the economic aspect of the treaty, and a delineation of the boundaries of Germany including cession of the colonies.[75] Upon his return, the President found the negotiations complicated by House's compromises,[76] and the necessity to introduce the reservations to the treaty necessary for future Senate ratification. He felt, however, that public opinion in the United States was back of him.[77] Clemenceau and Lloyd George had been aware of the President's loss of the November Congressional elections, they recalled Theodore Roosevelt's warning that Wilson had been discredited and could not speak for the American people at the Conference.[78] Knowing the peculiar nature of politics in the United States, they viewed with some doubt the American pledges at Paris,[79] which in turn hampered Wilson's bargaining position. The American amendments to the League Covenant weakened his strong moral position and permitted the opportunity for other nations to attempt changes serving their own interests.[80]

To add to the complexity of the negotiations, Wilson was stricken with influenza.[81] Again Colonel House acted for the President, indicating the President still trusted his confidante. House alone now attended sessions of the Council of Four, organized on Lloyd George's suggestion to expedite the business of the Conference. Lansing was indignant at being superseded! He wrote in his desk diary: "I need not express my feelings. If it was not for the critical state of affairs and popular temper I would ask to be allowed to return home. Patriotism and personal indignation are pulling in opposite directions. I suppose my sense of duty will swallow my pride."[82]

House saw the necessity for a swift peace and attempted to do what he could to achieve it, but reparations, then under discussion, seemed to bring forth verbal changes and delays, mostly on the part of the French, until both House and Wilson were displeased.[83] The President told Lansing he was disgusted with the slow movement of business, that he intended to call for a plenary session and to quit the Conference unless there were immediate agreements. The following day the Navy Department received a cable asking how soon the *George Washington* could be made ready. It was interpreted as a Presidential threat to leave the Conference, and occasioned much comment;

but Seymour doubts if it speeded up the business of the Conference.[84] On April 8, the President recovered sufficiently to return to the meetings.

First it had been the British elections, then the President's visit to Italy and England that had delayed opening of the Conference. Work had been further delayed by his return to Washington in February. The President realized that the situation in Europe was critical and like House he hoped for an early peace. Bela Kun in Hungary, the Russian Civil war, Allied forces in Siberia, Germany on a starving diet, hunger and dissatisfaction everywhere — this was the composite picture facing him. The relief ships moved slowly across their tracing map in Herbert Hoover's office, but there was never enough. Europe was a powder keg. Communism could sweep the West! Wilson threw his influence behind an early settlement, letting no delay stand in the way. Now that the League had been formed, the best thing to do was to make the best possible peace in the least possible time. The League would serve as a future instrument for correcting any errors.[85]

Creation of the Council of Four, consisting of the four principal Allied heads of state, to make the major decisions had resulted from this desire for an early treaty. The Japanese resented exclusion from the Big Four, but Wilson promised that they would be consulted and informed on the work of the Council before it was adopted. In case problems wider than Europe were discussed, Japan would be called into session.[86]

On April 21, Makino and Chinda called individually on Wilson and Lansing to prove the justice of Japanese claims in Shantung. Wilson proposed that the German rights be ceded to the five powers as trustees for disposition and that all spheres of influence in China be abrogated. The Japanese agreed with the latter proposal, meantime pointing out that the British and the French would not agree. They strongly maintained that the German rights must be ceded to Japan.[87]

Makino, on the following day, offered two drafts concerning Shantung to the Council of Four. He reviewed his statement of January 28 and defended the legality of the 1915 and 1918 agreements with China. Viscount Chinda supported his colleague's appeal with the admonition that they were under instructions from Tokyo and could not sign the treaty unless their terms were met. They claimed the support of the secret 1917 treaties with their Allies and gave a legal brief in defense of their arrangements with China, revealing that the latter had actually received 20,000,000 yen under the terms of the railway concessions of the 1918 treaty. Makino handed around a draft of the clauses Japan wished included in the Versailles treaty in relation to Shantung. With but minor changes these eventually became the articles accepted.

In reply to Japan's claim for support under the secret 1917 treaties, Lloyd George stated that his government would fulfill her agreement. He ventured to question, however, if it were advisable to put the settlement of the Shantung issue in the German treaty, since as a special item it might induce other powers to seek separate articles which would delay the peace. Chinda explained that as a developed leasehold it demanded special treaty mention, and that Japan must have the German rights in Shantung surrendered by treaty so she could in turn restore the territory to China.[88]

Wilson inquired for a more explicit statement on the railway provisions of the 1918 Sino-Japanese Agreement, especially regarding the joint administration of the railroads and the part the provided Japanese instructors were to play in their management. Such arrangements, the President declared, were a part of a series of things imposed on China. He inquired of the concessions for exploitation of the mineral wealth and the possible interference of the Japanese arrangements with the open door. Since Lloyd George and Clemenceau were tied by the secret treaties he felt he alone was free to judge in the matter. (Italy had withdrawn from the Conference for the time being over Wilson's refusal to grant them Fiume, but they were also in on the secret treaties.)

Wilson then launched into a biting moral harangue to the Japanese delegates. The peace of the Far East centered on China and Japan. He thought that Japan should think more of her duties to China — the idea of duty was central in the League. He desired to see Japan lead the Far East standing on the ideas

of the League. Two days previously he had proposed cession
of the German rights in Shantung to the five powers as trustees
to determine how the treaties were to be carried out. He sought
a definition of how Japan proposed to help China. He had
hoped the powers would pool their interests and give China a
chance for equality among the nations of the world. With a
population of 400,000,000, "if flames were put to it, the fire
could not be quenched." He desired to uphold the sanctity of
treaties, but he thought some would have been better not negotiated.[89]

The best opinion in Japan, replied Makino, favored Wilson's view; but he recalled that international affairs in China
had not always been on a very just basis. (Lloyd George here
vocally agreed.) As to Japan's plans to develop China, Makino
believed it must be by joint undertakings of their peoples. In
January, Premier Hara had said that Japan was ready to agree
to anything proposed in justice concerning extraterritoriality,
foreign troops, spheres of influence, Boxer indemnity, and such
matters in China. He thought his government was ready to
discuss these matters with the powers. At this point, Wilson
asked what was Japan's attitude on extraterritoriality in relation to Kiaochow. Makino replied that if the established principles of extraterritoriality changed in relation to the rest of China,
Kiaochow would be no exception. Wilson then suggested that
the Chinese should be brought to the Council of Four. Makino
made no objection to the Chinese being heard, but the Japanese delegation, not wishing to enter into a discussion of the
question, failed to be present that afternoon when China presented her case.[90]

Wilson opened the afternoon session with the Chinese delegation by mentioning that he had read the Sino-Japanese agreements and the British, French, Japanese treaties. (Lloyd George
interrupted to explain the origin of the British treaty was due
to the acute need of convoy aid in the Mediterranean in 1917.)
The President then read extracts of the various agreements and
stated that the Chinese could see the embarrassing position of
their case. Lloyd George and Clemenceau were bound by treaty
to support Japan; China was bound to the Japanese case by the

exchange of notes and a treaty. He observed that Koo had claimed before the Council of Ten in January that the war had cancelled the agreement with Germany, but it had not cancelled the Sino-Japanese agreements made before and after the entry of China into the war. Wilson then reviewed his efforts to alleviate the settlement for China; he had asked Japan to agree to a five power trusteeship, suggested it might be possible to modify the Sino-Japanese treaty, proposed all governments renounce their special rights in China — all to no avail. He then reviewed the Japanese position as presented in the morning session.[91]

Wellington Koo explained that the treaty of 1915 and the agreement of 1918, growing out of the former, were the outcome of the Twenty-One Demands, accepted under duress by China. He thought for this reason the whole matter of the Sino-Japanese agreements stood outside the regular treatment of treaties and international agreements. China had submitted to *force majeure*. He explained how by 1918 Japan had penetrated two hundred fifty miles into the interior of Shantung, established civil administration bureaus, levied taxes, and exerted judicial powers in the interior. (All of which Wilson knew to be true on the basis of Reinsch's reports.) Public feeling against the Japanese was so aroused, Koo claimed, that Peking had been forced to conclude the 1918 agreement to secure the delimitation of Japanese activities and thus quiet the people of China.[92]

The British Prime Minister asked if China would gain more by the treaty ceding the German rights in Shantung outright to Japan, or by having the Japanese retain the rights ceded under the 1915 and 1918 understandings with China. Koo replied that with Japan in Manchuria occupying the railroad and in Shantung doing likewise, Peking was in a Japanese pincer. After consulting his colleagues, he answered Lloyd George's question. He could not make a choice between a cession of German rights or a recognition of the 1915 and 1918 agreements. Both were unacceptable!

Wilson and Lloyd George attempted to show Koo that they wished to do what they could for China under the circumstances.

The President explained that both China and Japan would be members of the League, which would guarantee their territorial integrity and political independence. China would thus receive a protection she had never had before. He was himself prepared to advocate before the League that the special rights of all nations in China be abandoned. Japan had declared that she would support this position. He concluded that while there was doubt as to the legality of the treaty and of the notes between China and Japan, there was no doubt concerning the French and British treaties with Japan. Wilson viewed the alternatives for China as lying between the concession of the German rights to Japan and the recognition of that power's status in Shantung under the 1915 and 1918 agreements. He exclaimed that the heart of the world went out to China's 400,000,000 people, and any statesman who ignored them played a dangerous game.

Lloyd George and Clemenceau told the Chinese delegates that their governments must honor their Japanese treaty obligations. Both men promised to stand up for China in the League, but the war had been fought for the East as well as the West against German domination, and treaty obligations must be respected. The Chinese, however, were unconvinced that this should necessitate recognition of Japan's rights in Shantung, so Wilson asked them to consider the question further.

The matter as to whether China would best benefit from direct cession of the German rights to Japan or under the Sino-Japanese agreements was referred to a committee of experts. E. T. Williams, of the American mission consulted with his British counterpart Ronald Macleay. They found the proposal to grant Japan the rights enjoyed by Germany prior to 1914 objectionable since "Japan in Shantung is far more dangerous to China and to the peace of the Far East than Germany ever was." Williams thought, "To give her a fortified naval base for 78 years at Tsingtau and *permanent* control of the railways and mines of Shantung is to make a thrust at the very heart of China." However, the alternative would be worse. "The conventions of 1915 . . . ought not to be recognized at all in the settlement. Rather they ought to be declared not binding, for they are even more objectionable than the Treaty of Brest-

Litovsk." They were extracted under duress and their terms would give Japan a permanent settlement in Tsingtau. She would retain the mines and the railway; the latter she would continue to police. "Her offer for return of Kiaochow therefore is merely an offer of the shell. She would keep the kernel." Williams suggested, that Germany relinquish her rights in Shantung to the five powers, or Japan, now in possession of the rights, should relinquish them to China upon the latter's agreement to establish an international settlement at Tsingtau. Japan should then be reimbursed for her expenses in taking Kiaochow from Germany. As a concession to Japan, the mines might be operated under a Sino-Japanese company, but the railroad under no condition should be left in her possession. The American expert recalled Wilson's Mt. Vernon address stressing every settlement of the peace agreeing with the free will of the people concerned. Chinese opinion was determined in its resistance to the Japanese claims. "Nowhere have the people of a district spoken more plainly."[93]

On the same day, Wilson also received a letter from Lou Tseng-tsiang, chief of the Chinese delegation, reiterating the unacceptability of any alternative granting Japan the German rights in Shantung. It followed Koo's argument that the 1915 and 1918 agreements were accomplished under coercion, and that the principles accepted as the basis for the peace conference were incompatible with and superseded them. While in accord with the purpose to uphold the sanctity of obligations, it questioned if there were not "a higher obligation resting on the Council now to remove serious obstacles to the maintenance of a durable peace in the Far East as elsewhere."[94] Wilson's alternative recommendation followed the Williams' suggestions of a five power receivership, reimbursement of Japan for the capture of Tsingtau, and establishment of Kiaochow as an open port with an international settlement if desired.

At this time, Presidential Secretary Tumulty cabled Wilson that Japan's designs seemed as indefensible as Italy's. He asked, "Would it not be an opportune time to cast another die, this one in the direction of Japan that the whole world may know once and for all where America stands upon the greatest issue of the peace we are trying to make?" Tumulty advised, "Now is the time to use your heavy artillery and emphasize [the] danger of secret treaties and selfish designs of certain big nations."[95]

On April 24, Makino and Chinda called at the Crillon, American headquarters in Paris. Makino said Japan would not sign the treaty unless her informal promise to return Shantung to China was accepted as satisfactory. Somewhat sarcastically, he stated, "In Tokyo they do not seem to see why we should be the least-favored nation in our relations with Shantung simply because almost unaided, . . . we rescued the province from the German invaders." It was clear to Bonsal that Makino was "mad," and House's assistant was not surprised, considering the scurrilous treatment Japan was getting in the press.[96]

The Japanese demands for the German rights in Shantung were made opportunely. The German delegates were expected to arrive on April 28 to receive the terms of the treaty. Italy had left the conference over Fiume on April 23; Belgium threatened to do likewise unless German reparations included full payment of damages. The Chamber of Deputies in France and the British House of Commons called for a hard peace with Germany. Among the lesser delegates in Paris, there was dissatisfaction at the way the Council of Four was making decisions. Now Japan threatened refusal to sign the treaty if her objectives in Shantung were denied. Without Japan, Wilson thought the formation of the League would be endangered. The League was to be the means of settling the discrepancies in the treaty and of preventing future conflicts. Yet, the President's advices were contrary to granting Japan's desires. It was a difficult decision to make.[97] Meantime, the President did what he could in the interests of China.

Koo formally presented on April 25 the Chinese solution of a five power receivership of the German rights and the other points suggested in the Lou Tseng-tsiang letter to Wilson on April 25.[98] The Chinese suggestion was taken under advisement by the Council, and Wilson suggested that Lloyd George and Balfour see the Japanese as to what arrangements were possible on the proposal.[99]

After meeting with the American Delegation to discuss the Shantung situation, upon which he consulted them more than on any other issue,[100] Wilson asked Lansing to see the Japanese and attempt to persuade them to consider the proposal of an international trusteeship for Shantung. That evening the Secretary and E. T. Williams conferred with the Japanese.[101] It seemed they had answers to all questions. Lansing asked what Japan desired concerning Shantung. Chinda said she wanted fulfillment of her agreement with China. The Secretary protested "We looked upon the people of Shantung as a people wronged and oppressed [by Germany] and now that the enemy was removed we could not bear to see the evil continue through replacing one foreign nation by another." Chinda countered that Japan did not intend to treat the people like Germany had. The United States, Lansing declared, stood for the rights of nationalities and the self-determination of peoples. "O but the situation is quite different," Chinda said. "We have express conventions with China dealing with the question and we mean to insist upon their *exact fulfillment.*"[102]

Lansing then asked why Japan resisted a treaty statement of the exact conditions under which the return of Kiaochow was to be made to China. Chinda explained that the treaty was with Germany and not China, therefore, such a statement was not apropos, since Germany could not tell Japan what she should do with the rights ceded. Lansing protested that this did not prevent a statement by Japan of her generous intentions. The Viscount said that had already been done by Japan in her ultimatum to Germany. "He charged that we were always suspecting them, doubting their good faith . . . He asked if we came here to sit in judgment of them, saying that Japan could not submit to that; that we all came as representing sovereign states, compeers, and no one could call in question the action of another." Lansing denied these allegations and said America's sole aim was to reconcile the claims of Japan and China. Chinda attacked the propaganda methods of the Chinese delegation and said it was a point of honor with Japan to see that China fulfilled her obligations regarding Shantung under her treaty with Japan. He repeated they had had instructions from home that if the German rights were not renounced in favor of Japan, the Japanese delegates were not to sign the treaty.[103]

Lansing delayed informing the President,[104] who on the morning of April 28 called to ascertain the outcome of the meeting. At the early gathering of the Big Three the same morning, Balfour reported the results of his conference with the Japanese. They had been in most respects similar to those of Lansing. Japan was unwilling to modify the terms of the treaty and the understandings with China. However, she would give assurances that the Tsingtau concessions to Japan would not exclude other foreigners, and the Shantung railway rights would not be used to discriminate against other nations. This was something in the nature of a guarantee of Wilson's open door for the area.

The President speculated of telling Japan that the powers agreed to transfer the German rights to her, but that they refused to recognize her wartime arrangements with China, and required assurances that she would not use the rights for employing military forces in Shantung. He said the American public was firm in demanding that China not be oppressed by Japan, and they expected him to be "as solid" on this issue as he had been on Fiume.[105] This suggestion led to securing Japanese promises to restrict the use of her military forces in the former German leasehold. It also indicated Wilson was quite aware of the importance of his opposition to recognition of the 1915 and 1918 Sino-Japanese treaties which made Kiaochow a free port with a Japanese concession, gave the Japanese joint operation with the Chinese in the Shantung railroad but policed under Japanese direction, and otherwise extended the rights of the German concession.

Balfour attempted to put the Japanese position in a more favorable light. Japan had been asked to agree on a League wherein her petition for inclusion of racial equality had failed. If Japan's ambitions on both equality and Shantung were checked, her delegation's position would be serious. A decision on Shantung was necessary that day before the afternoon meeting of the plenary session. If Japan received Shantung, her spokesmen would make only an abstract resolution on racial equality, otherwise her delegation had been unable to say what her action would be.[106] This was the immediate decision demanded of the Council.

Wilson announced his decision: if the Japanese would cede their military and retain only their economic rights in Shantung, he would agree to the settlement; but when the League was organized he would propose the cession of all extraterritoriality in China.[107] The three agreed that Balfour write the Japanese the line the decision would take, which permitted Japan to receive the German rights in Shantung by direct cession, subject to the Wilson reservations on military force and a declaration concerning the railroads. The Japanese were requested to appear next day at the Council.[108]

That afternoon in the plenary session of the Conference, Japan made her mild statement of not pressing racial equality at the moment. The terms of the Council of Three had been made known to them. Japan had won out on the issue of Shantung, but her war time agreements and thus her right to deal with China in an unhampered manner remained unrecognized. Lansing confided to his diary that at the plenary session the President showed him a letter approved by the heads of State and addressed to Makino expressing sorrow that the Japanese claims had not been finally settled before the session. From this and the President's conversation, Lansing concluded "that a bargain has been struck by which the Japanese agree to sign the Covenant in exchange for admission of their claims. If so, it is an iniquitous agreement." The President was concurring on this "to avoid Japan's declining to enter the League of Nations." House, the Secretary thought, was at the bottom of the whole business. "I said to him today that to give Kiau Chau to Japan was to barter away a great principle. He replied, 'We have had to do it before.' I answered with some heat; 'Yes, it has been done and it is the curse of this Conference that that method has been adopted.' He made no reply, but that may have been because we were talking across a corner of the peace table in whispers." The Secretary believed it would be better to leave Japan out of the League than to abandon China and thus surrender American prestige in the Far East.[109] This was also the conclusion of both White and Bliss.

That evening Wilson asked Ray Stannard Baker, his press secretary, to secure information on the Chinese situation. Baker called on Hornbeck, and they discussed it until two in the morning. Baker returned to the Crillon and worked on the memoranda for the President until six. Three hours later, he laid before Wilson the notes and the memoranda from Williams, Hornbeck, Koo, Wei and others. Pinning up a map on the wall of the President's study, Baker made as good a case as he could for the Chinese position. When he concluded Wilson said, "Baker, the difficulty is not with the facts of the controversy, but with the politics of it." He then pointed out how the matter was tied up with the secret treaties, and expressed the fear that with Italy out of the Conference, Belgium discontented, the defection of Japan might break up the Conference and destroy the League.[110]

The Baker memoranda argued for America's moral duty to China and concluded, "The Japanese proposals amount to offering China the shell and securing for Japan the oyster." Hornbeck's notes warned against any acknowledgment of the Sino-Japanese agreements, but that refusal of the Conference to recognize Japan's claims would neither put her in possession of or drive her out of Shantung — she was there. If Japan failed to sign the treaty, the European questions would not be affected. He thought she would not withdraw from the conference if refused her demands but compensated with some mild compromise on the Shantung question. Baker's report included the statements and contracted obligations of Japan on Shantung and a French report to Clemenceau, calling Shantung "China's Alsace-Lorraine" and Japan the "Yellow Prussia."[111]

Other members of the American delegation resented bitterly the sacrifice of China's position in Shantung. General Bliss, with the approval of Lansing and White, sent a letter of protest to the President. The General admonished, "It can't be right to do wrong even to make peace." He protested the settlement as immoral in principle and unjust to China.[112] House had nothing to do with the protest. From the beginning he had held aloof from the other three members of the Commission who consulted with one another each morning. This aloofness, together with the confidence the Colonel seemed to enjoy of the President, had only added to Lansing's embitterment.[113]

At the Council on the same day, the Japanese were handed the settlement on which they had conferred with Balfour. It provided that Japan would receive Shantung from Germany and then transfer it in full sovereignty to China while retaining the economic privileges (the Wilson formula). Police forces along the railway were to be used for security of traffic only, while the instructors employed were to be selected by the company.[114]

The Japanese on the last of April agreed to the terms of the Big Three and gave the oral guarantee desired by Wilson:

> The policy of Japan is to hand back the Shantung Peninsula in full sovereignty to China, retaining only the economic privileges granted to Germany and the right to establish a settlement under the usual conditions at Tsingtau.
>
> The owners of the railway will use special police only to ensure security for traffic. They will be used for no other purpose.
>
> The police force will be composed of Chinese, and such Japanese instructors as the directors of the railway may select will be appointed by the Chinese Government.[115]

At the time of making their statement, the Japanese insisted on the validity of the war time agreements and maintained that if China failed to cooperate in the settlement as obtained in the Conference, the Japanese would insist on fulfillment of the 1915 and 1918 agreements. Wilson stated categorically that nothing he had done or stated must be taken as recognition of these agreements. If trouble were encountered in the future relations of Japan and China, he said, the League would be the mediator. Chinda persisted that in case of difficulty of a settlement with China, Japan would insist on the war-time arrangements.[116]

The Japanese draft of articles 156 through 158 with their slight amendments were given to Sir Maurice Hankey, Secretary of the Council, to send to the drafting commission for inclusion in the treaty. In them Germany renounced in favor of Japan her rights and privileges in Kiaochow, including the mines, railways, and cables. All movable and immovable property of the German state within Kiaochow was thus acquired by Japan, who was to receive all the related archives and documents from Germany within three months after the treaty came into force.[117] The statement of Japan concerning her guarantees was not included, for it had been made only with the understanding that it be of an informal nature. The deed was accomplished.

Actually, the decision by Wilson to give the German rights in Shantung to Japan was made on April 28, before the plenary session, and thus before his final consultation with the American experts through Baker. All his advices were against the step he took, but Wilson was convinced, and justly so, that it was necessary to keep Japan at the Conference and to obtain a League of Nations. The unpopularity of his decision was apparent to the President and he cabled Tumulty a précis of the business for use at such time as it came under public discussion. In his own words, the matter had been settled "in a way which seems to me as satisfactory as could be got out of the tangle of treaties in which China herself was involved. . . ."[118] Tumulty was sorry about the settlement and "afraid of the impression" it would make.[119]

Reaction to the settlement was various. House approved the decision.[120] Bonsal saw the chief argument for the decision in the unspoken climate of the conference: with Italy withdrawn, Russia absent, the Central Powers excluded, if Japan withdrew, "our world congress, or whatever it is, would dwindle to the proportions of a rump parliament."[121] Lansing thought it conceded all Japan claimed, and he anticipated a storm of protests from the United States "when it is known that we have abandoned China and given in to Japan." The President's sincere fear of the destruction of the League, the Secretary thought, had caused the decision. He believed the League had become a millstone around America's neck.[122] Henry White thought the decision "unfortunate to put it mildly."[123] At first when Bliss learned of the decision, he considered whether or not he should resign, or give notice he would not sign the treaty if the Shantung articles were retained.[124]

Thomas F. Millard, the Shanghai publisher, ran into the chief Far Eastern expert of the American Commission, E. T. Williams, it was April 30, and Paris was buzzing with the settlement. Williams exclaimed, "This is terrible! It may bring on war in Asia."[125] Another time Bonsal, while agreeing with Williams that China was a world problem, expressed the thought that Japan was due some recognition for her war contribution. Williams disagreed: "I am sorry for the poor Japanese peasant too. He is a pawn in the hands of his imperialistic leaders. They are after the conquest of Asia, as a preliminary to world conquest, and their first objective is the coal and iron of Shantung, which they need for their domestic economy as well as their wider, more far reaching plans of conquest." He saw the Japanese withdrawal of troops without effect, since coolies could always be hired in China to cause an incident and bring about Japanese intervention.[126]

The American delegation was displeased at the outcome, but the Chinese delegates were shocked when a press representative brought the news of Wilson's "surrender" of Shantung to Japan. "So absolutely did the Chinese rely on the friendship of America and her power to see justice done that the first message was not credited. . . ." They phoned Lansing for confirmation, but he knew nothing of the decision. Then confirmation came. "One Chinese flung himself on the floor in a paroxysm of despair and rage."[127] Baker late that evening brought the news from the President, but it was already known. The Presidential Press Secretary expressed Wilson's sorrow that he had been unable to do more for China, but the decision had been compelled to "save the League of Nations."[128] Some of the Chinese delegates were for issuing an immediate statement or for leaving Paris. Baker dissuaded them in this, but he found it "bitterly hard, where one believed in the justice of the claim (as I did in the justice of the Chinese demands) to argue that they be disregarded in order to accomplish some farther-sighted purpose."[129] Dr. Morrison, English adviser to the Chinese delegation, told Bonsal that the Chinese were more furious with Wilson than with Balfour whom they regarded "as his cat's paw." They insisted the President had said, "You can rely on me."[130]

On May 4, Lou Tseng-tsiang entered a "formal protest in the name of justice" concerning the settlement. He reiterated the Chinese case and proclaimed Japan, because of her proximity, a greater menace to China than Germany. His government, he stated, had relied on the Fourteen Points and their extension, the honorable relationship between states, and the justice and equity of the case to no avail.[131] Two days later, in the plenary session of the Conference, China submitted a formal protest against the decision. On May 7, the Chinese received their copy of the treaty which had been handed the German group at the plenary conference the day previous. It contained no statement safeguarding China's rights or territorial sovereignty in Shantung since the Japanese assurances on these points were informal. So great was the feeling among the Chinese, Koo feared for his life and told Bonsal, "If I sign the treaty — even under orders from Peking — I shall not have what you in New York call a Chinaman's chance."[132] However, the Chinese decided to sign the treaty subject to reservation of the future status of the German rights in Shantung. When this was refused, they asked for an annex to the treaty containing the same reservation. Again they were refused at the last moment; and when the treaty was signed at Versailles on June 28, the Chinese delegation was conspicuously absent from the fifty minute ceremony.[133] It was finally China who did not sign. China was weak; Japan was strong — so simply can the lack of concern over China's refusing to sign the treaty be explained.

On September 15, 1919, President Hsu Shih-chang proclaimed the restoration of peace between China and Germany. His country had already come into the League by the Austrian treaty. In January, 1920 the Versailles Treaty went into effect, and Japan attempted to enter into negotiations with China on the question of restoring Shantung under the Versailles articles; but China refused to negotiate, as she did again the following September. The situation thus produced in East Asia by her refusal, the coming date for renewal of the Anglo-Japanese Alliance, the question of British abandonment of the open door, and the load of world armaments, all combined to give China her opportunity to air the Shantung decision once again at the Washington Conference. This time she was successful in her attempt to have the German rights restored to her. On June 2, 1922, Japan and China ratified their new agreement on Shantung.[134]

On the Sunday following the Shantung decision in Paris, student demonstrations had begun in China. Organized first as a protest of the Peace Conference action, they grew into a boycott of Japan in which merchants, dockworkers, laborers and even peasants freely participated. Reinsch reported that the Conference decision had "destroyed all confidence in a league of nations which had such an ugly fact as its cornerstone."[135] Polk's cable carried the cryptic facts: "Advices from Peking indicate great resentment over Shantung. Chinese Minister to Japan assaulted by student mob. Tsao Ju-lin's house burned and he is refugee in legation. Situation such it might be capitalized by Southern leaders to overthrow govt. Should this happen Japan might intervene."[136]

When the Japanese delegates returned home in August, 1919, they were met with a demonstration protesting their failure to obtain a racial equality clause in the treaty. Japan's national pride had been injured, and for many months she had suffered at the hands of the United States Senators,[137] the reports of Asian correspondents, and the expressed opinion of the world. She had her own chauvinists who were ever willing to fan the flame of discontent, for the military was a powerful voice in politics. Newspapers were anti-American, and when the Shantung reservation was made by the United States Senate, Ambassador Morris informed the Department, "It appears to me quite clear that the military party is using the United States as the future menace, not sincerely but as a justification for increased army and navy appropriations."[138]

In the heat of the controversy over Shantung, it was forgotten both in China and the United States that Section II, Articles 128-134 of the treaty granted concessions to China, which in a more temperate time would have been hailed by her as great diplomatic gains.[139] These articles terminated the old "unequal" treaties with Germany and Austria-Hungary, gave China the German property in Tientsin, Hankow and elsewhere, cancelled the Boxer indemnity to the defeated powers, and returned the astronomical instruments taken by Germany in 1901.[140]

The Shantung issue at Paris was a gathering of a complexity of problems in East Asia. Racial equality and the island annexations, the inopportuness of the appearance of the question for settlement only added to the difficulty. Wilson yielded under pressure of the previous decisions against Japan, the secret treaties, China's own agreements with Japan on the issue, and the Japanese real threat to refuse signing the treaty and wreck the League through weakness. Wilson took these threats seriously, and no other argument was more influential in forcing his decision. It has since been proved that the Japanese threats were sincere, and the delegation was instructed to withdraw if Shantung was not conceded.[141] The President had secured oral guarantees on what he considered the main threats of Japan in Shantung, and he promised to bring the whole position of China in review before the League at a later day.

Wilson had prevented the recognition of the war time Sino-Japanese agreements which Japan had so carefully erected to assure her position in Asia. The Shantung articles thus were not the defeat they appeared to be; and certainly if Wilson's plans for the League had been accomplished, he was justified in foreseeing a happier ending to the tale. But to China, expecting miracles in a prosaic world, the efforts of a prudent friend were little appreciated. If failure there was, perhaps General Smuts was right when he said, "It was not Wilson who failed. . . . It was the human spirit itself that failed at Paris."[142] Even Nietzsche confessed, "Success has always been a great liar."

Wilson himself answered best the critics of Versailles in his address to the International Law Society at Paris. He no doubt had the recent Shantung issue in mind:

> May I say that one of the things that has disturbed me in recent months is the unqualified hope that men have entertained everywhere of immediate emancipation from

the things that have hampered them and oppressed them.
You cannot in human experience rush into the light. You
have to go through the twilight into the broadening day
before the noon comes and the full sun is upon the land-
scape; and we must see to it that those who hope are not
disappointed by showing them the processes by which hope
must be realized, processes of law, processes of slow disen-
tanglement from the many things that have bound us in the
past. You cannot throw off the habits of the individual
immediately. They must be slowly got rid of, or, rather,
they must be slowly altered. They must be slowly adapted.
They must be slowly shaped to the new ends for which we
would use them. That is the process of law if law is intelligently conceived.[143]

And he had hoped to put the world under the rule of law.[144]

CHAPTER TEN

The Course Is Run

WHAT DIFFERENCE DOES PARTY MAKE WHEN MANKIND IS
INVOLVED.

—Woodrow Wilson

Woodrow Wilson attended the signing of the Versailles
Treaty on June 28, 1919. The following day he sailed for home.
He was well aware of the Republican Senatorial cabal organized
to turn public opinion against the terms he had secured at
Paris.[1] The President had not been one to run from a fight.
Secretary Lansing said that the President "is going back with
blood in his eye and his loins girded for battle. He will, I
judge from what he says, be the attacking party and not stand
on the defensive. I have never seen him more pugnacious or
bellicose. Unless I am greatly mistaken he will 'carry the war
into Africa' and make a lively row for the enemy."[2]

Returning from the conference aboard the *George Washington,* Wilson had discussed the Shantung decision with Bernard
Baruch, Vance McCormick, Norman Davis, Thomas Lamont
and others. The President confessed it was the most difficult
part of the treaty to defend, but France and England had been
absolutely bound to the support of Japan. By making the
settlement, they had kept Japan in the conference and made
her a party to the Allied policy toward China in all other respects. As a member of the League, Japan would be forced into
accepting the open door, and the President thought something
might be done to force her release of any exclusive sphere of
influence in China. At any rate, the settlement had given Japan

economic not political control, and had extracted verbal assurances agreeing to pull out of Shantung, although she had refused to put the agreement in writing because it reflected Allied suspicion of her good faith.[3]

On July 10, two days after his return, Wilson presented the treaty to the Republican-controlled Senate. In talking to some of the League supporters at the capitol, he expressed his dissatisfaction with the Shantung settlement, but he thought Japan would deal fairly with China.[4] The Shantung articles had become one of the main points in the Republican attack on the treaty[5] and the agreed party position was to support a resolution eliminating the settlement as obtained at Paris.[6] When the Senate called on Wilson for a copy of the German-Japanese Treaty, rumored to have been negotiated the previous October, the debate ran into the Shantung issue, leading Senator Williams of Mississippi to warn against irresponsible accusations of secret understandings by Japan with the enemy. Senator William E. Borah of Idaho said if Japan wanted to take issue with the United States for not upholding the Shantung settlement, he was willing for the challenge of war to come. The United States, he declaimed, could not afford to cringe longer before Japan's threats.[7]

Before leaving Paris, Wilson through Lansing had sought to commit the Japanese formally to the assurances and obligations that were unofficially assumed by Makino and Chinda on Shantung.[8] He thought Makino would understand "that the interests of the United States are very deeply involved, and it ought to be clear to him, as it is to me, that extended unrest in China, which will certainly ensue unless the most explicit reassurance is given, might not only immediately but for a long time to come disturb the peace of the East and might lead to very serious international complications."[9] Lansing had seen Makino and presented him with a draft which the United States thought sufficient to cover the situation. However, Lansing and Henry White, his successor in the negotiations, failed to accomplish the desired official commitment.[10] The lack of any formal document to present to the public showing just what assurances Japan had given on Shantung became a matter of embarrassment to the President. The Republicans saw the political advantage in the issue and used it for all it was worth in their attack on Wilson and the treaty.

When Katsuji Debuchi, Counselor and Chargé d'Affaires of the Japanese Embassy called to see Polk on July 18, the Acting Secretary, on Wilson's instructions, told him that the President was surprised to note that the Japanese Minister of Foreign Affairs had announced that Japan would withdraw from Kiaochow under the 1915 and 1918 treaties. Polk informed Debuchi that the United States understood that the Paris arrangement superseded these private agreements between Japan and China. Debuchi intimated that the treaties were "little of our business," but Polk insisted that as a party to the Versailles settlement the United States was interested in its terms being observed. He indicated that American opinion was opposed to the Shantung settlement, but that the resentment would be increased if Japan insisted on holding onto her war-time arrangements with China.[11]

In London on the same day, Viscount Chinda, now Ambassador to Britain, went to the Foreign Office for a conversation with Viscount Curzon, who frankly protested Japan's attempts to achieve dominance of the Far East during the war. He warned that Japan had alienated the sympathy of the world by her actions in China. The times now called for a cooperative policy; the day of the division of China into spheres had passed. The British insisted that Japan make a public declaration promising the return of Kiaochow to China. Chinda protested that it had been ceded by Germany to Japan as a result of war. Curzon replied that many unfortunate treaties had been swept away by the course of events and that Japan should recognize the new course of affairs. He also protested Japan's attempts to perpetuate spheres of influence by claiming railroad rights, and stated that the Japanese railroads, built and contemplated, in Manchuria along with those in the rest of China should be internationalized.[12]

Meantime, Wilson saw individual members of the senatorial opposition in an attempt to state frankly his case to them. These meetings were undertaken only after it became obvious that

Chairman Henry Cabot Lodge[13] was unwilling to respond to a Presidential invitation for a meeting with the Senate Foreign Relations Committee.[14] He also sought out Senator Hitchcock, who was leading the Senate fight on the treaty for the administration. The President wanted the country to know that the Shantung decision was not as iniquitous as represented by his enemies. Senator Charles L. McNary, who opposed the treaty said, after a White House conference, that Wilson had facts on Shantung that changed his first impression of the decision.[15] When Lodge stated there would be a reservation on the Shantung decision, two members of the Chinese Mission to the Conference called to declare that they looked on the Senator as a friend of China.[16] When it was reported that the President took sole responsibility for the Shantung decision, the White House vigorously denied the story next day.[17] Wilson abjured any private correspondence for the time being on the subject and confined his statements to official channels.[18]

After expecting hourly a statement of the guarantees on the Shantung settlement from Tokyo, Wilson decided to release his own understanding of the obligations undertaken by the Japanese Government at Paris.[19] Third Assistant Secretary Long called in Debuchi and gave him an unofficial copy of the President's release.[20] It stated the terms under which Japan received the Shantung rights and disclaimed any American acknowledgment of the war-time treaties.

Debuchi then informed Long that a Japanese statement had been released in Tokyo. He said his government would take exception to the President's stand on the 1915 and 1918 agreements with China, for the Conference had not deprived Japan of these treaty rights, and no issue concerning them had been stated in the Lansing-Ishii Agreement. Furthermore, he thought there could be no understanding between Tokyo and Washington until the treaties were recognized.

Long pointed to the specific exception to these treaties made by Polk at the President's direction on July 18 in his talk with the Japanese Chargé. Then, as Secretary in charge of Far Eastern Affairs, Long presented a full-length discourse on the falseness of the Japanese pretensions which were losing her the friendship of the world and casting suspicion on her motives in China. He urged Debuchi, who had been Japan's representative in Peking during the Twenty One Demands, to recommend a new course for his government.

The Chargé confessed that he was a man of liberal views and that he disagreed with the military domination of Japanese foreign policy, but he would make no promises to Long concerning the future of Tokyo's policy or his own part in it.

In London the same day, Colonel House, at a Mandates Commission meeting, took Ambassador Chinda aside to advise that Japan publish an immediate statement on her intent to give up Shantung. The issue was strongly agitated in the United States, the Colonel argued, and Japan was doing herself an injustice by creating suspicion in the eyes of the world. Chinda assured House that Japan would make such an announcement.[21] Neither man was aware that the statement had already been issued in Tokyo.[22]

The Tokyo statement declared that Japan did not intend to claim any rights in Shantung affecting Chinese sovereignty there. Japan had made promises to China to return the territory and the promises would be fulfilled; but there was little Japan could do until three months after the Versailles Treaty went into effect, by which time Germany was to have completed her Shantung obligations to Japan under the treaty. Troops would then be withdrawn and the region returned to China.[23] The statement notably placed the settlement under the war-time treaties, for Tokyo still sought their recognition. The next day, Wilson's statement appeared in the press, reiterating the obligations undertaken by Japan at the Council of Four and definitely declaring that the 1915 and 1918 treaties with China were in no way involved.[24]

On the same day that the Japanese statement appeared in the press, Secretary Lansing gave testimony before the Senate Foreign Relations Committee. The Senators directed much of their questioning to the Shantung agreement, during which Lansing confessed that he thought the Japanese would have signed the treaty without it.[25] Again on August 11 Lansing appeared to testify as to his information concerning the 1917 secret treaties of Japan with the European Allies. Writing of his experience to Polk, now heading the American delegation in Paris, the Secretary confessed: "My endeavor on the hearings was to be loyal to the President and to avoid statements which indicated disagreements with him about the covenant or the mode of conducting the negotiations. . . . As to Shantung I was entirely frank because the Committee knew that I was radically opposed to the decision reached."[26]

President Wilson conferred with the Foreign Relations Committee at the White House on August 19.[27] The questions ranged the whole of the Versailles settlement. In relation to Shantung, Senator Borah asked when the United States gained its first knowledge of the secret treaties of the European Allies with Japan over the region. Wilson answered that his first knowledge of them came at Paris. He also confessed it was his first knowledge of the secret treaties adjusting matters in Europe.[28] Later to a question by Senator Johnson of California asking if the United States had been officially informed of agreements of Allied governments between the outbreak of the war and the armistice, he answered that it was not as far as he knew.[29]

The President also explained that the Japanese guarantees given at Paris in relation to Shantung were "technically oral, but literally written and formulated, and the formulation agreed upon." They were in the form of a *procés verbal*, but since the business of the meeting was recorded and agreed upon by the negotiators the terms were therefore really written. Senator Borah asked if granting the economic rights of Shantung to Japan did not virtually give her mastery of the province? Wilson replied that he thought such a view exaggerated. Senator Knox asked if it had not been through economic privileges that the Japanese acquired mastery in Korea, Inner and Outer Mongolia and in Manchuria? Wilson answered, "Yes, Senator; in the absence of a league of nations they have." He felt confident had the League been in existence such would not have occurred.[30]

As to Japan's return of Kiaochow to China, the President testified it was the Paris understanding that this was to take place as soon as possible, and that he had every confidence that it would. If the Treaty were to fail, however, he confessed Japan would be free to treat Shantung as she saw fit, as she had already done in Manchuria.[31]

Senator Johnson asked if the Shantung decision was reached because otherwise Japan refused to sign the treaty. Wilson replied: "No, I do not think it would be true to say 'yes' to that question. It was reached because we thought it was the best that could be got, in view of the definite engagements of Great Britain and France, and the necessity of a unanimous decision, which we held to be necessary in every case we have [sic] decided."[32] When confronted with Lansing's testimony that Japan would have signed the treaty without the inclusion of the Shantung agreement, Wilson said, "Well, my conclusion is different from his, sir." In the President's judgment Japan would not have signed. Later scholarship was to prove his view correct.[33] The testimony was reported in the press and Wilson hoped it had cleared the air.[34]

On August 23, the Foreign Relations Committee voted to amend the treaty by returning the German rights directly to China. Already the Senate had taken the initiative in calling disgruntled factions not heard at Versailles to their day in public hearings. The Committee then gravely proceeded to query representatives of these various peoples.[35]

Wilson wrote his cousin-in-law Samuel Woodbridge, the Shanghai editor now in the United States, a defense of the Shantung provisions of the treaty:

> But what you say leads me to believe that you have not thought the matter through. France and Great Britain absolutely bound themselves by treaty to Japan with regard to the Shantung settlement as it stands in the Treaty with Germany. What would you propose that we should do? To refuse to concur in the Treaty with Germany would not alter the situation in China's favor, unless it is your idea that we should force Great Britain and France to break their special treaty with Japan, and how would you suggest we should do that? By the exercise of what force?

Japan, as you know, has promised to retain much less than the terms of the treaty give her. She has consented to bind herself by all the engagements of the Covenant of the League of Nations, and if the United States is to be a party to this treaty and a member of the League, she will have an opportunity for serving China in all matters of international justice such as she has never had before, and such as she could not obtain by the course you suggest.

I beg that you will think these things over.[36]

As early as June 1, 1919, Presidential Secretary Joseph P. Tumulty, Wilson's close adviser in matters political, had suggested that the treaty must be taken to the people.[37] Congress had assembled in May, and it was evident that difficulty lay ahead. The *Springfield Republican* had urged that Wilson declare himself a candidate in the 1920 Presidential race for the purpose of securing ratification of the treaty.[38] This latter suggestion Wilson, after advising with Cummings, Glass, and others of his cabinet, was willing to consider. Tumulty, however, was of the opinion the announcement should be delayed until success in 1920 looked more promising, and after the President had gone to the country with the League; "then that time in my opinion will offer the psychological moment for you to say what really is in your heart about a third term, and thus help not only the party but the League of Nations so dear to our hearts."[39] Two days later, Tumulty prepared a tentative itinerary for the tour and advised the President that he must not give the administration's enemies a minute's rest after his return.[40] By June 17, the Secretary had outlined a thirty day trans-continental speaking trip which began in Washington, crossed the continent to San Francisco and returned.[41]

After Wilson's arrival from Paris there seemed to be little mention of a tour until opposition to the treaty became apparent.[42] The President was very tired from his activities during the strenuous eight months abroad, in addition to the treaty fight since his return. The strain was visible in his physique. Friends and Admiral Cary Grayson, his physician, warned him that he would be endangering his life to undertake a western tour. When a similar intimation of the danger to himself was mentioned in the Cabinet, Wilson "promptly replied that he would be willing to give his life for the cause."[43] Secretary Lansing thought the trip was unwise and that it was more important for the President to remain in touch with Congress where the treaty was having "rough sledding."[44] House, feeling the chill of the once-warm friendship, deplored the President's fight with the Senate and confided to his diary, "He is not a good pilot."[45]

Faced with the mounting criticism of the treaty in the Senate, Wilson decided to take the issue to the people. On his western trip, lasting from September 4 to 25, he traveled some eight thousand miles, and made thirty-seven speeches, sometimes as many as three in one day. He discussed the chief points in dispute: Article X which guaranteed the territorial integrity of member states of the League, the reservation from League control of the Monroe Doctrine, and of domestic affairs such as immigration, naturalization, and tariffs, the multiple votes of Great Britain in the Assembly, and the Shantung decision.[46]

In Indianapolis he explained that granting Japan the German rights in Shantung, with the understanding that they were to be returned to China, was a necessity under the agreed treaties of the Allies. The war had been fought in part to defend the sacredness of treaties; there was nothing for the United States to do but urge the guarantees which Japan had accepted. He did not fail to point out that under the Covenant of the League secret treaties could be outlawed.[47] In St. Louis, he urged, "It is all very well to talk about standing by China, but how are you standing by China when you withdraw from the only arrangement by which China can be assisted?"[48] Wilson confessed to his Des Moines audience that he did not like the Shantung settlement "any more than you do," but the circumstances were such that nothing else could be done. He asked, "Are you going to institute a war against Japan and France and England to get Shantung back to China?[49] Article X of the Covenant would preserve the territorial integrity and political independence of all member states. Article XI gave China an opportunity to call to the bar of world justice anyone encroaching upon her. Hence the Treaty was the future guarantee of China's sovereignty.[50]

In San Francisco, Wilson brought up the Republican record in relation to China. There had been no outcry when Japan received Port Arthur after the Russo-Japanese War, neither had there been protest earlier in 1898 at the German seizure of Kiaochow. He claimed the proposed League was the "first time in the history of the world that anything has been done for China. . . ." At Paris he had put the question "May I expect this will be the beginning of the retrocession to China of the exceptional rights which other Governments have enjoyed there?" The other negotiators had replied, "Yes, you may expect it."[51] So the League would bring a new security for China and freedom from her past.

The President waxed eloquent in Salt Lake City over the past sufferings of the Chinese: "I for one want to say that my heart goes out to that great people, that learned people, that accomplished people, hundreds of millions strong but never adequately organized for the exercise of force, therefore always at the mercy of anyone who has effective armies and navies, always subject to be commanded, and never in a position unassisted by the world to insist upon its own rights."[52] In his last speech of the tour at Pueblo, Colorado, while almost blinded with pains in his head, Wilson patiently explained the rights acquired in Shantung by Japan under the Versailles Treaty. He showed that these were not excessive of similar rights exercised by other powers in other parts of China. "For my part, my judgment, my moral judgment, is against the whole set of concessions. They were all of them unjust to China, they ought never to have been exacted, they were all exacted by duress, from a great body of thoughtful and ancient and helpless people." He confessed to a profound sympathy for China and to pride at having taken part in the formation of the League which promised her "the protection of the world."[53]

That night Wilson's illness was upon him. Two days more remained of the tour. The engagements were cancelled and the train hurried back to Washington bearing the ailing President. In Washington he walked from the train to his car.

Four days later, a thrombosis paralyzed his left side. Rumors multiplied. No one was officially informed of the President's condition. Lansing, on October 6, called the Cabinet into session, and Dr. Grayson informed them that Wilson had suffered a nervous breakdown. For days no official business was transacted. As his condition improved all necessary items were submitted to him in the form of memoranda through Admiral Grayson, his physician, and his second wife, Edith Galt Wilson, who consulted on matters with Presidential Secretary Tumulty. The chief usher, on October 20, practically discontinued his White House diary listing the official life of the President. There were only occasional diary entries throughout 1920.[54] The Presidential letter books which averaged one volume of five hundred pages for each six weeks of the administration now received infrequent letters. From the time of his illness until March 4, 1921, a period of eighteen months, only three-fourths of one letter book was filled.[55]

The President's illness was felt throughout the whole administration but nowhere more keenly than in the State Department where John V. A. MacMurray, Chief of the Far Eastern Division observed:

Perhaps the fundamental in the whole situation is the illness of the President. He has been so exclusively responsible for policies — particularly in the realm of foreign affairs — the whole administration has been so much a one man show — that his disability has paralysed the whole executive. One has that queer feeling of a ship at sea with engines stopped; there is a play of forces at work, amid which the ship is merely passive, and one is acutely conscious that no will or purpose is at work, with them or against them. Nobody takes any initiative; the responsibility for seeing and meeting situations is not taken; things drift until they have reached the stage of being urgent and overshadowing emergencies that have to be met in some way.[56]

Not until April 13, 1920 did Wilson attend a Cabinet meeting. Physically he was a shadow of his former self. His left side was affected; his leg dragged, and he who had been so jaunty now moved with the greatest of difficulty. He depended much on his subordinates, especially Houston, Baker, and Colby for the drafting of official communications.[57] His relations with Bainbridge Colby, the new Secretary of State, Lansing having left office on February 12, 1920, were close and cordial. But in a larger sense the Wilson administration waited on destiny both in the Far East and elsewhere. Without the pilot, the nation drifted in the eddy of the Republican rancor over the agitation of the treaty.

Senator Hitchcock, leading the defense of the treaty in the Senate, saw the President briefly on two occasions in November and again before the votes on the treaty.[58] Meanwhile, the treaty went through the processes on the Hill. It had been reported from Committee on September 10, 1919 with forty-five textual-amendments and four reservations, including the one on Shantung; by early November all were defeated — a victory for the Wilson Democrats. On November 6, 1919, Lodge presented his fourteen reservations, number six of which withheld American assent to the articles relating to Shantung and reserving full liberty of action in any controversy arising therefrom.[59] Senatorial voices were cleared and the debate began. It was long and at times acrimonious. The opposition was partly an attack on Wilson and partly an attack upon American departure from two main lines of traditional policy — that of guaranteeing China's political and territorial integrity and of opposing international commitments.[60] Wilson, feeling that the League reservations killed the treaty, asked the Senate Democrats to oppose them, and the next day, on November 19, the Lodge reservations were voted down. This really spelled defeat for the Treaty although it was to be further considered.[61]

After the reassembling of Congress, Wilson renewed the treaty battle by his Jackson Day letter of January 8, 1920 to a gathering of Democrats in Washington. He asked them "to give the next election the form of a great and solemn referendum" on the unchanged treaty.[62] On February 9, the Senate voted to reconsider the treaty, and between February 21 and March 7 succeeded in adopting or revising eight of the fourteen Lodge amendments. The Shantung reservation now omitted mentioning either China or Japan but it still refused assent to the terms.

Wilson informed Senator Carter Glass that he would withdraw the treaty rather than have the reservations, and on March 8 he wrote Hitchcock further "digging in his heels" against them. Eleven days and much maneuvering later, the treaty again came to a division; it failed for the lack of seven votes to give it a two-thirds majority.[63]

Cleveland Dodge, Wilson's life-long friend, thought that pushing the treaty into the 1920 presidential election as a "solemn referendum," would be very difficult "as there will be so many other issues that it will be almost impossible to get a fair referendum of the people of the United States on this very important subject. . . ."[64] His observations proved only too true for the election involved issues and personalities other than the treaty to such an extent that the "solemn referendum" was lost in the melee. The nation went Republican, and Warren G. Harding, who had been one of the leaders in the fight against the treaty, became the President-elect of the United States.

The Shantung question was not settled by the election, and it was not until the Washington Conference of 1921-1922 that Japan restored to China the leased territory of Kiaochow. The maritime customs at Tsingtau and the salt industry were likewise restored, and Japanese soldiers and police were then withdrawn. At the same time, the transfer of the Tsingtau-Tsinanfu Railway, the extensions of the railway, mining rights, and the former German cables were made subject to certain conditions designed to conserve the Japanese interests involved.[65] Japan in no sense lost her invested interest nor her political influence in China.

Upon the wrecking of the Versailles Treaty, and consequently the League as Wilson visualized it, the keystone for a new world order based on law and holding individual nations to an accounting of their compeers was lost. Whether it was an impractical dream, a culminating note in the desertion of traditional American policy of national interest for an intangible dream of internationalism is still a matter of contention. The long debate on the treaty, the accusations hurled at Japan, and the bellicose presentation of America's interest in the Far East did little to improve Japanese-American relations. These relations had been

further embittered by the quarrel over Yap, the naval arma-
ments race, a revival of California exclusion laws, and the
Tientsin fracas, in addition to the conflicts that raged over
Siberia and the terms of the New Consortium.

A source of friction between America and Japan growing
out of the Paris peace conference centered around the island of
Yap. The issue arose out of the war-time recognition of the
vital role played by communications in the modern world. The
lagging service across the Pacific had caused Wilson, at the suggestion of Walter S. Rogers, then a representative of Charles R.
Crane, to inform Lansing that he thought it an opportune time
to negotiate with Japan concerning improvement of the cable
and radio communications.[66] Rogers later joined the Committee on Public Information and there continued his interest
in improved cable services.[67] As the activities of the United
States increased in the Far East with Siberian intervention, commercial cable deliveries lagged ten to fifteen days behind sched-
ule, and cable rates were nearly a dollar a word from New York
to Yokohama. An Inter-Departmental Committee on Communications was then created to deal with the situation, headed by
Breckenridge Long of the State Department.[68] This Committee
was organized in the fall of 1918, three months before the end of
the war, and two of its members were later attached to the
American delegation at the peace conference. They discussed
communications with Wilson in Paris, and he considered formation of a policy of cooperation, which led to the calling of a
preliminary Conference on Communications at Washington.[69]

The island of Yap[70] came into the picture as the center of
the German cable radiating to the Dutch Indies, Shanghai, and
Guam. Thus through the Guam-Yap connection the ostensibly
American-owned Commercial Pacific Cable Company,[71] which
was the sole cable system across the North Atlantic, connected
with the German lines. In case of operational difficulties, and
breaks in the cables were frequent in the earthquake region, the
Americans could rely on the German route as an alternate connection to Asia. It could also be used to speed cable service when
necessary.[72]

Japan had occupied Yap, along with the other German islands north of the equator, in late 1914. She sealed the cables and left them out of operation even though the war-time load on the American line to the continent was burdensome.[73] When the whole question of the Pacific Islands came up for settlement at Paris, Wilson was well-aware of the situation.[74] Rogers, who had been interested in Pacific communications from the beginning, informed the President of the importance of Yap.[75] The Naval recommendations for the area had pointed to its importance as a communications base.[76] In the Council of Four, on April 21, 1919, while discussing the Japanese mandate for the region, Wilson reserved Yap from the mandate and said it should be internationalized because of its communication importance. Later, Lansing too made a reservation of Yap for further discussion and suggested that he would propose it be internationalized. On May 1, Wilson again stated that Yap should not pass into the hands of any one power. When the mandate was awarded to Japan on May 7, Lloyd George referred to it as a mandate over "certain" German islands north of the equator, but the President did not then specify Yap be excepted.[77] He signed the Versailles treaty carrying the award, apparently thinking that his declared exception of Yap had taken care of the situation.

In his appearance before the Senate Foreign Relations Committee on August 19, Wilson testified concerning his action on Yap at the Conference: ". . . I made the point that the disposition, or rather the control, of that island should be reserved for a general conference which is to be held in regard to the ownership and operation of the cables. That subject is mentioned and disposed of in this treaty and that general cable conference is to be held." Under further questioning, he affirmed that the secret British-Japanese treaty awarding the islands to Japan, in the light of the exception he had made, would in no wise include Yap. He confessed the stipulation regarding his reservation was not a formally signed protocol, "but nobody has any doubt as to what was agreed upon."[78]

Yap dissolved into the many other problems before the nation, and it was not until March 22, 1920 that it again crystallized in public attention with Senator Lodge's resolution inquiring of the President concerning a recent statement of Lloyd George that Yap had been awarded to Japan.[79] The Department of State was then in process of calling the international conference on communications and the whole issue opened to agitation.[80] On March 25, the Minister of the Netherlands expressed the concern of his government over the award of Yap to any third power,[81] while the Chinese were less diplomatic and protested the ownership of the Yap-Shanghai cable by Japan.[82]

The preliminary International Conference on Communications met in Washington from October 8 to December 14, 1920. Yap once more was back in the news. President Wilson protested to Lloyd George that previous to the Japanese mandate award of May 7, he had made reservations regarding Yap due to its cable importance and had so informed both Chinda and Makino.[83] This communication was followed up on November 9 by an American statement to the former Allied governments asserting that the communications center was not included in the mandate settlement.[84] Japan's reply was that she had received "the whole of the German islands north of the Equator," and was unable to consent to any decision excluding Yap.[85]

In the light of the position taken by the foreign governments that Yap was included in the mandate, and the contention within the preliminary communications conference then proceeding, the administration deemed it wise to have Norman Davis, then Acting Secretary of State, consult the Foreign Relations Committee of the Senate. Davis made the point that the United States would not object to any of its unfortified islands being open to use for international cables and insisted that the same attitude should be expressed on the part of the other powers. The Committee was unanimous in support of the administration's policy on Yap.[86]

A draft convention providing for a Universal Communications Union to have supervision over international radio, wire, and visual communication was meanwhile adopted in the preliminary communications conference.[87] The Republicans, however, seized upon the fact of American leadership in the field

of radio communications and refused any international cooperation under the proposed terms. As a result of this expressed
opposition to the agenda, the formal Conference which actually
was to negotiate a communications agreement was never called.[88]

Upon the failure of the United States to ratify the Versailles
Treaty, the remaining powers, without the official knowledge of
Washington, had awarded Japan a Class "C" mandate over the
North Pacific islands and drew up the administrative procedures.
This was, of course, the highest type of mandate and bordered
on outright transfer of sovereignty. On December 17, 1920, the
Council of the League confirmed the arrangement. The State
Department refused to recognize the action and protested the
League's award.[89] Thus Yap remained a point of conflict be-
tween Japan and the United States until the treaty of 1922,
growing out of the Washington Conference, which recognized
the Japanese mandate in return for American residential, cable,
and radio rights there.[90]

In the post-war period, Japanese-American tension was
intensified due to their increased naval programs in the Pacific.
Woodrow Wilson was the friend of a big naval program. In the
campaign of 1912 he had advocated expansion of the American
merchant fleet.[91] During the preparedness campaign of 1916,
he had told a St. Louis audience: "There is no other navy in the
world that has to cover so great an area of defense as the American
Navy, and it ought, in my judgment, to be incomparably the most
adequate navy in the world."[92] On August 29, 1919, in response
to the President's plans, Congress passed a naval appropriations
act authorizing a building program comprising 156 war vessels,
with 16 capital ships.[93] During the war, the program shifted
from capital ships to modern destroyers; and when the United
States returned to its original program at the end of the war,
Britain and Japan were disturbed. At the Paris Conference,
Wilson resisted Lloyd George's attempt to restrict the American
naval program.[94] In the summer of 1919, the American fleet
was divided, the heaviest and newest units were sent to the
Pacific. As part of the Western tours in September, 1919,
Wilson reviewed this newly created Pacific fleet.[95]

During the fiscal year 1919-1920, the United States added 1 battleship, 96 destroyers, 18 submarines, and 109 other vessels to its naval strength. It had under construction 11 battleships, 6 battle cruisers and 123 other ships. In Japan the "double-eight program" was adopted calling for the construction of 8 battleships and 8 cruisers, 75 destroyers and other craft to be completed by 1923.[96] While the United States possessed double the number of Japan's capital ships, Japan equalled American construction of post-Jutland type craft. Among naval experts, all craft of the prior-Jutland type were considered outmoded; so each keel laid was of utmost importance in the naval race then underway. Japan's *Nogato*, commissioned in December, 1920, was the most modern and largest battleship in the world.[97] In addition, Japan had undertaken a military program which would raise her armed manpower close to five million men.[98] This naval race existing in the midst of the post war misunderstandings and suspicions intensified the seriousness of American-Japanese relations following the conclusion of the war in Europe.

With the ending of the war the perennial problem of Japanese immigration once more arose to vex the Washington authorities. The California Oriental Exclusion League had been formed in 1919 with the avowed purpose of cancelling the Gentlemen's Agreement and barring Asiatics forever from American citizenship. In September, this program was presented to the Congressional Committee on Immigration,[99] and Senator James D. Phelan of California introduced an amendment to the immigration bill, effectively excluding the Japanese working class from entering the United States. Since the Senator's chief complaint was the number of Japanese women brought in each year as picture brides,[100] John MacMurray, new chief of the Division of Far Eastern Affairs, suggested that if Japan would curb this practice, Congress might not act on any exclusion.[101] Secretary Lansing, on November 21, 1919, advised the Japanese Ambassador that favorable action barring picture brides might deter further investigation of their legality or the adoption of Phelan's exclusion amendment. Since Congress reconvened in December, the Secretary was anxious for Japanese assurances so that he might prevent passage of the undesirable legislation.[102]

While the Senate criticized Japan concerning Shantung, the Siberian expedition provided points of conflict, details of the New Consortium were in dispute, the naval race mounted, and Yap emerged as an issue, Tokyo gave her assurances that effective steps would be taken to prohibit the immigration of picture brides to the United States.[103]

However, California went ahead to adopt initiative proposed legislation which prevented Japanese nationals from leasing or owning lands and implemented former restrictive laws by regulating the right of Japanese aliens to employ guardians, trustees, or holding companies in evading restrictions.[104] In Japan, news of the California legislation appeared in the same papers announcing the election of Warren Harding as President of the United States. The American Chargé in Tokyo reported that the first newspaper reaction to California's referendum was "hysterical."[105] Opposition papers exhausted their "stock of vituperation against [the] United States." But the Japanese press saw no hope of relief in the Republican victory, "The general assumption is that the Republican Party is more given to positive and imperialistic policies than the Democratic and therefore greater encroachment upon Japan may be expected in [the] future."[106] Both American political parties had included Oriental exclusion planks in their platforms.[107]

Morris and Shidehara meanwhile worked on the problem and drafted a treaty revision of the Gentlemen's Agreement, prohibiting further immigration of the families of resident Japanese laborers and providing for joint enforcement by Japan and the United States. In return the two powers were to guarantee equality of rights accorded to the citizens or subjects of other countries, excepting the right of naturalization. This provision would have abrogated the alien land legislation,[108] but the treaty was never submitted to the Senate. Opposition from the Coast was too strong,[109] and the nation fearing a deluge of immigration from war torn Europe went ahead to enact in May, 1921 the quota act, greatly restricting alien admission. Orientals being barred by previous legislation were not granted a quota in the new law.

A further source of irritation in American-Japanese relations sprang from a series of clashes between American and Japanese military units stationed in Tientsin, China. Between March 11 and 13, 1919 three provocative incidents occurred. Japan claimed they grew out of misconduct of American soldiers in the Japanese concession. Two American soldiers were arrested, one mistreated, and four seriously injured by the Japanese.[110]

Despite the protests of the United States, Japan failed to apologize for her nationals until nearly two months after the affair and then in such general terms that Washington refused acceptance.[111] The Tientsin incident of itself was not important, but mingled with the Siberian intervention and other differences, it provided fuel for increased animosity toward America in the Japanese press. American newspapers also expressed bitter differences with Japan on the multitude of issues, so much so that Acting Secretary Polk saw fit to call in representatives of the press and "had a heart to heart talk" with them.[112] American naval authorities at the time doubted "whether the [Japanese] military government wanted war but thought its actions and reports in the press might arouse popular feeling beyond the control of the government."[113]

So serious had American suspicion of Japan become by May, 1920 that Charles D. Tenney, chargé d'affaires ad interim in Peking, reported to Secretary Colby: "The Japanese Government and nation are drunk with ambition. They aspire to control the western share of the Pacific and the resources of the hinterland." While seeking to control the trade of Asia, they dream "of 'the day' when they can humble the United States and are systematically preparing for it." Their schemes were "flourishing" in both Siberia and China, and Tenney thought the American reaction "indulging in empty protests and displaying a feeling of suspicion and ill-will, constitute a pin prick policy the results of which will be worse than even blindness to what is going on." His solution was an Anglo-American understanding to supersede the Anglo-Japanese Alliance, then under serious criticism both in Canada and the United States.[114]

China was again the scene of Japanese and American differences when in January of 1919 Minister Reinsch proposed to the foreign representatives in Peking an embargo on foreign loans and arms to China until she became united. The policy was accepted by all the governments except Japan, who claimed she could not interfere with contracts already negotiated. However, in mid-March, Tokyo agreed to adhere to the policy. From the time it was suggested until she too consented to the American proposal, Japanese firms reportedly delivered yen 15,000,000 in arms and munitions to war-poised China. The prohibition of arms shipments aroused resentment in the South, where it was claimed Peking had already received adequate munitions to resume hostilities if the peace talks failed,[115] as they eventually did.

Enforcement of the arms embargo was an obligation for each of the twelve governments concerned. Of course, there were protests of violations, arguments concerning what was considered munitions, and recriminations, especially between Japan and the United States, with the nationals of both countries at times obviously violating the policy.[116] Although the intent was admirable in its conception, continuance of the policy under President Harding was disastrous, since it helped to drive Sun Yat-sen and the nationalists to seek aid of the Soviet Union.[117]

In China, the closing years of the Wilson administration produced little for future hope. On June 7, 1919, Minister Paul S. Reinsch in a letter of resignation also outlined his views on affairs there.[118] He found the general outlook discouraging. It was impossible to accomplish anything in China until the home governments were willing "to face the situation and to act." A strong policy was needed; and if not backed by the American people, "In its stead there will come a sinister situation dominated by the unscrupulous methods of the reactionary military regime centered in Tokyo, absolute in tendency, cynical of the principles of free government and human progress." Reinsch warned, "If this force with all the methods it is accustomed to apply remains unopposed there will be created in the Far East the greatest engine of military oppression and dominance that the world has yet seen." In such case he thought the brunt of the results would fall on the United States, as witnessed in the "bitter hostility and abnormal vituperativeness of the Japanese press with regard to America." His solution, like that of Tenney, was for Britain and the United States to stand together in opposition to Japan, for neither the League nor treaties would be security against her firm, quiet determination for a paramount position in Asia.

Reinsch believed there must be continuous support on the part of the American government of the missionaries, merchants and constructive forces in China. Lack of it during the war "drove Tuan and his followers into the arms of the Pro-Japanese agents. Instead of support we gave China the Lansing-Ishii note as interpreted by Japan." Since the war Japan had carried through her China policies by bluff, where formerly she had made veiled threats to align with Germany. The Minister suggested that someone in America should give continuous attention to China so that something might be accomplished. He confessed his work had suffered due to Washington's neglect of continuous attention to Far Eastern affairs.[119]

Commenting on the Reinsch letter, Breckenridge Long said while it was fair in its summation of the internal situation, it revealed the author's antipathy toward Japan. As Secretary in Charge of Far Eastern Affairs, Long felt "attention has been given to China and has been continuous."[120]

The Reinsch and Long letters were returned by the President to Lansing. Wilson thought Long's comments were "well founded, but Japan certainly has China very much in her grasp, and I am eager to concert methods by which China may be extricated and set free. We must devote our best thought to this matter at the earliest possible moment."[121] The Siberian venture and the New Consortium then under way were already steps in that direction.

Wilson had regretfully accepted Reinsch's resignation to become effective September 15, 1919.[122] It was not until January 19, 1920, however, that Mrs. Wilson at the President's request submitted the nomination: "To China, Mr. Charles R. Crane of Ill. and N.Y.; whose familiarity with oriental affairs is unrivaled and whose experience in dealing with oriental questions qualifies him as none else is qualified."[123] The *New York Times* commended the nomination of Crane as a man of wide experience in business and affairs, knowing well the situations and the men of the Orient. It thought his excellent knowledge of Russia would also be of advantage since the interests of that country, China and Japan met in Manchuria and Mongolia.[124] Tokyo had protested Crane's appointment to the same post by President Taft in 1909. Already Reinsch's attitude in Peking was considered hostile by the Japanese;[125] the new appointment did little to improve understanding and accord.

The post war years brought vital changes in the State Department personnel dealing with Far Eastern matters. From the time of his speech before the American Bar Association of September 4, 1919, Lansing had heard from the President only indirectly through Mrs. Wilson. It was apparent to all that the President and his Secretary were at odds. On February 11, 1920, Wilson requested Lansing's resignation, assigning for his reason the Secretary's differing viewpoint and the holding of unauthorized Cabinet meetings during the President's illness.[126]

A month after Lansing's resignation, Bainbridge Colby of New York, formerly of the Shipping Board, was called to assume the position as Secretary of State. The appointment was unexpected for the man was a lawyer without diplomatic experience, but Wilson had been attracted to his abilities and liberal views while in Paris, where Colby managed the knotty details of the shipping situation so effectively.[127]

The resignations of experienced personnel within the State Department following the peace conference were of great significance, especially since Wilson after his illness was limited in his direction of policy, and the department was thereby given a great deal of initiative in its formulation. On March 25, 1920, two days after Colby's assumption of office, William Phillips, the Assistant Secretary, resigned; and no replacement was made. In June, Frank L. Polk, the Undersecretary,[128] left the Department because of ill health, and Norman H. Davis replaced him. Breckenridge Long resigned the same month to run unsuccessfully for the Senate from Missouri. Van Santwood Merle-Smith assumed the duties of Third Assistant Secretary in charge, among other things, of Far Eastern Affairs. He was a young Princeton graduate, a Republican without knowledge of Asia who had been a major in the recent war and served with the Secretariat of the Peace Conference.

Chief of the Division of Far Eastern Affairs at this time, however, was John V. A. MacMurray who had been with the Department since 1907 and had served in both Peking and Tokyo. MacMurray had replaced Ransford S. Miller in the Division on August 20, 1919.[129] DeWitt C. Poole, the former Counselor to the Embassy in Russia, a rabid Siberian interventionist, became Chief of the Division on Russian Affairs in October of 1919 and continued throughout the remainder of the administration.[130]

Meanwhile in China, the Shantung decision had aroused the students in Peking to mass demonstrations. They burned the house of Tsao Ju-lin, demanded the dismissal of three pro-Japanese ministers by the government, and set afoot a boycott of Japanese goods. So effective was their work that on June 11, 1919 the suspect ministers were dismissed, but the boycott continued.[131] The American Minister advised, "It is in no sense in our interests to get into this matter unless circumstances should by right compel [it]. If events here can have their widened course the main result will be salutary."[132] Lansing had talked the situation over with the President in Paris, and they had determined upon a policy of noninvolvement.[133] The Japanese could not understand the Chinese viewpoint in the boycott for they proposed to look upon Japan's activities on the Asian continent as protecting the Oriental peoples from the West, hence Tokyo blamed the activities of British and Americans in China for the outburst of anti-Japanese feeling.[134] Premier Hara confessed to holding such views, but he himself reportedly worked against the Japanese military party for reconciliation with China.[135]

The Shanghai peace conference talks for a United China were called off on May 14, 1919. The Allied ministers presented their *memoirs* for continuance of the talks, but the appointment of a new Northern emissary in August was looked upon with disfavor and the Southern faction refused to renew the conversations.[136] Thus China was left in her governmental chaos, divided north and south, and engaged in factional war. In

July, 1919, the northern tuchuns permitted General Wu Pei fu to drive Premier Tuan and his pro-Japanese adherents from office, but the reform element and General Wu failed to gain control within the government. The tuchuns, Chang Tso-lin of Manchuria and Tso Kun of Chi-li, continued to dominate the northern government of President Hsu. China gave her adherence to the League of Nations and in December, 1920 was elected to the Council.[137] If anything, the Wilson years had witnessed a deterioration of China, politically speaking, and her internal weakness continued to imperil the peace and security of East Asia.

In the closing months of the Wilson administration, the President was occupied in organizing a relief committee to raise funds for the mitigation of the famine in China's Chihli, Honan, Shantung and Shansi provinces.[138] In his appeal to the American people, Wilson urged their earnest participation in the relief work since "To an unusual degree the Chinese people look to us for counsel and for effective leadership."[139] He named Thomas Lamont to head the committee. In his last week in office, the President purchased tickets to a ball being held in Washington for the benefit of the Chinese Famine Relief Fund; his words, even in such a small situation, were, "I am very glad to be of any assistance, however slight. . . ."[140] In many ways this was the summation of Wilson's career and policy — service to the welfare of mankind.

CHAPTER ELEVEN

Epilogue

THE LAW OF DEMOCRACY IS FOR THE PROTECTION OF THE
WEAK, AND THE INFLUENCE OF EVERY DEMOCRACY IN THE
WORLD SHOULD BE FOR THE PROTECTION OF THE WEAK
NATION, THE NATION WHICH IS STRUGGLING TOWARDS ITS
RIGHT AND TOWARDS ITS PROPER RECOGNITION AND PRIVI-
LEGE IN THE FAMILY OF NATIONS.

—Woodrow Wilson, December 7, 1920

In a consideration of Woodrow Wilson's relation to the
Far East three facets are involved: Wilson himself, the particular
situation, and the tradition of American policy. These three
elements were constants in their application to Far Eastern
policy throughout the period 1913-1921, eight years in which
the relationship of Asia to the West underwent a drastic change.
For it was in these years that the triangular balance of power
between Russia, Britain, and Japan in China was destroyed;
and the United States, which had traditionally sought to preserve
its "most favored nation" status in China by playing off the
contending powers against one another, found itself standing
alone, feeling obligated to preserve Occidental rights and interests against a Japan opportunely using the European war for
carving out her own security in Asia. At first this new position
of America in Asia was not apparent to the administration, but
the presentation of the Twenty-One Demands in January of
1915 awakened the President to the reality of the challenge in
the Far East.

Wilson was primarily concerned with the political rather than the economic influence of the United States. In his thinking, America stood for a moral ideal and the reign of justice in the world. America sought to champion the rights of man and the cause of humanity. Her strength was in her ideals, her contribution in the service to the betterment of mankind, her greatness in her moral character. But this was only one aspect of Wilson's thinking. He also realized that trade meant not only national prosperity, but it served as the means of conveying American ideals and character to other peoples of the world. A Manchester liberal, believing emphatically in its cult of individualism, the President was convinced that laissez faire must prevail in international trade and economic barriers and discriminations must be eliminated. He was thus utterly sincere in his devotion to the Open Door and the protection of the status quo of sovereignty in the Far East.

Wilson's ethical view of America's role in the world was implemented by the expansion of her commerce; however, he seriously warned against the danger of a foreign policy based on material interests. He sought to elevate the conduct of international relations onto a higher plane of morality, to place nations like individuals under law in which they would be held responsible for their every act. It was in these ideals that he was dogmatic; he was the soul of expediency and flexibility as to how they could be achieved.

A mature scholar of the functioning of governments, the President believed firmly in the Darwinian concept of the organic development of institutions. He was optimistic, a believer in the law of progress; yet, he realized that sound institutional growth depended on the experience of a people. While he believed in democracy as the height of a people's achievement in government, he realized that the United States could not export her institutions, but that she might by example, tutelage, and cultural exchange influence the world toward self-government in the evolution of the years. Wilson also believed that Christianity contributed to this development since it served to awaken the individual to the service of his fellow man — a necessary foundation in the development of self-government.

He therefore encouraged the growth and development of missionary activities, especially in China, where in 1913 he saw the Christian influence at the forefront in the awakening of that ancient land.

But a false picture is given if one emphasizes Wilson's ideals without giving proper place to the realism with which he attempted to realize them. He thought of himself as the practical-idealist. His approach was always, "What can be done?" In the Caribbean, this practical-idealism manifested itself in economic penetration and domination far beyond the accomplishment of the old "Dollar Diplomacy" school. In Asia, it brought him to proceed upon the historical policies of the Open Door and the preservation of the political and territorial integrity of China. The practical realities, without any conscious thought of historical consistency, however, shaped the policies pursued in these years.

In 1901 Wilson had seen the new frontage of the nations as being on the Pacific. In his *History of the American People,* he marked the Spanish American War as the turning point in America's new role as a world power. In the days before the Baltimore convention, he spoke out for an increased American merchant marine and for a venturesome capitalism to exploit the backward areas of the world. Ideologically he was in step with the nation as to its role in the world.

From the earliest days of his administration Wilson was forced to deal with Far Eastern problems. Each situation brought its individual response in action. There never was any master strategy beyond support for the historic policies pursued in relation to the area. As early as March 18, 1913, he refused to give the guarantees sought by the American Group for continuance in the International Consortium loan to China. The President resented the small number of American banks represented and the terms of the agreement, which he thought transgressive of China's sovereignty in the control of her financial affairs. Participation in such an arrangement tied the United States to a cooperative policy with the other powers and delimited her freedom of action. This kind of a Consortium ran counter to Wilson's view of the necessity for freedom and competition in international trade and policy. He refused therefore to sanction any guarantees to the bankers participating in the proposed loan, and the American group willingly withdrew from the Consortium.

Wilson continued his independent course of action in extending recognition to the Chinese Republic on May 2, 1913. He was filled with a hope that a new day was dawning in the political darkness of Asia, and he spoke of the Chinese government as newly awakened to a sense of duty to its people. He was fully aware that representative government was of slow growth and reluctant rootage; and as Yuan Shih k'ai emerged as the strong man in China, rather than the leader of a popular democratic cause, Wilson supported him as a stable element in the progressive development of her government. In 1915 he was even willing to recognize Yuan as the Emperor of China, providing the change was constitutionally accomplished and enjoyed popular support.

While Wilson in 1901 viewed America's duty in China as indirect, working through example and cultural exchange, he saw her influence in the Philippines based on a direct responsibility to the Filipino people. The islands offered a clear challenge as an American experiment for the development of a people along the pathway leading to self-government. Through training and moral example, the United States was to lift the natives to a stage of development where they could care for themselves. True self-government came only through the responsibility of governing. Thus Felix Frankfurter's recommendations for the initial administration policy in the islands, since it worked towards native responsibility, was accepted and put into practice. The so-called Jones Law, giving the government into native hands, represented Wilson's chief contribution to the development of the Philippines. The preamble of the law put the United States on record as promising ultimate independence. Working toward the goal of native responsibility Wilson realized meant the sacrifice of efficiency in governing for the wider goal of experiencing a generation in the process of government. He was willing to make this sacrifice.

The President's goal of eventual independence for the Philippines developed practically on a gradual basis, evaluating the gains as they were made, and then proceeding to the next step in its attainment. Although he publicly agreed with the Clark Amendment of 1916, which would have granted independence to the islands within four years, he privately admitted that he thought the legislation inopportune; and, through private intervention, he succeeded in having the amendment so changed as to place final control over what was to be done in the hands of the Chief Executive, thus removing any dangers to his policy of gradualism. Since he was then currently at odds with the Senate over the right of Americans to travel on belligerent ships, his agreement on the Amendment would appear to have been an expedient to serve as a sop to the disgruntled Senators. There was little danger in this tactic, since it was generally understood that the House would never pass the measure.

Since the end of the Russo-Japanese War, the American press had expressed a fear of Japanese ambitions on the Asian continent. Wilson in the early part of his administration discounted the expressions criticizing the hostile intent of Nippon. He shared then, and appreciated throughout these years, the general opinion within the State Department that Japan as a progressive, expanding nation must be permitted the wherewithal for her national development. He persistently followed the idea that Japan could gain economic hegemony over contiguous territory on the Asian mainland while China retained the political sovereignty of the region. During the crisis of the Twenty-One Demands, in 1915, this view was expressed in Bryan's recognition of the special interest of Japan in Shantung, Manchuria, and Eastern Inner Mongolia. It was somewhat less clearly reiterated in the Lansing-Ishii Agreement of 1917, which recognized that territorial propinquity creates special interests. At the Paris Conference, Wilson assented to Japan retaining the economic rights in Shantung while returning the political sovereignty of the region to China. However, in each of these diplomatic arrangements American policy was seeking an expedient within a particular situation, it was in no position to dictate, and it was not achieving its fullest goals.

Faced with the anti-Japanese measures of the California legislature in 1913, Wilson personally favored a treaty settlement guaranteeing equality of treatment for Japanese and European aliens in the United States. He recognized, however, that such a treaty had no chance of passing the Senate; and by private intervention with certain influential persons, he successfully prevented other states from following California's example. The California legislation produced a crisis in our relations with Japan; there was a sharp war scare which Wilson's sanity of action did much to calm.

Official Washington manifested a considerable sympathy for Japan's problems of population pressure and raw materials shortages. During the early course of the Twenty-One Demands, the President conceded to the Japanese viewpoint and refused to object to Group Two of the Demands which served to establish her hegemony in Manchuria and Eastern Inner Mongolia. This was not essentially new since in the days of President Taft the other concerned powers had already recognized Japan's position there. It was, however, in part due to American protests joining with those of the other powers in China that Japan relinquished pressing Group Four of the Demands which made vast inroads on China's sovereignty. Going a step farther, Counselor Robert Lansing drew up and Wilson approved a *caveat* excepting American recognition of the agreements growing out of the Demands which impaired "the treaty rights of the United States and its citizens in China, the political or territorial integrity of the Republic of China, or the international policy relative to China commonly known as the open door policy." Again, this was in the best vein of traditional American policy.

It was during the controversy of the Twenty-One Demands that Wilson came to visualize the United States as the guardian of the rights of the war-engaged Occidental nations in China. This was no cavalier assumption on his part, but it proceeded out of a recognition of American national interest in the Asian power balance; it was vital that this balance be not too severely jeopardized by Japan's advances during the war. In pursuing a course implementing this objective, Wilson found recourse to the support of the British Foreign Office to supplement his representations to Japan. After the Twenty-One Demands episode, the United States sought a status quo condition in Asia rather than a solution. Through legalisms and exceptions, it attempted to prolong settlement of the differences with Japan until the balance of power in Asia could be redressed more favorably to American advantage at war's end. There was, of course, the complicating factor of Japan's position in the Allied camp. Throughout the war years, as Germany attempted to entice Japan away from her Allied commitments, it became increasingly difficult to protest Japan's actions on the Asian mainland without increasing the possibilities of her disaffection.

The advantages of the war years played heavily into Japanese hands. She acquired the German position in Shantung as a result of ousting the enemy. China's need for funds, the absorption of the powers in the European war, and the disinterest of private American banking firms served to thrust the financing of China into the hands of Japan by default. By 1918 she dominated Chinese finances. Her influence extended into the inner circle of the Peking cabinet. Wilson, in withdrawing from the Consortium of 1913, had hoped to open Chinese loans to the free competition of international banking institutions. Now Japan had almost a closed market on Chinese loans.

Wilson had attempted to encourage American bankers to undertake Chinese investments. In the summer of 1913, he gave support to the Huai River Conservancy Project to prevent floods in the Huai River basin, to reclaim lands, and to improve the water communication on the Grand Canal. The European War made it impossible to proceed further with this project since funds could not be raised. In 1915 Wilson strongly supported the attempted Griswold loan for China, insisting that it be made on the basis of wide participation by a number of banks, but this, too, failed. Wilson learned how unattractive China loans were to American bankers and investors.

In the summer of 1916 an unsuccessful attempt was made to resurrect the Old Consortium; this failing, the organization of a Second Consortium in which the European and Japanese bankers would join an American-dominated organization took shape. However, in giving approval to the organization of an American Group, Wilson carefully warned that the sovereign rights of China must in all cases be respected. The American Group came into existence by July 10, 1918 as a bona fide banking organization, but the secret objective of the State Department was to use the bankers "to drive Japan out of China." It hoped to accomplish this by internationalizing all Chinese loans. The State Department was to pass upon all loans before they could be consummated. The inroads on China's sovereignty made by Japan through financial means during the war would be overthrown as these loans reverted to Consortium control. Japan, of course, was reluctant to join an American dominated banking consortium. Not until October 15, 1920, with inclusion of very definite restrictions on areas of Consortium interests, did Japan agree to become a member in the new international group. The New Consortium became the chief prop in American policy to redress the upset balance of power in Asia. Although it made no loans, it was credited with preventing further Japanese financial encroachment on China.

Concurrent with the consideration of the organization of the New Consortium, Wilson found himself being pressed to consent to Japanese intervention in Siberia as the mandatory of the Allied Powers. Both Britain and France insisted that such action was necessary to prevent the mass transfer of German troops to the Western Front where the Allied armies in the Spring of 1918 suffered grievously from the renewed German offensive. Wilson could not see the military importance of such a plan; his Washington advisers were of the opinion that it would not divert German strength, and he feared it might throw the Russians into the arms of Germany. He consistently opposed the Allied recommendations, although he momentarily weakened under pressure of the recommendation in the month of March. Reports of German war prisoners in cooperation with Bolshevik troops seriously endangering the Czechoslovak forces making their way out of Russia served as a basis for the Allies to renew their plea for intervention in Siberia. Marshal Foch and General Pershing recommended joint American-Japanese intervention. The French pictured conditions as such in Siberia that Japanese intervention was inevitable with or without Allied invitation. Wilson decided that if Japan went in the United States would also have to intervene in order to watch her. He arranged a bilateral oral understanding with the Japanese which limited the number of troops to be employed and stated guarantees for the respect of Siberian territorial integrity. On August 3, 1918, the United States reluctantly agreed to the intervention. As the Japanese expanded their forces under pretext of an American breach of the agreement, Wilson admitted that he completely lost confidence in their good faith.

At the peace conference, Wilson opposed Japan's plans for outright annexation of the former German Pacific Islands north of the equator. He favored the second point of the Japanese program calling for the inclusion of a racial equality statement in the Covenant of the League of Nations, but he was forced by circumstances to oppose its adoption. On the third point, the cession of the German rights in Shantung to Japan, Wilson reluctantly consented. In the face of the Japanese agreements with both China and the European Allies, the threat of Japan leaving the conference if her objectives were not met, the unsettled conditions in Europe necessitating an early peace, and as a means of saving the League, which was to be the keystone of the new world order, Wilson consented to Japan retaining the economic rights in Shantung while returning the political sovereignty to China. This decision gained public attention in the United States and became one of the main points of attack in defeating the treaty. No one noted that the President had successfully prevented recognition of the 1915 and 1918 Sino-Japanese agreements on which Japan based her war-time gains in China.

The Consortium, containment in Siberia, and continuance of a large naval building program constituted the three active points of American post-war Far Eastern policy. Japan viewed the American naval building program as aimed at a curtailment of her ambitions in Asia. She attempted to strengthen her position and a naval arms race developed. American naval expansion was an outgrowth of the war. Throughout the conflict neutral shipping had suffered at the hands of British sea power. In 1916 there was fear that the war might end with the German fleet supreme on the Atlantic. America undertook her naval rearmament in the light of these two facts. At war's end, Wilson was of the opinion that only an American fleet could serve with the disinterest necessary to enforce the justice of the League. Naval expansion enhanced the voice of the United States in the Orient, and some official and nonofficial Americans looked upon it as a weapon to contain Japan's Asian ambitions, but within presidential circles it appears that the naval program was not directed against Japan. However, the Pacific fleet was organized in the summer of 1919, and Japan viewed this as a direct challenge to her position in Asian waters.

The Wilsonian policy in Far Eastern relations then was not new. It followed in the well-worn channels of traditional policy for the area. The President's ostensive discard of Taft's policy for cooperative action with the powers in favor of an independent course, marked by the disavowal of support for the American Group in the Consortium, was more proclaimed than real. When the occasion arose, as in the attempt to contain Japan, to organize a New Consortium, to unify China, Wilson sought the cooperation of the powers. He increasingly relied, like Taft, on British backing in his policies. He carefully reiterated traditional American support of China's political and territorial integrity and the policy of the open door. Like his predecessors, without force necessary to implement his policies, with his Pacific position weakened by involvement in an European war, and thrown more or less alone *vis à vis* the dominant military might of Japan in the region, confronted with the fact not the theory of Japan's possession of the Pacific islands, her occupation of Shantung, her gains in China, and her invasion of Siberia under the guise of a limited intervention, he was reduced to diplomacy to circumvent what appeared to be Japan's inevitable dominant position in Asia.

Victory is seldom complete in diplomacy, but Wilson did succeed in the reduction of Japan's gains to a mandate over the Pacific islands. He obtained her promise to return Kiaochow to China while retaining the economic rights in Shantung. He avoided the keen desire of Japan to have her gains recognized under the 1915 and 1918 treaties with China which would have given her position a respectful legality. In the days of Japan's opportunity, he stood athwart her ambitions in Siberia. Of course, other factors in addition to American diplomacy aided in accomplishing this thwarting of Japan's program, not the least of which was resistance in Japan itself to the ambitious undertaking; but the Wilson administration must be given credit, for good or ill, of pacing the foreign opposition to Japan's ambitions and of keeping the situation fluid for a more suitable settlement of the problems.

Wilson recognized the ferment working in the Orient. He believed it should be left to its own course of development, although the United States should stand ready to serve China whenever called upon to do so by the Chinese people. He hoped to see the inequalities imposed on China by the powers abolished, and he warned that should China's 400,000,000 people be stirred to revolt, "the fire could not be quenched." At the same time, he recognized Japan's position in the Asia of his day. At Paris he expressed the desire to see Japan lead in the Far East, standing on the ideals embodied in the League of Nations.

As a student of government, Wilson was interested in what transpired in China. He confessed that it engaged his attention as much as any other country in the world. He admitted his agreement with many of the policies for which the revolutionary Sun Yat-sen stood, but the head of a state is circumscribed in what he can do to bolster the cause of reform by disaffected elements in another sovereign state. Wilson too was limited by his information on the nature of events transpiring in the Far East. Starting with a feeling for the uplift of the Orient, he acquired considerable in the way of an understanding of affairs there. While on the whole the State Department was anti-Japanese and considerably pro-Chinese in its attitude, this state of affairs was compatible with the support of policies which favored American interests in the area. Generally this meant support of China. The State Department and Wilson were aware that this played into Chinese hands, for they sought to cast the United States in the role of their defender against Japan.

At the same time, Far Eastern affairs were relatively unimportant in the diplomacy of the United States. The Pacific was broad in those days. Aside from American stakes in the Philippines, the economic interest in the area was insignificant. The Senate, acting on its own initiative in 1916, could vote to give up the Philippines. America's limited interests in Asia made any question of initiating a firm policy which might involve the United States implementation with force "quixotic in the extreme," to use Lansing's phrase.

Through the League, Wilson hoped to redress not only the provisions of Paris concerning China, but the whole arrangement of inequalities imposed upon her from the past. The League would also make the independence of the Philippines a possibility by bringing about the rule of law and providing for the security of small states. This Wilsonian concept of the League never came into being. None can say if it would have succeeded; but to us of a later day, it seems conditions were more opportune for its success in 1919 than at the half-turn of the "Century of Progress." If one agrees that the realities which govern men lie deeply clothed in the emotional caverns of his religious-idealistic nature, Wilson's insistence on this framework can be viewed with appreciation. If on the other hand man lives solely in a *machtpolitik* reality, divorced from the influence of ethics and value systems, Wilsonian idealism assumes all the symptoms of a fatal political blindness. We are no longer so sure of the improvability of man, but the challenge is ever present. Nietzsche himself confessed that success is a great liar. Nevertheless, the years of the Wilson administrations marked the first period of outright challenge to a responsible American policy in the Far East. Within the circumscription of the time, the challenge would seem to have been met adequately.

Notes

NOTES FOR CHAPTER ONE

1. This was generally the evaluation of his critics and the opposition. It gained public recognition during the contest over the Versailles Treaty when much was made of Wilson's wilful opportunism and dogmatic nature. See Henry Cabot Lodge, *The Senate and the League of Nations* (New York: 1925) passim; John M. Keynes, *The Economic Consequences of the Peace* (New York: 1920), pp. 38-55; *Harvey's Weekly* and the newspaper press, however, were more effective in giving this impression of Wilson.

2. A view shared by his biographer Ray Stannard Baker, *Woodrow Wilson Life and Letters,* 8 vols. (Garden City: 1927-1939) passim. Hereafter cited as *Wilson.* H. C. F. Bell, *Woodrow Wilson and the People* (Garden City: 1945); Harold G. Black, *The True Woodrow Wilson, Crusader for Democracy* (New York: 1946); E. M. Hugh-Jones, *Woodrow Wilson and American Liberalism.*

3. Arthur S. Link takes this view in his *Wilson the Road to the White House* (Princeton: 1948), pp. 96, 122-123, 179-184, 191-193, and also in *Woodrow Wilson and the Progressive Era, 1910-1917* (New York: 1954), pp. 74-75; James Kerney, *The Political Education of Woodrow Wilson* (New York: 1926) rather shares this viewpoint.

4. Woodrow Wilson, "The Ministry and the Individual," in Ray S. Baker and William E. Dodd (eds.), *The Public Papers of Woodrow Wilson,* 6 vols. (New York and London: 1925-1927), II, 184-185. Hereafter cited *Wilson Public Papers.* See also *ibid.,* I, 75; Kerney, *Political Education of Woodrow Wilson,* p. 72.

5. Woodrow Wilson, *Constitutional Government in the United States* (New York: 1908), pp. 56-57.

6. Joseph K. Fornance Notes from Wilson's Jurisprudence course, 1904, Lecture 8, in the Manuscripts Division of the Library, Princeton University.

7. Charles Seymour, *Woodrow Wilson and the World War* (New Haven: 1921), p. 15.

8. David F. Houston, *Eight Years with Wilson's Cabinet,* 1913-1920. 2 vols. (Garden City: 1926), II, 183. Hereafter cited as *Eight Years.* Eleanor Wilson McAdoo, *The Woodrow Wilsons* (New York: 1937), p. 155; Frederic C. Howe, *The Confessions of a Reformer* (New York: 1925), pp. 283-284.

9. As quoted in Lincoln Steffens, *The Autobiography of Lincoln Steffens* (New York: 1931), p. 739; also see J. Duncan Spaeth, "Wilson as I Knew Him and View Him Now," in William S. Myers, *Woodrow Wilson Some Princeton Memories* (Princeton: 1946), p. 73.

10. Quoted in Baker, *Woodrow Wilson,* IV. 55.

11. Bell, *Wilson and the People,* p. 10; also letter of John R. Mott to author, May 19, 1951.

12. Woodbridge to Wilson, April 7, 1910 in the Woodrow Wilson Papers, Manuscripts Division, Library of Congress, series II, box 6. Hereafter W will be used to denote letters to and from Wilson. This source is subsequently cited as Wilson Papers followed by series and box number. Also to Lockridge, Jan. 6, 1903, Wilson Papers, II, 6.

13. Harley Notter, *The Origins of the Foreign Policy of Woodrow Wilson* (Baltimore: 1937), p. 202. Hereafter cited *Origins Wilson's Foreign Policy.*

14. Baker, Wilson, III, 417-418.

15. *Ibid.,* III, 442.

16. That Wilson was reluctant to have Bryan in the Cabinet is shown in Charles Seymour, *The Intimate Papers of Colonel House* (4 vols., Boston and New York: 1926-1930), I, 97-98. Hereafter cited *Intimate House Papers.*

17. House to W, Jan. 30, 1913, in *ibid.,* I, 105.

18. *The New York Times,* Mar. 6, 1913, made light of the predictions that Bryan would dominate the President and referred to the fact that the Department of State was under the direct supervision of the chief executive.

19. The young man turned up in Nebraska declaring himself a Japanese follower of Bryan and attached himself to the family. See Wayne Williams, *William Jennings Bryan* (New York: 1936), p. 277. He later appeared at the Versailles conference in 1919 as evidenced in Yamashita to Wilson, June 2, 1919, Wilson Papers, VIII A, 38.

20. William J. Bryan, *Speeches of William J. Bryan* (2 vols., New York: 1913), II, 267, 272.

21. William J. and Mary B. Bryan, *The Memoirs of William Jennings Bryan* (Chicago: 1925), pp. 309-314, tells briefly of the journey. A fuller account is William J. Bryan, *The Old World and Its Ways: A Tour Around the World and Journey through Europe* (St. Louis 1909). See also Williams, *Bryan,* pp. 279-280.

22. During the trip home Bryan wrote *Letters to A Chinese Official Being A Western View of Eastern Civilization* (New York: 1906) in which he defended the progress of Western civilization and the merits of Christianity over and against the claims of Oriental culture and religion.

23. F. M. Huntington Wilson, *Memoirs of An Ex-Diplomat* (Boston: 1945), pp. 248-249, tells that when Bryan was arranging to leave the Department in the Counselor's charge, Huntington Wilson wrote him the following letter, March 16, 1913, Wilson Papers, VI, 245: "Of course I have frequently been in charge of the Department for months at a time. However I feel my responsibilities just at this juncture to be peculiarly heavy, because of the fact that you and the President have not yet had opportunity thoroughly to examine our foreign policies and convince yourselves, as I venture to believe

will be the case, that there is a continuity in the basic principles of American foreign policy quite aloof from all differences of opinion upon the issues of domestic politics."

24. Frederick V. Field, *American Participation in the China Consortium* (Chicago: 1931), pp. 97-100; George H. Blakeslee, *The Recent Foreign Policy of the United States* (New York: 1925), pp. 195-196; Mingchien J. Bau, *The Open Door Doctrine in Relation to China* (New York: 1923), p. 389. The most adequate recent treatment is found in Tien-Y Li, *Woodrow Wilson's China Policy, 1913-1917* (New York: 1952), pp. 23-48.

25. United States Department of State, *Papers Relating to the Foreign Relations of the United States, 1913* (Washington: 1920), p. 192. Hereafter cited *Foreign Relations*.

26. Yuan Shih k'ai to representatives of the Consortium, March 9, 1912, in *Foreign Relations, 1912*, p. 120.

27. *Ibid.*, pp. 122-123; J. V. A. MacMurray, *Treaties and Agreements with and Concerning China*. 2 vols. (New York: 1921), II, 1034-1035. Hereafter cited *Treaties*.

28. Willard Straight, "China's Loan Negotiations," in George H. Blakeslee, *Recent Developments in China* (New York: 1913), pp. 143-144.

29. Herbert Feis, *Europe: the World's Banker, 1870-1914* (New Haven: 1930), pp. 434-435.

30. Calhoun to Bryan, February 21, 1913, *Foreign Relations, 1913*, p. 164.

31. F. H. McKnight to J. P. Morgan and Company, Feb. 18, 1913, in State Department files, National Archives, 893.51/1341. Hereafter S. D. preceding file number will indicate source.

32. Memorandum by R. S. Miller, Feb. 21, 1913, S. D., 893.51/1341.

33. *New York Times*, March 11, 1913; Thomas W. Lamont, *Henry P. Davidson: The Record of a Useful Life* (New York and London: 1933), pp. 161-162; William Jennings Bryan and Mary Baird Bryan, *The Memoirs of William Jennings Bryan* (Chicago: 1925), p. 362. The latter hereafter cited *Memoirs*.

34. Josephus Daniels, *The Wilson Era: Years of Peace, 1910-1917* (Chapel Hill: 1944), pp. 158-159. Hereafter cited *Wilson Era, 1910-1917*. For a discussion of the discrepancies in the dates and reports concerning the meeting see Li, *Woodrow Wilson's China Policy*, footnote 54, p. 52.

35. From the Diary of Colonel Edward M. House, March 14, 16, 1913. The Diary is in the House Papers, Yale University Library. Hereafter cited House Diary.

36. Daniels, *Wilson Era, 1910-1917*, p. 159; Houston, *Eight Years*, I, 45.

37. *New York Times*, March 19, 1913.

38. Houston, *Eight Years*, I. 45.

39. *New York Times*, March 20, 1913.

40. The correspondence is found in the *New York Times*, March 21, 1913.

41. Field, *China Consortiums*, p. 117.

42. For the statement here and in the succeeding paragraphs see *Foreign Relations, 1913*, pp. 170-171.

43. Quoted in the Diary of Josephus Daniels, March 28, 1913 deposited in the Josephus Daniels Papers, Manuscripts Division, Library of Congress. Hereafter cited as Daniels Diary.

44. Baker, *Wilson*, IV, 75 explains that the reason Wilson broke with the cooperative policy was because he considered the objectives of the loan improper. Wilson believed in cooperation in Asia and was at the time seeking to act with the powers in relation to the problem of the opium trade.

45. See the campaign addresses in Woodrow Wilson, *The New Freedom A Call for the Emancipation of the Generous Energies of a People* (New York: 1913), pp. 3-7, 50, 57-63, 163-191.

46. Houston, *Eight Years*, I, 44.

47. Li, *Woodrow Wilson's China Policy*, p. 43. Of the twenty-eight letters on the subject in the White House files of the Wilson Papers only one is in dissent. The letters mentioned are found under dates March 19-21, 1913, Wilson Papers, VI, 227.

48. Bryan to W, March 23, 1913, Wilson Papers, II, 54.

49. Chargé to Bryan, March 25, 1913, *Foreign Relations, 1913*, p. 175. See also Charles F. Remer, *Foreign Investments in China* (New York: 1933), p. 130.

50. *New York Times*, March 22, 1913.

51. Brown to W, March 20, 1913, Wilson Papers, VI, 227.

52. Sammons to Lane, March 23, 1913, Wilson Papers, II, 35.

53. March 29, 1913.

54. Bau, *The Open Door*, p. 84; Henry Chung, *The Oriental Policy of the United States* (London and New York: 1919), p. 74.

55. Harley Notter, *Origins Wilson's Foreign Policy*, p. 231.

56. Remer, *Foreign Investments in China*, p. 130.

57. Japanese Ambassador to Bryan, March 24, 1913, *Foreign Relations, 1913*, pp. 173-174. For the best account of the background on Chinese recognition see Meribeth E. Cameron, "American Recognition Policy Toward the Republic of China, 1912-1913," in *Pacific Historical Review*, II, 1933, pp. 214-230.

58. Harley F. Mac Nair, *Modern Chinese History Selected Readings* (Shanghai: 1927), pp. 689-734 contains the documents pertaining to the abdication and the provisional constitution. For an account of the revolution as viewed by an American in Peking see Herbert Croly, *Willard Straight* (New York: 1924), pp. 413-448. See also Stanley K. Hornbeck, *Contemporary Politics in the Far East* (New York: 1916), pp. 3-17.

59. Edward Thomas Williams, *China Yesterday and To-Day*. 4th edition. (New York: 1924), pp. 564, 567-568. The author was American Chargé in Peking at the time. Hereafter cited *China*.

60. *Ibid.*

61. Lyon Sharman, *Sun Yat-sen: His Life and Its Meaning* (New York: 1934), p. 134.

62. Williams, *China*, pp. 569-573.

63. Acting Secretary of State to Presidential Secretary, Feb. 25, 1913, *Foreign Relations, 1913*, pp. 92-93. The previous July, Secretary Knox had

informed the foreign governments that public opinion would probably force American recognition. Knox, however, prevailed against such a move and handed the whole matter to Wilson. In January, Senator Bacon had introduced a joint resolution for recognition. Missionary groups, the China Society, and the Fourth Annual Conference on Foreign Relations at Clark University also urged recognition. For the fullest development of the forces making for recognition see Maribeth E. Cameron, "American Recognition Policy Toward the Republic of China, 1912-1913," in *The Pacific Historical Review*, II, 1933, pp. 214-230.

64. Chargé to Bryan, Mar. 18, 1913, *Foreign Relations, 1913*, pp. 96-98.

65. Chargé to Bryan, Mar. 28, 1913, *Ibid, 1913*, p. 100.

66. Houston, *Eight Years*, I, 49.

67. Daniels Diary, Apr. 1, 1913.

68. The original undated document is in Wilson's handwriting. On the bottom in Bryan's scrawl is an undated note to Tumulty: "Mr. Adee says this is O. K. Please show this President & send me copies enough for all nations." Wilson Papers, II, 34; also *Foreign Relations, 1913*, p. 108. The political assassination in China was brought up at the Cabinet on April 4 by Bryan. The question arose whether or not China had a government. Wilson was of the opinion it did since the Parliament had been elected without difficulty. Daniels Diary, Apr. 4, 1913.

69. Japanese Embassy to Department of State, Apr. 4, 1913, *Foreign Relations, 1913*, p. 109.

The Chinese nationalists later accused the treaty powers of thus backing Yuan, whom they labeled reactionary, against the reformer Sun Yat-sen, see Sir Frederick Whyte, *China and the Foreign Powers: An Historical Review of Their Relations* (London: 1927), pp. 14-15.

70. Chargé to Bryan, Apr. 11, 1913, *Foreign Relations, 1913*, p. 112. "The Pres. and the whole Cabinet devoutly hope that everything will go well in China today and the people will so demean themselves as to justify their recognition by the whole world and give the Chinese Republic an opportunity to take its place among the Republics of the earth." Daniels Diary, Apr. 8, 1913.

71. Chargé to Bryan, May 2, 1913, *ibid., 1913*, p. 115.

72. Bryan to Chargé, Apr. 6, 1913, *ibid., 1913*, p. 110.

73. Bryan to J. B. Moore, May 2, 1913, S. D., 893.00/1644.

74. Williams, *China*, p. 578.

75. W to Julean Arnold, May 23, 1913, Wilson Papers, VI, 227. Arnold later became the Commercial Attaché of the Peking legation.

76. Notter, *Origins of Wilson's Foreign Policy*, pp. 243-244.

77. Daniels, *Wilson Era, 1910-1917*, p. 160.

78. *The Outlook*, CIV, May 10, 1913, p. 4.

79. *The New York Times*, Apr. 28, 1913. At the Cabinet meeting Bryan read the newspaper account of China's call for prayers by the Christian world. "The President said he did not know when he had been so stirred as when he read that message in the paper this morning and he had in mind to request it. . . ." Redfield thought it a play for the support of the

Christian nations, but Wilson said he thought the appeal should be accepted as an honest one. Daniels Diary, Apr. 18, 1913.

80.   Harold M. Vinacke, *Modern Constitutional Development in China* (Princeton: 1920), p. 150.

81.   Hornbeck, *Contemporary Politics,* pp. 77-84, discusses the party battle during this period.

82.   Williams, *China,* p. 469.

83.   Vinacke, *Modern Constitutional Development in China,* p. 159.

84.   Bryan to Chargé, July 26, 1913, *Foreign Relations, 1913,* pp. 126-128.

85.   Williams, *China,* pp. 579-580.

86.   W to Bryan, Oct. 6, 1913, Wilson Papers, VI, 226.

87.   Yuan to W, Oct. 13, 1913, *Foreign Relations, 1913,* p. 135.

88.   Chargé to Bryan, Oct. 10, 1913, *ibid., 1913,* p. 134.

89.   Hornbeck, *Contemporary Politics,* p. 81.

90.   Chargé to Bryan, 2 telegrams of Nov. 5, 1913, S. D., 893.00/1993 and /1995.

91.   Bryan to W, Nov. 5, 1913, Wilson Papers, II, 41.

92.   Stuart, The Department of State, pp. 225-227.

93.   W to Eliot, Sept. 17, 1913, in Baker, *Wilson,* IV, 42.

94.   Notes of Joseph K. Fornance in Wilson's Jurisprudence, 1904, Princeton University, Lecture 21, Princeton Library. Wilson's teaching habit was to dictate for part of the period. These words are evidently his.

95.   Kerney, *Political Education of Wilson,* pp. 288-289.

96.   Williams, *Bryan,* p. 337.

97.   House Diary, Jan. 17, 1913.

98.   W to Eliot, Jan. 20, 1913, Ray Stannard Baker Collection, Eliot file, box 5 in the Library of Congress. Afterwards cited Baker Collection.

99.   Seymour, *Intimate House Papers,* I, p. 105.

100.   W to Eliot, Jan. 30, 1913, Baker Collection, Eliot, 5.

101.   W to Bryan, Feb. 5 [11], 1913, *ibid.,* Bryan, 3; also in Baker, *Wilson,* IV, 31.

102.   W to Bryan, Feb. 14, 1913, *ibid.,* Bryan 3.

103.   Bryan to W, Feb. 17, 1913, *ibid.,* Bryan 3.

104.   W to Dodge, Mar. 10, 1913, Baker, *Wilson,* IV, 31. Dodge sent a long cable along with messages from five or six other people to Mott, then in Seoul, Korea. This is evidenced in Dodge to W, Mar. 28, 1913, Wilson Papers, IV, 31.

105.   W to Mott, Mar. 21, 1913, Wilson Papers, VI, 214.

106.   W to Dodge, Apr. 5, 1913, Letter Book 2, Wilson Papers, VII, p. 106.

107.   Dodge to W, Mar. 30, 1913, Wilson Papers, VI, 259.

108.   W to Dodge, Apr. 10, 1913, Wilson Papers, VI, 259.

109.   Crane to W, Apr. 8, 1913, Wilson Papers, VI, 259.

110.   Mott to W, July 3, 1913, Wilson Papers, VI, 203.

111. Bryan to W, June 2, 1913, Wilson Papers, II, 54.

112. Kerney, *Political Education of Wilson*, P. 313.

113. Crane to W, Mar. 21, 1913, Wilson Papers, VI, 227.

114. Crane to W, Mar. 24, 1913, Wilson Papers, II, 252.

115. W to Davis, June 10, 1913, Letter Book 4, p. 212, Wilson Papers, VII.

116. W to Bryan, June 25, 1913, Wilson Papers, II, 54.

117. *The New York Times*, July 17, 1913.

118. Moore to Reinsch, Aug. 19, 1913, S. D. 123R271/2a.

119. Williams, *China*, p. 578.

120. John B. Powell, *My Twenty-Five Years in China* (New York: 1945), p. 47.

121. Paul S. Reinsch, *Intellectual and Political Currents in the Far East* (Boston and New York: 1911), p. vii.

122. Daniel J. Gage, "Paul S. Reinsch and Sino-American Relations" (unpublished dissertation, Ph.D., Stanford University, 1939), p. 67. Most of Dr. Reinsch's papers were destroyed when his family left China after his death, according to Gilbert H. Doane, Director of Libraries, University of Wisconsin, to author, July 18, 1950.

123. Paul S. Reinsch, *An American Diplomat in China* (Garden City, N. Y.: 1922), p. 63.

124. W to Bryan, Mar. 31, 1915, Letter Book 21, p. 282, Wilson Papers, VII.

125. Donald M. Souder to W, June 7, 1914, Wilson Papers, II. 55; W to James Sprunt, Feb. 1, 1913, Wilson Papers, II, 31.

126. H. C. Ives to W, Nov. 12, 1914, Wilson Papers, VI, 227.

127. "The Ministry and the Individual," an address delivered by Woodrow Wilson at the McCormick Theological Seminary, Chicago, Nov. 2, 1909, Baker and Dodd (eds.), *Wilson's Public Papers*, II, 118.

128. W to G. S. Eddy, Foreign Department of the Y. M. C. A., Dec. 9, 1914, Wilson Papers, VI, 227.

129. *The Boston Herald*, March 27, 1913.

130. Remer, *Foreign Investments*, pp. 273-274.

131. James K. Fornance notes of Wilson's course in Politics, Princeton, 1904, lecture 3, in Princeton University Library.

132. "Address of Woodrow Wilson to the McCormick Theological Seminary," Baker and Dodd, *Wilson Public Papers*, II, 183.

133. Baker, *Wilson*, IV, 61.

NOTES FOR CHAPTER TWO

1. Thomas A. Bailey, *Theodore Roosevelt and the Japanese-American Crises* (Stanford: 1934), pp. 15-18.

2. *Ibid.*, pp. 324-326.

3. John Bassett Moore, *The Collected Papers of John Bassett Moore* (7

vols., New Haven: 1944), VII, 21-22. Caminetti was later made Commissioner General of Immigration in the Labor Department.

4. Jeremiah Jenks, "The Roots of the Japanese-American Understanding," in the Bureau of Insular Affairs (afterwards B. I. A.) Records, National Archives, file 644/44.

5. W to ex-Mayor Phelan of San Francisco, undated, in *The Independent*, LXXIII, Oct. 10, 1912, p. 863.

6. A. Morgan Young, *Japan Under Taisho Tenno* (London: 1928), p. 68.

7. Dan E. Clarke, "Manifest Destiny and the Pacific," *Pacific Historical Review*, I, 1932, pp. 1-17, shows the growth of the imperial dream in America. James K. Eyre, "Japan and the American Annexation of the Philippines," *Pacific Historical Review*, XI, 1942, pp. 55-71; also Iichiro Tokutomi, *Japanese-American Relations* (S. Yanagiwara, translator, New York: 1922), pp. 21-27, for a Japanese view of American imperialism.

8. Paul H. Clyde, "The Open Door," in *Pacific Affairs*, XXII, 1930, pp. 210-214.

9. Scott Nearing and Joseph Freeman, *Dollar Diplomacy: A Study in American Imperialism* (New York: 1925), pp. 36-37.

10. Payson J. Treat, *Japan and the United States, 1853-1921* (Boston and New York: 1921), p. 192.

11. Kenneth Scott Latourette, *The History of Japan* (New York: 1947), p. 171.

12. *Foreign Relations*, 1910, pp. 234-237.

13. Robert T. Pollard, "Dynamics of Japanese Imperialism," in *Pacific Historical Review*, VIII, 1939, pp. 5-38, covers the growth of Japanese interests in Asia and the internal causation during this and subsequent periods.

14. Sir George Sansom, "Liberalism in Japan," in *Foreign Affairs*, XIX, 1941, pp. 551-560, shows that liberalism as we know it in the West was of no consideration in Japan; it was completely foreign to the ways of Japanese thought.

15. Thomas A. Bisson, *America's Far Eastern Policy* (New York: 1945), pp. 12-14.

16. Joseph E. Power, "The Japanese Constitution and the Militarists," in *Pacific Affairs*, XV, 1942, pp. 188-194.

17. Hornbeck, *Contemporary Politics in the Far East*, pp. 131-133.

18. Hamilton W. Mabie, "A Japanese Statesman on Japan: An Authorized Interview with Count Okuma," in *The Outlook*, CIV, June 14, 1913, p. 338.

19. Sansom, "Liberalism in Japan," in *Foreign Affairs*, XIX, 1941, pp. 555-556.

20. Young, *Japan Under Taisho Tenno*, pp. 20-21, 25-30; Hornbeck, *Contemporary Politics*, pp. 160-166; Smimasa Iditti, *The Life of Marquis Shigenobu Okuma* (Tokyo: 1940), pp. 359-366.

21. *The North China Herald*, Mar. 8, 1913, pp. 689-691.

22. *Ibid.*, Apr. 12, 1913, p. 81.

23. William Kend to Bryan, Apr. 7, 1913, Wilson Papers, II, 39.

24. Thomas A Bailey, "California, Japan, and the Alien Land Legislation of 1913," *Pacific Historical Review*, I, 1932, p. 53.

25. Houston, *Eight Years*, I, 51-52.

26. *Ibid.*, I, 60.

27. Moore, *Collected Papers*, VII, 21.

28. Bailey, "California, Japan and the Alien Land Legislation of 1913," in *Pacific Historical Review*, I, 1932, p. 39.

29. Mabie to W, Apr. 12, 1913, Wilson Papers, II, 34, wired that deep feeling was involved in the legislation.

30. Bryan to Hiram Johnson, Apr. 18, 1913, Wilson Papers, II, 35.

31. Houston, *Eight Years*, I, 60.

32. W to Corwin, Apr. 19, 1913, Letter Book 2, p. 414, Wilson Papers, VII.

33. *The New York Herald*, Apr. 25, 1913, enumerated the difficulties facing Bryan and carried the Wilson statement.

34. Moore, *Collected Papers*, VI, 434.

35. Baker, *Wilson*, IV, 83.

36. Moore, *Collected Papers*, VI, 435.

37. The following account of the speech is from a typescript copy, "Executive Joint Conference of the Legislature of California," April 28, 1913, in the William Jennings Bryan Papers, box 38, Manuscripts Division of the Library of Congress.

38. W to Bryan, Apr. 29, 1913, Letter Book 3, p. 62, Wilson Papers, VII.

39. W to Bryan, Apr. 29, 1913, Letter Book 3, p. 63, Wilson Papers, VII.

40. W to Bryan, Apr. 30, 1913, Letter Book 3, p. 90, Wilson Papers, VII.

41. W to Bryan, undated but between April 30 and May 2, 1913, Letter Book 3, p. 99, Wilson Papers, VII.

42. Bailey, "California, Japan and the Alien Land Legislation of 1913," in *Pacific Historical Review*, I, 1932, p. 46.

43. W to Hiram Johnson, May 6, 1913, Letter Book 3, p. 149, Wilson Papers, VII.

44. This is the conclusion of Paxton Hibben, *The Peerless Leader William Jennings Bryan* (New York: 1929), p. 328. Hibben disproves the statement of Tumulty to Ray Stannard Baker that "Wilson soon saw that Bryan was making a mess of it [the California negotiations] and took over the whole thing himself." This assertion was made to Baker by Tumulty in an interview of November 6, 1927. See R. S. Baker Papers, I-B, 38.

45. Houston, *Eight Years*, I. 61.

46. Related later in the *New York Herald*, May 13, 1913, but the action took place soon after Bryan's return to Washington.

47. *Foreign Relations*, 1913, pp. 627-628.

48. Chinda to Bryan, May 9, 1913, *Foreign Relations, 1913*, pp. 629-631.

49. Houston, *Eight Years*, I, 62.

50. Daniels Diary, May 13, 1913.

51. Houston, *Eight Years*, I, 54.

52. Daniels Diary, May 13, 1913, and appended Fiske to Daniels, May 13, 1913.

53. William C. Redfield, *With Congress and Cabinet* (Garden City, N. Y.: 1924), p. 71. Redfield was the Secretary of Commerce; Daniels, *The Wilson Era, 1910-1917*, p. 163. The Admiral George Dewey Papers, in the Manuscripts Division of the Library of Congress, reveal nothing on the meeting of the Joint Board.

54. Admiral Fiske Memorandum, May 14, 1913, in Daniels Diary, May 15, 1913.

55. Daniels, *The Wilson Era, 1910-1917*, P. 165. Daniels confessed if he knew as much of the Pacific problem when he became Secretary as he did three months later, he would have sent the fleet to the Pacific. Daniels Diary, May 16, 1913.

56. Houston, *Eight Years*, I, 66.

57. Redfield, *With Congress and Cabinet*, pp. 71-72.

58. Daniels, *The Wilson Era, 1910-1917*, pp. 163-164, 167; Daniels Diary, May 17, 1913.

59. *The New York Herald*, May 16, 1913.

60. Daniels Diary, May 17, 1913; also Daniels to Wilson, Apr. 10, 1915, in the Josephus Daniels Papers, box 12. This letter is a reminder to Wilson of his action in the matter.

61. *The New York Herald*, May 17, 1913.

62. *The New York Times*, May 18, 1913.

63. *The North China Herald*, May 17, 1913, p. 460; for Mott see *The New York Herald*, May 23, 1913.

64. *The New York Sun*, May 25, 1913.

65. *The New York Times*, May 20, 1913.

66. A. M. Pooley, *Japan's Foreign Policies* (London: 1920), p. 125.

67. Blanchard to Bryan, May 17, 1913, Wilson Papers, VI-B, 272A.

68. Baker, *Wilson*, IV, 82. Also Bryan, *Memoirs*, p. 367.

69. Moore, *Collected Papers*, VII, 22.

70. Bryan to Chinda, May 19, 1913, *Foreign Relations, 1913*, pp. 631-632.

71. Baker, *Wilson*, IV, 81.

72. Moore, *Collected Papers*, VII, 21.

73. Rikitaro Fujisaiwa, *The Recent Aims and Political Development of Japan* (New Haven: 1923), pp. 20-21.

74. Bryce to W, June 12, 1913, Wilson Papers, II, 36.

75. W to Garrison, June 12, 1913, Letter Book 4, p. 326, Wilson Papers, VII.

76. Memorandum of R. S. Miller of Far Eastern Affairs, undated, S. D., 893.00/1744.

77. Bryan to W, June 30, 1913; also Moore to Bryan, June 29, 1913, Wilson Papers, II, 36.

78. Bryan to Chinda, July 16, 1913, *Foreign Relations, 1913*, pp. 641-645.

79. Aide-Memoiré to Japanese Embassy, July 16, 1913, *Foreign Relations, 1913,* pp. 645-650; also Japanese Minister of Foreign Affairs to Japanese Ambassador, Aug. 23, 1913, *ibid.,* pp. 651-653.

80. Japanese Minister of Foreign Affairs to Japanese Ambassador, Aug. 23, 1913, *ibid.,* pp. 651-653.

81. W to Bryan, Sept. 11, 1913, Letter Book 6, p. 369, Wilson Papers, VII.

82. W to Bryan, Jan. 1914, Wilson Papers, VI-B, 272; also Guthrie to Bryan, Jan. 29, 1914, Wilson Papers, II, 45.

83. Seymour, *Intimate House Papers,* I, 108.

84. W to Palmer, Mar. 11, 1913, Letter Book 1, p. 122, Wilson Papers, VII.

85. Seymour, *Intimate House Papers,* I, 129.

86. W to Guthrie, Apr. 29, 1913, Letter Book 3, Wilson Papers, VII.

87. *The Outlook,* CIV, Mar. 28, 1917, p. 539; *The New York Times,* Mar. 9, 1917.

88. W to Guthrie, Dec. 11, 1916, Wilson Papers, II, 109.

NOTES FOR CHAPTER THREE

1. Link, *Wilson,* p. 27.

2. Baker and Dodd, *Wilson Public Papers,* I, 413-414.

3. *Ibid.,* I, 426.

4. *Ibid.,* I, 438-439.

5. Notter, *Origins Wilson's Foreign Policy,* p. 134.

6. *Ibid.,* p. 148.

7. Link, *Wilson,* p. 120.

8. *Ibid.,* p. 123. Wilson belonged to several liberal organizations, one being the Short Ballot Association of which he became President. There he was brought together with such men as Norman Hapgood, Henry J. Ford, Lawrence Abbott, William U'Ren, and the novelist Winston Churchill, all leaders in American progressive thought.

9. Woodrow Wilson, *Constitutional Government,* pp. 52-53.

10. Democratic National Committee, *The Democratic Textbook,* 1912 (New York: 1912), p. 30.

11. Bryan letter in the *Washington Post,* Apr. 29, 1906.

12. Williams, *Bryan,* p. 345.

13. Interview of Ray S. Baker with Senator John Williams, Mar. 11, 1927, in R. S. Baker Papers, I B, 41.

14. Grayson L. Kirk, *Philippine Independence* (New York: 1936), p. 44. As early as 1912 Quezon had supplied Wilson with data on the islands.

15. Republican National Committee, *Republican Textbook,* 1912 (New York: 1912), p. 276. Also Progressive National Committee, *A Contract with the People* (New York: 1912).

16. Baker and Dodd, *Wilson Public Papers,* II, 469.

17. *El Ideal,* Manila, Nov. 6, 1912.

18. William C. Forbes, *The Philippine Islands,* 2 vols. (Boston: 1928), II, 372.

19. President Taft's Message to Congress, Dec. 6, 1912, in *The Congressional Record,* 62nd Congress, 3rd Session, p. 208. Hereafter *Congressional Record,* 62nd Congress, 3rd.

20. As quoted in Kirk, *Philippine Independence,* p. 44.

21. Page to W, Jan. 1, 1913, Wilson Papers, II, 30; Redfield to W, Mar. 24, 1913, Wilson Papers, VI, 44, sent the same advice. The first and possibly most effective suggestion came from W. H. Page.

22. Forbes, *Philippine Islands,* II, 205.

23. The bank advanced $7,000 for this purpose. Edward Howe, Vice President of the Princeton Bank to W, Sept. 5, 1913, Wilson Papers, II, 30.

24. Frank McIntyre, Chief of the Bureau of Insular Affairs, to Forbes, Jan. 21, 1913, B. I. A., McIntyre Personnel File.

25. Forbes to W, Mar. 5, 1913, Wilson Papers, VI, 44.

26. W to Forbes, May 6, 1913, Wilson Papers, VI, 44.

27. *The Filipino People,* May, 1913, pp. 14-15.

28. W to Scott, May 16, 1913, Wilson Papers, VI, 44.

29. Wilson's expression in Woodrow Wilson, *A History of the American People,* 5 vols. (New York: 1902 [1901]), V, 300.

30. *The Filipino People,* June, 1913, p. 15.

31. Frankfurter to Secretary of War, Apr. 11, 1913, B. I. A., 141/76.

32. Garrison to W, Apr. 24, 1913, B. I. A., 141/78.

33. Dr. Charles W. Eliot who returned home from an Eastern investigation in 1913 favored retention of the islands. Eliot to W, May 9, 1913, Wilson Papers, VI, 203.

34. W to Garrison, Sept. 26, 1913, Wilson Papers, II, 44.

35. Ford to W, Apr. 30, 1913, Wilson Papers, II, 35.

36. See Ford to W, May 20, 1913, Wilson Papers, II, 35, for here and following.

37. Aguinaldo to W, May 23, 1913, Wilson Papers, VI, 44.

38. See Ford Report, undated, in B. I. A., Ford Personnel File, for here and following.

39. W to Garrison, July 24, 1914, B. I. A., Ford Personnel File.

40. Garrison to W, June 13, 1913, Wilson Papers, VI, 44.

41. W to Garrison, June 16, 1913, Wilson Papers, VI, 44.

42. Storey to W, June 9, 1913, Wilson Papers, VI, 44. There is no indication of the book having been read. Many of the pages are uncut.

43. John H. Watkins, New York attorney, to Mrs. F. J. Harriman, May 22, 1913, Wilson Papers, VI, 44.

44. Forbes to Ford, May 12, 1913, B. I. A., 364/296.

45. W to Garrison, Apr. 10, 1913, Wilson Papers, VI, 44.

46. Garrison to W, Apr. 24, 1913, Wilson Papers, II, 35.

47. Unfortunately the conversation is undated in Manuel L. Quezon, *The Good Fight* (New York and London: 1946), p. 126. Quezon dictated these memoirs while dying in Washington, a war exile from his native land. He had a keen imagination, but the tenor of the recollection seems to fit what he was saying to McIntyre and others at the time.

48. Bryan to W, Aug. 16, 1913, Wilson Papers, VI, 44.

49. Quezon to Bryan, Aug. 16, 1913, Bryan Papers. These papers are deposited in four volumes, arranged by date, in the National Archives. Place of deposit will differentiate them from other Bryan Papers in the Library of Congress.

50. W to Bryan, Aug. 18, 1913, Bryan Papers, National Archives.

51. Francis B. Harrison, *The Conerstone of Philippine Independence* (New York: 1922), p. 3.

52. W to Bryan, Aug. 20, 1913, Wilson Papers, VI, 44.

53. Garrison to W, Aug. 19, 1913, Wilson Papers, VI, 44.

54. W to Forbes, Aug. 25, 1913, Wilson Papers, VI, 44.

55. Bryan to W, Aug. 25, 1913, Wilson Papers, VI, 44.

56. *The Filipino People*, Sept., 1913, p. 4.

57. Aug. 20, 1913.

58. Aug. 21, 1913.

59. *The Outlook,* CV, Sept. 6, 1913, p. 7.

60. Harrison, *Cornerstone,* p. 3.

61. *Ibid.,* p. 56.

62. In B. I. A. 141/85; also in Harrison, *Cornerstone,* p. 50. The two sources differ in paragraphing and punctuation. Here Harrison is used since there is an obvious scramble of a sentence in the B. I. A. document. It is interesting to note that the message was cabled to Harrison in Japan on his way to Manila.

63. Bryan to W, Oct. 9, 1913, Wilson Papers, II, 40.

64. Harrison, *Cornerstone,* pp. 31-49.

65. *Ibid.,* pp. 66-67.

66. *Ibid.,* pp. 69-70. The American members were: Henderson S. Martin, Vice Governor; Winfred T. Denison, Secretary of the Interior; Clinton T. Riggs, Secretary of Commerce and Police.

67. Martin to Garrison, Feb. 5, 1914, B. I. A., 1239/102.

68. McIntyre to J. G. White, March 30, 1914, B. I. A., 1239/105.

69. McIntyre to Garrison, Jan. 17, 1914, Wilson Papers, II, 44, is a lengthy memorandum on the Quezon-McIntyre talks. The Chief of the Bureau of Insular Affairs had a habit of keeping lengthy memoranda on any subject with which he dealt.

70. McIntyre to Garrison, Jan. 17, 1914, Wilson Papers, II, 44.

71. *Ibid.*

72. *Ibid.*

73. *Ibid.*

74. Garrison to W, Jan. 19, 1914, Wilson Papers, II, 44.

75. "Bureau of Insular Affairs Memorandum re Bill to Provide a More Popular Government for the Philippine Islands, Submitted by Messrs. Quezon and Earnshaw," Feb. 21, 1914, Wilson Papers, II, 47.

76. *Congressional Record*, 63rd Congress, 2d, p. 16020.

77. McIntyre Memorandum, May 13, 1914, B. I. A., 4325/158.

78. Garrison to McIntyre, May 13, 1914, B. I. A., 4325/158.

79. McIntyre to Garrison, May 26, 1914, B. I. A., 4325/158.

80. W to Garrison, June 4, 1914, Wilson Papers, VI, 44.

81. W to Jones, June 11, 1914, Wilson Papers, VI, 44. This provided for a change from an absolute veto lodged in the Governor General to a veto which the legislature could override and with final veto power in the person of the President of the United States.

82. McIntyre to Harrison, June 8, 1914, B. I. A., 4325/66.

83. Garrison to W, June 5, 1914, Wilson Papers, II, 55.

84. Garrison to Harrison, July 2, 1914, B. I. A., 1239/133.

85. Garrison to W, June 9, 1914, B. I. A., 4325/71.

86. Garrison to Hitchcock, June 19, 1914, B. I. A., 4325/74.

87. Ross to Riggs, June 13, 1914, B. I. A., 4325/93a.

88. Riggs to Garrison, June 18, 1914, B. I. A., 4325/93.

89. Bryan to Quezon, July 23, 1914, in *The Filipino People*, July, 1914, p. 4.

90. *Congressional Record*, 63d Congress, 1st, pp. 2863-2865.

91. *Ibid.*, 63d Congress, 2d, pp. 15800-15811.

92. *Ibid.*, 63d Congress, 2d, pp. 1533-1538.

93. *Ibid.*, 63d Congress, 2d, pp. 16024-16025.

94. *Ibid.*, 63d Congress, 2d, p. 16074.

95. *Ibid.*, 63d Congress, 2d, p. 16090.

96. *Ibid.*, 63d Congress, 2d, p. 16092.

97. *Ibid.*, 63d Congress, 2d, p. 16134.

98. McIntyre to Harrison, Sept. 9, 1914, B. I. A., 4325/102.

99. McIntyre to Harrison, three communications, Sept. 26, Oct. 14, Oct. 17, 1914, in B. I. A., 4325/120; also *Congressional Record*, 63d Congress, 2d, p. 16628.

100. House Diary, Dec. 10, 1914.

101. Garrison to McIntyre, Dec. 10, 1914, B. I. A., 4325/120.

102. Harrison to Hitchcock, Dec. 12, 1914, B. I. A., 4325/122.

103. Marshall to Quezon, undated, in *Filipino People*, Dec. 1914, p. 6.

104. Harrison to McIntyre, Feb. 22, 1915, B. I. A., 4325/152. The Committee heard such notables as the former President William H. Taft, former member of the Philippine Commission Dean C. Worcester, incumbent Vice Governor H. S. Martin, Commissioner Manuel Quezon, and Secretary of War Lindley Garrison.

105. McIntyre to Garrison, Feb. 21, 1915, B. I. A., 4325/after 152.

106. W to Garrison, Feb. 24, 1915, Wilson Papers, VI, 44.

107. Garrison to W, Feb. 26, 1915, B. I. A., 4325/154 after.

108. McIntyre Memorandum for the Record, Mar. 4, 1915, B. I. A., 4325/155 after.

109. *Congressional Record,* 63d Congress, 3d, pp. 2839, 5342-5343.

110. Garrison to Harrison, Mar. 4, 1915, Wilson Papers, II, 94.

111. *Ibid.*

112. W to Harrison, Mar. 8, 1915, Wilson Papers, VI, 44. The draft written on Wilson's typewriter is in the B. I. A., 4325/157.

113. W to Harrison, Mar. 8, 1915, Wilson Papers, VI, 44.

114. W to Quezon, Mar. 12, 1915, Wilson Papers, VI, 44.

115. McIntyre to Harrison, Dec. 10, 1915, B. I. A., 4325/175.

116. Kincaid to McIntyre, Dec. 23, 1915, B. I. A., 4325/186.

117. Unsigned but probably McIntyre Memorandum, also undated, B. I. A., 4325/204 after.

118. *Congressional Record,* Jan. 11, 1916, 64th Congress, 1st, p. 846.

119. McIntyre, undated, B. I. A., 4325/204 after.

120. *Congressional Record,* 64th Congress, 1st, Jan. 24, 1916, p. 1426.

121. Wilson to Tumulty, radiogram, Jan. 23, 1916, Wilson Papers, VI, 44.

122. Jan. 24, 1916.

123. Quezon to W, Jan. 25, 1916, Wilson Papers, VI, 44.

124. McIntyre Memorandum, Feb. 6, 1916, B. I. A., 4325/204 after.

125. W to Garrison, Jan. 25, 1916, B. I. A., 4325/204.

126. McIntyre Memorandum, undated, B. I. A., 4325/204.

127. *Congressional Record,* 64th Congress, 1st, pp. 2107-2108.

128. *Ibid.,* 64th Congress, 1st, pp. 2109-2110.

129. *Ibid.,* 64th Congress, 1st, pp. 2110-2111.

130. *Ibid.,* 64th Congress, 1st, pp. 2111-2112.

131. *Ibid.,* 64th Congress, 1st, pp. 2115-2116.

132. *Ibid.,* 64th Congress, 1st, p. 2119.

133. *Ibid.,* 64th Congress, 1st, p. 2125.

134. McIntyre Report, Feb. 7, 1916, B. I. A., 4325/204 after.

135. Breckenridge to W, Feb. 7, 1916, B. I. A., 4325/210 after.

136. Daniels, *Wilson Era, 1910-1917,* p. 445.

137. Garrison to W, Feb. 9, 1916, B. I. A., Garrison Personnel File.

138. W to Garrison, Feb. 10, 1916, Wilson Papers, II, 93. The correspondence concerning the resignation is also in Houston, *Eight Years,* I, 174-180.

139. Garrison to W, Feb. 10, 1916, Wilson Papers, II, 93.

140. W to Garrison, Feb. 10, 1916, Wilson Papers, II, 93.

141. McIntyre to Harrison, Feb. 14, 1916, B. I. A., Garrison Personnel File.

142. McIntyre to Harrison, Feb. 24, 1916, B. I. A., 4325/217.

143. Charles W. Swift, Philippine Railway Company, to Jones, Feb. 18, 1916, B. I. A., 4325/216; also *The New York Journal of Commerce*, Mar. 3, 1916.

144. McIntyre to Harrison, Feb. 14, 1916, B. I. A., 1239/135.

145. Daniels, *Wilson Era, 1910-1917*, p. 449; also Seymour, *House Papers*, I, 109.

146. McIntyre Memorandum to Secretary of War, Mar. 16, 1916, and McIntyre to Baker, Mar. 16, 1916, B. I. A., 4325/225a.

147. Baker to W, Apr. 4, 1916, enclosing Harrison to Baker, B. I. A., 4325/227.

148. W to Jones, Apr. 26, 1916, Wilson Papers, VI, 44.

149. McIntyre to Tumulty, enclosing Martin, Apr. 27, 1916, Wilson Papers, VI, 44.

150. McIntyre to Harrison, Mar. 25, 1916, B. I. A., 4325/226.

151. *New York Sun*, Apr. 28, 1916.

152. Kincaid to W, Feb. 11, 1916, Wilson Papers, II, 93.

153. McIntyre to Harrison, Apr. 17, 1916, B. I. A., 4325/221.

154. *Congressional Record*, 64th Congress, 1st, pp. 7210-7211.

155. *The Boston Herald*, May 12, 1916.

156. Quezon was convinced of the Catholic influence on the vote. See his secretary, Maximo M. Kalaw, *The Development of Philippine Politics* (Manila: 1926), p. 347; Harrison, *Cornerstone*, p. 193. John Lind, Wilson representative in Mexico, thought it significant that eleven of the bolting Democrats were connected with Tammany or its Brooklyn annex. See George M. Stephenson, *John Lind of Minnesota* (Minneapolis, Minn.: 1935), p. 324.

157. Baker to W, May 3, 1916, B. I. A., 4325/236.

158. W to Baker, May 5, 1916, B. I. A., 4325/237.

159. These embodied many of the changes resulting from McIntyre's trip to the islands in 1915.

160. "Democratic Party National Platform" in Wilson's typescript. p. 25, Wilson Papers, II, 99.

161. Baker and Dodd, *Wilson Public Papers*, IV, 92.

162. John Dewey, "The Hughes Campaign," *The New Republic*, VIII, Oct. 28, 1916, p. 319.

163. W to Harrison, Nov. 15, 1916, B. I. A., Wilson Personnel File. On Wilson's reelection, Quezon informed the President that the news "filled my heart with genuine joy. The Filipino people have to a man rejoiced over your triumph, and we shall continue to lend to your Philippine policy for the administration of the Islands our whole hearted support as we have done heretofore." Quezon to W, Nov. 18, 1916, B, I. A., Wilson Personnel File.

164. *Congressional Record*, 64th Congress, 1st, pp. 12840-12841.

165. W to Osmena, Sept. 7, 1916, Wilson Papers, VI, 44; "I rejoice in the passage of the new legislation and hope that it will bring prosperity and happiness to the Filipino people."

166. *Congressional Record*, 64th Congress, 1st, p. 128389.

167. W to Baker, Sept. 7, 1916, Wilson Papers, VI, 44. Much of the credit for the success of the bill belonged to McIntyre, confessed Hitchcock to Baker, Aug. 23, 1916, B. I. A., McIntyre Personnel File.

168. The legislation dragged on so long in the American Congress that the bill came to be known in the islands by the familiar title "Bill Jones."

169. *The Statutes At Large of The United States of America* (Washington: 1917), XXXIX, part 1, 545-556.

170. W to Harrison, Oct. 14, 1916, Wilson Papers, VI, 44.

171. Baker to Harrison, August 18, 1916, Forbes, *Philippine Islands*, II, 259; also B. I. A., 141/91.

172. Bryan to Osmena, Sept. 2, 1916, B. I. A., 141/110.

173. John R. Hayden, *The Philippines, A Study in National Development* (New York: 1942), pp. 325-326; also Harrison, *Cornerstone*, pp. 202-215, discusses the development government under his administration. The Governor General throughout seems to have held that the only way to train a people for self-government was to permit them to govern. For a brief account of the independence movement see Paul H. Clyde, *The Far East, A History of The Impact of the West on Eastern Asia* (New York: 1948), pp. 618-640.

NOTES FOR CHAPTER FOUR

1. Henry James, *Charles W. Eliot*, 2 vols. (London: 1930), II, 218. Eliot met the Chinese leader while on an Oriental junket in 1912.

2. Williams, *China Yesterday and Today*, p. 583.

3. Reinsch, *American Diplomat*, pp. 1, 3.

4. Reinsch to Bryan, Dec. 23, 1913, *Foreign Relations, 1913*, p. 141.

5. Hornbeck, *Contemporary Politics*, p. 82.

6. W to Yuan, Feb. 11, 1914, Letter Book 10, pp. 271-272, Wilson Papers, VII.

7. George M. Dutcher, *The Political Awakening of the East, Studies of Political Progress in Egypt, India, China, Japan, and the Philippines* (New York: 1925), p. 132; also *Foreign Relations, 1915*, pp. 44-45.

8. Young, *Japan Under Taisho Tenno*, pp. 41-42.

9. Hornbeck, *Contemporary Politics*, p. 166.

10. Young, *Japan Under Taisho Tenno*, p. 43.

11. *Ibid.*, p. 45

12. *The North China Herald*, Apr. 25, 1914, pp. 253-254.

13. Robert K. Reischauer, *Japan Government and Politics* (Princeton: 1939), p. 130.

14. Fujisiawa, *Recent Aims and Political Development of Japan*, p. 28.

15. Reinsch to Bryan, June 12, 1914, S. D., 793.94/196.

16. Iditti, *Okuma*, p. 372.

17. Baker, *Wilson*, IV, 481.

18. *Ibid.*, V, 1, 8.

19. Grey to Greene, Aug. 1, 1914, George P. Gooch and Harold Temperley (eds.), *British Documents on the Origins of the War, 1914-1918* (11 vols. and parts, London: 1926-1938), XI, 256. Hereafter cited as *British Documents*.

20. Greene to Grey, Aug. 3, 1914, in *ibid.*, XI, 305.

21. Note by Sir William Tyrrell, Aug. 3, 1914, in *ibid.*, XI, 292.

22. Greene to Grey, Aug. 4, 1914, in *ibid.*, XI, 327-328.

23. Grey to Greene, Aug. 4, 1914, in *ibid.*, XI, 329.

24. Sir Edward Grey, *Twenty-Five Years, 1892-1916*. 2 vols. (New York: 1925), II, 99-100; Grey to Greene, Aug. 6, 1914, *ibid.*, Appendix II, X, part 2, p. 823.

25. Iditti, *Okuma*, pp. 373-374; also Gooch and Temperley, *British Documents*, Appendix II, X, part 2, p. 823.

26. MacMurray to Bryan, Aug. 3, 1914, *Foreign Relations, 1914*, I, 162.

27. Two telegrams, Bryan to MacMurray, Aug. 7, *ibid., 1914*, I, 163.

28. Page to Bryan, Aug. 11, *ibid., 1914, I.* 165-166.

29. Gerard to Bryan, Aug. 13, 1914, Wilson Papers, II, 60; also in *Foreign Relations, 1914, Supplement*, pp. 169-170.

30. Iditti, *Okuma*, pp. 374-376.

31. Guthrie to Bryan, Aug. 15, 1914, *Foreign Relations, 1914, Supplement*, pp. 170-171; also Charles N. Spinks, "Japan's Entrance into the World War," *Pacific Historical Review*, V, 1936, pp. 297-311.

32. Bryan to W, Aug. 16, 1914, Wilson Papers, II, 60.

33. Bryan to Guthrie, Aug. 19, 1914, *Foreign Relations, 1914, Supplement*, p. 172.

34. W to Bryan, Aug. 19, 1914, Letter Book 15, p. 434, Wilson Papers, VII.

35. Memorandum of the British Embassy to Bryan, Aug. 18, 1914, *Foreign Relations, 1914, Supplement*, p. 171.

36. *The North China Herald*, Aug. 22, 1914, pp. 566-567.

37. MacMurray to Bryan, Aug. 19, 1914, *Foreign Relations, 1914, Supplement*, pp. 172-173.

38. MacMurray to Bryan, Aug. 20, 1914, *ibid., 1914, Supplement*, pp. 173-174.

39. Bryan to MacMurray, Aug. 20, 1914, *ibid., 1914, Supplement*, p. 174.

40. The Imperial Rescript Left at the Department of State by the Japanese Ambassador, Aug. 23, 1914, *ibid., 1914, Supplement*, p. 175.

41. House to W, Aug. 22, 1914, House Papers.

42. House Diary, Aug. 22, 1914.

43. MacMurray to Bryan, Sept. 28, 1914, and Japanese Embassy to Department of State, Oct. 1, 1914, *Foreign Relations, 1914, Supplement,* pp. 182-183.

44. *The North China Herald* quoting the vernacular press, Sept. 12, 1914, p. 841.

45. Jefferson Jones, *The Fall of Tsingtau* (Boston: 1915) is an eyewitness account; also *The North China Herald,* Nov. 14, 1914, pp. 469-470.

46. Reinsch to Bryan, Nov. 28, 1914, Wilson Papers, VI, 1953.

47. Guthrie to Bryan, Oct. 8, 1914, *Foreign Relations, 1914, Supplement,* pp. 190-191.

48. Lansing to Reinsch, Nov. 4, 1914, *ibid., 1914, Supplement,* pp. 189-190.

49. Reinsch to Bryan, Dec. 18, 1914, *ibid., 1915, Supplement,* p. 204.

50. Treat, *Japan and the United States,* p. 209.

51. A. Whitney Griswold, *The Far Eastern Policy of the United States* (New York: 1936), p. 178.

52. Iditti, *Okuma,* pp. 381-383.

53. *Ibid.,* pp. 388-389.

54. Treat, *Japan and the United States,* p. 210.

55. Charles N. Spinks, "The Liberal Myth in Japan," *Pacific Affairs,* XV, 1942, p. 451.

56. Hosea B. Morse and Harley F. MacNair, *Far Eastern International Relations* (Boston: 1931), pp. 579-580.

57. Reinsch to Bryan, Feb. 10, 1915, S. D. 793.94/257 contains a summary of the negotiations to date.

58. Reinsch to Bryan, March 6, 1915, *Foreign Relations, 1915,* pp. 99-103. contains in parallel columns the Demands as handed to China and to the American minister.

59. Reinsch to Bryan, Jan. 23, 1915, *ibid., 1915,* p. 79.

60. Reinsch to Bryan, Feb. 10, 1915, S. D., 793.94/257.

61. House Diary, Jan. 25, 1915. Lansing succeeded Moore as Counselor in the State Department on April 1, 1914.

62. Lansing Desk Diary, Jan. to May, 1914, *passim.,* in Lansing Papers, Library of Congress. The Desk Diary was kept by Lansing throughout his service in the Department.

63. E. T. Williams, "The Crisis in China," Jan. 27, 1915, S. D., 793.94/211.

64. W to Bryan, Jan. 27, 1915, Bryan Letter Book II, p. 104, Bryan Papers, Library of Congress.

65. Morse and McNair, *Far Eastern Relations,* pp. 583-584.

66. Reinsch to Bryan, Feb. 1, 1915, Wilson Papers, II, 75.

67. Bryan to Page, Feb. 2, 1915, *Foreign Relations, 1915,* p. 82.

68. Guthrie to Bryan, Feb. 3, 1915 and same to same, Feb. 6, 1915, *ibid., 1915,* p. 83.

69. Reinsch to Bryan, Feb. 8, 1915, *ibid., 1915,* p. 83.

70. Japanese Foreign Office to Governments, Feb. 8, 1915, *ibid., 1915,* pp. 83-84.

71. W to Reinsch, Feb. 8, 1915, Letter Book 20, p. 234, Wilson Papers, VII.

72. Bryan to Wilson, Feb. 22, 1915, Bryan Papers, National Archives.

73. Williams to Bryan, Feb. 26, 1915, Bryan Papers, National Archives.

74. Lansing to Bryan, Mar. 1, 1915, in United States Department of State, *Papers Relating to the Foreign Relations of the United States. The Lansing Papers, 1914-1920.* 2 vols. (Washington: 1940), II, 407-408. Hereafter cited as *Lansing Papers* to differentiate them from the manuscript collection in the Library of Congress.

75. Instructions of Baron Kato to Minister Hioki, Dec. 3, 1914, *Foreign Relations, 1915*, p. 161.

76. W to Bryan, Feb. 25, 1915, *Lansing Papers*, II, 407 .

77. Williams to Bryan, Feb. 26, 1915, Bryan Papers, National Archives.

78. Bryan to Reinsch, Feb. 24, 1915, S. D., 793.94/236.

79. W to Bryan, Mar. 10, 1915, R. S. Baker Papers, I, State, 11.

80. Reinsch to Bryan, Mar. 13, 1915, *Foreign Relations, 1915*, p. 105.

81. Bryan to Japanese Ambassador, Mar. 13, 1915, *ibid., 1915*, p. 111.

82. W to Bryan, Mar. 16, 1915, S. D., 793.94/267½.

83. Guthrie to Bryan, Mar. 21, 1915, *Foreign Relations, 1915*, pp. 113-115

84. Bryan to W, Mar. 22, 1915, *Lansing Papers*, II, pp. 409-411.

85. Official Memorandum left by Chinda, Mar. 22, 1915, Bryan Papers, National Archives.

86. W to Bryan, Mar. 24, 1915, *Lansing Papers*, II, 411.

87. Bryan to Reinsch, Mar. 25, 1915, S. D., 793.94/266.

88. Bryan to W, Mar. 25, 1915, *Lansing Papers*, II, 413-414.

89. Reinsch to Bryan, Mar. 24, 30, 1915, *Foreign Relations, 1915*, pp. 116-118.

90. Reinsch to Bryan, Apr. 5, 1915, *ibid., 1915*, pp. 119-122.

91. MacMurray to W, Apr. 5, 1915, and Wilson Memorandum, undated, appended thereto, Wilson Papers, II, 78.

92. Charles F. Hubbard and others to W, Apr. 8, 1915, Wilson Papers II, 79.

93. W to Bryan, Apr. 12, 1915, Bryan Papers, National Archives.

94. Bryan to W, Apr. 15, 1915, Bryan Papers, National Archives.

95. Consul Sammons to Bryan, July 25, 1915, S. D., 793.94/446.

96. Reinsch to Bryan, Apr. 14, 1915, in Bryan Papers, National Archives.

97. W to Bryan, Apr. 14, 1915, *Lansing Papers*, II, 416.

98. Bryan to W, Apr. 15, 1915, Bryan Papers, National Archives.

99. Bryan to Reinsch, Apr. 15, 1915, *Lansing Papers*, II, 417.

100. W to Bryan, Apr. 16, 1915, Bryan Papers, National Archives.

101. Reinsch to Bryan, Apr. 24, 1915, S. D., 793.94/309.

102. W to Bryan, Apr. 27, 1915, *Lansing Papers*, II, 417-418.

103. Bryan memorandum for Ambassador Chinda, Apr. 27, 1915, Bryan Papers, National Archives.

104. Bryan to W, Apr. 28, 1915, Bryan Papers, National Archives.

105. W to Bryan, Apr. 28, 1915, Bryan Papers, National Archives.

106. Chargé Wheeler to Bryan, Apr. 28, 1915, *Foreign Relations, 1915*, p. 128.

107. Bryan to W, May 3, 1915, *Lansing Papers*, II, 418-422.

108. Reinsch to Bryan, May 4, 1915, *Foreign Relations, 1915*, pp. 131-132.

109. Bryan to W, May 4, 1915, and W to Bryan, May 5, 1915, Bryan Papers, National Archives.

110. Bryan to Reinsch, May 6, 1915, *Foreign Relations, 1915*, p. 143.

111. W to Bryan, May 6, 1915, Bryan Papers, National Archives.

112. Bryan to Okuma, May 6, 1915, *Lansing Papers*, II, 422-423.

113. Bryan to American Embassies in London, Paris, and Petrograd, May 6, 1915, *Lansing Papers*, II, 423.

114. Reinsch to Bryan, May 6, 1915, *Foreign Relations, 1915*, p. 143.

115. Lansing to Bryan, May 7, 1915, *Lansing Papers*, II, 424.

116. Page to Bryan, May 7, 1915, *Foreign Relations, 1915*, pp. 144-145.

117. House to W, May 7, 1915, House Papers; also Wilson Papers, II, 80.

118. Reinsch to Bryan, May 17, 1915, *Foreign Relations, 1915*, pp. 148-150.

119. Bryan to W, May 8, 1915 and W to Bryan, May 10, 1915, *Lansing Papers*, II, 426.

120. W to Bryan, May 10, 1915, *ibid.*, II, 426.

121. Bryan to Tokyo Embassy, May 11, 1915, *Foreign Relations, 1915*, p. 146.

122. Reinsch to Bryan, May 17, 1915, *ibid., 1915*, p. 151.

123. Reinsch to Bryan, Dec. 4, 1915, *Lansing Papers*, II ,429-430.

124. W to Bryan, Dec. 5, 1915, *ibid.*, II, 430.

125. Lansing to Reinsch, Nov. 4, 1914, *Foreign Relations, 1914, Supplement*, p. 190.

NOTES FOR CHAPTER FIVE

1. Pooley, *Japan's Foreign Policies*, pp. 132-133.

2. Guthrie to Bryan, Jan. 31, 1914, Wilson Papers, II, 45.

3. Phillips to Polk, Feb. 17, 1917, Frank L. Polk Papers, in Yale University Library. Hereafter cited as Polk Papers.

4. Stephenson, *John Lind of Minnesota*, p. 250.

5. G. C. Carruthers to Bryan, Feb. 5, 1915, Bryan Papers, Library of Congress.

6. James K. Eyre, "Japan and the American Annexation of the Philippines," *Pacific Historical Review*, XI, 1942, pp. 55-71.

7. Griswold, *Far Eastern Policy*, pp. 223-225.

8. Ford to W, Jan. 17, 1914, Wilson Papers, II, 44.

9. The United States maintenance of troops, fortifications, etc. in the islands were charged to national defense. Actual civil expenses of the govern-

ment were supported by insular taxation. "Memorandum Covering the Cost of the Philippine Islands to the United States," prepared by the Bureau of Insular Affairs, Jan. 1913, B. I. A., 1007/68.

10. Harrison to Garrison, May 8, 1914, B. I. A., 1239/113.

11. Hayden, *The Philippines*, p. 717. Theodore Nicholson just returned from the Philippines said that the Japapese were buying up every concern possible. On the day the Senate passed the Philippine bill some Japanese tried to buy his sugar refinery there; see interview in *Chicago Examiner*, June 22, 1916. Similar acts of the Japanese were reported in the *Philadelphia North American*, July 3, 1916. Commissioner Earnshaw in an interview with the *Seattle Times* of Jan. 19, 1917 said there were 20,000 Japanese in the islands. Harrison to B. I. A., Nov. 11, 1917, B. I. A., 6144/35 reported that the increased interest manifested by the Japanese in Philippine agriculture, the visits of their investors and officials, and expansion of Japanese interests, especially in Davao, "are a source of uneasiness to the people."

12. Denison to Garrison, Nov. 27, 1914, B. I. A., 6144/316.

13. *New York Times*, Jan. 29, 1914.

14. Seward W. Livermore, "American Naval-Base Policy in the Far East, 1850-1914," *Pacific Historical Review*, XIII, 1944, pp. 113-135. The Navy made plans in 1914 to transfer its fleet to the Pacific upon completion of the Panama Canal. See Outten J. Clinard, *Japan's Influence on American Naval Power, 1897-1917* (Berkeley, Calif.: 1947), p .110.

15. Jan. 24, 1915.

16. Hudson Maxim, *Defenseless America* (New York: 1915), pp. 63, 100.

17. (New York: 1908), p. 173.

18. James F. Abbott, *Japanese Expansion and American Policies*, 2d edition (New York: 1916), p. 6. See also Sidney L. Gulick, *America and the Orient* (New York: 1916), pp. 1-27; ————, *The American Japanese Problem* (New York: 1914), chapters xii-xiii. For the historic development of this ill feeling see David Starr Jordan, "Relations of Japan and the United States," in George H. Blakeslee, *Japan and Japanese American Relations* (New York: 1912), pp. 1-9.

19. *Washington Post*, Jan. 25, 1915.

20. *Makahlo Free Press*, Mar. 25, 1916.

21. *Filipino People*, Feb. 1915, p. 10.

22. Jan. 14, 1916, B. I. A., 364/310.

23. *Consolidacian Nacional*, Feb. 24, 1916.

24. *La Democracia*, May 4, 1916.

25. Werner Levi, "American Attitudes Toward the Pacific Islands, 1914-1919," *Pacific Historical Review*, XVII, 1948, p. 58. This article contains the results of an interview with Breckenridge Long, the Third Assistant Secretary of State.

26. Livermore, "American Naval-Base Policy," *Pacific Historical Review*, XIII, 1944, p. 134.

27. Lansing, *War Memoirs of Robert Lansing* (New York: 1935), p. 293. Lansing in his personal Diary, Jan. 10, 1918, in the Robert S. Lansing Papers,

Library of Congress, confesses to the knowledge of the secret agreement giving the islands north of the equator to Japan and south to the British Empire. Hereafter cited Lansing Diary which differentiates it from the Lansing Desk Diary.

28. Levi, "American Attitudes Toward the Pacific Islands, 1914-1919," *Pacific Historical Review*, XII, 1948, pp. 59-60. These documents were not conclusive however since they consisted only of telegrams from the Russian Ambassador suggesting the articles for such a treaty. It was not known that they were signed.

29. Sir George Sansom, *The Western World and Japan: A Study in the Interaction of European and Asiatic Cultures* (New York: 1950), pp. 363-364, states that had Japan adopted a constitution independent of any study of foreign constitutions, it would have produced one similar to that of Germany since it best fitted the situation.

30. Bryan to W, Apr. 26, 1915, Bryan Papers, National Archives.

31. W to Bryan, Apr. 27, 1915, Bryan Papers, National Archives.

32. Polk Diary, Dec. 15, 1915, Polk Papers.

33. House to W, Jan. 15, 1916, House Papers.

34. Marye to W, Jan. 25, 1916, S. D., 761.94/151 sent on to Lansing, Mar. 1, 1916, S. D., 761.94/157.

35. W to Lansing, Mar. 1, 1916, S. D., 761.94/157.

36. Japanese-Russian Treaty, Secret Document, July 3, 1916, S. D., 761.94/137½.

37. Ernest B. Price, *The Russo-Japanese Treaties of 1907-1916 Concerning Manchuria and Mongolia* (Baltimore: 1933), pp. 88-89.

38. Francis to W, July 7, 1916, as translated from the *Novoe Vieyma* of July 1, 1916, Wilson Papers, II, 102.

39. Phillips to Polk, July 10, 1916, Polk Papers.

40. Guthrie to Lansing, Aug. 21, 1916, *Foreign Relations, 1916*, p. 444.

41. Guthrie to Lansing, Aug. 1, 1916, received Sept. 28, 1916, S. D., 793.94/538½.

42. House to W, July 1, 1916, House Papers, also in Wilson Papers, II, 98.

43. British Ambassador to Japanese Foreign Minister, Feb. 16, 1917, in John V. A. MacMurray, *Treaties and Agreements*, II, 1167.

44. Memorandum of the Far Eastern Division, Mar. 5, 1918, S. D., 761.94/137½. The Russian Ambassador's telegram was of Jan. 26, 1917 so the negotiations were simultaneous.

45. W to Phelan, Oct. 10, 1912, *Independent*, LXXIII, Oct. 10, 1912, p. 863.

46. W to Bryan, Jan. 15, 1914, Wilson Papers, VI, B-272.

47. McIntosh to State Department, Oct. 24, 1914, Wilson Papers, II, 66.

48. Samuel Gompers, *Seventy Years of Life and Labor* (New York: [1925] 1948), pp. 60-61.

49. Guthrie to Bryan, Nov. 5, 1914, Wilson Papers, II, 67.

50. Episcopal Bishop's Office in Tokyo to W, Nov. 5, 1914, Wilson Papers, II, 67.

51.   Phelan to W, Nov. 13, 1914, Wilson Papers, II, 67.

52.   Bryan to W, Jan. 23, 1915, Bryan Papers, National Archives; also in Bryan Letter Book, II, pp. 95-97, Library of Congress.

53.   Bryan to W, Mar. 8, 1915, Bryan Papers, National Archives.

54.   Note of W to Bryan, Mar. 8, 1915, *Lansing Papers*, II, 401-402.

55.   Walter Parker to Tumulty, Apr. 12, 1915, Wilson Papers, VI, 272.

56.   W to Tumulty, undated note, Wilson Papers, VI, 272.

57.   Polk Diary, Feb. 1, 1917.

58.   Henry L. Day to Tumulty, Feb. 2, 1917, see also President's note attached, Wilson Papers, VI, 272.

59.   C. N. McArthur to Tumulty, Feb. 3, 1917 inclosing telegrams, Wilson Papers, VI, 272.

60.   W to J. A. Berst, June 4, 1917, and Berst to W, June 8, 1917, Wilson Papers, VI, 4020.

61.   W to Polk, June 16, 1917, Letter Book 41, p. 409, Wilson Papers, VII; also Polk to W, June 12, 1917, Wilson Papers, VI, 4020.

62.   W to Berst, Aug. 11, 1917, Wilson Papers, VI, 4020.

63.   Lansing to Tumulty, Wilson Papers, VI, 4020.

64.   For Report see *Foreign Relations, 1914*, p. 97.

65.   Boardman to W, July 12, 1913, Wilson Papers, II, 36.

66.   W to Boardman, July 23, 1913, Wilson Papers, II, 37.

67.   Boardman to W, July 25, 1913, Wilson Papers, II, 37.

68.   Boardman to W, July 26, 1913 and note of W to Tumulty, undated, attached, Wilson Papers, II, 37.

69.   J. B. Moore to W, Jan. 26, 1914, Wilson Papers, II, 45.

70.   Baker and Dodd, *Wilson Public Papers*, I, 90-91; also W to Moore, Feb. 6, 1914, *Foreign Relations, 1914*, p. 105.

71.   Boardman to W, Mar. 24, 1914, Wilson Papers, II, 48.

72.   W to Senator George F. Chamberlain, Apr. 7, 1914, Wilson Papers, VI, 227.

73.   Colonel W. L. Sibeil, Chief of Engineers, Arthur P. Davis and Professor D. W. Mead composed the party. Chinese Minister to Bryan, May 23, 1914, *Foreign Relations, 1914*, p. 109.

74.   George W. Davis to Chinese Minister, Oct. 31, 1914, *ibid., 1914*, pp. 115-116.

75.   Davis to Bryan, Dec. 19, 1914, *ibid., 1914*, pp. 117-118.

76.   Davis to Bryan, Jan. 6, 1915, *ibid., 1915*, p. 212.

77.   Reinsch to Bryan, Feb. 4, 1915, *ibid., 1915*, p. 214.

78.   Reinsch to Chinese Minister of Agriculture and Commerce, Jan. 14, 1916, *ibid., 1916*, p. 104.

79.   MacMurray, *Treaties and Agreements*, II, 1287-1291, 1304, 1309 contains the texts of the treaties.

80.   American Intelligence Corps to Lansing, June 29, 1916, *Foreign Relations, 1916*, p. 123.

81. Reinsch to Lansing, Jan. 2, 1917, *ibid., 1917*, p. 207.

82. For text of agreement see MacMurray, *Treaties and Agreements*, II, 1297-1302.

83. Lansing to Reinsch, quoting Straight, Jan. 8, 1917, *Foreign Relations, 1917*, p. 208.

84. Reinsch to Lansing, May 17, 1916, *ibid., 1916*, pp. 179-181.

85. Thomas E. La Fargue, *China and the World War* (Stanford University: 1937), p. 122.

86. Lansing to American Chargé in Peking, Sept. 11, 1913, *Foreign Relations, 1913*, p. 187.

87. J. B. Moore to Chinese Chargé and enclosures, Jan. 16, 1914, *ibid., 1914*, pp. 68-69, 71.

88. Reinsch to Bryan, Dec. 30, 1915, *ibid., 1915*, pp. 215-216.

89. Griswold to W, Apr. 10, 1915 and pencil note appended, Wilson Papers, II, 79.

90. Bryan to W, May 3, 1915, Bryan Papers, National Archives.

91. Griswold to Bryan, June 3, 1915, Bryan Papers, National Archives.

92. W to Bryan, June 7, 1915, Bryan Papers, National Archives.

93. The original revision is in the Bryan Papers, National Archives.

94. W to Griswold, June 10, 1915, Wilson Papers, VI, 227.

95. John Hayes Hammond and Jeremiah W. Jenks, *Great American Issues: Political, Social, Economic* (New York: 1921), pp. 225-232.

96. Lansing to W, June 15, 1916, S. D., 893.51/3009.

97. W to Lansing, Apr. 7, 1916, R. S. Baker Papers, I, State, 11.

98. Long to Polk, July 12, 1916, Polk Papers.

99. See the agreement of Nov. 16, 1916, *Foreign Relations, 1916*, pp. 138-143.

100. Lansing to Reinsch, Apr. 15, 1916, S. D., 893.00/2384.

101. Williams for Lansing, June 21, 1916, R. S. Baker Papers, I, State, 11.

102. Lansing to W, June 15, 1916, R. S. Baker Papers, I, State, 11.

103. The American Group to Lansing, July 26, 1916, *Foreign Relations, 1916*, pp. 134-138.

104. W to F. C. Howe, Aug. 7, 1916, Wilson Papers, VI, 226.

105. Reinsch to Lansing, Dec. 21, 1916, S. D., 893.51/1715.

106. W to Lansing, Dec. 3, 1916, R. S. Baker Papers, I, State, 11.

107. W to Lansing, Dec. 5, 1916, R. S. Baker Papers, I, State, 11.

108. La Fargue, *China and the World War*, pp. 125-126.

109. Morgan, Grenfell and Company to J. P. Morgan and Company, Mar. 2, 1917, *Foreign Relations, 1917*, p. 128.

110. Memorandum of Japanese Ambassador to Department of State, Jan. 25, 1917, *ibid., 1917*, pp. 117-118.

111. American Group to Lansing, Mar. 8, 1917, *ibid., 1917*, pp. 126-127.

112. Polk Diary, Apr. 3, 1917.

113.   Bau, *The Open Door*, p. 98; Remer, *Foreign Investments*, pp. 101, 114; also La Fargue, *China and the World War*, p. 142.

114.   P. S. Heintzlemann to Reinsch, Aug. 18, 1916, *Foreign Relations, 1917*, p. 243.

115.   Lansing to Guthrie, Sept, 6, 1916, *ibid., 1917*, p. 244.

116.   Williams to Polk, Oct. 11, 1916, Polk Papers.

117.   Guthrie to Lansing, Sept. 11, 1916, *Foreign Relations, 1916*, p. 245.

118.   Lansing to Guthrie, Sept. 13, 1916, *ibid., 1916*, p. 245.

119.   Reinsch to Lansing inclosing settlement as reported in *Peking Gazette*, Jan. 31, 1917, *ibid., 1917*, p. 249.

NOTES FOR CHAPTER SIX

1.   Charles C. Tansil, *America Goes to War* (Boston: 1938), p. 28.

2.   Bell, *Woodrow Wilson*, pp. 167-172, contains an excellent interpretation of the President's mind on the problem of participating in the war.

3.   John L. Heaton (ed.), *Cobb on "The World"* (New York: 1924), pp. 268-270.

4.   Joseph Tumulty, *Woodrow Wilson as I Knew Him* (Garden City: 1921), p. 256; Houston, *Eight Years*, I, 250.

5.   Lansing, *War Memoirs*, p. 212.

6.   Houston, *Eight Years*, I, 229.

7.   Lansing to Diplomatic Representatives in Neutral Countries, Feb. 3, 1917, in *F. R. 1917, Supplement, 1*, p. 108.

8.   Lansing, *War Memoirs*, pp. 285-287.

9.   MacMurray, *Treaties and Agreements*, II, 1368. Wilson's circular note was not designed to call any one country to follow American action in breaking relations with Germany, but Minister Reinsch so interpreted it in dealing with China. His haste was due in part to the temporary absence of the Japanese Minister from Peking. See Griswold, *Far Eastern Policy*, p. 201.

10.   Reinsch to Lansing, Feb. 7, 1917, *F. R., 1917, Supplement 1*, pp. 403-404.

11.   Reinsch to Lansing, Feb. 9, 1917, *F. R., 1917, Supplement 1*, p. 408.

12.   Lansing to Reinsch, Feb. 10, 1917, *F. R., 1917, Supplement 1*, p. 408.

13.   W on his own typewriter to Lansing, Feb. 10, 1917, R. S. Baker Papers, I, State 11; also Baker, *Wilson*, VI, 467.

14.   Lansing to Reinsch, Feb. 10, 1917, *F. R., 1917, Supplement 1*, p. 408.

15.   Reinsch to Lansing, Feb. 12, 1917, *F. R., 1917, Supplement 1*, pp. 408-409.

16.   Robert T. Pollard, *China's Foreign Relations, 1917-1931* (New York: 1933), p. 13.

17.   Anatol M. Kotenev, *New Lamps for Old, An Interpretation of Events in Modern China and Whither They Lead* (Shanghai: 1931), p. 103; also

Paul S. Reinsch, *Secret Diplomacy How Far Can It Be Eliminated* (New York: 1922), p. 128.

18. Lansing to Reinsch, Feb 17, 1917, *F. R., 1917, Supplement 1*, pp. 410-411.

19. Lansing to Reinsch, Feb. 25, 1917, *F. R., 1917, Supplement 1*, pp. 411-412.

20. Griswold, *Far Eastern Policy*, pp. 205-206; La Fargue, *China and the World War*, p. 97.

21. Pollard, *China's Foreign Policy*, pp. 14-15.

22. Reinsch to Lansing, Feb. 28, 1917, *F. R., 1917, Supplement 1*, p. 412.

23. Lansing to Reinsch, Mar. 2, 1917, in *F. R., 1917, Supplement 1*, p. 412.

24. Thomas A. Bailey, *The Policy of the United States Toward the Neutrals, 1917-1918* (Baltimore: 1942), p. 32.

25. Polk to W, Mar. 10, 1917, R. S. Baker Papers, I, State, 11.

26. Lansing to Reinsch, Mar. 26, 1917, *F. R., 1917, Supplement 1*, pp. 422-423. Before entering the war, China agreed to retain control of her military forces and munitions. See *F. R., 1917, Supplement 2, Part 1*, p. 696.

27. Robert Lansing, *War Memoirs*, p. 226; also W. H. Page to W, Sept. 10, 1917, in *F. R., 1917, Supplement 1*, pp. 147-148.

28. George S. Viereck, *The Strangest Friendship in History, Woodrow Wilson and Colonel House* (New York: 1932), p. 189.

29. Polk Diary, Feb. 26, 1917, in the Frank L. Polk Collection, Division of Manuscripts, Yale University Library.

30. Lansing, *War Memoirs*, pp. 226-228.

31. Polk Diary, Feb. 28, 1917, in the Polk Papers.

32. Lansing, *War Memoirs*, pp. 228-229.

33. Lansing Diary, Mar. 4, 1917. The entry as contained in his *War Memoirs*, p. 229, differs from the original. The information, however, is essentially the same. The Secretary changed its style and wording for publication.

34. Baker to W, enclosing Pershing to Adjutant General, Apr. 5, 1917, Wilson Papers, II, 116.

35. Baker, *Wilson*, VI, 474.

36. Lansing to House, Mar. 19, 1917, House Papers.

37. Daniels Diary, Mar. 20, 1917.

38. Colonel House seems to be the only one who definitely knew the contents of the President's address calling for war; see Seymour, *Intimate House Papers*, II, 467-470.

39. Address of Wilson to Joint Session of Congress, Apr. 2, 1917, *F. R., 1917, Supplement 1*, p. 202.

40. Wilson to Cleveland Dodge, Apr. 4, 1917, Baker, *Wilson*, VI, 515.

41. Reinsch to Lansing, Apr. 12, 1917, *F. R., 1917, Supplement 1*, pp. 425-427.

42. Lansing to Reinsch, Apr. 23, 1917, *F. R., 1917, Supplement 1*, pp. 431-432.

43. Polk Diary, April 26, 1917.

44. Two dispatches from Reinsch to Lansing, May 10, 1917, *F. R., 1917, Supplement 1*, pp. 445-449 and May 23, 1917, *F. R., 1917*, p. 47.

45. Reinsch to Lansing, May 30, 1917, *F. R., 1917*, p. 48.

46. Reinsch to Lansing, June 2, 1917, *F. R., 1917*, p. 48.

47. Lansing to Reinsch, June 4, 1917, *F. R., 1917*, pp. 48-49.

48. Sun Yat-sen to W, June 9, 1917, Wilson Papers, II, 120.

49. Lansing, *War Memoirs*, p. 288.

50. Child to House, June 7, 1917, Wilson Papers, II, 120.

51. Reinsch to Lansing, July 1, 1917, *F. R., 1917*, p. 79.

52. Lansing to Chargé Wheeler, July 3, 1917, *F. R., 1917*, p. 80.

53. Reinsch to Lansing, July 9, 1917, *F. R., 1917*, p. 86.

54. Lansing to W, July 2, and July 3, 1917, Wilson Papers, II, 122; also Lansing to W, July 2, 1917, *F. R., 1917*, p. 88.

55. Reinsch to Lansing, Aug. 3, 1917, *F. R., 1917*, p. 89.

56. Pollard, *China's Foreign Policy*, pp. 29-30, reveals the Young China Party supported the war while Sun Yat-sen and part of the Kuomintang opposed it. The older leaders in China feared the rise of the military power there. Powell, who interviewed Sun, in his *Twenty-Five Years*, p. 34, tells that Sun claimed China had no direct interest in the war.

57. Reinsch, *American Diplomat*, pp. 286-287. The Allies did agree to consider a Boxer indemnity suspension, an effective five per cent tariff; see Whyte, *China and the Foreign Powers*, p. 16.

58. Reinsch to Lansing, Aug. 23, 1917, *F. R., 1917*, pp. 99-100.

59. Reinsch to Lansing, Aug. 21, 1917, *F. R., 1917*, p. 99.

60. Woodbridge to W, Sept. 11, 1917, Wilson Papers, II, 126.

61. Abu Bekr to W, Aug. 25, 1917, Wilson Papers, II, 128.

62. House to W, Sept. 8, 1917, enclosing Child to House, House Papers; also Wilson Papers, II, 126. This was the famous Ishii Mission.

63. W to D. B. D. Warfield of Princeton, Oct. 30, 1917, Letter Book 45, p. 117, Wilson Papers, VII. Scott was the missionary at Tsingtau who corresponded regularly with the President. The book was a collection of the author's lectures delivered at Princeton Theological Seminary.

64. Reinsch to Lansing, Oct. 28, 1917, S. D., 123R271/61½. Reinsch confessed that he sought advice from the following men: John C. Ferguson, Counselor of the Chinese Foreign Office; George E. Morrison, the British adviser to the President of China; Roy S. Anderson, who had a wide acquaintance among Chinese officials; Admiral Tsai Ting Ken; W. H. Donald, the Australian journalist; and C. C. Wang, C. C. Wu and Wellington Koo.

65. La Fargue, *China and the World War*, p. 130.

66. Wheeler to Lansing, June 4, 1917, *F. R., 1917*, pp. 68-71.

67. Japanese Ambassador Sato to Lansing, June 15, 1917, *F. R., 1917*, p. 259.

68. Lansing to Sato, July 6, 1917, *F. R., 1917*, pp. 260-262.

69. W to Lansing, July 3, 1917, R. S. Baker Papers, I, State, 11.

70. Interview with Breckenridge Long by author, May 29, 1951.

71. House to W, July 8, 1917, Wilson Papers, II, 122.

72. Balfour to House, July 6, 1917 Wilson Papers, II, 122; for here and following.

73. Balfour to House, July 6, 1917, Wilson Papers, II, 122; for here and following.

74. Long never knew what was in the envelope House gave him and told him to guard with his life. Interview with Breckenridge Long by author, May 29, 1951.

75. House to W, July 8, 1917, Wilson Papers, II, 122.

76. Seymour, *Intimate House Papers*, III, 71-72.

77. W. H. Page to W, Aug. 14, 1917, Wilson Papers, II, 125.

78. House to W, July 17, 1917, Wilson Papers, II, 123.

79. Lansing to W, June 10, 1917, Wilson Papers, II, 120.

80. House to W, May 11, 1917, Wilson Papers, II, 118.

81. Sato to House, May 8, 1917, Wilson Papers, II, 118.

82. House to Sato, May 10, 1917, Wilson Papers, II, 118.

83. House to W, May 11, 1917, Wilson Papers, II, 118.

84. Polk Diary, June 20, 1917, in Polk Papers.

85. Long to House, Aug. 1, 1917, in House Papers.

86. "Report of Personnel of the Japanese Mission, 1917," in Polk Papers.

87. William G. Sharp to W, June 30, 1917, Wilson Papers, II, 121.

88. Lansing, *War Memoirs*, pp. 285-286.

89. Kikujiro Ishii, *Diplomatic Commentaries* (W. R. Langdon, translator, Baltimore: 1936), p. 112.

90. Griswold, *Far Eastern Policy*, p. 217.

91. Interview with Breckenridge Long by author, May 29, 1951.

92. The Carnegie Endowment for International Peace, *The Imperial Japanese Mission*, 1917 (Washington: 1918), *passim*.

93. Long to W, Sept. 1, 1917, and appended note, Wilson Papers, VI, 272.

94. Ishii, *Diplomatic Commentaries*, pp. 112-113.

95. Ishii, *Diplomatic Commentaries*, p. 115.

96. Lansing, *War Memoirs*, pp. 290-302.

97. *Lansing Papers*, II, 433.

98. *Lansing Papers*, II, 434.

99. *Lansing Papers*, II, 435.

100. Ishii, *Diplomatic Commentaries*, pp. 118-119.

101. Lansing Memorandum of Conference with Ishii, Sept. 22, 1917, *Lansing Papers*, II, pp. 435-436.

102. *Lansing Papers*, II, pp. 436-437.

103. Baker, *Wilson*, VII, 262-263.

104. W to Lansing, Sept. 26 (?), 1917 in *Lansing Papers*, II, 438. Baker, *Wilson*, VII, 282 thinks this interview was September 26, although the note is dated as of the day previous.

105. Ishii to Lansing, Nov. 2, 1917, *F. R., 1917*, p. 265.

106. "Protocol to the Lansing Ishii Agreement," *Lansing Papers*, II, 450-451.

107. Lansing, *War Memoirs*, pp. 305-306.

108. Lansing to Morris, Nov. 5, 1917, *F. R., 1917*, p. 267.

109. W to Lansing, Nov. 7, 1917, *Wilson Papers*, II, 129.

110. Lansing to Morris and to Reinsch (2 cables), Nov. 5, 1917, *F. R., 1917*, pp. 266-277, 278.

111. Lansing to Page, Nov. 6, 1918, *F. R., 1917*, p. 269.

112. Lansing to individual Allied Ambassadors in Washington, Nov. 5, 1917, *F. R., 1917*, p. 268.

113. Morris to Lansing, Nov. 16, 1917, *F. R., 1917*, pp. 271-272.

114. Chinese Minister to Lansing, Nov. 2, 1917 given Lansing Nov. 12, *F. R., 1917*, p. 270.

115. Memorandum of Lansing interview with Koo, Nov. 12, 1917, *Lansing Papers*, II, 451-453.

116. Morris to Lansing, Nov. 13, 1917, S. D., 793.94/602.

117. W. H. Page to Lansing, Nov. 13; T. N. Page to Lansing, Nov. 12; Sharp to Lansing, Nov. 15, 1917, S. D., 793.94/600,/599,/616.

118. Copenhagen Legation to Lansing, Nov. 19, 1917, S. D., 793.94/619.

119. Memorandum of MacMurray Conversation with Bakhmeteff, July 9, 1927, S. D., 793.94/609.

120. Griswold, *Far Eastern Policy*, p. 217.

121. La Fargue, *China and the World War*, pp. 138-139.

122. Ishii, *Diplomatic Commentaries*, p. 123.

123. The Japanese gave fullest honors to the dead Ambassador, returning the remains to the United States, with a military escort aboard a special cruiser. See Lansing to Wheeler, June 14, 1917, *Foreign Relations, 1917*, p. 847.

124. House to W, Sept. 18, 1917, House Papers.

125. Baker, *Wilson*, VII, 281.

NOTES FOR CHAPTER SEVEN

1. La Fargue, *China and the World War*, pp. 114-115; see also Griswold, *Far Eastern Policy*, p. 223; John K. Fairbank, *The United States and China* (Cambridge: 1948), p. 322.

2. British Embassy to Lansing, Oct. 3, 1917, and Jusserand to Lansing, Nov. 19, 1917, *Foreign Relations*, 1917, pp. 144-145, 154-155.

3. Memorandum of Japanese Ambassador to Department of State, Jan. 25, 1917, *ibid., 1917*, pp. 117-118; also La Fargue, *China and the World War*, pp. 125-126.

4. Long to Polk, July 12, 1917, Polk Papers.

5. Lansing to W, June 25, 1917, Wilson Papers, II, 121.

6. Lansing to W, July 3, 1917, Wilson Papers, II, 122.

7. La Fargue, *China and the World War*, p. 141.

8. Lansing Desk Diary, July-September, 1917, *passim*.

9. Lansing to Reinsch, Nov. 9, 1917, *Foreign Relations, 1917*, p. 153.

10. Page to Lansing, Nov. 12, 1917, *ibid., 1917*, pp. 153-154.

11. Jusserand to Lansing, Nov. 19, 1917, *ibid., 1917*, pp. 154-155.

12. Lansing to Sharp, Nov. 22, 1917, *ibid., 1917*, pp. 156-157.

13. Redfield to Lansing, Jan. 8, 1918, S. D., 793.94/662.

14. Lansing to Redfield, Jan. 11, 1918, S. D., 793.94/662.

15. Breckenridge Long, "Memorandum on the Chinese Consortium," undated, R. S. Baker Papers, I, Long file, 25. Since Long, after January, 1917, was the administration's representative in the negotiations for the New Consortium, this memorandum is an unusually valuable insight into its formation. It forms the basis of the story here and following. Hereafter cited as Long, "Consortium Memorandum."

16. Lansing to W, June 20, 1918, *Foreign Relations, 1918*, pp. 169-170.

17. *Ibid.*

18. Lansing Desk Diary, June 15, 1917.

19. Lansing to W, June 20, 1918, *Foreign Relations, 1918*, pp. 170-171 for here and following.

20. The treaty of Brest-Litovsk was signed on March 3, 1918, and German troops had taken up occupation in Southern Russia. However, it was Gregory Semenov's defeat in Siberia and retreat into Manchuria which aroused apprehension lest the Bolshevik forces supposedly implemented by German war prisoners would turn the border region into an active front. La Fargue, *China and the World War*, pp. 163-164.

21. Lansing to W, June 20, 1918, *Foreign Relations, 1918*, p. 171.

22. W to Lansing, June 21, 1918, *ibid., 1918*, p. 171.

23. Lansing to American Bankers, June 22, 1918, *ibid., 1918*, p. 172. The firms were: National City Bank, Kuhn-Loeb, J. P. Morgan, Guaranty Trust, First National, and Chase National of New York, Continental and Commercial Trust and Savings of Chicago, and Lee, Higginson and Company of Boston.

24. Those present were: J. P. Morgan, Frank A. Vanderlip, Jacob H. Schieff, Gordon Abbott and six others. Russell C. Leffingwell and another Treasury man with Breckenridge Long and E. T. Williams of the State Department represented the government. Lansing Desk Diary, June 26, 1918.

25. Long, "Consortium Memorandum," R. S. Baker Papers, I, 25.

26. *Ibid.* Italics are those of the present author.

27. Lansing Desk Diary, July 1, 1918.

28. *Ibid.,* July 18, 1918.

29. All information except where indicated based on "Consortium Memorandum," R. S. Baker Papers, I, 25.

30. *Ibid.*

31. Certain American Bankers to Lansing, July 8, 1918, *Foreign Relations 1918*, pp. 172-173.

32. *Ibid.*

33. Lansing to American Bankers, July 9, 1918, Long, "Consortium Memorandum," R. S. Baker Papers, I, 25.

34. *Ibid.*

35. Remer, *Foreign Investments in China*, p. 329.

36. Griswold, *Far Eastern Policy*, p. 209.

37. Lansing to Lord Reading, July 10, 1918, *Foreign Relations, 1918*, pp. 175-176.

38. *The New York Times*, July 2, 9, 11, 16 and 19, 1918.

39. Polk to W, July 24, 1918 and W to Polk, July 26, 1918, Wilson Papers, VI, 40.

40. Polk was serving as Acting Secretary of State during Lansing's absence at this time. The Polk statement is clearly a condensation of the Long letters appearing over Lansing's signature on July 9, 1918, and is found in *The New York Times*, July 30, 1918.

41. These are dispatches attached in the article to the Polk statement, *The New York Times*, July 30, 1918.

42. Lansing to Reinsch, June 21, 1918, S. D., 123R271/74a.

43. Lansing to W, Aug. 24, 1918, Wilson Papers, II, 147.

44. Reinsch to W, Aug. 31, 1918, Wilson Papers, II, 147, Throughout the Consortium negotiations the American Minister to Peking thought there were two things that halted action: outside influences and the provincialism of the New York bankers; see Reinsch, *American Diplomat*, p. 298.

45. Pollard, *China's Foreign Relations*, p. 45.

46. Lansing to Jusserand and inclosed memorandum, Oct. 8, 1918, *Foreign Relations, 1918*, pp. 193-196 for here and following.

47. *Ibid.*

48. Field, *China Consortiums*, pp. 148-152.

49. Long, "Consortium Memorandum," R. S. Baker Papers, I, 25.

50. *Ibid.*

51. David Hunter Miller, *My Diary at the Conference of Paris, with Documents*. 20 vols. (Privately printed: 1928), I, 100. Hereafter cited as Miller, *Diary.*

52. Long, "Consortium Memorandum," R. S. Baker Papers, I, 25.

53. Martin Eagan for Lamont to Long, Jan. 30, 1920, S. D., 793.94/1065. Lamont asked for information on the Twenty-one Demands and anything bearing on relations between China and Japan. Long ordered that he was to have anything except what was of an ultra confidential nature.
    Lamont recognized, "This job of getting the Japanese to come across and withdraw their reservations as to the scope of the consortium is going to be very difficult, but in any event, I am hopeful that my trip to the

Far East will result in giving us a closer insight perhaps in establishing friendly feelings in various directions." Lamont to Polk, Feb. 16, 1920, Polk Papers.

54. Lansing to Morris, Feb. 7, 1920, *Foreign Relations, 1920,* I, 497.

55. Polk to Morris, Feb. 28, 1920, *ibid., 1920,* I, 499.

56. Memorandum of Japanese Embassy to Department of State, May 2, 1920, *ibid., 1920,* I, 500-503.

57. Wright to Polk, Mar. 20, 1920, *ibid., 1920,* I, 517-518.

58. Colby to Davis, Apr. 6, 1920, *ibid., 1920,* I, 530-531.

59. Morris to Polk, Mar. 8, 1920, *ibid., 1920,* 1, 507.

60. Morris to Polk, Mar. 11, 1920, *ibid., 1920,* I, 508-509.

61. Colby to Chargé Tenney in China for Lamont from American Group, Apr. 22, 1920, *ibid., 1920,* I, 533-534.

62. Department of State to Japanese Embassy, Apr. 29, 1920, *ibid., 1920,* I, 536-538.

63. Memorandum of Long, Apr. 30, 1920, *ibid., 1920,* I, 538-539.

64. Long, "Consortium Memorandum," R. S. Baker Papers, I, 25.

65. Japanese Embassy to Department of State, May 8, 1920, *Foreign Relations, 1920,* I, 541.

66. Field, *China Consortiums,* pp. 162-163.

67. For the Agreement see *Foreign Relations, 1920,* I, 576-589.

68. Long, "Consortium Memorandum," R. S. Baker Papers, I, 25.

69. Henry K. Norton, *China and the Powers* (New York: 1927), p. 138.

70. When Feng cabled congratulations on Wilson's Mt Vernon Speech of July 4, 1918, the American President replied: "I am sure I need not tell you how genuine and constant the friendship of the people of the United States is for China or how anxious the Government of the United States is to find every means of manifesting that friendship. It is therefore with a very deep and genuine pleasure that I receive from you this message of friendship and concurrence of aim." Wilson's secretary, Charles R. Swem, noted on the Chinese message, "Is this the Chinese President?" W note to Department of State for drafting, July 16, 1918, Wilson Papers, VI, 226.

71. Williams, *China,* pp. 597-598.

72. W to Hsu Shih-chang, Oct. 10, 1918, quoted in Pollard, *China's Foreign Relations,* pp. 45-46.

73. Hsu Shih-chang to W, Nov. 20, 1918, Wilson Papers, VI, 226.

74. W to Lansing, and Lansing to W, Nov. 25, 1918, Wilson Papers, II, 157.

75. W to Lansing, Nov. 22, 1918, Wilson Papers, II, 156.

76. Miller to Lansing, Nov. 26, 1918, Wilson Papers, II, 156.

77. Reinsch to Lansing. Nov. 22, 1918, S. D., 793.94/734. This confirmation was sent by letter and did not reach the Department of State until after Miller's appraisal was sent to the President.

78. Japanese Embassy to Department of State, Oct. 25, 1918, *Foreign Relations, 1918,* p. 114.

79. Miller to Lansing, Oct. 25, 1918, Wilson Papers, II, 152.

80. Lansing to W, Oct. 26, 1918, Wilson Papers, II, 152.

81. W to Lansing, Nov. 5, 1918, Letter Book 55, p. 139, Wilson Papers, VII.

82. La Fargue, *China and the World War*, p. 174.

83. Foreign Intelligence Memorandum, Jan. 25, 1919, Polk Papers.

84. La Fargue, *China and the World War*, p. 178.

85. C. Burnell Olds, "Potentialities of Japanese Liberalism," *Foreign Affairs*, April, 1944, p. 437.

86. Fujisawa, *Recent Aims and Political Development*, pp. 79-83.

87. Morris to Lansing, Aug. 26, 1918, S. D., 894.50/6.

88. Morris to Lansing, Sept. 6, 1918, S. D., 894.50/9.

89. Fujisawa, *Recent Aims and Political Development*, p. 103; Young, *Japan Under Taisho Tenno*, p. 120.

90. Dutcher, *Political Awakening of the East*, pp. 209-214.

91. Unpublished report of German Consul Dr. Ohrt (translated by J. J. Ernster and John S. Hodgson of Tariff Commission) filed May 4, 1922, S. D., 894.50/8. See also Stanley K. Hornbeck, *Japan: Trade During the War* (for the United States Tariff Commission, Washington: 1919), pp. 13, 15, 23, 132-133. Hornbeck shows that during the war Japan's trade to Asia expanded in manufactured goods and to the United States in raw materials, chiefly raw silk. Foreign trade in Japan doubled between 1913-1917. In 1916 the United States became the leading importer of Japanese goods and exported 25% of its raw cotton to them. In 1917 iron and steel exceeded cotton in value of exports from American ports to Japan. The only decrease of exports flowing through United States' ports to Japan during the war years was in petroleum.

92. This observation was submitted to Reinsch by a member of the Japanese legation in Peking, who said, "Party competition reduces itself to who will favor the most aggressive action in foreign affairs." Reinsch to Bryan, S. D., 793.94/256.

93. Guthrie to Lansing, Nov. 5, 1915, Wilson Papers, II, 66.

94. Walter S. Rogers to George Creel, Aug. 13, 1917, Wilson Papers, II, 125.

95. W to Lansing, Oct. 9, 1917, Wilson Papers, II, 128.

96. George Creel, *How We Advertised America* (New York: 1920), pp. 253-254, 280.

97. House Diary, June 28, 1919.

98. Phillips to American Mission, inclosing Fleisher for Rogers, Mar. 22, 1919, and Morris to Polk, Mar. 20, 1919, Wilson Papers, VIII, 27.

99. For a detailed account see F. A. McKenzie, *Korea's Fight for Freedom* (New York: 1920), pp. 244-246, 251, 254-255; also see *The New York Times*, Mar. 13, 15, 23, 1919.

100. Young, *Japan Under Taisho Tenno*, p. 154.

101. Morris to Polk, Apr. 6, 1919, *Foreign Relations, 1919*, II, 460-461.

102. Bergholz to Polk, Jan. 29, 1919, *ibid., 1919*, II, 458.

103. Morris to Polk, Apr. 6, 1919, *ibid., 1919*, II, 460-461.

104. Syngman Rhee, Chairman of the Korean National Association, to W, Nov. 25, 1918, Wilson Papers, VIII, 4.

105. Polk Diary, Feb. 28, 1919.

106. Stephen Bonsal, *Suitors and Suppliants, The Little Nations at Versailles* (New York: 1946), p. 223.

107. Polk to Tumulty, June 16, 1919, Wilson Papers, III, 4991.

108. Polk to Morris for Seoul Consulate, Apr. 14, 1919, *Foreign Relations, 1919*, II, 462.

109. Phillips to American Mission, forwarding Morris, May 2, 1919, Wilson Papers, VIII, 44.

110. *The New York Times*, Sept. 12, 1945.

111. Phillips to American Mission, forwarding Crow to Sisson, Mar. 30, 1919, Wilson Papers, VIII, 30.

NOTES FOR CHAPTER EIGHT

1. Wilson, *Constitutional Government*, p. 29; Joseph K. Fornance, notes on Wilson's Jurisprudence lectures, 1904, Lecture 1, Princeton Library.

2. Lansing to Francis, Mar. 20, 1917, *Foreign Relations, 1918, Russia, I*, 12; also Baker, *Wilson*, VI, 501.

3. Scott, *Wilson's Foreign Policy*, pp. 282-283.

4. W to Long, May 7, 1917, R. S. Baker Papers, II, 9.

5. R. H. Bruce Lockhart, *British Agent* (New York and London: 1933), p. 207 for this estimation of Francis.

6. David R. Francis, *Russia From The American Embassy, April, 1916 - November, 1918* (New York: 1921), p. 130. The purposes of the mission are contained in W to Lansing, May 7, 1917, S. D., 861.77/98½.

7. This mission on which John R. Mott and Charles R. Crane, Wilson's intimate advisors served, was originally suggested on a governmental level by William Phillips, the Assistant Secretary of State, and had Lansing's approval. Lansing distrusted the optimistic report, Crane dissenting, of the mission concerning the provisional government. See Phillip C. Jessup, *Elihu Root* 2 vols. (New York: 1938), II, 362-363; Lansing Diary, II, Aug. 9, 1917; and Charles R. Crane to Richard Crane (sent to Wilson) July 21, 1917, Wilson Papers, VI, 288.

8. The Sisson, who represented Creel, and Francis controversy was among the earliest of the quarrels in these inter-group conflicts. Francis resented the public information man representing himself as the President's spokesman in Russia. It became a matter for Wilson to decide. He did so, saying it was best the Embassy not be identified with the American education program in Russia; see Lansing to Francis, Oct. 20, 1917, Wilson Papers, II, 131.

9. This view was also propounded by the Russian Ambassador in a memorandum left by Berton and sent to W, Dec. 14, 1917, Wilson Papers, II, 132; Pauline Tompkins, *American-Russian Relations in the Far East* (New York: 1949), pp. 71-72; Lansing, *War Memoirs*, p. 341.

10. W to Lansing, Oct. 24, 1917, Wilson Papers, II, 128.

11. House to W, July 23, 1917, Wilson Papers, II, 123.

12. W to Senator John S. Williams, Aug. 13, 1917, Letter Book 43, p. 149, Wilson Papers, VII.

13. House to W, Aug. 15, 1917, Wilson Papers, II, 125; for the Papal peace proposal see *Foreign Relations, 1917, Supplement 2*, I, 162-164; for Wilson's reply see Lansing to Page, Aug. 27, 1917, *Foreign Relations, 1917, Supplement 2*, I, 177, 179; Baker, *Wilson*, VII, 221-223 contains Wilson's notes on the proposal, the original of which are in Wilson Papers, II, 125.

14. Lansing advised Wilson that American inaction was playing into Red hands. He proposed support of General Kaledin of the Don Cossacks in an effort to restore Russia as an effective participant in the war. See Lansing Diary, Dec. 7, 1917. The Reinsch advice is contained in a letter to Lansing, Dec. 6, 1917, *Foreign Relations, 1918 Russia*, II, 5.

15. Reinsch to Lansing, Dec. 8, 1917, *Foreign Relations, 1918, Russia*, II, 8.

16. The offer as made by General Tanak, Japanese General Staff, to General Nakajima, Japanese Special Agent at Harbin, is contained in Consul Moser to Lansing, Apr. 4, 1918, Wilson Papers, II, 138.

17. Elena Varneck and H. H. Fisher, *The Testimony of Kolchak and Other Siberian Materials* (Stanford University: 1935), pp. 114-115. For a description of the leading Siberian leaders, including Semenov see Emil Lengyel, *Siberia* (New York: 1943), pp. 224-225, 238-239.

18. Kolchak's movement was never widely popular and depended upon Allied backing from the beginning. See Griswold, *Far Eastern Policy*, p. 236.

19. *Ibid.*, pp. 229-230, 240-241.

20. Bliss approved of the Foch request; see Baker to W, July 6, 1918, Wilson Papers, II, 144; also Frederick Palmer, Newton D. Baker, *America at War*, 2 vols. (New York: 1931), II, 317, 319; Griswold, *Far Eastern Policy*, p. 226.

21. Lansing Desk Diary, Dec. 21, 24, 26, 27, 1917.

22. Memorandum of Sato and Spring-Rice Talk, inclosed in Spring-Rice to W, Dec. 29, 1917, Wilson Papers, II, 134.

23. Lansing Diary, Dec. 31, 1917.

24. Sir Robert Cecil to ?, Jan. 1, 1918, Wilson Papers, II, 133. On the same day, Lansing reported on the Soviet peace appeal to the President and charged: "Lenine, Trotsky and their colleagues are so bitterly hostile to the present social order in all countries that I am convinced nothing could be said which would gain their favor and render them amenable to reason." See Lansing to W, Jan 2, 1917, Wilson Papers, II, 134. The Polk Diary, Jan. 3, 1918 contains similar sentiments.

25. Commander of Asiatic Fleet to Lansing, Jan. 3, 1918, Wilson Papers, II, 134.

26. In preparing his speech Wilson had the report of S. E. Mezes, D. H. Miller and Walter Lippman before him. It recommended a statement of policy to show America was relying on diplomacy as well as force in achieving its war aims. Baker, *Wilson*, VII, 426, 451.

27. Wilson's address to the Congress, Jan. 8, 1918, in Scott, *Wilson's Foreign Policy*, pp. 354-363.

28. W to Charles Eliot, Jan. 21, 1918, R. S. Baker Papers, I, Eliot file, 5.

29. Polk Diary, Jan. 9, 10, 16, 1918.

30. Department of State to American Embassy at Tokyo, Jan. 19, 1918, Polk Papers.

31. House to W, Jan. 31, 1918 inclosing Balfour cable, Wilson Papers, II, 135.

32. House to W, Feb 2, 1918, Wilson Papers, II, 135; also in House Papers.

33. W to Thomas W. Lamont, Jan. 31, 1918, Wilson Papers, VI, 64.

34. W to Senator John S. Williams, Feb. 6, 1918, Wilson Papers, VI, 64.

35. Morris to Lansing, Jan. 17, 1918, *Foreign Relations, 1918, Russia*, II, 30.

36. Morris to Lansing, Feb. 8, 1918, Wilson Papers, II, 135.

37. Telegram no. 624 to Foreign Office, Feb. 15, 1918, Wiseman Papers.

38. Bliss to March, Feb. 20, 1918, Polk Papers; also Wilson Papers, II, 136.

39. Bliss to Adjutant General, Feb. 20, 1918, Wilson Papers, II, 136.

40. Bliss to Polk, Feb. 25, 1918, Polk Papers.

41. Two telegrams of Balfour to Reading, Feb. 26, 1918, Wilson Papers, II, 136. On February 27, Morris to Lansing, S. D., 861.00/1165 told of the Irkutsk situation where German prisoners were being armed by the Reds.

42. Substance of a telegram received by the British Ambassador, being a summary of one from the French Ambassador in Tokyo, Feb. 27, 1918, Wilson Papers, 11, 126.

43. Lansing to W, Feb. 27, 1918, *Lansing Papers*, II, 354-355.

44. Draft in *Lansing Papers*, II, p. 355; original in S. D., 861.00/1245.

45. Spring-Rice had died the previous month and had been succeeded by Reading.

46. Polk Diary, Mar. 1, 1918.

47. House Diary, Mar. 2, 1918.

48. Polk was left in charge during Lansing's absence from March 2 to 14 in Augusta, Georgia, as revealed in Lansing Desk Diary of dates.

49. Memorandum for Polk by Bullitt, Mar. 2, 1918; sent to Wilson at House's request, Wilson Papers, II, 138.

50. House to W, Mar. 3, 1918, Wilson Papers, II, 137.

51. House Memorandum given Auchincloss, Mar. 3, 1918, House Papers.

52. House Diary, Mar. 3, 1918.

53. Brigadier General Judson, and Acting Chief of Staff Lt. Col. Sherman Miles to W, Mar. 4, 1918 objected to Japanese intervention. Long in a letter of the same date approved it. Wilson Papers, II, 137.

54. See *The New York Times*, Mar. 2-5, 1918.

55. When Polk read the new message to the Japanese Ambassador, he stressed that the reason for American objection was its possible effect on Russia. Polk Diary, Mar. 6, 1918.

56. The Wilson message was handed to Polk, Mar. 5, 1918, S. D., 861.-00/1245. An account is in Polk to Lansing, Mar. 5, 1918, R. S. Baker Papers, I, State, 11. The House Diary, Mar. 4, 1918 states that the President was disturbed over his letter and held up the note to Japan. House cabled Balfour, Mar. 4, 1918, that consent to Japan's intervention would throw Russia into the arms of Germany and destroy the moral position of the United States before the world. Wilson Papers, II, 137.

57. See *The New York Times* report, Mar. 4, 1918.

58. House Diary, Mar. 4, 1918.

59. Japanese Foreign Office to British Embassy in Washington, Mar. 7, 1918, House Papers.

60. Balfour to House, Mar. 6, 1918, delivered to W, Mar. 7, 1918, Wilson Papers, II, 137.

61. Polk to W, Mar. 6, 1918, Wilson Papers, 137.

62. Military Attaché to War Department, Mar. 8, 1918. Wilson Papers, II, 137.

63. House to W, Mar. 10, 1918, Wilson Papers, II, 137.

64. Polk advised the message be delivered to the Russian people through the Congress of Soviets to avoid it being treated with contempt. Polk Diary, Mar. 11, 1918. The message was used as an occasion for an attack on the capitalistic United States within the Congress of Soviets, as shown in Caldwell to Lansing, Mar. 17, 1918, S. D., 861.00/1309.

65. The United States had a representative present. W to House, Mar. 20, 1918, House Papers.

66. Balfour to W, presented by Reading, Mar. 18, 1918, Wilson Papers, II, 137.

67. Polk Diary, Mar. 18, 1918.

68. Lansing Diary, Mar. 18, 1918.

69. Lansing Desk Diary, Mar. 19, 1918.

70. Polk Diary, Mar. 21, 1918.

71. Lansing to W, Mar. 19, 1918, Wilson Papers, II, 137.

72. Lansing Desk Diary, Mar. 21, 1918.

73. Morris to Lansing, Mar. 19, 1918, S. D., 861.00/1334.

74. Lansing to Morris, Mar. 20, 1918, S. D., 861.00/13605.

75. Wilson consistently sought the views of his military men on military questions. Only in the matter of the Siberian and Murmansk expeditions did he go contrary to their advices. Peyton C. March, *The Nation At War* (Garden City: N. Y.; 1932), p. 113.

76. W on his typewriter to Lansing, Mar. 20, 1918, R. S. Baker Papers, I, 11.

77. Lansing Diary, Mar. 22, 1918.

78. B. H. Liddell Hart, *The Real War, 1914-1918* (Boston: 1930), p. 387.

79. Jusserand to Secretary of State, Mar. 25, 1918, S. D., 861.00/1363; also Masaryk Memorandum, April 10, 1918 in Wilson Papers, II, 139. Masaryk's recommendation was for recognition of the Bolsheviks. He believed the

Allies must fight the German in Russia and that Japanese intervention would work to German propaganda advantage.

80. Lansing to Morris, Mar. 28, 1918, S. D., 861.00/1358. The Japanese at this time were making overtures to Hovart as revealed in Consul Morse to Lansing, Apr. 4, 1918 transmitting Japanese secret documents. Wilson Papers, II, 138.

81. W to Lansing, Apr. 4, 1918, S. D., 861.00/1439½. Count Tolstoy was also calling for intervention as shown in Woods to W, Apr. 17, 1918, Wilson Papers, VI, 64.

82. Lansing Diary, Apr. 6, 1918.

83. Lansing to Francis, Apr. 5, 1918, *Foreign Relations, 1918, Russia,* II, 100-101.

84. Caldwell to Lansing, Apr. 6, 1918, *ibid., 1918, Russia,* II, 105.

85. Lansing Diary, Apr. 10, 1918.

86. W to Daniels, Apr. 8, 1918, Daniels Papers.

87. Paraphrase of telegram from Balfour to Reading, Apr. 19, 1918, Wilson Papers, II, 138.

88. House Diary, Apr. 24, 1918.

89. House to W, Apr. 24, 1918, Wilson Papers, II, 139.

90. Lansing Desk Diary, Apr. 28, 1918.

91. Lansing to W, Apr. 29, 1918, Wilson Papers, II, 139.

92. Reinsch to Lansing, May, 16, 1918, Wilson Papers, II, 140.

93. W to Lansing, May 20, 1918 and Lansing's answer of May 21, Wilson Papers, II, 140.

94. Miles Memorandum, May 21, 1918, Wilson Papers, II, 140.

95. Reading to Lansing, May 21, 1918 sent to W with two inclosures, Wilson Papers, II, 140.

96. Wiseman Memorandum for Sir Eric Drummons, May 30, 1918, Wiseman Papers.

97. Palmer, *Baker,* II, 315.

98. House to W, June 11, 1918, Wilson Papers, II. 141.

99. Page to W, June 11, 1918, Wilson Papers, II, 142.

100. Stovall to W, June 11, 1918, Wilson Papers, II, 142.

101. Vance Thompson for Maklakoff to W, June 13, 1918, Wilson Papers, II, 142.

102. Baker to W, June 19, 1918, Wilson Papers, II, 142.

103. March, *Nation At War,* p. 118.

104. Palmer, *Baker,* II, 317.

105. Balfour to Reading, quoting Foch to W, June 30, 1918, Wiseman Papers.

106. W to Jusserand, June 25, 1918, Wilson Papers, II, 142.

107. Balfour to Reading, June 30, 1918, Wiseman Papers.

108. Lansing Diary, July 4, 1918.

109. Caldwell to Lansing, June 25, 1918; also sent by Admiral Knight to Navy Department, June 26, 1918, Wilson Papers, II, 142.

110. Balfour to Reading, June 28, 1918, Wiseman Papers.

111. Reading to W, June 28, 1918, Wilson Papers, II, 142.

112. Balfour to Reading, July 2, 1918, Wiseman Papers.

113. Balfour in Paris to Reading, July 2, 1918, Wilson Papers, II, 143. House wrote Wilson, July 6, 1918, Wilson Papers, II, 144: "It has been my opinion for a long time that unless Japan was treated with more consideration regarding the rights of her citizens to expand in nearby Asiatic undeveloped countries, she would have to be reckoned with — and rightly so."

114. Peyton C. March, "Japanese Strategy in the Far East," *Yale Review,* XXIII, 1933, p. 84. Lansing's account of this meeting is revealed in his Diary of the date. It states that Japan and America agreed to send 7,000 troops each and to await developments before thinking of increasing the number.

115. Lansing Diary, July 6, 1918.

116. Lansing Desk Diary, July 8, 1918.

117. W to House, July 8, 1918, House Papers.

118. Lansing Desk Diary, July 7, 1918.

119. Wiseman to Foreign Office, July 8, 1918, Wiseman Papers.

120. House Diary, July 9, 1918.

121. Lansing to W, July 9, 1918, Wilson Papers, II, 144.

122. British Embassy to Foreign Office, July 9, 1918, Wiseman Papers.

123. British Embassy to Foreign Office, July 10, 1918, Wiseman Papers.

124. Lansing to W, July 10, 1918, Wilson Papers, II, 144.

125. Polk Diary, July 15, 1918.

126. Polk Diary, July 16, 1918.

127. British Embassy to Foreign Office, July 15, 1918, Wiseman Papers.

128. Balfour to Reading, July 13, 1918, Wiseman Papers.

129. The American Military Attache to War Department, July 23, 1918, Wilson Papers, II, 145, bore out Ishii's contention that to put an exact limit on the strength of the intervention would upset the Government.

130. Polk to W, inclosing Japanese statement, July 24, 1918, Wilson Papers, II, 144. That Henri Bergson was in Washington at this time and saw the President on intervention is revealed in Polk Diary, July 25, 1918.

131. Polk Memorandum, July 25, 1918, Polk Papers.

132. House Diary, July 25, 1918.

133. Polk to W, July 26, 1918, Wilson Papers, II, 145.

134. British Embassy to Balfour, July 23, 1918, Wiseman Papers.

135. Polk Diary, July 26, 1918; also Jusserand to W, July 29, 1918, Wilson Papers, II, 145.

136. Polk to W, inclosing Knight, Aug. 1, 1918, Wilson Papers, II, 145. Lansing to Wilson, Aug. 14, 1918, Wilson Papers, II, 146, informed the President that since 1917 only the Czech troops were capable of action along the

Russian front. Since March they had been moving from the Ukraine, because of the withdrawal of Russia from the war. At Irkutsk Reds were
supposed to have surrounded four hundred Czechs, who overcame their
attackers and took over the town.

137. W to Daniels, Aug. 1, 1918, Wilson Papers, II, 145.

138. Polk Diary, Aug. 2, 1918.

139. Polk to W, Aug. 3, 1918, Polk Papers; also Wilson Papers, II, 145.

140. Polk Diary, Aug. 3, 1918.

141. William S. Graves, *America's Siberian Adventure, 1918-1920* (New
York: 1931), p. 4. Hereafter cited as *Siberian Adventure*. When Masaryk
congratulated Wilson on his decision, the President replied, "Your letter of
August 5th is greatly appreciated as I have felt no confidence in my personal
judgment about the complicated situation in Russia, and am reassured that
you should approve what I have done." Letter Book 52, p. 495, Wilson
Papers.

142. Graves, *Siberian Adventure*, pp. 5-10.

143. Graves to Adjutant General, Oct. 19, 1918; also W to Baker, Oct. 21,
1918, Wilson Papers, II, 151.

144. Polk Diary, Aug. 13, 1918. The agreement had been general and there
was no intent that Japan should control policy.

145. Polk Diary, Aug. 8, 1918. On August 23, 1918 Wiseman informed
Reading that President Wilson was beginning to feel that the Allies were
attempting to trick him into a policy of reconstitution of the Eastern front
when he had committed himself only to the rescue of the Czechs. Five days
later, Balfour informed Barclay that the United States refused to accept
the serious situation of the Czechs, but thought it was a British attempt to
involve Washington more deeply in Siberia. It looked all the worse for the
British since Masaryk failed to confirm their reports of the situation concerning the Czech troops.

146. Barclay to Reading, Aug. 10, 1918, Wiseman Papers.

147. Polk Diary, Aug. 10, 1918.

148. Lansing Desk Diary, Aug. 15, 1918.

149. Polk left on August 13 for Bar Harbor and Wilson on the day
following for a few days with House. See Lansing Desk Diary of Aug. 13, 14,
1918.

Later when Lansing had Long to call in Ishii concerning the excess
number of troops, the Japanese Ambassador insisted that the United States
had violated the Agreement by sending in an excessive number and that
this had released Japan from the understanding. Lansing and Long called
on Baker who insisted that 7,000 troops had been sent. March was brought
in and blandly stated some 2,000 additional non-combatants had been sent.
Baker, Lansing, and Long were dumbfounded. Lansing had Long talk very
plainly to Ishii and tell him that if his government intended to throw over
the whole understanding because 2,000 noncombatants in excess of the understanding had been sent in by the United States, then it was time that
Washington found a new policy to pursue in Siberia. Interview of the author
with Breckenridge Long, May 29, 1951.

150. Polk left for Bar Harbor on August 13, the following day Wilson departed for a visit to House. Lansing Desk Diary of Aug. 13, 14, 1918.

151. Lansing Desk Diary, Aug. 27, 1918.

152. Military Attaché of Japanese Embassy to War Department, sent on to W, Aug. 27, 1918, Wilson Papers, II, 147.

153. W to Lansing, Sept. 5, 1918, R. S. Baker Papers, I, State file, 11.

154. W to Lansing, Sept. 2, 1918, *Lansing Papers,* II, 380.

155. Masaryk to Lansing, Sept. 24, 1918, Wilson Papers, 148; the House Diary, Sept. 24, 1918, states that Wilson was thoroughly satisfied with the authenticity of the Lenine-Trotsky papers, revealing their German connections.

156. Lansing was also of the opinion that Graves' instructions of political neutrality should be changed in view of the "blood-thirsty" character of the Bolsheviks. Lansing Desk Diary, Sept. 25, 1918.

157. Balfour to Barclay, Oct. 2, 1918, Wiseman Papers.

158. Graves to Adjutant General, Oct. 19, 1918, Wilson Papers, II, 151.

159. W to Baker, Oct. 21, 1918, Wilson Papers, II, 151.

160. Graves to Adjutant General, Oct. 25, 1918, Wilson Papers, II, 151.

161. Miles to Lansing, Oct. 28, 1918 and Morris to Lansing, Oct. 25, 1918, Wilson Papers, II, 152.

162. Graves to Adjutant General, Oct. 31, 1918, Wilson Papers, II, 152.

163. Baker to W, Nov. 6, 1918 inclosing Graves of Oct. 1, 1918, Wilson Papers, II, 155.

164. Polk Diary, Nov. 6, 14, and 19, 1918. McCormick insisted to Wilson that American troops be sent along the Trans-Siberian.

165. Baker to W, Nov. 27, 1918, Wilson Papers, II, 151. The railroads served to supply Kolchak's forces and were vital to his movement. See Louis Fischer, *The Soviets in World Affairs,* 2 vols., 2d edition (New York: 1951) I, 186.

166. Polk to American Mission, Jan. 6, 1919, Wilson Papers, VIII, 7.

167. Polk to American Mission, Jan. 31, 1919, Wilson Papers, VIII, 16 and Mar. 29, 1919, Wilson Papers, VIII, 30.

168. Frederick L. Schuman, *American Policy Toward Russia Since 1917* (New York: 1928), pp. 117-122.

169. Polk to American Mission, Dec. 23, 1918, Wilson Papers, VIII, 4.

170. Polk to American Mission, Jan. II, 1919, Wilson Papers, VIII, 9.

171. Lansing to Polk, Jan. 10, 1919, Wilson Papers, VIII, 9.

172. Polk Diary, Feb. 18, 1919.

173. Lansing to Polk, Jan. 10, 1919, Wilson Papers, VIII, 9.

174. Polk to Lansing, Jan. 14, 1919, Wilson Papers, VIII, 9.

175. Polk Diary, Jan. 16, 1919.

176. Stevens to Lansing, Apr. 10, 1918 and Apr. 29, 1918 *Foreign Relations, 1918, Russia,* III, 229, 231.

177. Sharp to Lansing, Sept. 18; di Cellere to Lansing, Sept. 20; Barclay to Lansing, Oct. 3, 1918, *Ibid., 1918, Russia,* III, 259, 261, 272.

178. Morris to Lansing, Oct. 13, 1918, *Ibid., 1918, Russia,* III, 277.

179. *Ibid., 1918, Russia,* III, 239-240.

180. W to Lansing, Jan. 10, 1919, Wilson Papers, VIII, 9.

181. W Peace Conference Notes, Jan. 12, 1919, Wilson Papers, VIII, 9.

182. Bliss to Col. Archibald Hopkins, Feb. 12, 1919, Bliss Papers, box 232.

183. Lansing to Polk, Feb. 11, 1919, Polk Papers.

184. *Ibid.*

185. W to American Mission, Feb. 19, 1919, House Papers.

186. Francis to W, Mar. 1, 1919, Wilson Papers, VIII, 22. Francis wanted 50,000 American to join 30,000 to 40,000 troops each from Britain and France to put down the Reds.

187. Polk to Lansing, Mar. 13, 1919, Wilson Papers, VIII, 23.

188. Lansing to W, Mar. 22, 1919, Wilson Papers, VIII, 27.

189. Opnav to Amnav, Mar. 21, 1919, Wilson Papers, VIII, 27.

190. Extract of Knox Telegram to Lansing in Lansing to W, Mar. 22, 1919, Wilson Papers, VIII, 27.

191. Phillips was an ardent interventionist and a severe critic of what he thought was Graves' policy of extreme caution and political negativism in Siberia.

192. Phillips to American Mission, Mar. 28, 1919, Wilson Papers, VIII, 29.

193. Phillips to American Mission, Mar. 29, 1919, inclosing Harris, Wilson Papers, VIII, 30.

194. American Mission to Phillips, Apr. 2, 1919, Wilson Papers, VIII, 31.

195. Phillips to American Mission for Baker to W, Apr. 4, 1919, Wilson Papers, VIII, 32. Polk believed Semenov and Hovart were doing more to injure Siberia than all the Bolsheviks. See Polk Diary, Apr. 8, 1919.

196. American Mission to Phillips, Apr. 11, 1919, Wilson Papers, VIII, 35.

197. Polk Diary, Apr. 10, 11, 1919.

198. Polk to American Mission relaying Morris, Apr. 22, 1919, Wilson Papers, VIII, 39.

199. Polk to American Mission, May 5, 1919, Wilson Papers, VIII, 46.

200. Polk to American Mission, May 6, 1919, Wilson Papers, VIII, 46.

201. Bliss to W, inclosing Baker, May 9, 1919, Wilson Papers, VIII, 46; also Baker's interview with Polk, Polk Diary, May 10, 1919.
Polk writing Lansing, May 7, 1919, Polk Papers, said: "To my mind we have got to be pretty firm with the Japanese in the near future. They are behaving like the devil all over the shop, and I think a little mail fist would be useful in our relations. They understand that better than any other arrangement we could make."

202. Meeting of the Council of Four, May 9, 1919, *Foreign Relations, 1919, Russia,* pp. 345-347.

203. Letter of the Powers to Kolchak, June 13, 1919, *Foreign Relations, 1919, Russia,* pp. 367-370.

204. French Chargé at Omsk to French Foreign Minister, June 4, 1919, Wilson Papers, VIII, 56.

205. W to Tumulty, May 14, and May 16, 1919, Wilson Papers, VIII, 48.

206. McCormick to W, May 17, 1919, Wilson Papers, VIII, 49.

207. There was some delay in Morris leaving to see Kolchak. The original suggestion was made on May 17, 1919; see Lansing to W, June 6, 1919, Wilson Papers, VIII, 57.

208. Morris to Lansing, Aug. 4, 1919, *Foreign Relations, 1919, Russia,* pp. 403-405.

209. Morris to Lansing, Aug. 8, 1919, *Ibid., 1919,* pp. 407-408.

210. Morris to Lansing, Aug. 11, 1919, *Ibid., 1919,* pp. 408-410.

211. Lansing Desk Diary, Aug. 16 to Sept. 29, 1919.

212. Phillips to Polk, Sept. 26, 1919, Polk Papers.

213. Phillips to Polk, Sept. 26, 1919, Polk Papers. Phillips in the same letter reported that Wilson had not replied to Lansing's telegram explaining the Bullitt testimony. The Assistant Secretary was worried over the relations between the two men.

The Graves problem was much the concern of the State Department. Baker to W, Mar. 3, 1919, Wilson Papers, VIII, 22, said: "I think you will be very much interested to know that all of my late reports from Siberia show that General Graves has been conducting himself with discretion and good judgment, and has won the hearty commendation of Mr. Morris, American Minister to Japan, and others who have come in contact with him. At one time, you will recall, you and I were disposed to doubt his good judgment." McCormick wrote Wilson, on May 7, 1919, Wilson Papers, VIII, 49, inclosing a communication from Polk expressing doubts as to Graves being the man for Siberia. McCormick said he got the same information from all sources. Polk to Lansing, May 19, 1919, Polk Papers, repeats his hostility towards Graves: "Siberia is a problem. If they had only taken your advice in the beginning and sent some one else in the place of Graves, I have a feeling that half our troubles would have been avoided." So great were the representations against the General that Wilson ordered Morris, going to Omsk to see Kolchak, to also investigate Graves. See W to Tumulty, May 14, 1919, Wilson Papers, VIII, 48. Baker continued loyal to Graves, however, and on May 21, 1919, Wilson Papers, VIII, 51, wrote the President: "I feel from all the information that we have that General Graves is carefully and intelligently carrying out orders under trying circumstances, and that the efforts made to involve him in hostile operations against some part of the Russian population are insidious and baffling."

214. W to Julius H. Bauer, United States Wheat Director, Oct. 22, 1919, Wilson Papers, II, 171.

215. W to Lloyd George, Nov. 3, 1919, Wilson Papers, II, 171. For an appraisal of Kolchak see William H. Chamberlin, *The Russian Revolution,* 1919-1921, 2 vols. (New York: 1935), I, 185-187.

216. Lansing Desk Diary, Oct. 8, 1919.

217. Lansing to Ray Atherton, Chargé in Japan, Aug. 30, 1919, *Foreign Relations, 1919, Russia*, pp. 575-578.

218. Morris to Lansing, Oct. 31, 1919, *Ibid., 1919*, pp. 588-592.

219. Japanese Embassy to Department of State, Dec. 8, 1919, S. D., 861.-00/6109.

220. Morris to Lansing, Dec. 27, 1919, *Foreign Relations, 1920*, III, 485.

Lansing confided to his diary on November 30, 1919 that he favored American withdrawal as soon as practicable from Siberia. He thought the Japanese would be displeased but would accept it with good grace. "My belief is that they will send reenforcements to Siberia and attempt to strengthen Seminov's forces. I cannot see how the Japanese Government can adopt any other policy in view of the very real peril to Japan if the Bolsheviks should gain a foothold in Manchuria and cooperate with the Korean revolutionists. Certainly in the circumstances we ought not to raise any objection to Japan sending a sufficient force to check the Bolshevik advances for the spread of Bolshevism in the Far East would be a dreadful menace to civilization." In his *War Memoirs*, Lansing did not mention Siberia, but he took credit for the non-recognition of the Bolsheviks, p. 345.

221. Lansing to W, Dec. 23, 1919, *Lansing Papers*, II, 392-393.

222. Interview of the author with Breckenridge Long, May 29, 1951.

223. Lansing to Shidehara, Jan. 9, 1920, *Foreign Relations, 1920*, III, 487-490.

224. Graves, *Siberian Adventure*, p. 304 reported on December 29, 1919 he had been ordered to concentrate his command and that he would receive orders for withdrawal.

225. W to Senator James H. Lewis, July 24, 1918, Wilson Papers, II, 144, said, "I don't think you need fear any consequences of our dealings with the Bolsheviks, because we do not intend to deal with them." The growth of his antipathy and fear of Bolshevism is shown in Grant Squires, New York Attorney, to W, Nov. 9, 1918, Wilson Papers, II, 155, "You spoke with a rare insight into the near future, when you predicted to me a few weeks ago, of the dangers of Bolshevism likely to show themselves in this country as well as abroad."

NOTES FOR CHAPTER NINE

1. Interesting appraisals of the chief delegates at the Conference are found in Herbert C. Hoover, *America's First Crusade* (New York: 1942), pp. 31-32. Paul Birdsall, *Versailles Twenty Years After*, pp. 16-20, discusses the objectives of the various delegations.

2. George Creel, *Rebel At Large, Recollections of Fifty Crowded Years* (New York: 1947), pp. 254-255.

3. *The New York Herald*, Jan. 30, 1919.

4. Gallagher makes no mention of House's preparation to handle Far Eastern affairs; yet the Colonel through his influence with Wilson and the fact that the Inquiry had been set up under his direction made him a key

figure in the Paris negotiations. His close relations with the State Department had over the years kept him closely informed on the Orient, although his interests were mainly European. See Seymour, *Intimate House Papers*, III, 170-171.

5. Charles H. Haskins and Robert H. Lord, *Some Problems of the Peace Conference* (Cambridge, Mass.: 1920), p. 7; George Bernard Noble, *Policies and Opinions at Paris in 1919* (New York: 1935), pp. 72-80 observes that Wilson's support in France came largely from the groups on the Left.

6. *The New York Herald*, Jan. 30, 1919.

7. Stephen Bonsal, *Suitors and Suppliants*, pp. 227, 231; Morse and Mac-Nair, *Far Eastern Relations*, pp. 601-602. For a picture of the delegation see Denna F. Fleming, *The United States and the League of Nations* (New York: 1932), opposite p. 110.

8. For South China delegation see *Foreign Relations, Paris Conference*, I, 244.

9. For the Chinese delegation see La Fargue, *China and the World War*, pp. 180-182.

10. James T. Shotwell, *At the Paris Peace Conference* (New York: 1937), pp. 132-133, 136.

11. Polk to American Mission, transmitting Reinsch, Jan. 6, 1919, *Foreign Relations, Paris Conference*, II, 520-525.

12. *Ibid.*, II, 525-526.

13. Reinsch telegram of Jan. 6, 1919 and E. T. Williams' comment, Jan. 16, 1919, in House Papers.

14. *Foreign Relations, Paris Conference*, III, 755-756; also Birdsall, *Versailles Twenty Years After*, p. 87.

15. House Diary, Feb. 4-6, 1919; also *Foreign Relations, Paris Conference*, III, 755-756.

16. Birdsall, *Versailles Twenty Years After*, pp. 90-93; also House Diary, Feb. 12, 1919.

17. Miller, *Diary*, V, 215. The Wilson-House draft amendment proposed that "The equality of nations being a basic principle of the League of Nations, the High Contracting Parties agree to accord, as soon as possible, to all alien nationals of States members of the League equal and just treatment in every respect, making no distinction, either in law or in fact, on account of their race or nationality." David H. Miller, *The Drafting of the Covenant*, 2 vols. (New York: 1928), I, 183.

18. *Ibid.*, I, 114.

19. Miller, *Diary*, XIX, 45.

20. Long to W, Mar. 4, 1919, Wilson Papers, VIII, 22.

21. Long to W, Mar. 4, 1919 and inclosure of Japanese Memorandum, Wilson Papers, VIII, 22.

22. Miller, *Diary*, VI, 441; Polk to American Mission, Mar. 15, 1919, Wilson Papers, VIII, 23.

23. Miller, *Diary*, XVII, 254, 345-346.

24. Acting Secretary Phillips to American Mission, quoting Tokyo Embassy, Mar. 25, 1919, Wilson Papers, VIII, 28.

25. Stephen Bonsal, *Unfinished Business* (Garden City, N. Y.: 1944), pp. 169-170.

26. House Diary, Mar. 29, 1919.

27. Bonsal, *Unfinished Business*, pp. 178-179.

28. Phillips to American Mission, Apr. 7, 1919, Wilson Papers, VIII, 33.

29. Polk to American Mission, transmitting Fleisher to Rogers, Apr. 10, 1919, Wilson Papers, VIII, 34.

30. J. S. Dunnigan, Clerk of the Board of Supervisors, to American Delegates at Paris, Apr. 7, 1919, Wilson Papers, VIII, 33.

31. Miller, *Diary*, I, 243, 245.

32. *Ibid.*, VIII, Document 267.

33. *Ibid.*, I, 246.

34. House Diary, Apr. 12, 1919, records, "I urged the President to stay with the British, which he did, and in a speech made the arguments I gave him."

35. Birdsall, *Versailles Twenty Years After*, pp. 95-100.

36. Bonsal, *Unfinished Business*, pp. 197-198.

37. Miller, *Diary*, XX, 69.

38. Birdsall, *Versailles Twenty Years After*, p. 101; Ray Stannard Baker, *Woodrow Wilson and the World Settlement*, 3 vols. (Garden City, N. Y.: 1922), II, 239.

39. State Department Memorandum prepared by E. T. Williams, Jan. 22, 1918, Polk Papers.

40. Memorandum for Chief of Naval Operations by Planning Committee, Dec. 2, 1918, Wilson Papers, VIII, 1.

41. General Board to Secretary of the Navy, Jan. 24, 1918, Wlson Papers, VIII, 1.

42. *Foreign Relations, Paris Conference*, II, 512-513; also Levi, "American Attitudes Toward Pacific Islands," *Pacific Historical Review*, XVII, 1948, pp. 60-61.

43. *Foreign Relations, Paris Conference*, III, 741-743.

44. Wiseman Memorandum, Jan. 27, 1919, Seymour, *Intimate House Papers*, III, 294.

45. House to W, Jan. 28, 1919, Wilson Papers, VIII, 15. House added in pen at the bottom of the letter, "I have written this with a full knowledge of this case."

46. Seymour, *Intimate House Papers*, IV, 282.

47. *Ibid.*, IV, 295.

48. Smuts' Resolution on Mandates, Jan. 1919, Seymour, *Intimate House Papers*, IV, 319-320.

49. Miller, *Diary*, I, 100.

50. Long recommended return of the islands to Germany. See Long to Harrison, Dec. 14, 1918 and inclosure, *Foreign Relations, Paris Conference,* II, 511-515; also Miller, *Diary,* I, 99-100

51. Birdsall, *Versailles Twenty Years After,* p. 74.

52. Miller, *Diary,* I, 100.

53. See above, Chapter Nine.

54. *Foreign Relations, Paris Conference,* XIII, 299; also "Why They Struggle for Shantung," *The Literary Digest,* LXXII, Jan. 21, 1922, pp. 28-29.

55. Morse and MacNair, *Far Eastern Relations,* pp. 577-578.

56. Mac Murray, *Treaties and Agreements,* II, 1231.

57. La Fargue, *China and the World War,* pp. 185-186.

58. American Mission to Polk, Jan. 14, 1919, Wilson Papers, VIII, 5.

59. Li Shengto, President of the Senate, and Wang Yi tang, Speaker of the House, to W, Mar. 4, 1919, Wilson Papers, VIII, 22.

60. Memorandum prepared by United States Naval Advisors Staff, Dec. 19, 1918, Wilson Papers, VIII, 3.

61. Outline of Tentative Report and Recommendations Prepared by the Intelligence Section, Feb. 13, 1919, p. 36, Wilson Papers, VIII, 20.

62. Report of R. S. Baker to W, Apr. 29, 1919, Wilson Papers, VIII, 42.

63. *Foreign Relations, Paris Conference,* III, 739-740.

64. La Fargue, *China and the World War,* p. 185.

65. See Thomas A. Bailey, *Woodrow Wilson and the Lost Peace* (Combined edition, New York: [1944] 1947), pp. 144-149.

66. *Foreign Relations, Paris Conference,* II, 520-525.

67. Miller, *Diary,* XIX, 171-174.

68. Lansing had denied the rights of Japan in Shantung; see *Foreign Relations, 1917,* p. 117. For Reinsch's report see *ibid., Paris Conference,* II, 510.

69. *Ibid.,* III, 738, 755-757.

70. Lansing Desk Diary, Jan. 28, 1919.

71. Robert Lansing, *The Peace Negotiations, A Personal Narrative* (Boston: 1921), p. 253.

72. La Fargue, *China and the World War,* p. 206.

73. W to Lansing, Feb. 7, 1919, Wilson Papers, VIII, 18.

74. Lansing Diary, Feb. 3, 1919.

75. The misunderstanding between House and Wilson on the points of this program, especially the way they were carried out by the Colonel, was never healed according to Baker, *Wilson and the World Settlement,* 1, chapter xvii. See also Seymour, *Intimate House Papers,* IV, 329, 366-376.

76. Edith B. Wilson, *My Memoir,* pp. 245-246, recalls that after House had informed Wilson of the action taken in his absence, she went to his room. "The change in his appearance shocked me. He seemed to have aged ten years, and his jaw was set in that way it had when he was making superhuman effort to control himself." She asked what was wrong, and her

husband replied, "House has given away everything I had won before we left Paris."

77. Lansing to Polk, Mar. 14, 1919, Polk Papers, asked, "Am I wrong in feeling a little skeptical as to the unanimity of public opinion of which he [Wilson] seems convinced?"

78. Bailey, *Wilson and the Lost Peace*, pp. 72-73.

79. Winston L. S. Churchill, *The World Crisis*, 2 vols. (New York: 1923-1929), II, 149-150, 191-192.

80. Bailey, *Wilson and the Lost Peace*, p. 215.

81. Bonsal, *Suitors and Suppliants*, pp. 263-264; also Wold, *Mr. President How Is Your Health?* p. 177. Wilson's colleagues noted a change in the personality of the President following his illness — his remoteness, inability to follow argument and his cantankerousness.

82. Lansing Desk Diary, Apr. 4, 1919. When Wilson returned to Washington in February, the business of the Conference was still in the Council of Ten and Lansing with House represented the President, but by April the Council of Four had been formed and House's appointment to represent Wilson at the sessions was considered an insult by Lansing.

83. Seymour, *Intimate House Papers*, IV. 402-403.

84. *Ibid.*, IV, 403-404.

85. Baker, *Wilson and World Settlement*, II, 499, 514.

86. Bonsal, *Suitors and Suppliants*, p. 228.

87. Baker, *Wilson and World Settlement*, II, 247-248; *Foreign Relations, Paris Conference*, V, 109-111.

88. Miller, *Diary*, XIX, 177-180.

89. *Ibid.*, XIX, 183-184.

90. *Ibid.*, XIX, 184-187; Baker, *Wilson and World Settlement*, II, 249-252.

91. *Ibid.*, II, 253-255.

92. The argument of the Chinese position here and following is found in Miller, *Diary*, XIV, 186-187; Baker, *Wilson and World Settlement*, II, 252-258.

93. E. T. Williams to W, Apr. 24, 1919, Wilson Papers, VIII, 40.

94. Lou Tseng Tsiang to W, Apr. 24, 1919, Wilson Papers, VIII, 40.

95. Tumulty to W, Apr. 24, 1919, Wilson Papers, VIII, 40.

96. Bonsal, *Suitors and Suppliants*, p. 235.

97. Lansing, *Peace Negotiations*, p. 265.

98. Miller, *Diary*, XIX, 193-194.

99. *Foreign Relations, Paris Conference*, II, 249-250; Baker, *Wilson and World Settlement*, II, 259-260.

100. Lansing, *Peace Negotiations*, p. 266.

101. Lansing Desk Diary, Apr. 26, 1919.

102. The interview here and following is from Lansing's Memorandum of the event, dated Apr. 26, 1919, Wilson Papers, VIII, 41.

103. Lansing, *Peace Negotiations*, pp. 254-255.

104. Lansing and House left to visit the Somme battlefield and were thus gone on Apr. 27. House seemed to have been seeing less of the President at this time; on Apr. 25, Lansing notes in his Desk Diary that House said he had not seen Wilson for four days, that his only information as to what was going on came through Wiseman. For the meeting of Apr. 28, except where otherwise indicated, both here and following, see Miller, *Diary*, XIX, 195-198.

105. Tumulty to W, Apr. 26, 1919, Wilson Papers, VIII, 41, advised, "It appears to me from this end that the Japanese demands will soon produce another crisis. If such a crisis arises, I hope you will in any statement you make emphasize again America's purpose and her unwillingness to consent to any imperialistic peace. The whole country will be with you in the matter as never before. . . . In the Italian situation you took the offensive in the matter of secret treaties, plots, etc. You can't yield for a moment no matter what the consequences."

106. There is scant mention of Balfour's contribution in Blanche E. C. Dugdale, *Arthur James Balfour, First Earl of Balfour,* 2 vols. (New York: 1937), II, 199-200.

107. *Foreign Relations, Paris Conference,* II, 316-318.

108. Miller, *Diary,* XIX, 195-198.

109. Lansing Diary, Apr. 28, 1919. This entry is quoted in his *Peace Negotiations,* pp. 255-256, but in a revised form. There is no mention of House in the printed version.

110. Ray S. Baker, *American Chronicle, The Autobiography of Ray Stannard Baker* (New York: 1945), pp. 413-414.

111. Report of Baker to W, Apr. 29, 1919, Wilson Papers, VIII, 42. The Naval Advisory Staff, Dec. 19, 1918, Wilson Papers, VIII, 3, and the Intelligence Section Report, Wilson Papers, VIII, 20, recommended return of Kiaochow to China.

112. Bliss to W, Apr. 29, 1919, in Lansing, *Peace Negotiations,* pp. 257-261.

113. Bonsal, *Unfinished Business,* p. 42.

114. Miller, *Diary,* XIX, 199.

115. *Ibid.,* XIX, 200.

116. Baker, *Wilson and World Settlement,* II, 263-264.

117. Carnegie Endowment for International Peace, *Shantung: Treaties and Agreements* (Pamphlet 42, Washington, 1921), p. 98.

118. W to Tumulty, Apr. 30, 1919, Wilson Papers, VIII, 43.

119. Tumulty to W, Apr. 30, 1919, Wilson Papers, VIII, 43. Later Tumulty wrote, "Even I felt bitterly critical of what seemed to me to be the President's surrender to Japan in the matter of Shantung. But when he returned and told me the whole story and explained the complicated and delicate world situation which confronted him, I agreed with him that he had obtained out of a bad mess the best possible settlement." See Tumulty, *Wilson As I Know Him,* p. 390.

120. Seymour, *Intimate House Papers,* IV, 454.

121. Bonsal, *Suitors and Suppliants,* p. 237.

122. Lansing, *Peace Negotiations,* pp. 264-265.

123. Allan Nevins, *Henry White: Thirty Years of American Diplomacy* (New York: 1930), p. 445.

124. Lansing Diary, May 1, 1919. In another diary entry of Aug. 21, 1919, Lansing wrote that Bowman told him that conversations with the experts at Paris revealed that House favored the surrender of Shantung to keep Japan from pressing the racial equality issue. The Colonel also pressed the President to surrender the Pacific islands. (At this point Lansing's feelings towards House was such that these criticisms were probably welcome news.)

125. Thomas F. Millard, *Conflict of Policies in Asia* (New York and London: 1924), pp. 84-85.

126. Bonsal, *Suitors and Suppliants,* p. 240. On June 28, 1919, Williams gave the inside negotiations and information on the Shantung affair to the State Department; see Polk Diary of date.

127. Henry T. Hodgkin, *China in the Family of Nations,* 2d edition (London: 1928), p. 153.

128. Lansing, *Peace Negotiations,* p. 261.

129. Baker, *American Chronicle,* pp. 416-417, relates he found Williams and Hornbeck openly sympathizing with and helping the Chinese. He talked with Lansing who said he was for the right regardless of consequences. Baker asked even if it meant the breaking up of the conference, and Lansing answered, "Even that, if necessary."

130. Bonsal, *Suitors and Suppliants,* p. 239.

131. Miller, *Diary,* XVIII, 108, 111.

132. Bonsal, *Suitors and Suppliants,* p. 244.

133. Koo to W, June 27, 1919, Wilson Papers, VIII, 67, is China's appeal to Wilson for aid in obtaining consent to the reservation. For the signing ceremony see Miller, *Diary,* I, 458-459 and *Foreign Relations, Paris Conference,* VI, 710.

134. Miller, *Diary,* XIII, 300.

135. Reinsch, *American Diplomat,* 359.

136. Polk to American Mission, May 4, 1919, Wilson Papers, VIII, 44.

137. Fleming, *The United States and the League,* pp. 250, 252, 266-267, 303, 326-328.

138. *Foreign Relations, 1919,* II, 416-417.

139. Harold W. V. Temperley (ed.), *History of the Peace Conference of Paris,* 6 vols. (London: 1920-1924), III, 181.

140. Carnegie Endowment, *Shantung, Treaties and Agreements* (Washington: 1921), pp. 96-98.

141. See Russell H. Fifield, "Japanese Policy toward the Shantung Question at the Paris Peace Conference," *Journal of Modern History,* XXIII, 1951, pp. 265-272; the same author's *Woodrow Wilson and the Far East, The Diplomacy of the Shantung Question* (New York: 1952), Chapters 3-7 is an excellent account of the Shantung question at Paris.

142. Jan Christian Smuts, *Wilson's Place in History* (Boston, 1921), pp. 5-6.

143. Address of Wilson before the International Law Society, Paris, May 9, 1919, Wilson Papers, VIII, 48.

144. This was most succinctly stated in his Mt. Vernon address of July 4, 1918, "What we seek is the reign of law, based upon the consent of the governed and sustained by the organized opinion of mankind." Baker and Dodd, *Wilson Public Papers*, V, 234.

NOTES FOR CHAPTER TEN

1. Fleming, *United States and the League*, pp. 205-231. The British Ambassador told Polk that he had been approached by the Republicans, who said they would have to attack the British and take sides with the Irish due to the way Britain followed Wilson's lead in Paris. Polk Diary, Apr. 26, 1919.

2. Lansing to Polk, June 4, 1919, Polk Papers. House recorded in his Diary, June 29, 1919, that he advised Wilson to be conciliatory with the Senate on the treaty. The President replied, "House, I have found one can never get anything in this life that is worthwhile without fighting for it."

3. Vance McCormick Diary, July 5, 1919, p. 119 deposited in the Library of Congress.

4. *New York Times*, July 11, 1919.

5. Fleming, *United States and the League*, pp. 201-203, 266-267, 299, 326-328.

6. *New York Times*, July 14, 1919.

7. *Ibid.*, July 16, 1919.

8. The original suggestion came from Hornbeck in a report to Lansing which was transmitted to Wilson, June 3, 1919, Wilson Papers, VIII, 55. To the suggestion Wilson replied promising his "most thoughtful consideration" and admitting, "I realize the difficulties and the dangers very fully." W to Hornbeck, June 10, 1919, Wilson Papers, VIII, 60. Wilson wrote Lansing June 12, 1919, Wilson Papers, VIII, 61, to present the matter to the Japanese "in the light of the desirability, not to say necessity, of quieting opinion in China and making the fulfillment of the treaty provisions possible without serious friction. I think you cannot urge it upon him too strongly."

9. W to Lansing, June 20, 1919, Wilson Papers, VIII, 64.

10. Hornbeck Report on Far Eastern Affairs, July 24, 1919, Polk Papers.

11. Polk to Long, July 18, 1919, Polk Papers.

12. Earl Curzon to Mr. Alston, July 18, 1919, Wiseman Papers.

13. Lodge was not anti-Japanese like many of the other opponents of the League such as Johnson, Hearst, and Phelan. Tokutomi, *Japanese-American Relations*, p. 125.

14. *New York Times*, July 18, 1919.

15. *Ibid.*, July 19, 1919.

16. *Ibid.*, July 22, 1919.

17. *Ibid.,* July 23, 24, 1919.

18. W to Charles W. McAlpine, July 31, 1919, in the Woodrow Wilson Papers deposited in the Library of Princeton University.

19. Long to Polk, Aug. 6, 1919, Polk Papers. On August 6 Lansing called Wilson's attention to the Japanese statement given out in Tokyo and suggested it presented an opportunity for the United States to make a declaration. The Secretary objected to the terms being based on the 1915 and 1918 agreements and drafted reservations. Lansing to W, Aug. 4, 1919, Lansing Papers, II, 454.

20. Long Memorandum on Conversation with the Japanese Chargé, Aug. 6, 1919, Polk Papers for here and following. Concerning the memorandum, Long confessed to Polk, "The length of it I feel was more or less necessary, because of the experience I have had with the representatives of a certain Government and the advisability therefrom of making detailed memoranda."

21. House Diary, Aug. 7, 1919.

22. *New York Times,* Aug. 5, 1919.

23. *Ibid.,* Aug. 6, 1919.

24. *Ibid.,* Aug. 7, 1919.

25. United States Senate Document Number 106, 66th Congress, 1st Session, *Hearings on the Treaty of Peace with Germany,* X, 182. Hereafter cited *Senate Document 106,* 66th Cong., 1st Sess., X.

26. Lansing to Polk, Aug. 14, 1919, Polk Papers.

27. Head Usher's Diary, Aug. 19, 1919, Wilson Papers, I.

28. *Senate Document 106,* 66th Cong., 1st Sess., X, 518; also see Mary R. Frear, "Did President Wilson Contradict Himself on the Secret Treaties?" in *Current History,* XXX, June, 1929, pp. 435-443. The existence of the treaties was known, but it was generally believed in Washington that the peace would bring a new day in international relations superseding such secret agreements. Interview with Breckenridge Long by author, May 29, 1951.

29. *Senate Document 106,* 66th Cong., 1st Sess., X, 525.

30. *Ibid.,* X, 520.

31. *Ibid.,* X, 522.

32. *Ibid.,* X, 528. This was a difficult question for the President to answer publicly. He had consistently maintained that Japan would not have signed unless the Shantung settlement had been granted. For proof that his position was justified see Russell H. Fifield, "Japanese Policy toward the Shantung Question at the Paris Peace Conference," *Journal of Modern History,* XXIII, 1953, pp. 265-275.

33. *Senate Document 106,* 66th Cong., 1st Sess., X, 529.

34. W to Thomas Lamont, Aug. 21, 1919, Letter Book 57, p. 470, Wilson Papers, VII. The President wrote: "I hope now that all forces will be concentrated upon promoting the policy of keeping all reservations or interpretations out of the formal act of ratification, and embodying those that can be accepted in a separate document."

35. Fleming, *The United States and the League,* pp. 326, 328-329.

36. W to Woodbridge, Sept. 2, 1919, Letter Book 58, p. 141, Wilson Papers, VII.

37. Tumulty to W, June 1, 1919, Wilson Papers, VIII, 55.

38. For a discussion of Wilson and the third term see Thomas A. Bailey, *Woodrow Wilson and the Great Betrayal* (New York: 1945), pp. 408-411.

39. Tumulty to W, June 3, 1919, Wilson Papers, VIII, 55.

40. Tumulty to W, June 5, 1919, Wilson Papers, VIII, 56.

41. Tumulty to W, June 17, 1919, Wilson Papers, VIII, 63.

42. Houston, *Eight Years*, II, 20.

43. Jesse Jones wrote Wilson, July 5, 1919: "In making your speaking trip through the country, I believe you should go as far as your strength will permit, and let as many people as possible see you, and talk to as many people as possible. I believe that this trip will do a great deal to settle the unrest of the country, but as much as I believe that, I hope that you will not undertake such a program as to overtax yourself. The world is going to need you as much during the next few years as those just passed." R. S. Baker Papers, I, Jesse Jones file, 8. Long also felt the President's tour would force ratification of the treaty. Long to House, Sept. 5, 1919, House Papers.

44. Lansing to Polk, Sept. 2, 1919, Polk Papers. On August 20 Wilson told Lansing that considering the selfishness of the European powers he was almost of a mind to withdraw from joining the League. It was the third time he had made such a statement to the Secretary, and he added, "Foreign affairs certainly cause a man to be profane." Lansing Diary, Aug. 20, 1919.

45. House Diary, Sept. 21, 1919.

46. Houston, *Eight Years*, II, 20.

47. Baker and Dodd, *Wilson's Public Papers*, VI, 618.

48. Shaw, *Messages and Papers of Woodrow Wilson*, II, 764.

49. Baker and Dodd, *Wilson's Public Papers*, VI, 24-25.

50. *Ibid.*, VI, 134.

51. *Ibid.*, VI, 221-225.

52. *Ibid.*, VI, 363.

53. *Ibid.*, VI, 407, 409.

54. Chief Usher's Diary, Wilson Papers, I. See also Irwin H. Hoover, *Forty-two Years in the White House* (Boston and New York: 1934), pp. 100-108.

55. Letter Books, Wilson Papers, VII.

56. MacMurray to Morris, Feb. 7, 1920 in the Roland Morris Papers, deposited in the Library of Congress.

57. Viereck, *The Strangest Friendship in History*, p. 342; Houston, *Eight Years*, II, 47, 75.

58. Bailey, *Wilson and the Great Betrayal*, p. 148.

59. *Ibid.*, p. 162.

60. Robert E. Hosack, "The Shantung Question and the Senate," *The South Atlantic Quarterly*, XLIII, 1944, pp. 191-192.

61. Hitchcock and Wilson hoped thereby to gain moderate changes. See Lansing to Polk, Nov. 17, 1919, Polk Papers.

After leaving office, Wilson wrote George Creel: ". . . I could not accept any amendments because it was not within the right of any one of the signatory powers to amend the treaty in any particular, and I was obliged to reject all the amendments suggested to me because they were not made in good faith but intended as nullifications as I stated at that time. The amendments were suggested by Lodge and were intended to nullify and undo the work at Versailles as far as we were concerned." W to Creel, Jan. 19, 1923, R. S. Baker Papers, I, Creel file, 3.

62. Lawrence, *Wilson*, pp. 291-292.

63. The best account of the treaty in the Senate is found in Bailey, *Wilson and the Great Betrayal*, chapters 12-17.

64. Dodge to Tumulty, March 30, 1920, Wilson Papers, VI, 307.

65. *Foreign Relations, Paris Conference*, XIII, 300.

66. W to Lansing, Oct. 9, 1917, Letter Book 44, p. 372, Wilson Papers, VII.

67. House Diary, May 10, 1918.

68. Minutes of Interdepartmental Committee on Pacific Communications, Aug. 10, 1918, Polk Papers.

69. Undated Memorandum prepared by Breckenridge Long for Baker in R. S. Baker Papers, I, Long file, 25.

70. For a concise treatment of the subject see Griswold, *Far Eastern Policy*, pp. 264-268.

71. Actually owned by the British as revealed in 1921; see Leslie B. Tribolet, *The International Aspects of Electrical Communications in the Pacific Area* (Baltimore: 1929), p. 22.

72. *Ibid.*, pp. 233-236.

73. *Ibid.*, pp. 231-232.

74. Long had drawn up a memorandum on the importance of the islands both strategically and as a communication center. Dec. 14, 1918, *Foreign Relations, Paris Conference*, II, 512-515.

75. Wilson himself suggested Rogers draw up an outline of the best way to solve the communication question in the Pacific, "possibly under international supervision." W to Rogers, Jan. 31, 1919, Wilson Papers, VIII, 16.

76. Testimony of the President before the Foreign Relations Committee of the Senate, in the *New York Times*, Aug. 20, 1919.

77. Acting Secretary Davis to the Ambassador in Great Britain, Dec. 4, 1920 summarizes the conference action and presents the American legal case. *Foreign Relations, 1921*, II, 265-268.

78. *New York Times*, Aug. 20, 1919; also Senate Document 106, 66th Cong., 1st Sess., X, 506.

79. *New York Times*, Mar. 23, 1920.

80. The invitation to the various governments was issued on March 30, 1920, *Foreign Relations, 1920*, I, 116.

81. Netherlands Minister to Department of State, Mar. 25, 1920, *ibid., 1920*, I, 115-116.

82. Memorandum of Assistant Chief of Division of Far Eastern Affairs, Aug. 9, 1920, *ibid.*, *1920*, I, 126-127.

83. W to Lloyd George, Nov. 3, 1920, Wilson Papers, II, 171.

84. Colby to Ambassadors in Great Britain, Japan, France, Italy, Nov. 9, 1920, *Foreign Relations, 1921*, II, 263.

85. Chargé Bell in Japan to Colby, Nov. 19, 1920, *ibid., 1921*, II, 264.

86. *New York Times*, Dec. 11, 1920.

87. Report of Subcommittee on Universal Communications and Annexations, *Foreign Relations, 1920*, I, 149-168.

88. Long Memorandum on Communications for Baker, undated, R. S. Baker, I, Long file, 25.

89. George H. Blakeslee, "The Mandates of the Pacific," *Foreign Affairs*, I, 1922, p. 100.

90. Yap Treaty, *Foreign Relations, 1922*, I, 599-604.

91. Baker and Dodd, *Wilson's Public Papers*, II, 374-375.

92. *New York Times*, Feb. 4, 1916.

93. Outten Jones Clinard, *Japan's Influence on American Naval Power, 1897-1917*, p. 171, concludes "That the Naval Construction Act of 1916 was directed against Japan, there can be little doubt. The attitude of the President and of Congress shows this clearly. The Japanese themselves were convinced that the new fleet could have been authorized for no other purpose than to defeat 'Japanese pretensions in the Pacific and Far East'."
   A more reasonable explanation of the American 1916 Naval program is given in Hector C. Bywater, *Navies and Nations: A Review of Naval Developments Since the Great War* (London: 1927), pp. 104-105. The contention is made that Wilson adopted the 1916 program in fear of Germany emerging from the war with her navy intact and thus posing a threat to the United States. At the end of the war, Wilson and his advisers saw the American navy as the surest guarantee of world peace, for only the United States could be trusted to never abuse the possession of sea power, which the British had wielded as it wished during the war. The President even asked for naval appropriations which he never intended to use in order to strengthen his bargaining position at Versailles. Also see "No War With England," *Nation*, CXII, May 11, 1921, p. 681.

94. Josephus Daniels, *The Wilson Era, Years of War and After, 1917-1923* (Chapel Hill: 1946), p. 382.

95. George T. Davis, *A Navy Second to None: The Development of Modern American Naval Policy* (New York: 1940), pp. 251-252.

96. Henry R. Mussey, "Our Armament Race with Japan," *Nation*, CXII, Feb. 2, 1921, p. 179.

97. Hector C. Bywater, "Japan and American Naval Power," *Atlantic Monthly*, CXXVIII, Nov., 1921, pp. 704-712.

98. Alexander Powell, "Are We Giving Japan A Square Deal?" *ibid.*, CXXVIII, Nov., 1921, p. 695.

99. Tokutomi, *Japanese-American Relations*, pp. 98-99.

100. Japanese girls who were often selected from photographs by resident Japanese in the United States.

101. MacMurray Memorandum, Nov. 19, 1919, *Foreign Relations, 1919*, II, 415-416.

102. Lansing to Morris, Nov. 21, 1919, *ibid., 1919* II, 417-418.

103. The Appointed Ambassador from Japan Shidehara to Lansing, Dec. 13, 1919, *ibid., 1919*, II, 419.

104. Stephens to the Acting Secretary of State, Dec. 9, 1920, *ibid., 1920*, III, 20-21; I. Yenaga and Denoske Sato, *Japan and the California Problem* (New York and London: 1921), pp. 138-141; MacMurray to Morris, June 16, 1920, *Foreign Relations, 1920*, III, 1.

105. Chargé Bell to Secretary of State, Nov. 4, 1920, *ibid., 1920*, III, 17-18.

106. Chargé Bell to Secretary of State, Nov. 5, 1920, *ibid., 1920*, III, 18-19.

107. Tokutomi, *Japanese-American Relations*, pp. 106-107.

108. Morris to Acting Secretary of State, Jan. 25, 1921, *Foreign Relations, 1921*, II, 343-349.

109. Griswold, *Far Eastern Policy*, p. 369.

110. Phillips to Morris, Apr. 4, 1919, *Foreign Relations, 1919*, II, 424-425.

111. MacMurray Memorandum, Dec. 4, 1919, *ibid., 1919*, II, 441.

112. Polk to Lansing, Apr. 17, 1919, Polk Papers.

113. Naval Operations to American Naval Party, Mar. 21, 1919, Wilson Papers, VIII, 27.

114. Tenney to Colby, May 20, 1920, S. D., 793.94/1092.

115. Reinsch to Acting Secretary of State, June 6, 1919, *Foreign Relations, 1919*, I, 330-331.

116. *Ibid., 1920*, I, 534-550, 738-754.

117. Whyte, *China and the Foreign Powers*, pp. 18-19.

118. Reinsch, *American Diplomat*, p. 382.

119. Reinsch to W, June 7, 1919, S. D., 123R271/101.

120. Long to Lansing, Aug. 5, 1919, S. D., 123R271/105.

121. W to Lansing, Aug. 14, 1919, Letter Book 57, p. 442, Wilson Papers, VII.

122. Lansing to Reinsch, Aug. 15, 1919, S. D., 123R271/104a.

123. Edith B. Wilson to Lansing, Jan. 19, 1920, R. S. Baker Papers, I, Lansing file, 8.

124. *New York Times*, Feb. 27, 1920. Crane had formerly been appointed to the China post by President Taft. He was in San Francisco ready to sail when he was called back to Washington to answer reported indiscretions disclosing American policy towards the Six Power Consortium Loan. When Secretary of State Philander Knox made it a matter of choice between retaining himself or Crane, Taft asked the Minister to resign. Crane broke with the Republican Party and contributed to Wilson's election. He had been since 1913 a close adviser of the President on the Far East and Russia, where he had scattered business interests. See the *New York Times*, Feb. 25, 1920.

125.   Department of State to Reinsch, Apr. 12, 1919, S. D., 123R271/92.

126.   Breckenridge Long to Brand Whitlock, Feb. 16, 1920, Breckenridge Long Papers, Library of Congress, Confidential file, number 5.

For the resignation see Lansing, *Peace Negotiations,* 268-280; Tumulty, *Wilson As I Know Him,* pp. 444-445; Houston, *Eight Years,* II, 67-68; Bailey, *Wilson and the Great Betrayal,* pp. 404-405.

127.   John Spargo, "Bainbridge Colby," in Bemis (ed.), *The American Secretaries of State,* X, 180-182.

128.   Dating from July 1, 1919, the Counselor was known as the Undersecretary of State.

129.   United States Department of State, *State Department Register, 1919, passim.*

130.   See Poole to American Delegation, Feb. 5, 1919, in Francis, *Russia from the American Embassy,* pp. 322-323.

131.   "China in 1919," *The North China Herald,* Jan. 24, 1920, p. 205.

132.   Reinsch to Lansing, June 9, 1919, quoted in Polk to American Mission, June 11, 1919, Wilson Papers, VIII, 61.

133.   Lansing to Polk, June 14, 1919, Wilson Papers, VIII, 63.

134.   Morris to Acting Secretary of State, June 20, 1919, *Foreign Relations, 1919,* I, 704-708.

135.   Morris to Acting Secretary of State, June 15, 1919, *ibid., 1919,* I, 701.

136.   *The North China Herald,* Jan. 24, 1920, p. 118.

137.   Dutcher, *Political Awakening of the Far East,* pp. 82, 136-137.

138.   Quarterly Report, Peking Legation, inclosure in Crane to Colby, Jan. 26, 1921, *Foreign Relations, 1920,* II, 475.

139.   W statement, Dec. 9, 1920, Wilson Papers, VI, 227.

140.   W to Shigeo Ito, Feb. 25, 1921, Wilson Papers, II, 174.

Bibliography

I. MANUSCRIPT SOURCES: OFFICIAL AND PRIVATE PAPERS CONSULTED

Official

Department of State, National Archives, 1913-1921.

The decimal files are exceptionally rich in Far Eastern materials. Most of the really important documents have been printed in the *Foreign Relations* volumes for the period, but consular reports, letters, and inter-departmental memoranda showing the creation of policy abound. Much of the material is reproduced in the Wilson Papers. Such files as 763.72, Political Conditions in Japan; 761.94, the Secret Documents Published by the Bolsheviks; 893.00, Relations of China and Japan; 793.92, the Lansing-Ishii Agreement; 861.00, Political Conditions in Russia and Japanese Intervention are extremely useful. For the most part the files are chronologically arranged.

Department of the Interior, Bureau of Insular Affairs, National Archives, 1913-1921.

These records were formerly in the War Department, since it was charged with Philippine affairs, but they have been shifted to the Interior Department records. The files are very rewarding. All personnel dealing with Philippine affairs are covered in personal files. There are long excerpts from speeches and official papers as well as clippings covering the views and contributions of individuals to insular affairs. General McIntyre's habit of keeping close memoranda is especially rewarding to the researcher on insular affairs for the period of the Wilson years.

Private

Baker, Ray Stannard. Collection in the Division of Manuscripts, Library of Congress.

An invaluable source of materials gathered in the preparation of Wilson's biography. It contains the written reports of Baker's numerous interviews with people associated with Wilson throughout life. Some of the materials are of a surprising nature that one would not expect to find in such a collection, e.g., the Long Memorandum on the Consortium. Copies of the more important State Department documents are also included.

Bliss, Tasker H. Collection in the Division of Manuscripts, Library of Congress.

A well arranged collection largely important for the views expressed in the Supreme War Council on Siberian intervention. The Diary shows the attitude of Bliss on current matters at the peace conference. The letters reveal that Bliss thought the best thing for the United States to do was to get out of Europe as fast as possible. He feared the revolutionary wave sweeping over the continent following the war.

Bryan, William Jennings. Collection in the Division of Manuscripts, Library of Congress.

Chronologically arranged, the papers reveal Bryan's undisciplined manner of working. Many of the notes are in pencil or scratched on the bottom of official communications. The papers reveal that Wilson and Bryan worked closely together, especially on Far Eastern affairs wherein the collection is especially rich.

Bryan, William Jennings. Collection in the National Archives.

Consists of four volumes of original letters many from Wilson on his own typewriter. This collection while smaller is much more rewarding than the materials in the Library of Congress. Arranged chronologically, it is indispensable for any study of foreign affairs during Bryan's incumbency as Secretary of State.

Daniels, Josephus. Collection in the Division of Manuscripts, Library of Congress.

The diary is especially rewarding for the period of the Japanese war scare in May, 1913. The papers are more voluminous than the Wilson Papers and impress the researcher that Daniels never had a wastebasket in his office. They are valuable too for an understanding of the functioning of the naval preparedness program and show Daniels as being often consulted politically by Wilson.

Dewey, Admiral George. Collection in the Division of Manuscripts, Library of Congress.

A small collection that proved unrewarding in indicating the intent of the Joint Army and Navy Board in adding to the war scare of May, 1913. Dewey was the chairman of the Board, but there is no mention of the meeting in his papers.

Frankfurter, Felix. Letter of March 26, 1951, to author. In author's possession.

Reveals that his Philippine recommendations in 1913 which were initially followed by the Wilson administration were the result of a routine call of the new Secretary of War for suggestions.

Garrison, Lindley K. Collection in Division of Manuscripts, Princeton University Library.

A small collection containing little material on the Philippines which came under Garrison as Secretary of War.

House, Edward M. Collection in Division of Manuscripts, Yale University Library.

The Diary is especially rewarding as showing House's relations with Wilson and infrequent comments of the Colonel on the Far East. The collection of letters from and to Wilson, bound separately, is rewarding and easy of access. Seymour in the printed collection has omitted much that is inane.

Lansing, Robert. Collection in the Division of Manuscripts, Library of Congress.

Arranged chronologically in books the materials are easy of access. There is little indication, however, when materials came into Lansing's hands. The personal diary is interesting as revealing Lansing's thought on various subjects, and especially Far Eastern affairs. Of great value are the desk diaries which he kept from 1914 to 1920 revealing his appointments, subjects discussed, and occasional comment. The desk diaries indicate that Far Eastern Affairs were much in the consideration and action of the Department during these years.

Long, Breckenridge. Collection in the Division of Manuscripts, Library of Congress.

From 1917 to 1920 Long served as Third Assistant Secretary of State in charge of Far Eastern Affairs. His papers are especially valuable on Siberian intervention, the Second Consortium, and the Chinese Eastern Railway.

Long, Breckenridge. Letter of February 11, 1951, to author, in author's possession.

Long explains Lansing's neglect of Far Eastern affairs in 1917 and 1918 in a more reasonable light than contained in Werner Levi's report of an interview with the former Third Assistant Secretary. The Levi report is found in "American Attitudes toward the Pacific Islands, 1914-1919." *The Pacific Historical Review,* XVII, 1948, pp. 55-64.

Morris, Roland. Collection in the Division of Manuscripts, Library of Congress.

This collection contains little beyond the printed materials found in *Foreign Relations* or the reports found in the Department of State files.

Mott, John R. Letter of May 19, 1951, to author, in author's possession.

Mott who served as Secretary of the International Y.M.C.A. and was a leading figure in the world mission movement states that Wilson was deeply interested in China. The letter contains brief answers to a series of questions asked by the author.

Polk, Frank L. Collection in the Division of Manuscripts, Yale University Library.

The letters are an important source of State Department attitudes on Far Eastern Affairs from 1915 to 1920. The

Long, Polk, Lansing letters are especially valuable. Polk's diary contains many documents and his own views are often expressed.

Student Notes Collection. Collection in the Division of Manuscripts, Princeton University Library.

This collection is an attempt to secure classnotes of all of Wilson's courses at Princeton. The notes of Joseph K. Fornace, Charles D. Besore, and William P. Vail are especially valuable. These notes would indicate Wilson's liberalism was a basic attitude towards life rather than something flowering suddenly upon his entering politics as maintained by Link and Kerney.

Thomas, James A. Collection in the Division of Manuscripts, Duke University Library.

Contains comments on Chinese politics during the Wilson years. There are some letters manifesting an interest of the Chinese American Bank in the organization of the New Consortium, 1918-1920.

Wilson, Woodrow. Collection in the Division of Manuscripts, Library of Congress.

A voluminous and indispensable collection of 1,183 boxes of materials which range from the most trivial to the most vital documents. Divided into nine numbered files Series I contains miscellaneous items, II the more personal collection, III a collection of notes and manuscripts concerned primarily with Wilson's life as a scholar, IV a closed file of two boxes containing letters of Wilson to his first wife, V the New Jersey papers, VI the White House Office File, VII the letter books, VIII the Peace Conference materials, and IX the post-Presidential years. The papers are rich in materials on Far Eastern affairs.

Wiseman, Sir William. Collection in the Division of Manuscripts, Yale University.

These papers are poorly arranged but prove valuable on Siberian intervention and British policy in working with Washington and Wilson. Wiseman was Balfour's agent in this country.

II. CITED PRINTED SOURCES

Official Documents

The Democratic National Committee. *The Democratic Textbook,* 1912. New York, 1912.

Gooch, G. P. and Harold Temperley. *British Documents in the Origins of the War.* London, 1926-1938. 11 vols.

Hornbeck, Stanley. *Japan: Trade During the War.* A report for the United States Tariff Commission. Washington, 1919.

Progressive National Committee. *A Contract with the People.* New York, 1912.

Republican National Committee. *Republican Textbook, 1912.* New York, 1912.

Temperley, H. W. V. (ed.) *History of the Peace Conference.* London, 1920. 6 vols.

United States Congress. *Congressional Record, Proceedings and Debates, 1913-1921.* Sixty-third through the Sixty-sixth Congress. Washington, 1913-1921.

United States of America. *The Statutes at Large of the United States of America.* Vol. XXXIX. Washington, 1917.

United States Department of State. *Papers Relating to the Foreign Relations of the United States, 1912-1922.* Washington, 1919-1938. 22 vols.

United States Department of State. *Papers Relating to the Foreign Relations of the United States. The Lansing Papers, 1914-1920.* Washington, 1939. 2 vols.

United States Department of State. *Papers Relating to the Foreign Relations of the United States, 1919. The Paris Conference.* Washington, 1942-1947. 13 vols.

United States Department of State. *Papers Relating to the Foreign Relations of the United States, 1919, Russia.* Washington, 1937.

United States Senate Document No. 106, Sixty-sixth Congress, First Session. *Hearings on the Treaty of Peace with Germany.* Washington, 1919.

Cited Official Documents Unofficially Published

The Carnegie Endowment for International Peace. *The Imperial Japanese Mission, 1917.* Washington, 1918.

The Carnegie Endowment for International Peace. *Shantung's Treaties and Agreements.* Washington, 1921.

MacMurray, John V. A. *Treaties and Agreements with and Concerning China.* New York, 1921. 2 vols.

Miller, David Hunter. *My Diary at the Conference of Paris, with Documents.* Privately printed, 1928. 20 vols.

Varneck, Elena and H. H. Fisher. *The Testimony of Kolchak and Other Siberian Materials.* Stanford University, 1935.

Cited Published Letters, Diaries, Memoirs, Speeches, etc.

Baker, Ray S. *American Chronicle: The Autobiography of Ray S. Baker,* New York, 1945.

Bryan, William Jennings. *Letters to a Chinese Official, Being a Western View of Eastern Civilization.* New York, 1906.

Bryan, William Jennings. *The Old World and Its Ways, A Tour Around the World and Journey Through Europe.* St. Louis, 1907.

Bryan, William Jennings. *Speeches of William Jennings Bryan.* New York, 1913. 2 vols.

Bryan, William Jennings and Mary Baird Bryan. *The Memoirs of William Jennings Bryan.* Chicago, 1925.

Creel, George. *How We Advertised America.* New York, 1920.

Creel, George. *Rebel At Large, Recollections of Fifty Crowded Years.* New York, 1947.

Daniels, Josephus. *The Wilson Era, Years of Peace-1910-1917.* Chapel Hill, 1944.

Daniels, Josephus. *The Wilson Era, Years of War and After, 1917-1923.* Chapel Hill, 1944.

Francis, David R. *Russia from the American Embassy, April, 1916-November, 1918.* New York, 1921.

Gompers, Samuel. *Seventy Years of Life and Labor.* New York [1925], 1948.

Graves, William S. *America's Siberian Adventure, 1918-1920.* New York, 1931.

Grey, Sir Edward. *Twenty-Five Years, 1892-1916.* New York, 1925. 2 vols.

Harrison, Francis B. *The Cornerstone of Philippine Independence.* New York, 1922.

Heaton, John L. (ed.) *Cobb of "The World": A Leader in Liberalism. Compiled from His Editorial Articles and Public Addresses.* New York, 1924.

Hoover, Irwin H. *Forty-two Years in the White House.* Boston and New York, 1934.

Houston, David F. *Eight Years with Wilson's Cabinet, 1913 to 1920.* Garden City, 1926. 2 vols.

Howe, Frederic C. *The Confessions of a Reformer.* New York, 1925.

Ishii, Viscount Kikujiro. *Diplomatic Commentaries.* W. R. Langdon, translator, Baltimore, 1936.

Jones, Jefferson. *The Fall of Tsingtau.* Boston and New York, 1915.

Lansing, Robert. *The Peace Negotiations, A Personal Narrative.* Boston, 1921.

Lansing, Robert. *War Memoirs of Robert Lansing.* New York, 1935.

McCormick, Vance. *Diary of Vance McCormick.* Privately published, n.d., n.p. In the Manuscript Division, Library of Congress.

Moore, John Bassett. *The Collected Papers of John Bassett Moore.* Yale University, 1944. 7 vols.

Powell, John B. *My Twenty-Five Years in China.* New York, 1945.

Quezon, Manuel Luis. *The Good Fight.* New York and London, 1946.

Redfield, William C. *With Congress and Cabinet.* Garden City, 1924.

Reinsch, Paul S. *An American Diplomat in China.* Garden City, 1922.

Seymour, Charles. *The Intimate Papers of Colonel House.* New York, 1926-1930. 4 vols.

Steffens, Lincoln. *The Autobiography of Lincoln Steffens.* New York, 1931.

Wilson, F. M. Huntington. *Memoirs of An Ex-Diplomat.* Boston, 1945.

III. WILSON MATERIALS

Cited Works by Woodrow Wilson

Wilson, Woodrow. *Constitutional Government in the United States.* New York, 1908.

Wilson, Woodrow. *A History of the American People.* New York, 1901. 5 vols.

Wilson, Woodrow. *The New Freedom*: *A Call for the Emancipation of the Generous Energies of a People*. New York, 1913.

Cited Collections of Woodrow Wilson's Works

Baker, Ray Stannard and William E. Dodd. *The Public Papers of Woodrow Wilson*. New York and London, 1925-1927. 6 vols.

Scott, James B. (ed.) *President Wilson's Foreign Policy*: *Messages, Addresses, Papers*. New York, 1918.

Cited Works about Wilson

Baker, Ray Stannard. *Woodrow Wilson Life and Letters*. Garden City, 1927-1939. 8 vols.

Baker, Ray Stannard. *Woodrow Wilson and the World Settlement*. Garden City, 1922. 3 vols.

Bell, H. C. F. *Woodrow Wilson and the People*. Garden City, 1945.

Black, Harold G. *The True Woodrow Wilson, Crusader for Democracy*. New York, 1946.

Diamond, William. *The Economic Thought of Woodrow Wilson*. Baltimore, 1943.

Hugh-Jones, E. M. *Woodrow Wilson and American Liberalism*. New York, 1949.

Kerney, James. *The Political Education of Woodrow Wilson*. New York, 1926.

Link, Arthur S. *Wilson the Road to the White House*. Princeton University, 1947.

Link, Arthur S. *Woodrow Wilson and the Progressive Era, 1910-1917*. New York, 1954.

McAdoo, Eleanor Wilson. *The Woodrow Wilsons*. With the assistance of M. Y. Caffey. New York, 1937.

Myers, William S. (ed.) *Woodrow Wilson Some Princeton Memories*. Princeton University, 1946.

Notter, Harley. *The Origins of the Foreign Policy of Woodrow Wilson*. Baltimore, 1937.

Smuts, Jan Christian. *Wilson's Place in History*. Boston, 1921.

Tumulty, Joseph P. *Woodrow Wilson as I Know Him*. Garden City, 1921.

Viereck, George S. *The Strangest Friendship in History, Woodrow Wilson and Colonel House.* New York, 1932.

Wilson, Edith Bolling. *My Memoir.* New York [1938], 1939.

Wold, Karl C. *Mr. President — How is Your Health?* St. Paul, Minnesota, 1948.

IV. CITED SECONDARY WORKS

General Accounts and Special Studies

Abbott, James F. *Japanese Expansion and American Policies.* Second edition. New York, 1916.

Bailey, Thomas A. *The Policy of the United States toward the Neutrals, 1917-1918.* Baltimore, 1942.

Bailey, Thomas A. *Theodore Roosevelt and the Japanese-American Crises.* Stanford University, 1934.

Bailey, Thomas A. *Woodrow Wilson and the Great Betrayal.* New York, 1945.

Bailey, Thomas A. *Woodrow Wilson and the Lost Peace.* New York, 1944.

Bau, Mingchien J. *The Open Door Doctrine in Relation to China.* New York, 1923.

Bemis, Samuel Flagg (ed.) *The American Secretaries of State and Their Diplomacy.* New York, 1927-1929. 10 vols.

Birdsall, Paul. *Versailles Twenty Years After.* New York, 1941.

Bisson, Thomas A. *America's Far Eastern Policy.* New York, 1945.

Blakeslee, George H. (ed.) *Japan and Japanese-American Relations.* New York, 1912.

Blakeslee, George H. (ed.) *Recent Developments in China.* New York, 1913.

Blakeslee, George H. *The Recent Foreign Policy of the United States.* New York, 1925.

Bonsal, Stephen. *Suitors and Suppliants, The Little Nations at Versailles.* New York, 1946.

Bonsal, Stephen. *Unfinished Business.* Garden City, 1944.

Bywater, Hector C. *Navies and Nations: A Review of Naval Developments Since the Great War.* London, 1927.

Chamberlain, William H. *The Russian Revolution, 1917-1921.* New York, 1935.

Chung, Henry. *The Oriental Policy of the United States.* London and New York, 1919.

Churchill, Winston S. *The Aftermath: The World Crisis, 1918-1928.* New York, 1929. 4 vols.

Clinard, Outten J. *Japan's Influence on American Naval Power, 1897-1917.* Berkeley and Los Angeles, 1947.

Clyde, Paul H. *The Far East, A History of the Impact of the West on Eastern Asia.* New York, 1948.

Croly, Herbert. *Willard Straight.* New York, 1924.

Davis, George T. *A Navy Second to None: The Development of Modern American Naval Policy.* New York, 1940.

Dugdale, Blanche E. C. *Arthur James Balfour, first Earl of Balfour.* New York, 1937. 2 vols.

Dutcher, George N. *The Political Awakening of the East, Studies of Political Progress in Egypt, India, China, Japan, and the Philippines.* New York, 1925.

Fairbank, John K. *The United States and China.* Cambridge, 1948.

Feis, Herbert. *Europe: The World's Banker, 1870-1914.* New Haven, 1930.

Field, Frederick V. *American Participation in the China Consortium.* University of Chicago, 1931.

Fifield, Russell H. *Woodrow Wilson and the Far East, The Diplomacy of the Shantung Question.* New York, 1952.

Fischer, Louis. *The Soviets in World Affairs, A History of the Relations between the Soviet Union and the Rest of the World, 1917-1929.* Princeton [1930], 1951. 2 vols.

Fleming, Denna F. *The United States and the League of Nations.* New York, 1932.

Forbes, William Cameron. *The Philippine Islands.* Boston, 1928. 2 vols.

Fujisaiwa, Rikitaro. *The Recent Aims and Political Development of Japan.* Yale University, 1923.

Gage, Daniel J. "Paul S. Reinsch and Sino-American Relations." An unpublished doctoral dissertation. Stanford University, 1939.

Griswold, A. Whitney. *The Far Eastern Policy of the United States.* New York, 1936.

Gulick, Sidney L. *America and the Orient.* New York, 1916.

Gulick, Sidney L. *The American Japanese Problem.* New York, 1914.

Hammond, John Hayes and Jeremiah W. Jenks. *Great American Issues: Political, Social, Economic.* New York, 1921.

Hart, Captain B. H. Liddell. *The Real War, 1914-1918.* Boston, 1930.

Haskins, Charles H. and Robert H. Lord. *Some Problems of the Peace Conference.* Cambridge, 1920.

Hayden, Joseph R. *The Philippines A Study in National Development.* New York, 1942.

Hibben, Paxton. *The Peerless Leader William Jennings Bryan.* New York, 1929.

Hodgkin, Henry T. *China in the Family of Nations.* Second edition. London, 1928.

Hoover, Herbert. *America's First Crusade.* New York, 1942.

Hornbeck, Stanley K. *Contemporary Politics in the Far East.* New York, 1916.

Hornbeck, Stanley K. *Japan: Trade During the War.* Washington, 1919.

Idditti, Smimasa. *The Life of Marquis Shigenobu Okuma, A Maker of New Japan.* Tokyo, 1940.

James, Henry. *Charles W. Eliot.* London, 1930. 2 vols.

Jessup, Philip C. *Elihu Root.* New York, 1938. 2 vols.

Kalaw, Maximo M. *The Development of Philippine Politics.* Manila, 1926.

Keynes, John M. *The Economic Consequences of the Peace.* New York, 1920.

Kirk, Grayson L. *Philippine Independence, Motives, Problems, and Prospects.* New York, 1936.

Kotenev, Anatol M. *New Lamps for Old, An Interpretation of Events in Modern China and Whither They Lead.* Shanghai, 1931.

La Fargue, Thomas E. *China and the World War.* Stanford University, 1937.

Lamont, Thomas W. *Henry P. Davidson: The Record of a Useful Life.* New York and London, 1933.

Latourette, Kenneth S. *The History of Japan.* New York, 1947.

Lea, Homer. *The Valor of Ignorance.* New York, 1909.

Lengyel, Emil. *Siberia.* New York, 1943.

Li, Tien-Y. *Woodrow Wilson's China Policy, 1913-1917.* New York, 1952.

Lockhart, R. H. Bruce. *British Agent.* New York and London, 1933.

Lodge, Henry C. *The Senate and the League of Nations.* New York, 1925.

McKenzie, F. A. *Korea's Fight for Freedom.* New York, 1920.

Mac Nair, Harley F. *Modern Chinese History Selected Readings.* Shanghai, 1927.

Maxim, Hudson. *Defenseless America.* New York, 1915.

Millard, Thomas F. *Conflict of Policies in Asia.* New York, 1924.

Miller, David H. *The Drafting of the Covenant.* New York, 1928. 2 vols.

Morse, Hosea B. and Harley F. McNair. *Far Eastern International Relations.* Boston, 1931.

Nearing, Scott and Joseph Freeman. *Dollar Diplomacy: A Study in American Imperialism.* New York, 1925.

Nevins, Allan. *Henry White: Thirty Years of American Diplomacy.* New York, 1930.

Noble, George B. *Policies and Opinions at Paris, 1919.* New York, 1935.

Palmer, Frederick. *Newton D. Baker, America at War.* New York, 1931. 2 vols.

Pollard, Robert T. *China's Foreign Relations, 1917-1931.* New York, 1933.

Pooley, Andrew M. *Japan's Foreign Policies.* London, 1920.

Price, Ernest B. *The Russo-Japanese Treaties of 1907-1916 Concerning Manchuria and Mongolia.* Baltimore, 1903.

Reinsch, Paul S. *Intellectual and Political Currents in the Far East.* Boston and New York, 1911.

Reinsch, Paul S. *Secret Diplomacy, How Far Can It Be Eliminated?* New York, 1922.

Reischauer, Robert. *Japan Government and Politics.* Princeton University, 1939.

Remer, Charles F. *Foreign Investments in China.* New York, 1933.

Sansom, Sir George B. *The Western World and Japan: A Study in the Interaction of European and Asiatic Cultures.* New York, 1950.

Seymour, Charles. *Woodrow Wilson and the World War, A Chronicle of Our Own Times.* Yale University, 1921.

Sharman, Lyon. *Sun Yat-sen: His Life and Its Meaning.* New York, 1934.

Shotwell, James T. *At the Paris Peace Conference.* New York, 1937.

Stephenson, George M. *John Lind of Minnesota.* University of Minnesota, 1935.

Tansill, Charles C. *America Goes to War.* Boston, 1938.

Tokutomi, Iichiro. *Japanese-American Relations.* S. Yanagiwara, translator. New York, 1922.

Tompkins, Pauline. *American-Russian Relations in the Far East.* New York, 1949.

Treat, Payson J. *Japan and the United States, 1853-1921.* Boston and New York, 1921.

Tribolet, L. B. *The International Aspects of Electrical Communications in the Pacific Area.* Baltimore, 1929.

Unterberger, Betty Miller. "America's Siberian Expedition, 1918-1920: A Study of National Policy." Doctoral dissertation, Duke University, 1950.

Varneck, Elena and Fisher, H. H. *The Testimony of Kolchak and Other Siberian Materials.* Stanford University, 1935.

Vinacke, Harold M. *Modern Constitutional Development in China.* Princeton University, 1920.

Whyte, Sir Alexander Frederick. *China and Foreign Powers An Historical Review of Their Relations.* Second edition, revised. Oxford University, 1927.

Williams, Edward T. *China Yesterday and Today.* Fifth edition, revised. London, 1933.

Williams, Wayne. *William Jennings Bryan.* New York, 1936.

Yenaga, I. and Kenoshe Sato. *Japan and the California Problem.* New York and London, 1921.

Young, A. Morgan. *Japan Under Taisho Tenno.* London, 1928.

Articles

Bailey, Thomas A. "California, Japan, and the Alien Land Legislation of 1913," *The Pacific Historical Review,* I, 1932, pp. 36-59.

Blakeslee, George H. "The Mandates of the Pacific," *Foreign Affairs,* I, 1922, pp. 98-115.

Bywater, Hector C. "Japan and American Naval Power," *Atlantic Monthly,* CXXVIII, Nov., 1921, pp. 704-712.

Cameron, Meribeth E. "American Recognition Policy toward the Republic of China, 1912-1913," *The Pacific Historical Review,* II, 1933, pp. 214-230.

Clarke, Dan E. "Manifest Destiny and the Pacific," *The Pacific Historical Review,* I, 1932, pp. 1-17.

Clyde, Paul H. "The Open Door Policy of John Hay," *The Historical Outlook,* XXII, 1931, pp. 210-214.

Dewey, John. "The Hughes Campaign," *The New Republic,* VIII, October 28, 1916, p. 319.

Eyre, James K. "Japan and the American Annexation of the Philippines," *The Pacific Historical Review,* XI, 1942, pp. 55-71.

Frear, Mary R. "Did President Wilson Contradict Himself on the Secret Treaties?" *Current History,* XXX, June, 1929, pp. 435-443.

Fifield, Russell H. "Japanese Policy toward the Shantung Question at the Paris Peace Conference," *Journal of Modern History,* XXIII (1951) pp. 265-272.

Hosack, Robert E. "The Shantung Question and the Senate," *The South Atlantic Quarterly,* XLIII, 1944, pp. 181-193.

Levi, Werner. "American Attitudes toward the Pacific Islands, 1914-1919," *The Pacific Historical Review,* XVII, 1948, pp. 55-64.

Livermore, Seward W. "American Naval-Base Policy in the Far East, 1850-1914," *The Pacific Historical Review,* XIII, 1944, pp. 133-135.

Mabie, Hamilton W. "A Japanese Statesman on Japan: An Authorized Interview with Count Okuma," *The Outlook,* CIV, June 14, 1913, pp. 333-338.

March, Peyton C. "Japanese Strategy in the Far East," *Yale Review,* XXIII, 1933, pp. 78-87.

Mussey, Henry R. "Our Armament Race with Japan," *Nation,* CXII, February 2, 1921, p. 179.

Olds, C. Burnell. "Potentialities of Japanese Liberalism," *Foreign Affairs,* XXII, 1944, pp. 433-443.

Pollard, Robert T. "Dynamics of Japanese Imperialism," *The Pacific Historical Review,* VIII, March, 1939, pp. 5-35.

Powell, Alexander. "Are We Giving Japan A Square Deal?" *The Atlantic Monthly,* CXXVIII, November, 1921, pp. 688-698.

Power, Joseph E. "The Japanese Constitution and the Militarists," *Pacific Affairs,* June, 1942, XV, pp. 188-194.

Sansom, Sir George. "Liberialism in Japan," *Foreign Affairs,* XIX, 1941, pp. 551-560.

Spinks, Charles N. "Japan's Entrance into the World War." *The Pacific Historical Review*, V, 1936, pp. 297-311.
Spinks, Charles N. "The Liberal Myth in Japan," *Pacific Affairs*, XV, 1942, pp. 450-456.

Newspapers Cited

The Boston Herald.
The Chicago Examiner.
Consolidacion Nacional.
El Ideal.
The Filipino People.
The Makahlo Free Press.
The New York Herald.
The New York Journal of Commerce.
The New York Sun.
The New York Times.
The North China Herald.
The Philadelphia North American.
The Seattle Times.
The Washington Post.

Index

Index

Abbott, James F., 135

Aguinaldo, Emilio, Filipino leader, 18, 72, 73

Allies, the, Siberian fracas, 213-48, 318; rehabilitation of Eastern Front after Bolshevik revolution, 237; secret treaties with Japan, 290; *see also* France; Great Britain, etc.

American International Corporation, 147

American Red Cross, the Huai River project, 144-46

Anfu faction in China, 207

Asia, *see* Far East

Austin, Richard W., Congressman, 88

Australia, Paris Peace Conference, 259

Axson, Stockton, Wilson's brother-in-law, 67

Baker, Newton D., becomes Secretary of War, 93; Philippine policy, 95, 97; Siberian intervention, 235, 238, 239, 243, 246

Baker, Ray Stannard, 42, 164, 277

Bakhmeteff, Boris A., Russian Ambassador to United States, 183, 216, 222

Balfour, Arthur James, 227, 280; U. S. negotiations for capital ships from Britain, 171; Siberian intervention, 219, 223, 224; Paris Peace Conference, 275

Banking interests and the Consortium, 24

Bashford, J. W., Methodist Bishop at Peking, 35

Bekr, Abu, Professor of the Mosque in Peking, quoted, 168

Belgium, Paris Peace Conference, 273

Bergholtz, Leo, American Consul in Seoul, 211

Bernstorff, Count Johann von, German Ambassador to U. S., 157, 162

Bethlehem Steel Company, improvement of Fukien harbor, 118

Blanchard, A. Bailey, U. S. Chargé in Tokyo, 59

Bliss, Tasker H., opposes Japanese intervention in Siberia, 220; on Bolshevism, 241; at Paris Peace Conference, 250, 277, 279

Boardman, Mabel T., the Huai River project, 144, 145, 146

Bonsal, Stephen, at Paris Peace Conference, 255, 257, 279

Borah, William E., opposes Shantung settlement, 286, 290

Brazil, 30

Breckenridge, Henry, Assistant Secretary of War, 91, 92

Brent, Charles H., Bishop, 73

Britain, *see* Great Britain

Brown, Arthur J., quoted, 25

Bryan, James W., Congressman, policy for the Philippines, 85

Bryan, William Jennings, 33, 57, 108; appointed Secretary of State, 16-18; Consortium loan to China, 21; hails Wilson anti-Consortium stand, 25; recognition of Chinese Republic, 30; Yuan's dissolution of Kuomintang, 34; Far Eastern appointments, 34, 37; suggested as ambassador to China, 35; the California crisis: the issue of Japanese immigration and land rights, 50 ff., 141, 142; the Philippines, 67, 75, 77, 84, 97; China's situation in World War, 105; Japan's entry into World War, 106,